American Independent Cinema

For Siân and Roman

American Independent Cinema

An Introduction

Second Edition

Yannis Tzioumakis

EDINBURGH
University Press

Edinburgh University Press is one of the leading university presses in the UK. We publish academic books and journals in our selected subject areas across the humanities and social sciences, combining cutting-edge scholarship with high editorial and production values to produce academic works of lasting importance. For more information visit our website: edinburghuniversitypress.com

First edition published 2006

Edinburgh University Press Ltd
The Tun – Holyrood Road, 12 (2f) Jackson's Entry, Edinburgh EH8 8PJ

Typeset in Arno, Myriad and Rockwell by
R. Footring Ltd, Derby, UK, and
printed and bound in Great Britain by
CPI Group (UK) Ltd, Croydon CR0 4YY

A CIP record for this book is available from the British Library

ISBN 978 1 4744 1682 5 (hardback)
ISBN 978 1 4744 1684 9 (paperback)
ISBN 978 1 4744 1683 2 (webready PDF)
ISBN 978 1 4744 1685 6 (epub)

Images on pp. 25, 64 and 184 courtesy of The Kobal Collection.
Images on pp. 54 and 112 courtesy of United Artists/The Kobal Collection.
Image on p. 137 courtesy of AIP/The Kobal Collection.
Image on p. 160 courtesy of Lion Productions/The Kobal Collection.
Image on p. 210 courtesy of Orion/The Kobal Collection.
Image on p. 236 courtesy of Cineville/Film 4 International/The Kobal Collection.
Image on p. 250 courtesy of View Askew/The Kobal Collection.
Image on p. 266 courtesy of Fox Searchlight/Photofest.
Image on p. 281 courtesy of Magnolia Pictures/Photofest.

Contents

Tables

Case studies

Figures

Acknowledgements for the first edition

During the first year of my postgraduate research degree in 1998 I complained to Warren Buckland, then lecturer in Screen Studies at Liverpool John Moores University, that there were very few studies of American independent cinema. Warren agreed with my remark and suggested that perhaps one day I would write one. For this reason I would like to express my first big thank you to Warren for putting the idea of this book in my head when I least expected it as well as for all his support and friendship in the last eight years. I would also like to thank Professor Steve Neale who became another early supporter of the idea for the book.

Then I would like to thank Ian Ralston for setting up a meeting with the American Studies Commissioning Editor from Edinburgh University Press, Nicola Ramsey, and for his friendship and generosity over the years. I would also like to thank Nicola who offered me valuable editorial advice during the writing stage and guided me through some difficult times.

This book would not have been possible without some generous funding from the School of Media, Critical and Creative Arts at Liverpool John Moores University, which allowed me to visit a number of research libraries in Los Angeles, California to gather the necessary material and to interview important figures in the independent sector such as Eric Pleskow and Mike Medavoy. The School also financed a year-long study leave that allowed me to research the topic further and write a large section of the book. I would like to thank everyone involved, especially Trevor Long, Nickianne Moody, Andy Ruddock, Chris Frost and Timothy Ashplant.

I would also like to thank my other colleagues for supporting me in various ways: Ruth McElroy, David Llewellyn, Ros Merkin, James Frieze, Helen Rogers, Colin Harrison, Nicole Matthews, Joanna Price, Claire Horrocks, Elspeth Graham, Tamsin Spargo, Joe Moran and Olga Guedes; and my colleagues in Screen Studies: Corin Willis, David Sorfa, Alex Irving, Noel Odger, Bill Sweeney, Ben McCann and especially Judith Jones who is the other big fan of American independent cinema in my department. Additionally, I would like to thank all the support staff in the School of Media for their efforts to minimise my administrative responsibilities during the period of research, especially Cathy Cromby and Julie Quine.

The staff at Aldham Robarts Learning Resource Centre provided me with assistance almost on a daily basis. I would like to thank each and every one of them, especially Sheena Streather, Frank Halligan and Julie Bulger who made the research stage of the project as easy as possible. Also I would like to thank Julie Butler, Tim Lees, Cath Gorton, Linden Sweeney, Chris Lucas, Ann Keeley, David Carroll, Jill Harrison, Grace Smith, Sharon Jarman-Stulberg, Dean Toth, Ian McColl, Mike Wilson, Doreen Azzopardi and the late Nick Spalton. Special thanks also to Annie Afferson at the interlibrary loans office and Denise Minde.

I would like to thank a number of friends and my family in Greece who offered me their views on a number of independent films during my summer visits: Panayiotis Tzioumakis, Christina Tzioumakis, Leonidas Tzioumakis, Patroula Vrantza, Panayiotis Koutakis, Dimitra Kavatha, Fenia Koutakis, Ioanna Koutakis, Harris Tlas, Harris Papadopoulos, Maria Goulimari, Alice Samouilidou, Dora Samouilidou and Yannis Stratis. Many thanks also to my friends who did the same thing in Liverpool, especially Joanne Whiteside, Paresh Ladd, Paul Shaughnessy, Yolanda Akil-Perez, Lisa Anderson, Ben Howarth and Jay Lally. Amanda Greening became an inexhaustible source of inspiration and support during the final stages of the writing period.

Special thanks must go to a number of film and media scholars who read chapters of this book and whose constructive criticism improved the manuscript vastly: Peter Krämer, Alison McMahan, Rigas Goulimaris, Claire Molloy and, especially, Julia Hallam and Gary Needham. Lydia Papadimitriou once again contributed her time, friendship and scholarship, especially in the final stages of the book.

Also I would like to express my gratitude to Sarah McLoughlin, who acted as my research assistant and who undertook a large number of menial aspects of the research stage, always with a smile. Without her organisational skills and patience, this book would have taken much longer to complete.

Finally I would like to thank all the students who took my course on American Independent Cinema and whose insightful contributions shaped my approach to the subject in fundamental ways. In particular, I would like to thank the Screen Studies students who took the course when it ran for the first time in 2002, as it was those students who actively encouraged me to write the book: Katie Algar, Suzy Baldock, Martin Boothman, Caroline Boyd, Clare

Gabbott, Natalie Garwin, Paul Hagen, Rebecca Hardy, Rachel Heyes, Sarah Holmes, Ameena Khan, Andrew Lister, Claire Manson, Catherine Roche, Sophie Sharp, Steve Simpson and Janine Ward.

Acknowledgements for the second edition

While I would like to extend my gratitude to everyone mentioned in the acknowledgements in the first edition, this new edition provides me with an opportunity to say a few additional 'thank you's.

I would like to start with Gillian Leslie, who commissioned this new edition and who identified American independent cinema as a key subject for Edinburgh University Press, which over the past few years has published some excellent studies on the topic. As always, she was very patient with me (especially as I turned out to be a few months late in submitting the manuscript) and as usual she was a great pleasure to work with on the details of the book. I would also like to thank Richard Strachan for also being extremely patient with me and for overseeing yet another one of my books on independent film, Rebecca Mackenzie for helping me choose and designing the wonderful cover of the book, Eddie Clark for managing the book's production process and Ralph Footring for his painstaking copy-editing job, which improved the manuscript vastly.

Many thanks to Anne Hurault Paupe and Céline Murillo, editors of the special issue of the *Revue française d'études américaines* (no. 136) under the title 'Et le cinéma indépendant?', as well as Hélène Le Dantec, the journal's editor in chief, for granting me permission to use some extracts from my article 'American Independent Cinema in the Age of Convergence', published as part of that issue in 2013.

As always, my colleagues in the Department of Communication and Media at the University of Liverpool have been a great source of support and inspiration and I would like to thank them all, especially the Head of the Department, Kay Richardson, and my new partner in crime in teaching film and media studies, Gary Needham, who reviewed some of the new case studies that appear in this edition. Lydia Papadimitriou read drafts of all the new material and offered me invaluable advice and feedback, as did Rigas Goulimaris, who checked some of the material I had to update throughout the book, while Jennifer Jones helped with aspects of the research for the new material. A special thank you to all of you.

As always, I would like to thank my parents, Panayiotis and Christina, my brother, Leonidas, and the rest of my family and friends in Greece, especially Panayiotis Koutakis and Alkisti Charsouli, as well as Harris Tlas, Annalies McIver, Paul Shaughnessy, Yolanda Akil Perez, Ben Howarth and Joanne Whiteside in the UK.

I have dedicated this book to my wife, Siân Lincoln, and my son, Roman Tzioumakis, both of whom have been the greatest source of happiness in my life! But I would like to close these acknowledgements by giving a mention to all those scholars who have done work on aspects of American independent cinema and whose work has influenced my own in productive ways. The majority of them were only 'names' back in 2006 when this book was first published. Eleven years later I have the great fortune to call most of these people friends. In no particular order: Warren Buckland, Peter Krämer, Chris Holmlund, Justin Wyatt, Thomas Schatz, Hilary Radner, Janet Staiger, Patricia Zimmermann, Alisa Perren, Tino Balio, Matthew Bernstein, the late Jim Hillier, Frederick Wasser, Julia Hallam, Phil Drake, Claire Molloy, Claire Perkins, Linda Badley, Michele Schreiber, James Lyons, Steve Neale, Denise Mann, Kathleen McHugh, Janet Wasko, J. J. Murphy, Michael Z. Newman, Sarah Sinwell, B. Ruby Rich, James Schamus, Murray Smith, Chuck Kleinhans, R. Barton Palmer, Peter Stanfield, Brian Taves, Glyn Davis, Chuck Tryon, Hayley Trowbridge, John Berra, Sherry B. Ortner, Annette Insdorf, Betsy McLane, Peter Lev, Greg Merritt, Rob Stone, Diane Carson, Steve Rawle, Rona Murray, Mary Erickson, Doris Baltruschat, Mark Gallagher, James Macdowell, Cynthia Baron, Christina Lane, R. Colin Tait, Nolwenn Mingant, Paul McDonald and of course Geoff King – great many thanks to all of you! Here is to continue studying and debating independence in American cinema!

Preface to the second edition

Looking back at 2006, when *American Independent Cinema: An Introduction* was first published, one cannot fail to see how remarkably different the independent film landscape in the US was then compared with its current shape. The sector was dominated by the so-called studio specialty film divisions such as Focus Features and Fox Searchlight, whose films such as *Brokeback Mountain* (Ang Lee, 2005) and *Little Miss Sunshine* (Faris and Dayton, 2006) were exemplars of a cinema that was perceived to be as close to that of the Hollywood majors as it was to the independent sector. Often labelled 'indiewood', this kind of cinema was aspired to and practised by a number of standalone companies such as the then newly established Yari Film Group Releasing and Weinstein Company, with films such as *The Illusionist* (Burger, 2006) and *The Matador* (Shephard, 2005), respectively, both with considerable commercial potential, given the presence of stars, stories that take place within clear generic frameworks and strong production values. Indiewood was also practised occasionally by larger divisions of the Hollywood conglomerated majors, such as New Line Cinema's *The New World* (Malick, 2005), as well as by diversified mini-majors such as Lions Gate (later Lionsgate), whose *Akeelah and the Bee* (Atchison, 2006) was very different from the company's more obviously commercial titles. Even more occasionally, indiewood could be found in the release slates of the Hollywood majors themselves, with Sony backing (financially and as a distributor) *Marie Antoinette* (S. Coppola, 2006) and Warner Bros. releasing *Syriana* (Gaghan, 2006).

At the lower end of the US independent film market, less commercial and often more daring and challenging filmmaking continued to take place. Driven by developments in digital technology, which had become increasingly both user-friendly and affordable, low-end independent filmmaking, quality and beyond, was expanding dramatically in terms of number of titles. However, very rarely were these kinds of film attracting any attention or becoming crossover successes. With the number of distributors operating in the US theatrical market in 2006 having reached 150, the marketplace had become incredibly congested.[1] Of these 150 distributors, more than 100 failed to reach the $1 million mark in terms of total theatrical box office gross from all the films they released (though many released just one), while more than 60 were unable to reach even the $100,000 mark. The latter category nonetheless distributed films that attracted some critical attention and were discussed by some academic studies, such as *Man Push Cart* (Bahrani, 2006), while the former category (grossing between $100,000 and $1 million) distributed some films, such as *The Puffy Chair* (Duplas, 2005), that were critically recognised as part of 'mumblecore', a loose cycle of films attached to the increasingly successful SXSW Festival. At the theatrical box office, these two films grossed $36,608 and $194,523 and found themselves in the 505th and 377th places of the annual box office charts, respectively. Of course, their theatrical release was minimal, given that their distributors could not afford a large campaign, while the absence of any traditionally commercial elements in both films necessitated such a distribution approach, with the former film released in one screen over two weeks and the latter in seven screens, which was the maximum number it played in over 15 weeks. Instead, these and hundreds of other low-end independent films at that time would try to find a larger audience through the DVD market and exposure in film festivals, with *Man Push Cart* screened at 16 festivals in 2006 alone and *The Puffy Chair* in three festivals (with both films also having been shown at festivals in 2005).[2]

Some other films, however, were trying to exploit what seemed to be a brave new world in 2006 – the world of social media and the opportunities it afforded for hosting, publicising and even exhibiting audio-visual content. With their present ubiquity, it is hard to believe that in 2006 social media were still at a nascent stage. The now much less prominent and rebranded Myspace (established in 2003) had made the first big splash in the media world as a social networking site, becoming particularly well known for being populated by musicians advertising their work. Facebook was established in 2004, YouTube in 2005, Twitter in 2006 and Tumblr in 2007, each providing a variation in social networking and the ways in which it could carry audio-visual content and therefore exploited for distribution/exhibition purposes. From these and other less successful social media sites, YouTube quickly emerged as the foremost video-sharing platform, which made it a key destination for low-end independent filmmakers (and others) in their efforts to locate spaces where they could advertise their work for free. Indeed, back in 2006 several US independent filmmakers were making their first steps in this new landscape with a view to increasing their chances of distribution. This was especially as distribution was being extended beyond the theatre and home video/DVD markets, with several on-demand services being launched around the same time as bandwidth continued to improve and delivery of larger digital files to computers and laptops was becoming easier than before. For instance, it was 2006 when Apple started offering feature films and television shows through its iTunes service for rental or outright purchase,[3] while in the same year giant online retailer Amazon introduced Amazon Unbox, a video download service that eventually evolved into what is known now as Amazon Video.[4] With Netflix (back in 2006 being exclusively a DVD mailing service) announcing itself in January 2007 as a new video streaming service,[5] it was clear that the distribution landscape was in the process of being reshaped.

The extent of these changes, however, the speed with which they took place and the radical way they reconfigured and continue to reconfigure American independent cinema both as an industry and as a film practice within a broader, converged media landscape were impossible to foresee at that time. This was especially as American independent cinema as an academic field of study had only just been constructed. Despite some important work in the 1980s that explored the outburst of low-end quality independent films in the late 1970s and early 1980s that are now considered to be part of a movement that marked the beginning of contemporary American independent cinema,[6] film scholars did little to take this forward in the 1990s.[7] And while at the same time a lot of historical work on American cinema was becoming increasingly interested in questions of independence, from the studio era all the way to the conglomeration of Hollywood in the 1960s and 1970s, with a handful of exceptions its main focus remained on the films of the Hollywood majors and the companies behind them.[8] On the other hand, outside academia, American independent cinema started attracting significant attention in the 1990s with a number of journalists, film critics and industry practitioners providing book-length studies that were recording activity in the sector.[9] These culminated in 1999 with *Variety* critic Emanuel Levy's 600-page *Cinema of Outsiders*, the most comprehensive effort to map the contemporary (1980s–90s, with a few examples from earlier years) independent cinema landscape.

However, since the 2000s, scholarly work on the topic started appearing much more frequently, with Jim Hillier's reader of articles on the subject that had appeared in the UK magazine *Sight and Sound* setting the scene.[10] Following this, E. Deidre Pribram's *Independent Film in the United States, 1980–2001*, Geoff King's *American Independent Cinema* and Chris Holmlund and Justin Wyatt's collection *Contemporary American Independent Film: From the Margins to the Mainstream* together with *American Independent Cinema: An Introduction* became the studies that constructed the field.[11] With Pribram and King interested solely in recent (1980s–90s) manifestations of independence from a number of perspectives, Holmlund and Wyatt expanding the field substantially to include less obvious forms of independence (avant garde, exploitation, pornography) and my own study providing a macro-historical account of how independence had been defined discursively, it is not surprising that questions of contemporary practice did not feature high on the agenda of all these studies. Indeed, such questions remained on the periphery in the next few years, until new book-length studies such as Berra's *Declarations of Independence*, King's *Indiewood USA*, Murray's *Studying American Independent Cinema*, Newman's *Indie*, Perren's *Indie Inc.* and my own *Hollywood's Indies* represented a significant effort to research the field in depth through a number of methodological approaches and specific focal points.[12] In this respect, despite the occasional journal article and work in magazines that cover the sector (such as *Filmmaker* magazine) it is only in the past three or four years that major studies in the field have started to examine the transformation of cinema in the sector and its shift from the theatres to other screens (see for instance King's *Indie 2.0*, some essays in King's collection *A Companion to American Indie Film* as well as in Badley, Perkins and Schreiber's collection *Indie Reframed*).[13]

In many respects, the new material in this edition responds to these developments under the prism of media convergence, with approximately half of a new chapter (Chapter 9) examining the ways in which digital technology has altered the fabric of American independent cinema, especially its low-end sector. As part of a study that adopts a historical perspective, it surveys some of the changes that took place in the fields of finance, production and distribution, while offering an examination of the film *Tangerine* (Baker, 2015) as an extensive case study. Furthermore, this second edition closes with a new epilogue that explores the actual present and immediate future of American independent cinema (to the extent that this can be predicted, given the rapid developments in global converged media), focusing specifically on independent film's complex relationship to other media, especially television. However, before discussing those issues, Chapter 9 also takes stock of the ways in which media convergence impacted the sector in other areas, especially the practice of indiewood filmmaking, and contains a second case study, indiewood film *par excellence*, *Sideways* (Payne, 2004). By placing indiewood (and independent cinema more broadly) within the context of media convergence, the new material in the book sees developments in the sector as part of wider shifts that have impacted media industries more generally, rather than being symptomatic of the independent film sector alone.

Placing these recent developments within this context and discussing American independent cinema as part of a broader converged media industries landscape also prompted me to rethink particular developments that took place before the publication of the first edition in 2006. For this reason, the new edition has substantially reworked Chapter 8, which discusses the institutionalisation of American independent cinema, primarily in the 1990s and early 2000s, with a number of updates and correctives. This is especially as aspects of the sector that seemed key at that time did not prove to have longevity after 2006 – and the reverse, as elements that were seen as insignificant have become more prominent recently. For instance, the Association of Independent Video and Film-makers, one of the pillars of support for independent filmmaking in the US from the 1970s onwards, ceased to exist in 2006, while Revolution Studios, a paradigmatic 'neo-indie' production company in the early 2000s, became much less prominent in later years, shifting its core business to licensing its library of titles in ancillary markets.

Although Chapters 8 and 9 contain most of the new material, this edition also includes three other new case studies as part of other chapters – *Stagecoach* (Ford, 1939) in Chapter 1; *Detour* (Ulmer, 1945) in Chapter 2; and *Macabre* (Castle, 1958) in Chapter 4. Together with the case studies from the previous edition and the new case studies that appear as part of Chapter 9, they illustrate a variety of points pertaining to understanding the multifaceted phenomenon that American independent cinema has been over the course of more than 100 years.

20 December 2016
Liverpool, UK

Notes

1 All the figures in this paragraph are taken from The Numbers, online, http://www. the-numbers.com/market/2006/top-grossing-movies (accessed 20 December 2016).

2 Details of the films' festival participation are taken from the Internet Movie Database. For *Man Push Cart* see http://www.imdb.com/title/tt0464105/releaseinfo?ref_=tt_dt_dt and for *The Puffy Chair* see http://www.imdb.com/title/tt0436689/releaseinfo?ref_=tt_ dt_dt (both accessed 20 December 2016).

3 Knapp, 2006.

4 Kirkpatrick, 2006.

5 Anderson, 2007.

6 See especially two special issues of the *Journal of the University Film and Video Association*: vol. 35, no. 2 and vol. 38, no. 1 (the latter under the journal's new title, *Journal of Film and Video*).

7 An exception here were two collections published in 1998 that included a number of key essays on the topic: Neale and Smith, 1998, and Lewis, 1998.

8 See for instance major histories of Hollywood cinema in the studio era such as Schatz, 1996, and Balio, 1995, both of which discuss questions of independence in some detail. For an example of work that puts questions of independence in that context centre stage, see Wyatt, 2002, pp. 142–59.

9 See for instance Lyons, 1994, Pierson, 1995, and Andrew, 1998.

10 Hillier, 2001.

11 Pribram, 2002, King, 2005, Holmlund and Wyatt, 2005, and Tzioumakis, 2006.

12 Berra, 2008, King, 2009, Murray, 2011, Newman, 2011, Perren, 2012, and Tzioumakis, 2012a.

13 King, 2014, King, 2017 (especially chapters by Tryon and by Sinwell) and Badley et al., 2016 (especially chapters by Pederson and Zimmermann and by McHugh).

Introduction: problems of definition and the discourse of American independent cinema

American independent cinema has always been a notoriously difficult concept to define. This is primarily because the label 'independent' has been widely used since the early years of American cinema by filmmakers, film critics, industry practitioners, trade publications, academics and cinema fans, to the extent that any attempt towards a definition is almost certainly destined to raise objections.

For the majority of people with a basic knowledge of American cinema, independent filmmaking consists of the low-budget projects of (mostly) young filmmakers with a strong personal vision, away from the influence and pressures of the few major conglomerates that tightly control the mainstream American film industry. Far from the clutches of, among others, Time Warner, Sony (Columbia) and Viacom (Paramount), which are mainly in the business of producing expensive star vehicles and special-effects-driven films as part of franchises that bring larger profits from DVD sales, streaming and merchandising than from theatre admissions, independent filmmakers create films that stand against the crass commercialism of mainstream Hollywood while often pushing the envelope in terms of subject matter and representation. As film critic Emanuel Levy put it, 'ideally, an indie is a fresh, low-budget movie with a gritty style and offbeat subject matter that express the filmmaker's personal vision'.[1]

This 'ideal' definition immediately brings to mind films such as *Return of the Secaucus 7* (Sayles, 1980), *Stranger than Paradise* (Jarmusch, 1984), *She's Gotta Have It* (Spike Lee, 1986), *Poison* (Haynes, 1991), *Straight Out of Brooklyn* (Rich, 1992), *Clerks* (Smith, 1994), *Welcome to the Dollhouse* (Solondz, 1996), *The Blair Witch Project* (Sanchez and Myrick, 1999), *Lost in Translation* (S. Coppola, 2003), *Juno* (Reitman, 2007) and many other films that emerged post-1980 as low-budget 'alternatives' to the considerably more polished, expensive and conservative films produced and distributed by the conglomerated Hollywood majors. Despite its popularity in public discourse, however, this is only one definition of independent film and, significantly, fails to demonstrate what all the above films are independent from, while also excluding other groups of films that could also lay claim to the label 'independent'.

For industry practitioners and trade publications like *Variety* and *Screen International* independent film can assume a completely different meaning. For instance, on 9 June 2003 a *Variety* article featured a quote by Graham King, head of the Initial Entertainment Group, about the production/distribution company's then new project, *The Aviator* (Scorsese, 2004), a $115 million Howard Hughes biopic starring Leonardo DiCaprio. The quote read: 'It's the biggest independent movie ever made, unless you count *Lord of the Rings*'.[2] On 8 February 2002, *Screen International* had published a table with the 'Top 20 Independent Movies of All Time' (in the US market). Leading the table while still in release was *The Lord of the Rings: The Fellowship of the Ring* (Jackson, 2002), while other films included: *Rush Hour* and *Rush Hour 2* (Ratner, 1998 and 2001); *Austin Powers: The Spy Who Shagged Me* (Roach, 1999); *Teenage Mutant Ninja Turtles* (Barron, 1990); *Spy Kids* (Rodriguez, 2001); *Scary Movie* (K. I. Wayans, 2000); *Dumb and Dumber* (Farrelly, 1994); *Good Will Hunting* (Van Sant, 1997); and *The Blair Witch Project*.[3]

With the exception of the ultra-low-budget novelty horror *The Blair Witch Project*, none of the other films included in the *Screen International* table would be considered independent in the 'ideal' sense of the term. For the trade publication, however, independence has nothing to do with low-budget films with gritty visual style and offbeat subject matter. Instead, an independent film is any film that has not been financed, produced and/or distributed by a conglomerated major: Columbia (a Sony subsidiary), Paramount (a Viacom subsidiary), Warner Bros. (a Time Warner subsidiary), MGM/UA (currently self-run but owned by numerous conglomerates in the past 40 years), Disney, Universal (a Comcast subsidiary), 20th Century Fox (currently a 21st Century Fox subsidiary but back in 2002 a News Corp. subsidiary) and Dreamworks SKG (initially independent but later corporately attached to Paramount and Disney).[4] Indeed, of the 20 films that appear on the list, nine were distributed by New Line Cinema, eight by Miramax (and its sister company, Dimension Films), while of the remaining three, Sony Pictures Classics, Artisan and USA Films distributed one film each. As *The Lord of the Rings* was financed and distributed by New Line Cinema and despite its $300 million price tag (for all three instalments) it can justifiably be considered an independent film, the most commercially successful one, for that matter. Equally, as IEG was the primary financer and worldwide distributor of *The Aviator* (with the exception of the US, where Miramax held the theatrical distribution rights), the $115 million film can also be considered an independent film.

However, even this definition of independent film (a picture financed, produced and/or distributed by any company outside the Hollywood majors) is problematic. This is because New Line Cinema and Miramax/ Dimension were once standalone companies before they became subsidiaries of major entertainment conglomerates (Time Warner and Disney, respectively) while Sony Picture Classics, from its establishment in 1992, has remained a company owned corporately by Sony. In this respect none of these companies can be perceived as truly independent. Depending on arrangements, they might have operated with a large degree of autonomy from their respective parent companies but they have always been financially accountable to them. This means that their parent companies have had the power to close these units, sell them, reorganise their management structures, decrease their production/ distribution/acquisition budgets, interfere in their decision-making and so on. Indeed, these and other practices did take place in the late 2000s, when both New Line and Miramax as well as other Hollywood major specialty film subsidiaries were shuttered by their parent companies. This leaves only Artisan and USA Films as 'independent' companies, neither of which has existed as a corporate entity since 2004. But even here the label 'independent' is relative. USA Films was a specialty film division of the USA Network before its participation in a series of mergers in 2002 helped create Focus Features, NBC Universal's (later Comcast's) specialty film distribution company. Artisan, on the other hand, was taken over by Lions Gate (now Lionsgate), which is currently one of the very few successful production-distribution companies that does not have a corporate relationship with a conglomerated major – in other words, an independent but with a slate of films that ranges from small genre productions to *The Hunger Games* franchise (2012–15).

Even if one is prepared to see beyond the problems that ownership of companies like Miramax and Sony Pictures Classics by a conglomerated major presents and perceive of them as distributors of independent films – after all, Miramax in particular has been associated heavily with American independent cinema in the minds of cinema-goers in the world around – film critics and industry analysts often have been reluctant to attach the label 'independent' to these companies, especially to Miramax. Having made a name by releasing successfully a number of 'ideal' or paradigmatic independent films such as *sex, lies, and videotape* (Soderbergh, 1989), *Reservoir Dogs* (Tarantino, 1992), *Clerks* and *Dead Man* (Jarmusch, 1995), by the late 1990s and early 2000s Miramax had shifted increasingly towards the finance and distribution of considerably more expensive, star-studded genre pictures, including *Gangs of New York* (Scorsese, 2002), *Captain Corelli's Mandolin* (Madden, 2001) and *The Aviator*. This shift resulted in an identity crisis that could be seen clearly in the words chosen by the trade press to describe the company. For instance, a *Variety* editorial of 11 November 2002 labelled Miramax a 'mini major'.[5] Five months later (7 April 2003), the same publication proclaimed that 'Miramax ha[d] evolved to the point that it resemble[d] a major'.[6] On 8 March 2004, Miramax, New Line Cinema and United Artists were described by *Variety* as 'semi indies',[7] while on 14 July of the same year another *Variety* article christened Miramax 'a production driven quasi studio with franchises, mega-grossing hits and mega-budget offerings'.[8]

Film academics, on the other hand, have preferred to use the label 'major independent' to describe companies such as Miramax and New Line Cinema. According to Justin Wyatt, this label captures well the hybridity of the companies in terms of structure and position in the market and distinguishes them from both the conglomerated majors, the other Hollywood majors' specialty film subsidiaries and the independent (i.e. standalone) companies.[9] If nothing else, the words 'mini major', 'major', 'semi indie', 'quasi studio' and 'major independent' demonstrate that Miramax could not be labelled an independent company, certainly not after becoming a Disney division (and until its closure by Disney in 2010). As a similar argument can be advanced with even greater conviction about New Line Cinema (shuttered as a film distributing division by Time Warner in 2008), one could suggest that 17 of the 20 most commercially successful American independent films on the *Screen International* list are not actually independent.

A different approach to what constitutes independent film can reveal a whole new set of potential candidates. A large number of widely regarded mainstream filmmakers and industry practitioners have established their own independent production companies which physically produce (and often finance) pictures. Examples of such companies by filmmakers include Lucasfilm (George Lucas; independent until 2012, when it became a Disney subsidiary), Amblin Entertainment (Steven Spielberg) and Lightstorm Entertainment (James Cameron), while well-known independent companies by industry practitioners include Jerry Bruckheimer Films (Jerry Bruckheimer) and Phoenix Pictures (Mike Medavoy and Arnold Messer). Films by these companies are distributed primarily by the majors, some of which have exclusive distribution deals with individual production companies (for instance, Phoenix had an exclusive deal with Sony until 2001) while others operate independently and approach the major distributors once finance is in place. This would mean that such definitive Hollywood films as Spielberg's *Minority Report* (2002) and *War of the Worlds* (2005), Lucas's first six instalments of the *Star Wars* saga (1977–2005), Phoenix's *The 6th Day* (Spottiswoode, 2000) and *Shutter Island* (Scorsese, 2010), and Cameron's *The Abyss* (1989), *True Lies* (1993), *Titanic* (1997) and *Avatar* (2009) can all be considered independent productions.

Although it is tempting to dismiss these films as independent productions on the basis that such a status has been conferred on a legal technicality (Cameron's Lightstorm Entertainment might have physically produced the $200 million *Titanic*, though Fox and Paramount shared the costs of the budget and therefore were really 'in charge' of the production), other cases point to the contrary. If it is difficult to perceive *Titanic* as an independent film, it is equally difficult to think of the three *Star Wars* prequels, *The Phantom Menace*, *Attack of the Clones* and *The Revenge of the Sith* (Lucas, 1999, 2002 and 2005) as such. All three films were produced by Lucasfilm for Fox and, like *Titanic*, they carried a very large production cost. Unlike *Titanic*, however, in this case the distributor did not provide the finance. It was Lucasfilm that funded as well as produced the three films, which makes them clearly independent productions while, according to *Variety*, the filmmaker has enjoyed an autonomy that 'is unique in the history of the entertainment industry'.[10] Equally, a number of Amblin films are partly financed by Dreamworks SKG, a major distribution company Steven Spielberg co-founded with David Geffen and Jeffrey Katzenberg. Although financial pressures made Dreamworks' independence short lived, as the company in the 2000s found itself affiliated with conglomerated majors in various arrangements, during the period when it was partly owned by Spielberg Dreamworks allowed the filmmaker freedom to pursue less commercial projects, such as *Amistad* (1997) and *A.I. Artificial Intelligence* (2001) while still making franchise pictures for other majors such as the *Jurassic Park* films for Universal.

If, despite this evidence, one is still tempted to disqualify Spielberg and Lucas as independent filmmakers because of their association with the majors, should this not be the case for all filmmakers whose work is financed or distributed by the majors? Take, for instance, Spike Lee and Wes Anderson, two filmmakers who are much easier to label 'independent', as throughout the years they have produced a number of low-budget, offbeat films permeated by a strong personal vision. Lee, in particular, is often credited with putting black American independent cinema on the map through a series of challenging films that dealt forcefully with questions of race from the mid-1980s onwards. What is interesting, however, is that after his breakthrough feature, *She's Gotta Have It* (produced by Lee's 40 Acres and a Mule Filmworks and distributed by the short-lived independent Island Pictures) in 1986, the next seven films Lee wrote and directed were financed and/or distributed by the majors: *School Daze* (1988) by Columbia; *Do the Right Thing* (1989), *Mo' Better Blues* (1990), *Jungle Fever* (1991) and *Clockers* (1995) by Universal; *Malcolm X* (1992) by Warner Bros. and *Crooklyn* (1994) by Paramount. More recently, Lee's films have been financed and distributed by various other companies, including Buena Vista, Disney's distribution arm, which released *Summer of Sam* (1999), *The 25th Hour* (2002) and *Miracle at St. Anna* (2008), and independent distributors such as FilmDistrict (*Oldboy*, 2013) and Variance Films (*Red Hook Summer*, 2012).

Disney is also responsible for financing and distributing some films by Wes Anderson, one of the most original voices in contemporary American cinema. Since his debut feature, *Bottle Rocket* (1996), a Columbia Pictures-financed remake of a 13-minute short that Anderson had produced in 1994 under the same title, the filmmaker has established himself with such famous 'indie' pictures as *Rushmore* (1998), *The Royal Tenenbaums* (2001) and *The Life Aquatic with Steve Zissou* (2004). Even though these three films were produced by Wes Anderson and Owen Wilson's production company, American Empirical Pictures, they were nevertheless co-financed and distributed by Buena Vista. Still, despite the obvious similarities with the finance, production and distribution of *Titanic*, the films by Anderson and Lee are more easily perceived of as independent, while Cameron's film epitomises mainstream Hollywood at its most excessive.

The above examples demonstrate clearly the significant problems involved in any attempt to define the term 'independent' in contemporary American cinema that privileges an industrial-economic perspective. If, as Jim Hillier has remarked, 'historically, "independent" has always implied work different from the dominant or mainstream, whether this relationship is defined primarily in economic terms (production and distribution) or in aesthetic or stylistic terms', these distinctions have not been clear cut in recent times, certainly not in terms of economics.[11] Independent production companies like IEG are in a position to finance films budgeted in excess of $100 million away from the majors. An independent distributor, Newmarket Films, scored $370.7 million at the US box office with its $20 million production *The Passion of the Christ* (Gibson, 2004), which is more than what blockbusters such as *Jurassic Park: The Lost World* (Spielberg, 1997) and *The Matrix* (Wachowski and Wachowski, 1999) have grossed. Another major independent, New Line Cinema, produced and distributed *The Lord of the Rings*, a film franchise that brought approximately $1 billion net profit, with the third instalment of the trilogy (*The Return of the King*, 2003) having out-grossed any film produced and or/distributed by New Line's 'mainstream' sister label Warner Bros.[12] Under the umbrella of the same conglomerate, Time Warner, one also finds Warner Independent Pictures (for some critics a contradiction in terms) which in its short-lived history (2003–8) financed and distributed low-budget, 'personal, taboo-breaking and experimental films' such as *A Scanner Darkly* (Linklater, 2006).[13] And still within the structures of Time Warner, over different periods there were also Fine Line Features (1990–2005), a specialty film subsidiary New Line Cinema created when it started moving to more expensive films, and Picturehouse

(2005–8), a specialty film subsidiary established between New Line and HBO (another Time Warner division).

If the distinctions in terms of economics are murky and the boundaries between independent and major companies forever blurred, an approach that sees independent filmmaking as different from mainstream in terms of aesthetics or use of film style produces equally, if not more, problematic results. With mainstream American cinema generally exemplified by what some critics have called a 'classical aesthetic', one would expect that independent films depart from some or all conventions associated with classical narrative and film style.[14] In terms of narrative, such conventions include: cause–effect logic; goal-oriented, psychologically motivated characters; an equilibrium–disequilibrium–new equilibrium structure; the transformation of the main characters by the end of the story; the formation of the heterosexual couple (or, alternatively, of the family unit); and narrative closure. In terms of visual style, one would expect a break of the rules of continuity editing (180-degree rule, eyeline match, point-of-view cutting, match-on-action cut and so on), which ensure that the spatial, temporal and causal relationships between characters in the film are clear at all times and that the spectator is always aware of his or her position in relation to the narrative. Continuity editing produces an unobtrusive or 'transparent' film style that is always at the service of the narrative and does not attract attention to itself. In other words, it allows the spectator to attend to 'the story being told and not to the manner of its telling'.[15]

With mainstream Hollywood cinema bound by so many conventions, independent films can depart from the dominant and the established in a large number of ways. *Pulp Fiction* (Tarantino, 1994; produced by A Band Apart and financed and distributed by Miramax), for instance, follows the rules of continuity editing within individual sequences. However, its move back and forth in time from scene to scene without explicit markers of flashback or flashforward (blurred images, intensification of music, framing of a character in a close-up to suggest that he or she is remembering or imagining something, and so on) disorients the spectator. *Memento* (Nolan, 2000; produced by I Remember Productions, Newmarket Capital Group, Summit Entertainment and Team Todd and distributed by the standalone/independent Newmarket) is edited in such a way that half its scenes (the ones in colour) unfold in reverse chronological order and are intercut with the other half (the ones in black and white), which move forward in time. Only towards the end of the film, when the last black and white scene 'meets' the last (chronologically first) colour scene is the spectator able to understand that all scenes in black and white take place before the scenes in colour and that this is a relatively linear narrative that has become complicated through editing. In the end, however, this assumption is thwarted as the film confounds audience expectations of a satisfactory narrative closure, as there are shots whose place in the narrative is not clear (for instance Leonard in bed with his wife and the words 'I did it' tattooed on his chest).

Other films break dominant conventions more forcefully. Harmony Korine's films *Gummo* (1997; produced by Independent Pictures and distributed by Fine Line Features) and *Julien Donkey-Boy* (1999; produced and distributed by Independent Features) can be more easily described as a loosely structured assemblage of scenes than anything close to a classical narrative. In David Mamet's films, especially *House of Games* (1987; produced by Filmhaus Productions and distributed by Orion Pictures), *Homicide* (1991; produced by Cinehaus and distributed by Triumph Releasing)] and *Oleanna* (1994; produced by Bay Kinescope and distributed by the Samuel Goldwyn Company), the specific logic of his scripts determines the choice of film style. This means that if the script calls for unclear psychological motivations on the part of the characters, for gaps in the narrative that cannot be explained, for interruptions in the cause–effect logic of the shots and scenes, and even for a lack of realism in the unfolding of the story, then the film's style would not attempt to cover these 'problems' as a mainstream film might try to do. Furthermore, Mamet's actors deliver their lines in such a non-emotive manner that the convention of the illusion of the character – upon which mainstream acting has been founded – is clearly shattered. Although in many ways structured in a classical manner, Kevin Smith's *Jay and Silent Bob Strike Back* (2001; produced by View Askew Productions and distributed by Miramax) contains so many references to Smith's previous films that lack of prior knowledge of the films can render *Jay and Silent Bob Strike Back* incomprehensible. In Todd Solondz's *Palindromes* (2004; produced by Extra Large Pictures and distributed by Wellspring Media), seven actors of different age, race and body shape play the same character, with only the costume they are wearing providing continuity from scene to scene.

The above examples demonstrate clearly the extent to which independent films can depart from the conventions that characterise mainstream filmmaking. On the other hand, it is also clear that several aspects of the classical narrative and style remain in place. This means that in terms of aesthetics, independent films retain a certain grounding on mainstream traditions, the extent of which varies from film to film. Especially in terms of narrative, as Geoff King has argued, 'it is rarely if ever the case that [it] is entirely absent in the more commercial/industrial independent sector'.[16]

Even though this argument seems to differentiate a very large category of films from the more mainstream fare (which would include the expensive blockbuster films made by the Hollywood majors), pointing perhaps towards a less controversial definition of American independent cinema, it nevertheless presents one major problem. It is not unusual for a mainstream film, especially an effects-driven action/adventure blockbuster, also to depart from the classical conventions. Stylistic and narrative patterns often associated with the blockbuster film include: loose narrative structure; narrative as a showcase for special effects; increasing emphasis on spectacle; characters as plot functions; and genre hybridity. For many film critics, the blockbuster film has gradually become an expression, or even a celebration, of a conglomerated entertainment industry, which attempts to entice a very large, increasingly young, audience to a specific kind of entertainment that can be reiterated ad infinitum through the multiple distribution channels that the same industry controls.[17] For this reason, certain pillars of the classical aesthetic, such as cause–effect narrative logic, psychological character motivation and clear-cut generic frameworks, have been replaced by elements of a new aesthetic that increasingly foregrounds narrative fragments rather than narrative structure in order to encourage spin-offs and tie-ins in various ancillary markets. This aesthetic has been labelled 'post-classicism' by some critics and, as in the case of independent cinema, it is characterised by both departures from and continuities with classical cinema.

The term 'post-classicism' has been employed also in critical discussions of 'the high-concept film', certainly a type of film associated with mainstream cinema. According to Justin Wyatt, the constituent elements of the high-concept film can be found in the construction of narratives as vehicles for advertising, to the extent that advertising and narrative have gradually become increasingly integrated, thereby changing the look and the sound of the film. Despite 'important aesthetic ties' with classical cinema, the considerably tighter relationship between economics and aesthetics of the high-concept film creates a style of filmmaking that differs considerably from the classical one.[18] And as with independent cinema, the extent of the breaking of the classical conventions varies from film to film.

As this stylistically determined approach to defining American independent cinema is also plagued with problems, one wonders whether it is, indeed, possible to come up with a comprehensive definition. Furthermore, up to this point I have been referring to examples of films that could be construed as independent strictly from the post-1980 period, which has attracted considerable critical attention in recent years.[19] Commercial independent filmmaking in the US, however, is as old as mainstream Hollywood, which for many film historians extends back to the second decade of the twentieth century. This means that, historically, independent cinema has assumed a large variety of forms and functions, some of which differ considerably from others. For instance, during the studio years (mid-1920s to late 1940s) the label 'independent' could be attached to prestige-level pictures made by producers such as Samuel Goldwyn, Walt Disney and David O. Selznick, who used United Artists (and later other companies) to release films they made through their respective production companies (in arrangements that are not very dissimilar from the examples of Lucas and Spielberg I discussed above). Among these independent films one could find *Gone with the Wind* (Fleming, 1939), a film widely considered the epitome of mainstream Hollywood under the studio system, which nevertheless was produced by Selznick through his Selznick International Pictures. The label 'independent', however, could be also attached to low-budget pictures, such as the singing-cowboy western *Tumbling Tumbleweeds* (Kane, 1935), produced and distributed by 'Poverty Row' studios (see Chapter 2) such as Monogram and Republic Pictures and destined for the low part of double bills in the 1930s and 1940s. It could also be attached to ultra-low-budget films that targeted the various ethnic populations in America, which were produced, distributed and exhibited mainly outside the California-based film industry.

To account for all these different forms and expressions of independent filmmaking during the last 100 years, this study approaches American independent cinema as a discourse that expands and contracts when socially authorised institutions (filmmakers, industry practitioners, trade publications, academics, film critics and so on) contribute towards its definition at different periods in the history of American cinema. The concept of discourse is well suited to sidestepping some of the problems involved in defining 'independent' filmmaking. According to Michel Foucault, discourses 'bring cultural objects into being by naming them, defining them [and] delimiting their field of operation'.[20] By creating objects of knowledge such as American independent cinema (and mainstream Hollywood cinema for that matter), various institutional forces such as academia, the trade press, filmmakers and industry practitioners highlight specific practices and procedures associated with filmmaking upon which individual definitions are founded. These practices 'realise and set the conditions for discourse, while discourse, reciprocally, feeds back utterances which facilitate practice'.[21]

A good illustration of the usefulness of this approach is provided by the case of Disney. One obvious practice that has consistently characterised the discourse of American independent cinema from the mid-1920s has been the production of films through production companies other than the major studios. One of the most successful such companies was Disney, which managed to curve a niche market with its animated films. In recent years, however, Disney has become one of the largest entertainment conglomerates and an undisputed member of the major powers in American cinema. The practices associated with the 'rise' of Disney from a relatively small independent production company to a major conglomerate – the establishment of a distribution apparatus, diversification in ancillary markets, its merger with giant television network ABC, its emphasis on tentpole films with potential for stratospheric profits, its distribution contracts with other production companies like Pixar (bought outright by Disney in 2006) which provide it with product – influenced the 'Disney discourse' to such an extent that it ceased to be part of the discourse of American independent cinema. Equally, following developments in the American film industry (including Disney's transformation to a conglomerate), the discourse of American independent cinema was shaped accordingly to exclude Disney from its remit.

The concept of discourse is also well suited for approaching American independent cinema because it involves questions of power. As discourses are produced and legitimated by socially authorised groups, it is obvious that there are parties who stand to gain through their association with American independent cinema (and through the exclusion of other parties or groups). Not surprisingly, numerous sub-groups within the above institutions have appropriated the term 'independent' in order to achieve particular objectives as well as to define the field. Nowhere is this more evident than in the manner in which sub-groups of filmmakers and industry practitioners have used the label to include themselves and exclude others. For instance, even as early as 1909, a number of filmmakers who opposed the tactics of the Motion Picture Patents Company created a distinct identity for themselves by choosing to be called independent. In the studio times, top-rank producers like Howard Hughes, David O. Selznick and Charles Chaplin used the concept of independence to differentiate their own productions – such as *Hell's Angels* (Hughes, 1930), *Gone with the Wind* and *The Great Dictator* (Chaplin, 1941), respectively – from the routine films associated with the Hollywood studios, often referred to as sausage factories. In the late 1950s and early 1960s, a group of experimental filmmakers on the East Coast dismissed all Hollywood-based filmmakers (including those with their own production companies) as cogs in an institutionalised film industry, claiming instead the label 'independent' for themselves and their own ultra-low-budget and technically unpolished personal projects.

Finally, it is certainly because of its association with questions of power relations between contending groups that the discourse of American independent cinema became so pervasive and prominent in the post-1980 period. With the major entertainment conglomerates tightening their grip on everything related to American cinema and with Reaganite entertainment defining mainstream cinema and reigning supreme at the box office, it became a cause for celebration when films that were financed, produced and distributed outside the majors met with (relatively) wide commercial success. This was particularly the case when the films also dealt with important social issues that were absent in the majors' productions or when their filmmakers employed challenging visual styles and/or narrative structures that were markedly different from the formal contours of the dominant aesthetic regime.

As the label 'independent' was also attached to productions such as *Heartland* (Pearce and Smith, 1979), *Return of the Secaucus 7, Smithereens* (Seidelman, 1982) and *Stranger than Paradise* and to a large number of films that were characterised by one or more of the above defining features in the following years, it acquired additional meanings. Besides signifying one or more of the above-cited characteristics, 'independence' also connoted a particular brand of quality that was perceived as absent from the considerably more refined (and expensive) but impersonal mainstream Hollywood productions. In other words, independence in American cinema became associated with intelligent, meaningful, often challenging, but always full of spirit, filmmaking, while, conversely, production by the majors was associated with conservative, conventional, formulaic and spiritually empty efforts at entertaining an increasingly young audience.

With the label 'independent' acquiring such distinct meanings, it was not long before small-scale distributors started using it as a marketing category. Especially during the early 1990s, a low-budget film's independent status could prove its only chance to attract a sizeable audience and return a profit to its producer and distributor. This was clearly understood by the majors, which managed to appropriate the term and use it for their own financial gain for the rest of the 1990s and the 2000s. Sponsoring their own brand of an increasingly expensive 'independent' filmmaking through specialty film divisions such as Sony Pictures Classics, Fox Searchlight and Warner Independent Pictures, the majors secured their presence in one more film market, while at the same time putting a significant dent in the profit margins of standalone companies. The majors' appropriation of the label for a large number of films that originated under their corporate umbrellas once again demonstrates the power struggle involved in the usage of 'independence' and in effect justifies an approach to American independent cinema as a discourse.

Although power relations are certainly important to the present study, the main emphasis is placed on industrial and economic factors and how those shaped the discourse of American independent cinema at various historical trajectories. This means that this study privileges an examination of the production of the discourse from one particular perspective, the industrial-economic one, though it resorts to numerous socially authorised institutions to achieve this objective. It draws on: the work of historians of American cinema (where questions of independence usually were dealt with in a surprisingly brief fashion until American independent film studies boomed in the 2000s); interviews with industry practitioners; legal documentation about independent production companies from archival collections; and trade publications. The study also contains a number of case studies. These include discussions of individual pictures as examples of independent filmmaking from specific periods in the history of American cinema. This book provides the reader not only with a history of the subject, but also with a concrete framework within which individual films can be discussed as independent.

Notes

1 Levy, 1999, p. 2.
2 Synder, 2003, p. 9.
3 Goodridge, 2002, p. 33.
4 At the time of the first edition, MGM/UA was in the process of being taken over by Sony, while Dreamworks was being taken over by Viacom. Despite this and other changes in their corporate status, these companies remained parts of the main group of conglomerated Hollywood majors and therefore will continue to be referred to as majors in this edition of the book.
5 Oppelaar, 2002, pp. 1 and 62.
6 Harris, 2003, pp. 1 and 54.
7 Brodesser, 2004, p. 53.
8 Rooney, 2004b, pp. 1 and 57.
9 Wyatt, 1998a, pp. 86–7.
10 Cohen 2005, pp. 1, 58–9.
11 Hillier, 2001, p. ix.
12 Oppelaar, 2003, p. 11.
13 See http://wip.warnerbros.com (accessed 10 January 2006).
14 The key study on Hollywood cinema as a 'classical' art is Bordwell, Staiger and Thompson's *Classical Hollywood Cinema: Film Style and Mode of Production to 1960* (1985). Although the study examines American cinema prior to 1960, in the penultimate chapter of the book the authors argue that the classical mode of film practice has persisted since 1960 (pp. 367–77). Equally Kristin Thompson's *Storytelling in the New Hollywood: Understanding Classical Narrative Technique* (1999) extends this argument to American cinema of the 1980s and 1990s.
15 Allen and Gomery, 1985, p. 81.
16 King, 2005, p. 60.
17 Schatz, 1993, pp. 23 and 33.
18 Wyatt, 1994, p. 18. Examples of high-concept films include *Flashdance* (Lyne, 1983), *Footloose* (Ross, 1984) and *Top Gun* (Scott, 1986).
19 At the time of the publication of the first edition there were only a few book-length studies that focused strictly or mainly on American independent cinema in the post-1980 period. These were; Rosen and Hamilton, 1990, Lyons, 1994, Pierson, 1995, Andrew, 1998, Levy, 1999, Pribram, 2002, Biskind, 2005, and King, 2005. Two edited collections also emphasised the post-1980 period: Hillier, 2001, and Holmlund and Wyatt, 2005. There was also a study that focused on independent filmmaking during the studio times (mid-1920s to late 1940s), Aberdeen, 2000; and only one study that examined independent filmmaking

in the US throughout the twentieth century, Merritt, 2000. After the publication of the first edition of this book in 2006, American independent cinema studies flourished, with a large a number of studies examining the sector from a variety of perspectives and approaches. Those that have exerted most influence in the field include: Murphy, 2007, Berra, 2008, Mann, 2008, King, 2009, Newman, 2011, Perren, 2012, Tzioumakis, 2012a, and King, 2014. The field has also seen a book series dedicated to it, American Indies (Edinburgh University Press, 2009–), with volumes including Tzioumakis, 2009, Needham, 2010, Molloy, 2010, King, 2010, and Davis, 2011. Additionally, the 2010s have seen the publication of three new collections: King, Molloy and Tzioumakis, 2013, Badley et al., 2016, and King, 2017.

20 Stam et al., 1992, p. 211, discussing Foucault.

21 Stam et al., 1992, p. 211.

Part I

American independent cinema in the studio years (mid-1920s to late 1940s)

Part I

American independent cinema in the studio years (mid-1920s to late 1940s)

Independent filmmaking in the studio era: tendencies within the studio system

The independent producer is a man who is dependent on the exhibitors, the studios and the banks.
Walter Wanger, independent producer[1]

Introduction

During the studio era, the American film industry was dominated by eight companies, the 'Big Five' – Paramount, Loew's (MGM), 20th Century Fox, Warner Bros. and RKO – and the 'Little Three' – Columbia, Universal and United Artists. The Big Five were vertically integrated companies: they produced their films at self-owned studios; they developed a network of offices in the US and around the world to market their films and deliver them to the theatres; and they owned a relatively small number of theatres in the US and in key European countries where they exhibited their own (as well as each other's) films. The Little Three were organised in the same way as the Big Five but were not integrated on the same level: Columbia and Universal produced and distributed their own films but did not own any theatres, while United Artists was mainly a distribution company even though, for a time, it owned a small number of theatres in certain key markets. According to Douglas Gomery, the eight studios produced about three-quarters of all features made, while this product was responsible for about 90 per cent of box office takings.[2]

This suggests that roughly one-quarter of all films in the US were made and distributed outside the eight studios, while 10 per cent of all dollars spent on cinema-going were for films produced and distributed by non-studio outfits.

This picture of the studio era, however, is not characteristic of the entire period from the mid-1910s, which is widely regarded as when the American film industry started to take shape. Although many production and business practices that were adopted at the beginning of this period remained in place throughout the years, it was not until the mid-/late 1920s that the overall structure of the industry became clear. For instance, RKO, the last member of the Big Five, was not established until October 1928, almost 14 years after Fox Film Corporation became one of the earliest examples of a vertically integrated film company. In 1925, the structure of the industry was very different. Instead of the Big Five and the Little Three, there were three major, vertically integrated companies (Paramount, Loew's and First National – with the Fox Film Corporation slightly trailing them), while Warner Bros., Columbia, Universal and United Artists were far more marginal than they were later. In this respect, even though the same few companies (with the exception of First National) would dominate the industry in the 1930s and 1940s, the balance of power in the American film industry did not remain unchanged since the formation of Fox Film Corporation in 1914, and the relationship between major and minor studios continued to evolve. In actual fact, almost all of the above companies had been associated with forms of independent film production and distribution before they became the masters of the American film industry in the late 1920s. Once in a position of power and control, they actively tried to suppress new independent production and distribution.

This raises two important issues. Firstly, one cannot talk about independent filmmaking in the studio era until the structure of the film industry became clear, until the five major and three minor studios became the forces which independent producers sought to avoid being 'dependent on'. Secondly, and as an extension of the first issue, independent production has a 'pre-history', from the mid-1910s to the mid-1920s, that involves earlier incarnations of the major studios, that is, before the studios assumed their producer-distributor-exhibitor guise; that period of industry consolidation had ended by the late 1920s. What links the two periods is the concept of independent production as a form of resistance to any attempts to monopolise the American film industry. During the early years of US cinema, independent film production and distribution became banners under which a number of companies actively sought to prevent the formation of trusts and syndicates that would threaten competition in the newly established film industry. During the studio years, independent film production fought the system of oligopoly, while rejecting key features of the studio-based system of production.

The first independents

The discourse of independent cinema appears perhaps for the first time in 1908–9, with the formation of the Motion Picture Patents Company (MPPC, also known as the Patents Company or simply the Trust) and its antagonists, which became known as independents. The company was established on 1 January 1909 by 10 film manufacturing outfits – led by Edison and Biograph – in an attempt to license all three branches of filmmaking (production, distribution and exhibition) in the US and, thereby, control the American film market.[3] By that time, the motion picture business was driven by the exponential growth of nickelodeons, the number of which had increased from 2,500 in 1906 to 8,000 in 1908.[4] The MPPC sought to become the main holder of various patents associated with cinematographic technology and put an end to long legal battles about who had the right to use this technology, at least in the US. By controlling the patents involved in the manufacturing of cameras, projectors and other items necessary for the production and exhibition of motion pictures, the MPPC started to charge a fee for the use of this equipment. It also made a deal with Kodak to provide raw film stock exclusively to members and its licensees, and, as a result, made it extremely difficult for other companies to photograph, develop, print or exhibit a film without its consent.[5]

In April 1910, the MPPC created the General Film Company (GFP) in an effort to exert similar influence on film distribution and to control the market further. The GFP gradually took over all but one of the licensed exchanges whose function was to ensure the smooth delivery of films from producers to distributors. The exception was an exchange in New York run by William Fox. Under the new status, production companies agreed to be paid a flat rate of 10 cents per foot of film by GFP in exchange for distribution rights. For the Patents Company, film was seen as a 'standardised, undifferentiated product' which was one reel long (roughly 14–15 minutes in duration) and was sold by the foot. There was no concern for the content or the quality of the product.[6]

The Trust's efforts to monopolise the American film industry, however, did not remain unchallenged. Between 50 and 100 companies, which were not considered by the MPPC significant forces in the embryonic film industry, were excluded from membership of the Patents Company and had to pay weekly fees for the right to use their licensed equipment.[7] Also, the General Film Company was not successful in absorbing the Greater New York Film Exchange owned by William Fox, as we saw earlier. Resistance began only one month after the formation of MPPC, in February 1909. These 'rebels' refused to respond to an initial deadline to abide by MPPC regulations, and decided to continue business through any means. They used illegal equipment, imported film stock from abroad or relocated their companies to geographical areas where the Trust's representatives would find it difficult to reach them and bring legal action against them. By 20 February 1909 an exchange appropriately called the Anti-Trust Film Company of Chicago had already been established. These 'unlicensed outlaws' attached the label 'independent' to their practices and, to a certain extent, became responsible for the failure of the Patents Company to monopolise the market.[8] Within six months from the establishment of the MPPC, independent companies were more than a few isolated presences in the American market. They were part of an *independent movement*, which directly opposed the plans of the Trust to dominate the market.

While the Patents Company was establishing the GFC to control film distribution (April 1910), a number of independent producers were in the process of forming their own apparatus to handle distribution for independent product, the Motion Pictures Distributing and Sales Company (MPDSC or the Sales Company). Representing the most important independents, including Carl Laemmle, future head of Universal, the Sales Company quickly became the GFC's main rival. Within eight months from its inception, the Sales Company was in a position to claim that 'in the year 1910 [they] succeeded in splitting the business of the country between the trust and [them]selves on a 50 percent basis'.[9]

In its attempt to organise the independent sector, however, the Sales Company found itself following several of the trade practices established by or associated with the Trust, rather than developing practices of its own.[10] Faced with the danger of having to substitute one form of dependence for another, several independent producers, who had also been hostile and antagonistic to each other, withdrew from the Sales Company and went on to form new distribution establishments. These included National Film Manufacturing and Leasing, the Film Supply Company (which grew into the Mutual Film Company, one of the key distributors in the early and mid-1910s) and the Universal Film Manufacturing Company (which eventually became Universal, one of the eight powers during the studio era).

As is clear from this account, independent filmmaking in the early years of American cinema was mainly a reaction to any attempt towards monopolisation of the film industry. In this respect, 'independence' is defined here by a production company's refusal to succumb to the pressures applied by one or more organisations that actively seek total control of the film market. This essentially means that a company's status as an independent is shaped by its position outside an established (or semi-established) industrial-economic system designed to suit one company organised in a particular way. The overall purpose of this system is to eliminate competition from existing players and/or discourage competition from potential entrants to the market. In other words, independence is perceived purely in industrial terms, without any reference to possible qualitative differences that the independents' films might demonstrate in comparison with the films made by the Patents Company members.

These early independents, however, did break away from certain production and distribution practices of the Trust. One of the major advantages the independents had over the Patents Company was that they were willing to experiment. Unlike the production companies working for the Trust, which were making one-reel films under the assumption that the public was indifferent to the quality of the product and which would get their 10 cents per foot of film produced regardless of content or quality, some independent producers consciously strove to differentiate their product. For that reason, when audience demand for more pictures with 'Little Mary' became evident, it was the independent companies that read correctly the public's increasing fascination with particular screen performers and it was Carl Laemmle and his Independent Motion Picture Company (before he formed Universal) who lured Florence Lawrence and Little Mary (aka Mary Pickford) away from Biograph, a member of the Patents Company. Despite the fact that the MPPC adopted the star system almost at the same time as the independents, in many ways this was a response more to practices initiated by independents than to the signs of the times that pointed to the emergence of film stardom.[11]

Similarly, it was another independent, Adolph Zukor and his Famous Players Film Company who realised the potential of feature-length films (at least four reels long as opposed to the two-reel maximum length practised by the Patents Company) for much greater profits. Although multi-reel films imported from Italy had appeared in the US market as early as 1910, it was the success of *Queen Elizabeth* (Desfontaines and Mercanton, 1912), a four-reel film imported by Zukor and starring Sarah Bernhardt, that paved the way for the eventual triumph of this film format as the mainstay of American cinema. With the General Film Company refusing to distribute anything longer than two reels – as this would mean a much higher distribution cost for a company that was buying films by the foot – Zukor resorted to other distribution strategies, such as road showing and promoting his films via the states rights market.

In road showing, films were branded as special events and toured around the country playing mostly in legitimate theatres and more rarely in prestigious exhibition sites such as town halls. Admission prices were as high as $1 (at a time when standard prices were around 25 cents) and the film played for as long as each market sustained it. Once demand for the film decreased, the producer would seek to make more profits through the states rights market. States rights was a system of film distribution whereby a small exchange company acquired the rights of a film and exploited it in a number of theatres in a delimited territory or state, usually for a flat fee. Operating outside the control of the General Film Company exchanges, which dealt specifically with one- and two-reel films, states rights distributors became specialised in the marketing and selling of multi-reel films, which were gradually becoming increasingly important as money-earners for their production companies.[12] It was partly due to the success of feature films in the states rights market that a national system of distribution finally emerged in 1915–16, primarily through the work of W. W. Hodkinson, who was originally in charge of one of these states rights exchanges.

These production and distribution methods practised by the first independents precipitated the decline and eventual collapse of the Motion Pictures Patents Company and its distribution arm, therefore salvaging the neophyte film industry from the claws of monopolisation. It was some of these same independents, however, that would try to become the next masters of the US film industry.

Independents before the formation of the studios

With the Patents Company out of the picture, Adolph Zukor's Famous Players Film Company set out to become the next ruler of the American film industry. Together with the Feature Play Company, owned by Jesse Lasky, Samuel Goldfish (later Goldwyn) and Cecil B. DeMille, Zukor's company understood the potential of a new system of national film distribution devised by Hodkinson and implemented through his company, Paramount (formerly Progressive). Under this system Paramount would finance the production of feature films by advancing funds to production companies in exchange for exclusive distribution rights for a set period. In this manner, producers would be in a position to dedicate their efforts solely to the making of the films, leaving their marketing, promotion and advertising to a specialised distribution company that was adequately equipped to reach a nationwide audience.

As one of Paramount's first clients, Zukor experienced at first-hand the benefits of the new distribution system. Within two years of their initial agreement, in 1914, Zukor and Lasky took over Hodkinson's company and in the process found themselves in charge of a giant production-distribution outfit as they also merged Famous Players with Feature Play into Famous Players-Lasky. The power of the company became such that before the end of 1916 it introduced the practice of block booking.[13] Under this trade practice, exhibitors were forced to accept a company's annual output in one large or a few smaller blocks of films, despite the fact that the majority of a company's films were of a dubious quality, with lesser or no stars, and production values often down to an absolute minimum. In order for exhibitors to secure a company's top-rate and therefore most desirable productions (for instance, the Mary Pickford films at Paramount), they would have also to accept the rest of the company's productions.

As we shall see later in this chapter, this particularly oppressive trade practice kept films made and distributed outside the studios from reaching specific cinemas and, to a certain extent, defined the parameters of independent filmmaking during the 1928–48 period. Block booking, moreover, provided the spark for another movement of resistance to Zukor's attempt towards monopolisation, a movement which, once again, can be labelled 'independent'. Unlike its predecessor, however, which had its roots in 'outlaw production', this independent movement started with disenfranchised film exhibitors.

By the mid-1910s a small number of newly built, centrally located theatres in several large American cities were accommodating the increasingly large motion pictures audience. Although these theatres represented a very small percentage of the theatres in the country at the time (approximately 200 out of 14,000),[14] they nevertheless held the power to dominate exhibition. This was because films in first run were guaranteed maximum exposure and publicity as well as much larger profits than in smaller, second-run theatres.

The first-run exhibitors were dissatisfied with Paramount's trade practices – especially with block booking – and as they gradually became aware of the power their sites had in controlling exhibition they organised resistance against Zukor. In April 1917, 26 key first-run exhibitors representing the biggest markets in the country formed the First National Exhibitors Circuit, a distribution company whose objective was 'to acquire outstanding pictures made by independent producers'.[15] With a distribution network in place and with exhibition secure in all key territories, First National proceeded to attract talent from various outfits.

The company's greatest success was to lure Charlie Chaplin and, especially, Mary Pickford from Mutual and Paramount, respectively. History repeated itself: in the same way Laemmle's Independent Motion Picture Company had managed to lure Pickford away from the Patents Company, it was now First National that managed to lure the same star away from another company that was attempting to exert control over the industry. By 1920 First National had become a great force in the industry, controlling 639 theatres, 244 of which were first-run houses.[16] Zukor 's response was to try to merge Paramount (as Famous Players-Lasky was eventually renamed) with First National, aiming to create a vertically integrated super-company. When the merger did not materialise, Zukor chose to do the next best thing: he proceeded to an aggressive programme of theatre acquisition which would not only make Paramount vertically integrated but would also end First National's domination of the exhibition circuit. From that moment on and for almost a decade, the history of the American film industry was defined by endless corporate battles, mergers and takeovers as other companies, in all three branches of the film business, tried to emulate Zukor's example, to stay in the game. The end result of this corporate restructuring was further consolidation until the industry reached its mature oligopoly phase in the mid-/late 1920s.

First National can be perceived as an independent company that opposed Paramount's march towards monopolisation of the American film market. However, the company is also important as a distributor that set out to acquire films made by independent producers. As a distributor-exhibitor (but not a producer) First National's practice of setting up creative individuals as independent producers with, sometimes, complete creative control in exchange for exhibition and distribution rights became the blueprint for one of the main forms of independent production in the studio era. It also paved the way for the birth of a distribution company which would handle the bulk of independent production during the era of oligopoly, United Artists (UA). It is not coincidental that prior to the formation of UA two out of its four founders (Charles Chaplin and Mary Pickford) were independent producers releasing through First National, while the other two (D. W. Griffith and Douglas Fairbanks) were set up as producers of their own films at Paramount/Artcraft but with less creative control than Chaplin and Pickford.

The formation of United Artists (Figure 1.1) was a direct response to the rumours of the merger between First National and Paramount. Star-producers Chaplin, Pickford and Fairbanks (whose contract with Paramount was close to expiring) and director-producer Griffith announced their intention to form their own production-distribution company. In their first press release (15 January 1919) they articulated clearly their vision of the role and function of their company:

> We believe this is necessary to protect the exhibitor and the industry itself, thus enable the exhibitor to book only pictures that he wishes to play and not force upon him … other program films which he does not desire … We also think that this step is positively and absolutely necessary to protect the great motion picture public from threatening combinations and trusts that would force upon them mediocre productions and machine-made entertainment.[17]

Under the spectre of a 'threatening combination' that the potential merger between Famous Players-Lasky and First National would create, and with the memories of the Trust's efforts to monopolise the industry still fresh, UA was officially incorporated on 17 April 1919. Although originally envisaged as a production-distribution outfit, UA was eventually set up purely as a distribution company, with the mission to supply theatres with films made by independent producers outside the studios, in addition to films made by its four founders. As we shall see in the next section, not only did UA come to represent one of the very few avenues – certainly the most prestigious – for independent production during the 1930s, it also actively shaped American independent cinema as a discourse for the same period. This was mainly because UA was created, as Tino Balio argued, 'for the benefit of the independent producer in an era dominated by big business and an oligopolistic market structure',[18]

Figure 1.1 The birth of United Artists: D. W. Griffith signs the papers finalising the company's incorporation, surrounded from left to right by Douglas Fairbanks Sr, Charlie Chaplin, Albert Bahnzaf (lawyer), Dennis O'Brien (lawyer) and Mary Pickford.

despite the fact that it eventually became an integral part of that same market structure it was set up to counter.

Despite its ambiguous position in the American film industry, UA ensured the continuation of a particular format of independent production, which can be labelled 'top-rank independent production' (as opposed to the 'low-end' format of independent production associated with the Poverty Row studios, which is examined in Chapter 2). Top-rank independent production was practised by a small number of filmmakers who could produce artistically minded and commercially successful films but who were unwilling to follow some of the rules of the studio system, for a variety of reasons. Some of these reasons included: disagreement with studio policies; lack of creative control during the production process; exclusion from profit participation schemes; and, more rarely, aspirations to make 'different' films, which the studios would probably never produce. Although one could argue that producers like Samuel Goldwyn, Walt Disney, David O. Selznick and Howard Hughes 'depended', each to a different extent, on certain resources of the studio system, they nevertheless provided American cinema with a product that often led the way in a number of areas of the film art and business. As Thomas Schatz put it:

> While the big studios emphasised efficiency and productivity, Selznick and other major independents like Sam Goldwyn and Walt Disney produced only a few high-cost, high-yield pictures annually. These filmmakers were in a class by themselves turning out prestige pictures that often tested the economic constraints and the creative limits of the system or challenged its usual division of labour and hierarchy of authority.[19]

Specifically, films by these producers tested the tolerance of the Production Code, a self-regulation framework instigated by the industry itself in 1930, notably Selznick's *Prisoner of Zenda* (Cromwell, 1937), *Gone with the Wind* and Hughes's *The Outlaw* (1943). They pushed the limits of technological innovation, as with Disney's *Snow White and Seven Dwarfs* (1937), and were credited with ushering Hollywood to a new era of mature representations on screen, for instance with Goldwyn's *The Best Years of Our Lives* (Wyler, 1946) and Selznick's *Duel in the Sun* (Vidor, 1946). Furthermore, the same producers repeatedly broke conventional distribution and marketing strategies in an attempt to maximise the box office revenues of their films (*Duel in the Sun* was one of the first films to be released simultaneously in a number of cities; *The Outlaw* was marketed on a city-by-city basis by the producer himself). They advocated the use of scientific audience research at a time when the studios took their audience for granted (Selznick and Goldwyn were among the first producers in Hollywood to make use of the Audience Research Institute, which was established by George H. Gallup to study the Hollywood industry and its audience). Their films repeatedly outperformed the studio films (*Gone with the Wind, The Best Years of Our Lives* and *Duel in the Sun* grossed more than $10 million each at a time when $5 million gross was considered outstanding business). Finally, in what was a unique arrangement in the studio era, Disney's short-subject films were used as hooks by distributor RKO to sell its – sometimes substandard – feature films (the opposite was true for all the other studios).

One could argue then that top-rank independent filmmaking during the studio era was associated with prestige-level film production, which became a particularly significant production trend in American cinema during the 1930s. Prestige-level films were high-cost productions (between $1 and $4 million) and were normally based on firmly established, pre-sold properties to ensure audience recognition. Such properties included nineteenth-century literature, Shakespearean plays, best-selling novels, popular Broadway productions, and biographical and historical subjects.[20]

As a result, prestige-level films could be of different genres and styles, as their emphasis was on production values (high budget, lavish settings, special effects, top stars, glamour) and especially on the films' marketing potential.[21] Although all the major studios adopted this trend, it was a small group of independent producers that, by and large, set the standards and defined the potential of such productions. And it was the success of these independently produced films which occasionally pioneered innovation in several areas of the three branches of Hollywood filmmaking: production, distribution and exhibition.

Independents in the age of oligopoly

There are two main periods in the history of top-rank independent production during the era of mature oligopoly (the era of the Big Five and the Little Three). The first period covers the years between the mid-/late 1920s and 1939. During this period top-rank independent production was a relatively isolated phenomenon in the American film industry and was mainly characterised by a small group of elite producers, which apart from Goldwyn, Selznick, Disney and Hughes included, among others, Walter Wanger, Joseph Schenck and Darryl Zanuck (before their company 20th Century Pictures merged with the Fox Corporation), Chaplin and Pickford. These producers had formed their own companies and were in the business of making only a few, mostly high-cost, prestige-level films per year.[22] Their films were handled theatrically by United Artists, which represented the main outlet for distribution of independently produced films during those years.

The second period of top-rank independent production in the studio era spans 1940 to 1948. This time it was characterised by an industry-wide shift to this type of filmmaking. A cluster of factors that included the growing demand for prestige-level films (especially during the World War II years), the increasing power and leverage of a relatively large number of above-the-line studio employees (actors, directors and, more rarely, writers) and the effects of changes in the taxation system for the duration of World War II encouraged a much larger number of film producers than in the previous period to go independent. Thus, by the end of World War II in 1945 there were 50 independent producers, while two years later the number had risen to 90.[23] Apart from the change in volume, what differentiates this phase of independent production from the earlier one was that the studios became active players in fostering this type of filmmaking. Starting with RKO, which had already signed Walt Disney from United Artists in 1938 and had become a major competitor for UA by 1940, all the major studios (with the exception of MGM) gradually opened their gates to independent producers and established an environment within which an increasing number of newly formed production companies were located. This of course raises questions about the degree of independence of those producers from the studios, questions that are tackled later on in this chapter.

The first period (mid-/late 1920s to 1939)

The first period of top-rank independent production is intricately linked with the trade and business practices of United Artists, the company that was set up with the explicit mission to function as a distribution avenue for filmmakers who produced self-financed films through self-owned companies. As the only distributor to be established by the talent and the only one of the eight dominant film companies in the 1920s and 1930s without a production or an exhibition arm, UA was certainly an oddity in the studio system. Despite the fact that it has always been considered by film historians as one of the eight oligopolists and, especially, a member of the Little Three, United Artists did not also cease to be what Douglas Gomery calls a 'specialised studio', located 'further on the fringe' alongside companies such as Monogram and Republic.[24] If the specialisation of the Poverty Row outfits was in producing and distributing cheap action films, especially westerns (see Chapter 2), the specialisation of United Artists lay in the distribution of prestige-level films and/or star vehicles by a small number of creative producers. United Artists was the only company outside the studios that was allowed access to the first-run houses, which had the power to dominate exhibition. With the other studios' doors firmly closed, top-rank independent producers needed United Artists' distribution apparatus to get access to those theatres.

By the time the structure of the American film industry stabilised in the late 1920s, there were over 20,000 theatres in the US. Although the five majors owned less than 20 per cent of those theatres, their assets included 80 per cent of the first-run theatres and a large number of the best second-run ones. Concentrated in major metropolitan areas, those studio-owned theatres were responsible for between 50 and 80 per cent of all box office revenues generated in the US, figures disproportionately high given the five studios' low ownership percentage.[25] Furthermore, these theatres and a small number of studio-affiliated theatre circuits were excluded from block-booking practices, which meant that they were free to book the most commercial titles from all eight studios, while in exceptional circumstances (when they could not fill all their playdates) they were prepared to accept independent films distributed by companies other than United Artists. Finally, the five major studios had divided neatly the exhibition market among themselves (Paramount controlled the South, New England and Upper Midwest; Fox, the West Coast; RKO and Loew's each controlled a large part of New York, New Jersey and

Ohio; and Warner Bros. dominated the mid-Atlantic states),[26] to the extent that no newcomer could enter the exhibition market without their approval.

With the danger of being shut out of the lucrative first-run theatre market clearly visible, United Artists, under the management of Joseph Schenck (1924–34), devised a programme of first-run theatre acquisitions. Once the major studios realised that the small distributor of independently made films was ready to play their game, that is, expand into the theatrical exhibition market, they agreed to allow UA-distributed films in their first-run theatres. This was under the condition that the company remain solely in the business of film distribution and therefore abort its expansion (and integration) programme. As the studios were in no position to produce a combined output of prestige-level films that would cover the exhibition requirements of the first-run theatre market, United Artists' product would certainly make for a welcome contribution, from which both parties would stand to profit: the studios through ticket sales, which were expected to be high, given the quality of the independently produced films; UA through distribution fees and rentals from first-run sites across the country, which were bound to be higher than the revenues the company would earn had it exhibited its films solely in its own theatres.[27] Between 1928 and 1931 all five major studios signed deals with UA whereby they agreed to exhibit a fixed number of its films in their first-run theatres, while UA refrained from further expansion into the field of exhibition.

Although these agreements secured United Artists' future, on the one hand, they also compromised the company's status as a vehicle for independent filmmakers' resistance to the integrated majors. Securing its future essentially meant becoming an integral part of the same oligopolistic structure the company originally set out to oppose. On the other hand, the majority of the independent filmmakers distributing through UA were prominent figures in American cinema and it was in their best interest to maintain a symbiotic relationship with the dominant forces of the industry rather than adopt a clearly oppositional stance. For that reason, even though UA, unlike the other studios, continued to avoid applying controversial trade practices such as block booking and blind bidding (the practice of forcing exhibitors to buy films sight unseen), it did become a member of the eight controlling companies of the American film industry. Indeed, its collusion with the five majors in the first-run theatre market was beyond doubt when in 1938 the Antitrust Division of the US Justice Department decided to charge UA, alongside the other studios, with violating the Sherman Antitrust Act.

Despite this ambiguous status, however, United Artists' access to first-run theatres ensured that there existed at least one serious distribution outlet for top-rank independent filmmakers. Not surprisingly, then, the company attracted almost all of the few individuals who, for various reasons, defied

Table 1.1 US production companies distributing through United Artists, 1926–39

Production companies	Period of association with UA (+ indicates continued association after 1939)	No. of films
Samuel Goldwyn Company (Samuel Goldwyn)	1926–39+	46
Art Cinema Corp. (Joseph Schenck)	1927–33	29
20th Century (Joseph Schenck, Darryl Zanuck)	1933–5	18
Walter Wanger Productions (UA, Walter Wanger)	1937–9+	13
Selznick International Pictures (David O. Selznick)	1936–9+	9
Reliance Pictures (Edward Small, Harry Goetz, Joseph Schenck)	1933–6	8
Caddo Productions (Howard Hughes)	1927–32	7
Elton Productions (Douglas Fairbanks)	1926–32	5
Hal Roach Studios Inc. (Hal Roach)	1938–9+	5
Joseph M. Schenck Productions (Joseph Schenck)	1926–9	5
Swanson Producing Corporation (Gloria Swanson)	1927–33	5
Mary Pickford Company (Mary Pickford)	1926–33	4
Charles Chaplin Productions (Charles Chaplin)	1926–39+	3
Buster Keaton Productions (Buster Keaton, Joseph Schenck)	1927–8	3
Inspiration Pictures (Walter Camp Jr)	1927–8	3
Edward Small Productions (Edward Small)	1938–9+	3
Inspiration-Carewe (Walter Camp Jr, Edwin Carewe)	1929–30	2
Art Cinema-Goldwyn (Joseph Schenck, Samuel Goldwyn)	1931	2
Pickford-Fairbanks (Mary Pickford, Douglas Fairbanks)	1929	1
Pickford-Lasky (Mary Pickford, Jesse Lasky)	1936	1
Walt Disney Pictures (Walt Disney)	1937	1
D. W. Griffith Productions (D. W. Griffith)	1932	1
Patrician Productions (Walter Camp)	1932	1
Halperin Productions (Edward Halperin)	1932	1
B. F. Zeidman Productions (Bennie F. Zeidman)	1933	1
John Krimsky and Gifford Cochran Inc. (Krimsky and Cochran)	1933	1
Viking Productions (King Vidor)	1934	1
Total		179

the studio-based system of film production and ventured into independent production by forming their own corporations. Table 1.1 contains details of the 27 American-based production companies, the individuals behind them and the number of films they delivered to United Artists for distribution during the period 1926–39 (the + symbol indicates that the company concerned continued producing for UA in the post-1939 period).[28]

Of the 27 American production outfits which were responsible for the 179 (out of 223) films United Artist released in those 14 years,[29] 11 made just one or two films for the company. These included ex-founder Griffith, who had sold his stake in UA by 1924 to return to studio-based filmmaking but arranged a one-off deal as an independent producer in 1932, and Walt Disney, who made a large number of shorts but only one feature-length film for the company. Of the 16 remaining production companies, United Artists' chairman Joseph Schenck was involved in five (Art-Cinema, 20th Century, Reliance Pictures, Joseph M. Schenck Productions and Buster Keaton Productions), while the three remaining founders, Chaplin, Fairbanks and Pickford, produced their films through individually owned companies. This left Goldwyn, Wanger, Selznick, Hughes, Hal Roach and Edward Small (who produced most of their films for United Artists post-1939), Gloria Swanson and Walter Camp, who produced films through three different outfits: Inspiration, Inspiration-Carewe and Patrician Productions.

It is clear then that the independent producers who supplied United Artists with product on a regular basis or throughout an extensive period of time were a particularly small group, which becomes even smaller if one tries to locate the individuals who were in the business of making only prestige-level pictures.[30] This suggests that top-rank independent production was a modest and relatively isolated phenomenon in American cinema until the late 1930s, which explains why it was represented mainly by one specialised distribution company.

Economic constraints

The reasons behind the relative shortage of successful or well established independent producers are several and can be traced in the specific market conditions that characterised American cinema during the late 1920s through to the late 1930s, the years of the Great Depression. In the years prior to the Depression, the independents faced two main problems: obtaining production finance and accessing the studio-owned first-run theatres. With Wall Street banks interested only in film companies with tangible assets – the studios – it was extremely difficult for independent companies to obtain production loans or secure any other form of investment, especially as they were not guaranteed access to the all-important first-run theatres (until United Artists came to an agreement with the majors in 1928). As a result, independent production was limited to a few individuals such as the UA partners who had established outstanding track records in terms of box office revenues since the early 1910s and millionaires like Howard Hughes, who was in a position to self-finance his productions.

These conditions did not particularly improve as the 1920s drew to a close, even though both production finance and access to the first-run theatres seemed to become somewhat easier to obtain than earlier in the decade. This time, it was the complex problems the industry faced during the period of the conversion to sound (1926–8) that proved prohibitive for a large-scale turn to independent filmmaking.[31] Even the few established producers who distributed through UA had to wait until October 1928 to release a film with synchronised sound, approximately 10 months after the release of *The Jazz Singer*.[32] This was because almost all available sound equipment was utilised for studio production, which meant that the independents had very few opportunities to make sound films.

The next decade, however, seemed to be somewhat more promising. Ironically, the major factor that slightly improved market conditions for established and new independent producers was the Great Depression and its impact on the studios and the film industry in general. Having borrowed heavily during the late 1910s and early 1920s to acquire hundreds of theatres and having extended financially even more in the late 1920s during the conversion to sound, the studios found themselves in an extremely fragile state when the Depression eventually hit the film industry late in 1930. One of the measures the studios took to deal with the effects of the Depression was to adopt a more tolerant attitude towards independent filmmakers. This was especially so when the latter started specialising in prestige-level pictures, films that turned out to be the biggest money-makers during the 1930s. Furthermore, the studios changed their system of production to reflect the flexibility of the independents' approach to filmmaking, while even developing their own brand of 'independent' production. All the above changes, however, took place after the studios collectively put an end to a radical independent project initiated by David O. Selznick. This was based on an idea that was only slightly ahead of its time and entailed the establishment of an independent company within the structures of a major studio, RKO.

Selznick attempted to create an independent company which would consist of a small number of units headed by filmmakers. The company would produce about 12 prestige-level films per year and, according to Selznick, would provide the answer to the considerable number of bad films that had flooded the US film industry in the early 1930s.[33] During his stint at Paramount, Selznick had suggested the idea to his superiors but the studio was not interested. After leaving Paramount, Selznick tried to obtain the necessary funds to get the company off the ground but he was unsuccessful. Instead, he decided to accept an offer to become RKO's vice president in charge of production in October 1931 and establish his company within the structures of the studio. By that time RKO was in a desperate financial situation (the Depression had started leaving its mark on that studio, with $5.7 million net losses for 1931) and, therefore, was willing to try new approaches to film production.[34]

The other studios interpreted Selznick's project as a move that would take creative and administrative control away from the studios' owners and top executives and give it to filmmakers or mid-echelon managers, and in effect undermine the traditional structure of the industry. In a perfect example of collusion, the studios ensured that Selznick's independent venture was killed off.[35] He had to wait until 1935 to form Selznick International Pictures (SIP), the structure of which reflected his original idea of a company made of a few units. Like other top-rank independents, SIP made an agreement with United Artists for distribution.

Although Selznick's idea had its foundation on unit production, a system of film production that had been practised informally in some studios since the late 1920s,[36] it nevertheless proved particularly threatening for the studios at a time when their revenues and profits were decreasing rapidly. With their combined profits dropping from $55 million in 1930 to $6.5 million in 1931, the studios were reluctant to allow the extra competition that Selznick's company would certainly create.[37] More importantly, though, the studios were not ready to formalise unit production and accept the partial handover of control of film production from studio owners or top executives to filmmakers. As it turned out, Selznick had put his idea forward only one or two years early. By 1933, as the eight studios collectively recorded $26 million net losses and the need for a more strict fiscal policy became evident, they were ready to replace the dominant central producer system of production with the producer-unit system.[38] Like any leading business enterprises in any other industry, they were ready to accept new practices when the benefits to them were clear or when market conditions left them with no alternative.

Independent production vs studio-unit production

Under the central producer system, which had been the dominant system of production since the mid-1910s, one executive – usually a top-class producer or a manager – supervised a large quantity of films per year (normally between 30 and 50). This system was best exemplified by managers like Irving Thalberg at MGM, who had input into every single production of their respective companies. The producer-unit system, however, decentralised management control, transferring it from one executive or a committee of executives to an elite group of top-rank producers/executives per studio. Each of these producers was in charge of a unit of studio-contracted employees and delivered just a few films, normally between three and six per year. The benefits were many, including: better cost and quality control per film as one person supervised fewer films; a more enhanced sense of teamwork among unit members; further product differentiation within a studio and across the industry as each unit revolved around a particular star, director or producer who made specific types of films; and more efficient use of a studio's assets, which meant lower overhead costs.[39]

This new system of film production had a number of features in common with top-rank independent production. The main ones included: a creative individual in charge of the production process; a tightly knit group of employees working only for one producer; a small number of films produced per year; occasional participation of unit-producers in their films' profits; and production of films of a particular type/trend/style. This suggests that at the time when a handful of producers were making films independently for United Artists there was a much larger number of producers who were heading their own units and were making films for the other studios. In other words, there was a significant number of producers, many of whom specialised in prestige-level and A-class films, who preferred the small degree of autonomy that the security of unit production provided over the larger degree of autonomy that the uncertainty of independent production promised. As we shall see in the next section, many of these unit producers became the independents who defined the 1940–8 period.[40]

This raises the question of the degree of independence for both unit and independent producers. According to Matthew Bernstein, the producer-unit system was only a slight modification of older production models initiated for the benefit of talent that sought more creative control (such as the Famous Players-Lasky's Artcraft arrangement for Mary Pickford in 1916 and First National's agreements for Chaplin and Pickford in 1917 and 1918, respectively).[41] As a result, Bernstein continues, when unit production became dominant in 1932–3, it was only an independent production model that was appropriated by the studios and was adapted to the needs of the existing mode of production. As he puts it:

> Although they correspond to different corporate and contractual arrange-
> ments, the different terms 'unit' and 'independent' production actually
> denoted differences in the degree of autonomy rather than differences in kind.
> In practice from the mid-1920s onward unit production and independent
> production for major studio distribution were interchangeable.[42]

Even though Bernstein seems to be refuting the existence of 'real' independent production in the studio era, he nevertheless does not refer to the producers who released through United Artists when he talks about 'independent' production. Instead, he refers to another brand of independent producers, such as Walter Wanger and Edward Small (before they both started producing for United Artists), Lewis Milestone, Jesse Lasky and a few others whose production companies established distribution deals with the majors. Although in many respects similar to the independents who distributed through United Artists, this particular brand of independent production was characterised by the various forms of control the studio/distributor was able to exercise. Furthermore, as the studios were members of the Motion

Picture Producers and Distributors Association (MPPDA) all the films they distributed (including their in-house independent/unit productions) were subject to approval by the Production Code Administration (PCA), a division of the MPPDA that regulated the films' content through the enforcement of the Production Code. For all these reasons, these productions' 'independent' status was severely compromised.

One particularly interesting example is provided by the treatment of independent production company JayPay's first film for Paramount, the Walter Wanger-produced *The President Vanishes* (Wellman, 1934). The film, which deals with the efforts of a group of industry leaders to force the US president to enter the war in Europe so that they will increase their profits, was subjected to a number of changes by Paramount and the PCA, which did not agree with the representation of various industry professions and the film's overtly liberal political content. As Bernstein argues, Wanger, who otherwise had enjoyed complete freedom in the production process, had actually chosen this format of independence to avoid 'the kind of meddling' that the studio and the PCA routinely exercised on their in-house productions. While Wanger's contract with Paramount specified that he was obliged to make any changes dictated by the PCA, it did not have any clauses that allowed for Paramount's interference with the film's content. Despite that, Paramount board members demanded cuts from the film, while the studio's president, John Otterson, dictated an opening title which would emphasise the film's fictional status and deny any potential for truth value in the events represented.[43] Producing independently for a major (a practice that Bernstein calls 'semi-independence' and equates to unit production), therefore, did not guarantee complete creative control, and Wanger, after a short stint as a (semi)-independent producer at Paramount, in 1936 moved to United Artists in search of a more enhanced form of independence.

The producers who distributed through United Artists, however, were 'a case apart', not least because United Artists did not have any in-house productions to which its independent films could be compared.[44] Like the other studios, United Artists was also a member of the MPPDA and had to distribute films that carried the seal of approval from the PCA. Unlike the studios, though, United Artists did not influence the production process or, indeed, demand any non-PCA-related changes in the films of its producers. On the contrary, the company made it an informal policy to stand by its producers' films, which often tested the tolerance of the PCA and the patience of its administrators. Aside from specific ideological reasons (the owners of the company were producers themselves and were more sensitive to questions of creative control than studio executives), United Artists was not in a position either to influence a production or to demand changes in a final cut. This was because all the producers who released through the company arranged their own financing. As a matter of fact, United Artists provided no finance to independent producers during the 1926–39 period, with the notable exception of Walter Wanger Productions when it joined UA in 1936.[45] As a result, the producers who distributed through UA were able to exercise creative control of their productions, unlike their counterparts who had distribution deals with the studios.

Financing for independent production in the 1930s was available only for an elite group of producers, while the size of guarantees financial backers asked for to make production funds available ensured that the group of independent producers would continue to remain small. With UA refusing to provide any form of financing, the only other avenue open to independent producers was commercial banks, which nevertheless agreed to bankroll producers who had established a good track record of box office revenues. For instance, Goldwyn and Selznick, perhaps the two most commercially successful independent producers in the studio era, arranged financing for their films in the form of residual loans from a small number of banks. To qualify for such a loan for a proposed picture, the producer was asked to secure a distribution contract, to surrender any profits from the proposed film until the loan was covered and to mortgage any earlier films that were still returning profits for the period of the loan agreement.[46] The more successful the earlier pictures and the more promising the proposed one, the more easily the bank would agree to a loan. This of course made it very difficult for any aspiring independent producer to secure production funds and partly explains why there were so many producers who delivered only one independently produced film for United Artists in the 1926–39 period.

Some economic opportunities

Despite the problems, however, top-rank independent production was also essential for the Depression-hit film market. Burdened by the heavy borrowing for the conversion to sound, the studios had started decreasing their output gradually, from 393 releases in 1929, to 362 in 1930, to 324 in 1931, to 318 in 1932.[47] Along with the slowdown in production, the studios also emphasised films 'that would add to the bottom line' rather than take gambles with ambitious projects.[48] Although this decrease was accompanied by a much more substantial drop in the number of theatres in the US (4,000 theatres closed between 1930 and 1932),[49] exhibitors' demand for product was nevertheless increased exponentially. This was because of the introduction of the double bill (or double feature presentation), a practice that saw the billing of two films together as part of an evening's programme. The double feature normally consisted of a major production, which was the main attraction (the

A film), and a lesser-known film, which got the lower half of the billing (the B film). Less than a year after its introduction, the double bill had become a norm in the field of exhibition as more than 8,000 theatres adopted the practice.[50] The A/B film combination was deemed good value for money for a bargain-hunting public and consequently can be considered responsible for keeping theatre attendance at a relatively respectable level during the nadir of the Depression (1932–3).

Although the double bill proved extremely beneficial for the low-end independent producers at Poverty Row (which is why we shall examine it in more detail in Chapter 2), it also provided top-rank independents with considerable gains. Firstly, because of the extraordinary demand for product, exhibitors (including the prestigious first-run theatres) turned more often to independent producers to acquire the necessary number of films to fill in their playdates than in the past. This resulted in the consolidation of the independents' status as essential components of the American film industry. Secondly, as they specialised in the production of prestige-level and solid A-class films, independent producers saw their films in constant demand for the top half of double bills.[51] Although top-rank independent producers such as Goldwyn and Selznick were completely against the concept of the double bill (they thought that coupling their own productions with lesser films would degrade the former as well as deprive them of a percentage of the rentals),[52] ticket sales in theatres playing double bills were consistently higher than in the theatres that exhibited one film. In other words, the independent producers stood to profit more from double bills despite their position that their films should be exhibited on their own.

Finally, and more importantly, the combination of great demand for film along with the studios' trend to emphasise the production of films that would add to the bottom line elevated the already prestigious independent film product to an even higher status. Top-rank independent producers became the champions (and gatekeepers) of outstanding production values and overall quality in filmmaking, while their films epitomised the level of artistic excellence that US cinema was capable of achieving. In the words of Thomas Schatz:

> Just as any studio needed its occasional prestige picture to reinforce its artistic credibility, so had the industry at large needed independent producers like Selznick and Sam Goldwyn to define the high-class motion picture – so long as they were not too independent and their pictures reinforced rather than challenged or changed the dominant notions of value and quality in feature filmmaking.[53]

As the film industry started bouncing back from the effects of the Depression in the mid- to late 1930s, the few top-rank independent production companies had not only managed to survive, but also had become an integral part of the film industry. The major studios had realised that not only were the independents' contributions essential for the smooth running of the industry, they also did not pose any real threat to the studios' domination of the film market. This was mainly because the most important of these independents (Goldwyn, Selznick, Disney and Wanger) operated as mini-studios and in effect replicated a number of production and business practices associated with studio filmmaking. These practices included, among many other things, the adoption of a detailed division of labour during the production process, the making of genre films and the placement of stars, directors and other creative personnel on long-term contracts. Furthermore, they could not pose any real threat to the studios because, despite whatever their claim to financial independence, they had to use some of the studios' resources, whether these were their sound stages, their directors or their stars. Most importantly, they had to use their theatres, because without the studios' theatres they would not be in a position to bring their films to profitability and therefore secure funding for more pictures.

Where they differed from the studios, the in-studio (semi-)independents (like JayPay Productions) and the studio units were in the ways top-rank independents adapted certain dominant production practices to allow for greater collaboration during all stages of the production process,[54] and in the ways they 'pushed the envelope' in several aspects of film production, distribution and exhibition. As a result, the vast majority of the films produced by these companies did not present major aesthetic differences from the films produced by the studios. Surely, there were films with transgressive moments in terms of the use of film style, the construction of narrative, the politics of representation and in terms of bypassing the limitations of the PCA. Those moments, however, were not pervasive enough to suggest the existence of an 'alternative' cinema, movement or film culture that ran parallel to the mainstream studio cinema. Rather, they constituted isolated instances of un-conventional filmmaking at a time when the films of a small number of studios seemed to be made within the boundaries of a particular aesthetic paradigm, which Bordwell, Staiger and Thompson called 'classical'.[55]

Although it would be easy to dismiss these types of films as nothing more than studio copycats that were made outside the studio system simply because their producers wanted a share of the profits, such a characterisation would entirely miss the point. This is because the purpose of top-rank independent production during this period was not to revolutionise American cinema or even to articulate an alternative voice. Instead, it was to resist the claws of an oligopoly which since the late 1920s was closing tighter and tighter on the American film market. With five vertically integrated corporations exerting almost total control of the market, the threat of a film industry that would turn out films 'like sausages' became visible once again.

Independent production, then, sought on the one hand to prevent an extreme standardisation of American cinema towards which the centripetal tendencies of its oligopolistic structure seemed to be leading it. At the same time, it provided American cinema with product differentiation that was based mainly on the high level of quality that the films brought on to the screen. Not surprisingly, independent producers specialised mainly in prestige-level films, which were defined by their level of quality, production values, spectacle and artistic competence rather than by particular genre/star/style combinations that characterised the vast majority of studio films. In this respect, independent production set trends, standards and fashions which were often imitated by the studios, while on several occasions pushing the limits of Hollywood's aesthetic paradigm. On the other hand, however, top-rank independent producers respected and therefore did not seek to change or even challenge certain fundamental aspects of American cinema: its organisation as a capitalist enterprise; its function solely as a narrative medium; and its emphasis on entertainment.

For all these reasons, it is not constructive to perceive top-rank independent production in the late 1920s and 1930s as a failed effort to establish an alternative aesthetic paradigm in American cinema. Rather, it should be seen as a successful experiment that prevented the integrated majors from achieving total control of the film market, while occasionally providing films which demonstrated the possibilities for an alternative American cinema.

Case study 1.1 Top-rank independent production in the 1930s: Walter Wanger, John Ford and *Stagecoach*

> *Stagecoach* (John Ford, 1939, 96 min.), produced by Walter Wanger Productions, distributed by United Artists.

Stagecoach is a film that was linked with a number of independent production outfits before it was eventually produced by Walter Wanger Productions in 1938. In the mid-1930s, director John Ford was under contract to 20th Century Fox, although he was allowed to do the occasional picture outside the studio. Ford signed a two-picture deal with Pioneer Pictures, an independent company run by filmmaker Merian C. Cooper and backed financially by millionaire Jock Whitney (Schatz, 2003, p. 23). Pioneer itself had a six-picture deal with Technicolor, the company responsible for the development of the three-strip colour process in 1932 (Schatz, 1996, p. 180). In April 1937, Ford bought the screen rights to a short story entitled 'Stage to Lordsburg', published in *Collier's* magazine, for $2,500 (Schatz, 2003, p. 23), though other sources (Bernstein, 1994, p. 146) place the cost of the property at $7,500. As westerns were not considered prestigious films in the 1930s, Ford intended to make it cheaply with B-movie stars Claire Trevor and John Wayne playing the main leads. Although such a project did not fit with Pioneer's Technicolor spectacles like *Becky Sharp* (Mamoulian, 1935) and *Dancing Pirate* (Corrigan, 1936), nevertheless Cooper agreed to the production of *Stage to Lordsburg*.

In spite of Cooper's agreement, the project also needed David O. Selznick's approval. In the summer of 1936, Selznick had taken charge of Pioneer Pictures in order to exploit its Technicolor contract for films made by Selznick International Pictures. As Jock Whitney was also the main financial backer of SIP (Bernstein, 1993, p. 47), he and Selznick orchestrated the deal, driven by their common desire to produce *Gone with the Wind* with the best three-colour process supplier. Although Pioneer and SIP never officially merged, Pioneer's projects nevertheless became Selznick's properties. When Ford and Cooper approached Selznick with *Lordsburg* (in the summer of 1937) Selznick suggested that SIP would be interested in producing the film, if the filmmakers revamped the project and replaced the two leads (Wayne and Trevor) with big stars such as Gary Cooper and Marlene Dietrich, in other words, if they upgraded the picture into a prestige-level film. Merian Cooper and Ford refused and they left SIP taking the property with them (Bernstein, 1994, p. 147). At that point Ford tried with fellow director Tay Garnett and actor Ronald Coleman to establish their own independent company (Renowned Pictures) to produce the film (Aberdeen, 2000, p. 146). That venture, however, did not take off and Ford accepted studio assignments at 20th Century Fox as well as a deal for a prestige-level film with Samuel Goldwyn Productions, *Hurricane* (1937) (Bernstein, 1994, p. 147). Still, on the side, Ford pitched the *Lordsburg* idea to major studios but Fox, Paramount, Columbia, MGM and Warner Bros. all declined (Schatz, 2003, p. 24).

In the summer of 1938, Ford approached Walter Wanger with the idea (Bernstein, 1994, p. 147). Wanger had been the first independent producer to agree a multi-picture deal with United Artists, whereby the distributor would provide finance for the pictures of Walter Wanger Productions (WWP) (Balio, 1976, p. 140). Formed in July 1936, at a time when United Artists was desperate for product, WWP would provide the distributor with A-class and prestige-level films, while United Artists would guarantee the company's production bank loans, pay the producer a straight salary and split the profits of his films. Although WWP provided UA with the additional product the distributor needed, the first group of films proved financial failures (Bernstein, 1994, pp. 437–8). Only in 1938, after the release of *Algiers* (Cromwell), did Wanger give a solid hit to the distributor. It was around the time of the release of *Algiers* when Ford asked Wanger to look at his property, which was renamed *Stagecoach*.

Wanger agreed to produce the picture at a cost of approximately $1 million (Bernstein, 1994, p. 147). Under his contract with United Artists, however, he had to seek the distributor's permission for films with a cost of more than $750,000 (Balio, 1976, p. 140). To avoid a potential rift with the company at a time when United Artists had yet to see a profit for a film released by WWP, Wanger agreed to produce the film on a lower budget. As a matter of fact, Ford had already budgeted the film for just $490,700, as both his salary and the other key collaborators' salaries were much lower than studio standards (Schatz, 2003, p. 25). Specifically, Ford's fee was $50,000, Dudley Nichols's fee (as the screenwriter) was $20,000, while the two leads would cost only $18,000 ($15,000 for Trevor and $3,000 for Wayne). To cut costs even further and to compensate Ford for his sub-par salary, Wanger offered the director a 20 per cent share of the producer's profits (Schatz, 2003, p. 29), which according to his contract with United Artists represented 75 per cent of a film's box office gross once the exhibitors' take, the distribution fee, and advertising and negative costs were deducted (Bernstein, 1994, p. 180).

Ford's control over the production of the film was complete and exceptional for the era. He was involved in virtually every phase between the film's development and shoot, and while he did not participate in the editing stage he was confident enough to let the film's editors put together the takes he had sent them (Schatz, 2003, p. 29). Ford was fully supported by his producer, who endorsed the director's authorship and promoted it in publicity material. Reviews in the national US press were very positive, with a reviewer for the *New York Times* writing about cinema as the 'director's medium' (Schatz, 1999, pp. 80 and 82) years before auteur theories informed any type of film reviewing and criticism. The film was released on 3 March 1939 and was a commercial hit. It grossed $1,103,757 and returned a profit of $297,639 (Bernstein, 1994, p. 439), to be shared between United Artists and Walter Wanger Productions in a 25 per cent 75 per cent split. Furthermore, the film was nominated for seven Academy Awards, including one for Best Picture, no small feat for a western in the year when films like *The Wizard of Oz* (Fleming), *Wuthering Heights* (Wyler), *Mr Smith Goes to Washington* (Capra), *Ninotchka* (Lubitsch), *Love Affair* (McCarey) and *Of Mice and Men* (Milestone) represented a particularly strong set of prestige-level films, by both studios and independents, led by Selznick's epic *Gone with the Wind* (Aberdeen, 2000, p. 13).

The remarkable degree of control Ford enjoyed during the production process – in a role normally associated with the independent producer – clearly attests to the film's independent status. Equally importantly, however, the film presents a number of characteristics, as these have been discussed by Thomas Schatz, that also make it a key 'independent' production for the 1926–39 period. Firstly, it was one of the earliest examples of high-budget westerns to usher the genre to the A-class/prestige-level category of films. Between 1939 and 1941 a significant number of high-budget westerns, released by the studios and a few independents, gave credibility to a genre that throughout the 1930s had been identified strongly with Poverty Row outfits, especially with Republic Pictures (Schatz, 2003, p. 21).

Secondly, despite its kinship with the other A westerns of the period, *Stagecoach* maintained also a certain distance from them, primarily by refusing to ground in history the events it depicted. Indeed, while the other

A westerns emphasised the historical dimension of their subjects (on a par with prestige-level pictures which dealt with biographical/historical subjects), *Stagecoach* avoided an overt historicism by also highlighting mythic elements of the West (particularly the mythology of the American frontier – the film opens with the invocation of Geronimo's name, once again threatening white settlers) (Schatz, 2003, p. 22).

Thirdly, and as an extension of the second characteristic, *Stagecoach* is different from other A westerns of the era as it co-opts and reworks a number of B western conventions and methods of filmmaking more generally. These include: the casting of lesser stars like Wayne and Trevor; the characterisation of Ringo (Wayne), which was based on the actor's persona developed in a series of westerns for Poverty Row outfit Monogram; the use of other actors associated with B films; the use of stunts (especially during the chase sequence); and even the execution of some studio-based scenes in the Republic Pictures studio space (Schatz, 2003, pp. 28–9). These distinct characteristics of the film demonstrate why it differs from the other A westerns and partly explain why the studios kept rejecting Ford's idea: his vision of what the film would look like was at odds with the studios' vision of the prestige/A western.

Despite those differences, it was *Stagecoach* that exerted the greatest influence on the A western, so much so that it was labelled the 'Renaissance western par excellence' (Schatz, 2003, p. 36). In this respect, it fulfilled the most important function of top-rank independent production in the 1930s: it defined the high-class, high-quality picture even in a genre like the western, which until then had been in disrepute.

The second period (1940–8)

If during the 1926–39 period independent production was a relatively isolated phenomenon, merely tolerated by the major studios and serviced primarily by one distributor, this was not the case after 1940. In the new decade independent film production became an industry-wide phenomenon, with the studios opening their gates to a large number of independent filmmakers and with United Artists gradually losing its distinct identity as the first-choice distributor for top-rank independents.[56] As a matter of fact, from 1945 and until the end of the studio period, going independent meant going only with the major studios as United Artists failed to attract any distinctive new producers. A number of problems within the company but mostly the other studios' active encouragement of independent production from the early 1940s onwards convinced a large number of new independents to snub United Artists and, instead, sign distribution deals with the majors. As a result, independent production became an integral part of studio filmmaking, unlike in the previous decade when it occupied a marginal position within it. This meant that the studios were now in a position where they could control and, consequently, influence independent production directly, while in the 1920s and 1930s they maintained their control indirectly, mainly through ownership of first-run theatres. On the other hand, independent production also influenced studio filmmaking in substantial ways and laid the foundations for a number of production and business practices that characterised American cinema as a whole in the following decades.

If there was a landmark achievement of independent film production during the previous era, this was undoubtedly the Selznick International Pictures-produced film *Gone with the Wind*. The film 'pushed the envelope' in a number of areas:

- it cost three to four times the budget of the average prestige-level film ($4.1 million);
- it was widely credited as a model of a faithful film adaptation (from Margaret Mitchell's titular novel);
- it employed state-of-the-art Technicolor cinematography;
- it ran for three and a half hours (almost double the length of an average studio film);
- it was launched amidst an unprecedented level of publicity;
- it received the highest number of Academy Awards until that time (eight – including one for Best Picture);
- it effected a minor but still very substantial victory against the Production Code Administration (the PCA allowed the inclusion of the word 'damn', a word explicitly forbidden by the Production Code until then);
- it grossed $20 million only from road showing (before its general release and subsequent runs), more than any other film in the history of sound cinema until that year.[57]

The phenomenal success of *Gone with the Wind* and the less spectacular but still very strong box office business of another Selznick International Pictures-produced film, *Rebecca*, the following year (Hitchcock, 1940), resulted in a unique occurrence in the history of American cinema. In 1940 SIP became the first independent company to record more profits in one year than any of the major studios ($10 million compared with $8.7 million for the second-ranked company, MGM, and $6.4 for the third, Paramount).[58] What makes SIP's achievement even more impressive, however, was that the company's profits came from only two films, as opposed to 47 for MGM and 48 for Paramount.[59] What is more, *Gone with the Wind* was also responsible for at least half of MGM's profits, as Selznick chose that studio to distribute his film, despite having a distribution contract with United Artists at the time. Realising that the box office potential of the film was enormous, MGM charged a 70 per cent distribution fee for a long period during the film's release and ended up with very good profits in a year when its own films underperformed.

Selznick's success demonstrated clearly the great potential for profit of independently produced prestige-level films. MGM's profits, on the other hand, convinced the studios that they could stand to earn a massive part of their income from independent production simply by using their distribution savvy and the power of their exhibition sites. As a number of independent producers had voiced strong complaints and doubts about United Artists' ability to market independent pictures effectively and to secure the best possible exhibition terms,[60] the studios were in a position to offer independent production companies considerably superior distribution expertise. In fact, Selznick opted for MGM instead of United Artists mainly because of the major's 'unparalleled sales and exhibition operations', which he considered to be greatly superior to United Artists' distribution resources.[61]

Although United Artists' competence in film distribution was questioned throughout its history by various independent producers, the company's distinct identity as the only distributor that could guarantee independents access to the first-run theatres ensured that it had always been the first destination for any top-rank independent producer. In the late 1930s, however, it got competition. In 1937 UA lost Walt Disney to RKO, while a year later George Schaefer, UA's general manager in charge of domestic distribution, left the company, also for RKO. As the new president of the studio, Schaefer immediately put into practice a programme of recruitment of independent producers, in effect adapting the United Artists model to the resources of a major studio. Within a few years RKO became a haven for independent filmmakers, with Samuel Goldwyn, Leo McCarey, Orson Welles and Alfred Hitchcock following Walt Disney and distributing their films through the company. Equally, Universal, Columbia and even Warner Bros., the most factory-oriented studio of the 1930s, moved to embrace deals with independent filmmakers in the early 1940s, thereby providing additional competition to United Artists.

The industry-wide shift

Besides the lessons that Selznick and *Gone with the Wind* were 'teaching' Hollywood in the late 1930s and early 1940s, there were other factors that convinced the studios to accept independent production as a very significant industry-wide paradigm for filmmaking. These included: the impact of the consent decree of 1940 (which limited substantially the practice of block booking and eliminated entirely the practice of blind bidding); the effects of

World War II (mainly the slowing down of film production, the increase in theatre attendances and, especially, the introduction of a system of taxation that encouraged the establishment of independent companies); and certain changes in film financing which opened up more options for independent producers. By the final months of 1947, when market conditions started deteriorating and independent production was no longer encouraged by the industry, there existed 90 active independent producers specialising in prestige-level or A-class features.

When the US Justice Department charged the eight major companies with violating the Sherman Antitrust Act on 20 July 1938, it initiated a legal battle that would last for more than a decade. Acting on behalf of the independent US exhibitors, which owned more than 60 per cent of the country's theatres but claimed a disproportionately low share of film rentals compared with studio and studio-affiliated theatre circuits,[62] the Justice Department filed a lawsuit against the Big Five and the Little Three to address this inequality. The lawsuit was aimed primarily at putting a stop to the practice of block booking, which forced all theatres – with the exception of the studio-owned first-run houses – to buy the studios' films in large blocks, sometimes as large as blocks of 50. Furthermore, and as an extension of this objective, the lawsuit was also about discontinuing the practice of blind bidding, which was also used routinely by the major studios. On a more general level, however, the Justice Department's lawsuit was aimed at separating the branch of production from distribution and exhibition, to stimulate competition in an industry that in the course of less than three decades had succeeded in erecting enormous entry barriers. Consequently, it focused its attention on the vertically integrated Big Five studios. After months of deliberations, negotiations, political manoeuvring and 13 trial postponements, the US government and the five big studios drafted a consent decree which was signed by the relevant parties on 29 October 1940.

Although the 1940 decree had several main points, the one that became important for independent production was the studios' agreement to reduce the number of block-booked films to five and to replace blind bidding with trade showing, a form of advanced screening of studio films for prospective buyers. The consequences were immediate. In order to make the block of five films as appealing to exhibitors as possible, the studios started placing more emphasis on the films' production values, especially in terms of the use of stars and spectacle in individual films.[63] As a result, they gradually phased out B-movie production but, more importantly, slowed down their overall production schedules to allow for more attention to their top films. The production slowdown had two very positive effects for independent production. Firstly, it made studios look once more to the established independents to supply the extra product. Secondly, the demand for top-rank pictures became so high that it created a need for more independent companies to provide those pictures to the studios.

The studios' renewed emphasis on quality and production values caused a particularly important shift in the balance of power, from executives to above-the-line talent. While in the 1920s and 1930s films were sold on the basis of the studios' brand names, the limiting of block booking to groups of five decreased the value of the studio brand name as a bargaining tool. Instead, it was the films' stars, directors and stories that became the focal point for programme differentiation, as well as the main marketing strategy the major distributors employed. Consequently, this above-the-line talent found itself in a position of growing power and increased leverage over the production process. The studios had no alternative but to accommodate a substantial number of directors, stars and, more rarely, writers who sought more creative and administrative responsibility of their pictures. This accommodation took the form of allowing (and later actively encouraging) talent to establish their own in-house independent shops, sometimes with extremely favourable terms. As Thomas Schatz put it, 'the studios were willing to consider deals with outside producers and other top talent, often on unprecedented terms, simply to secure proven filmmakers who could reliably deliver A-class pictures'.[64]

At the vanguard of this new independent movement were the 'hyphenates', filmmakers who undertook a second and, more rarely, a third role in the production process, in addition to their normal roles. Unlike the majority of independent producers in the 1930s, who were originally studio executives or had an industrial or business background, these new independents were mainly creative personnel who established their own companies, while also adding extra responsibilities to their job description. Thus directors became director-producers (John Ford, Leo McCarey, Cecil B. DeMille, Frank Capra); writers became writer-producers (Herman Mankiewicz, Sidney Buchman, Nunnally Johnson) and writer-directors became writer-director-producers (Preston Sturges).

As the above internal changes in the American film industry had already cultivated a positive climate for a more widespread practice of independent production, the effects of the United States' entry to World War II created even better market conditions for the film industry in general and the independents in particular. Even before the country's entry in the war in December 1941, the film industry had started reaping the benefits of an increasingly strong economy that was driven by massive investment in the country's defence build-up. Theatre attendance had started to increase and so had the studios' profits, which almost doubled from 1940 to 1941.[65] These trends continued throughout the years America was at war (1942–5). With employment rates at record levels, salaries up 65 per cent (from 1942 to 1945) and an overwhelming part of war-industry production taking place in and around the urban centres where the studios' theatres were located, attendance and profits surpassed pre-Depression totals in 1943 and continued at this level until the end of the war.[66]

The type of film that led the impressive box office revenues during this boom period was the prestige-level film. With approximately a third of all studio personnel serving in the armed forces and with a number of bans imposed on the use of essential raw material for film manufacturing, the studios had to cut back further on their yearly output (from 358 films in 1942, to 289 in 1943, to 262 and 270 in 1944 and 1945, respectively).[67] As the output was getting lower, demand for films, particularly for prestige-level productions, remained high and the studios were in an even greater need for such films. Under these conditions, independent production was not only welcomed but was also actively encouraged by a film industry that was desperate for product. Even the traditionally thorny issue of production financing was suddenly not such a great problem. The huge box office success of independently produced films such as *Sergeant York* (Hawks, 1941), *Since You Went Away* (Cromwell, 1944) and *The Bells of St Mary's* (McCarey, 1945) convinced Wall Street banks that independent filmmaking could be an enterprise as lucrative as studio production.[68] Consequently, they started financing independent companies, often without asking for the types of guarantees that had made production financing almost impossible in the previous decade.

Even though the system of production financing for independent films would be perfected after the end of the studio era, its main characteristics were introduced in the early 1940s. In general, there were three 'categories of money' which normally were differentiated by the degree of risk attached to them and which had to be obtained from different sources:

- *First money* financed up to 60 per cent of the production and was normally borrowed from a bank. It was termed so because it was the first debt to be paid back once the film was released.
- *Second money* or 'risk' money financed the remaining 40 per cent of the film and was normally raised by salary and other types of deferments or by straight cash from an outside party like a film distributor.
- *Completion money*, although the arrangement varied greatly from film to film, normally involved the signing of a bond by a guarantor who undertook the responsibility to provide the funds necessary for the completion of a film.[69]

The most important source of financing in this arrangement was the second money. It was on the basis of securing the second money (and of producing a distribution contract) that the banks would agree to provide the first money, as it was rare for a film in the 1940s not to return enough rentals to cover the 60 per cent of its budget that the banks provided.[70] On the other hand, if a film did indeed do bad business at the box office, the 'second money' group could stand to lose all their investment, which is why second money was also known as 'risk' money.

While market conditions were constantly improving, it was the introduction of a wartime system of taxation that perhaps played the most important part in the exponential increase in the number of independent producers in the 1940s. In order to finance the war, one of the US government's measures was to increase the income tax rates for all high-salaried employees. With the introduction of the Revenue Act of 1941, the top tax bracket was lowered from $5 million to $200,000, a figure which the salaries of many stars and top studio executives exceeded. For those individuals, income tax rates could be as high as 80 or 90 per cent, which meant that in 1941 a star like James Cagney would be able to keep only $70,000 on annual earnings of $350,000.[71] On the other hand, though, if such an individual was not earning this income as straight salary but receiving it instead as part of an investment in a corporation, the individual had the right to present this income as capital gains and be taxed at a rate of only 25 per cent. Forming an independent company or a partnership after 1941 then became the main avenue for stars or top executives to maintain their high earnings and to 'sequester returns from films in investments, deferments and other methods of remuneration than straight salaries'.[72]

Not surprisingly, the Revenue Act of 1941 provided above-the-line talent with even more impetus to enter independent production. As Ernest Borneman put it in an article in *Harper's* magazine, stars, directors and writers were starting their own companies by 'clutching the banner of freedom in one hand and an income tax blanket in the other'.[73] By 1946, the number of independents had risen to 70 and the capital gains tax loophole seemed to have created a new type of independent company, the single-picture collapsible corporation. Under this configuration, a producer would set up an independent company to make one feature and as soon as that feature was released he or she would dissolve the company and have the profits taxed at capital gains rate before moving on to the creation of a new single-picture corporation. This system proved very appealing not only for new producers but for established ones as well. In particular, Samuel Goldwyn produced his wartime films through different corporations each time (such as Avalon, Regent, Beverly and Trinity Productions) to exploit the low capital gains rate.[74]

The above developments signalled clearly the fact that top-rank independent production had become an industry-wide phenomenon. Equally importantly, however, they also demonstrated the remarkable adaptability of the studios, which retained control of the industry despite the shift to independent production. When the benefits of this format of film production became clear, the studios were quick to reorganise their production practices and make way for this type of filmmaking, proving that they were not monolithic organisations steeped in tradition but dynamic business enterprises with the power to adapt to new industry trends.

The end of the wartime boom

The rise in independent production continued after the end of the war. Even when the US government repealed the capital gains tax break in 1946, the number of independent companies continued to rise. In the following year an additional 20 new companies joined the independent ranks, bringing the total number to 90. By that time, however, market conditions had started deteriorating. Rising production costs, declining theatre attendances (after a peak in 1946) and the introduction of quotas and other protective measures in various European markets, which resulted in a steep decrease in the films' non-US box office revenues, cast a giant shadow over the future of both studio and independent production.

The studios responded immediately by tightening up operation costs. One of the first items in their agenda was reviewing and, on many occasions, revising the unprecedented deals they had made with independent producers during the war years. With the studios' gates closing as suddenly as they had opened, a large number of independent producers, especially hyphenate filmmakers (who were more specialised in the creative than the business side of production), found it hard to obtain financing for their films.[75] Consequently, many independent producers were forced to take a step back and sign with the studios as unit producers in order to secure their future. Furthermore, even the normally reliable United Artists was not in a position to support independent production, as the company was heading for bankruptcy after years of mismanagement and fierce battles among its partners.

Having lost its distinct identity at the beginning of the 1940s, United Artists had seen most of its key producers deserting the company for the superior resources of studios (Disney and Goldwyn to RKO, Wanger to Universal), while also failing to attract any major 'hyphenate' filmmakers with the exception of James Cagney (who also left the company in 1948) and Stanley Kramer (who made his presence felt in the post-1948 period). In 1942 United Artists resorted to the extreme measure of purchasing a package of 23 films from Paramount to fill in its release schedule for the 1942–3 season. The majority of these films, which were bought for $4.3 million in total, were B-class films, including 12 Hopalong Cassidy westerns that were made for less than $100,000 each.[76]

Besides contributing to the loss of United Artists' prestige as a company that released only the work of top-rank independent filmmakers, the Hopalong

Cassidy westerns were also responsible for reversing the company's 24-year-strong sales policy. As they were cheap genre pictures normally destined for the low end of a double bill, United Artists distributed them in blocks, a strategy never before practised by the company. Additionally, United Artists also distributed 'streamliners', light comedy featurettes, the duration of which did not exceed 50 minutes (20 out of the 29 films that producer Hal Roach delivered to the company were streamliners).[77] With complaints about the company's inability to secure the best possible distribution terms for independent films surfacing on a regular basis, it is no surprise that UA was not the top destination for independent filmmakers in the 1940s. It was also the only one of the eight main companies to record net losses during the wartime boom years.[78]

The industry-wide shift to independent production signalled the appropriation of this format of film production by the studios, to the extent that the label 'independent' must be questioned. If the independent producers of the previous decade tried to prevent the total domination of the industry from the forces of oligopoly as well as maximise their share of the profits from their films, then what was the purpose of top-rank independent producers in the post-1940 period? And what was their contribution to American cinema besides supplying theatres with additional prestige-level product when the studios slowed down their production?

As the majority of top-rank independent producers established distribution and financing deals with the studios, there was no doubt that this brand of independence was somewhat different from the one associated with UA in the previous decade and therefore more akin to unit production. As Thomas Schatz put it, on the one hand, there were those 'filmmakers who maintained their own production units but operated within the physical and administrative purview of [a] studio'.[79] On the other hand, though, the rapid increase of independent producers and especially their penetration of the major studios caused a major shift in the use of film style.

Until the early 1940s, film style was institutional, with many studios characterised by a distinct 'house style' which was the product of a creative interplay of stars, genres and budgets. As the studios decreased their output and started releasing more and more independently produced films, their distinct house styles started gradually dissipating, while different, individualised film styles were being developed primarily by the 'hyphenate' filmmakers.[80] In only a few years' time studio house styles would disappear completely while this model of independent production would become the dominant model of production in American cinema in general.

Case study 1.2 James Cagney as actor-producer at United Artists: *Johnny Come Lately, Blood on the Sun, The Time of Your Life*

> *Johnny Come Lately* (W. K. Howards, 1943, 93 min.); *Blood on the Sun* (F. Lloyd, 1945, 98 min.); *The Time of Your Life* (H. C. Potter, 1948, 105 min.), all produced by Cagney Productions, distributed by United Artists.

James Cagney was the first major Hollywood star to create his own production company, in the 1940s. Although there were other stars during the first phase of the studio period (like Gloria Swanson) who left the studios and formed their own companies in order to gain control of their careers, Cagney was the first to exploit the specific market conditions that gave rise to the wave of 'hyphenate' filmmakers in the post-1940 years. Together with his brother William, they formed Cagney Productions and arranged a finance and distribution deal with United Artists. Even though it was William Cagney whose name accompanies the word 'producer' in James's films, one can nevertheless assume that James Cagney was the first major actor-producer in the 1940s.

Cagney had a long and very substantial record of problems with Warner Bros., the company that offered him his first contract. in 1930. By 1936 he had left the studio three times after clashes with the studio heads about his salary, the number of films he was contracted to make per year, the quality of his films, the billing of his name, the marketing of his films and, most importantly, the stereotypical roles he was given to play. Specifically, in a four-year period (1932–5) Cagney made 19 films (approximately one-third of his entire filmography), which on the one hand established him as one of the major stars in the studio and, eventually, increased his income exponentially. On the other hand, though, Cagney found Warner Bros.' (and as an extension Hollywood's) system of mass-production degrading. For, despite the rise in his income and the growth of his stature as a star, his films were still made on the cheap, with little in terms of production values. Regardless of the quality of the productions, however, Cagney's films returned profits consistently, making him a particularly valuable commodity for the studio, which used Cagney films to block book lesser titles. For that reason, Warner Bros. was always ready to welcome him back after each walkout and offer him increasingly improved contracts.

By 1939 Cagney was in the top league of star performers, with a contract that granted him several powers (produce only A-class films, star in no more than three films per year, participate in his films' profits) and which would have earned him $1,650,000 from salary alone if he saw it to the end, until 1943 (Hagopian, 1986, p. 20). However, despite Warner Bros.' concessions, the studio was still trying to enforce on Cagney formulaic stories which highlighted the star 's street-smart, tough-guy image as it was established in the early-1930s Warner films such as *The Public Enemy* (Wellman, 1931) and *Smart Money* (Green, 1931). Desperate to shed this image and acquire more control over his career, Cagney announced his intention to go independent in 1941, after completing *Yankee Doodle Dandy* (Curtiz, 1942), which gave him an Academy Award for Best Actor and enhanced his visibility as a top Hollywood commodity.

Cagney's move to independence coincided with the introduction of the Revenue Act of 1941. As he was the actor with the highest income in Hollywood during that year ($365,000) Cagney was in danger of being taxed at an 80–90 per cent rate. His decision to go independent, then, was also motivated by his desire to reduce his income tax bill, as through Cagney Productions he would be able to present his earnings as capital gains, which would be taxed at a much lower rate.

Although by that time studios like RKO, Universal and Columbia had made numerous deals with independent filmmakers, the Cagneys chose United Artists. Having lost a number of independent producers to the studios, UA was desperate to attract new talent and therefore was prepared to offer finance on top of a distribution contract for a promising producer.

The deal between Cagney Productions and United Artists was for five pictures starring Cagney and a number of other pictures produced by the brothers. The first money would be provided by the banks and guaranteed by United Artists, while Cagney himself would supply most of the second money, primarily through salary deferrals. UA would put in the remainder of the second money, including funds to purchase properties, and pay the salaries of contractors to Cagney Productions. In terms of distribution, UA would collect a 25 per cent distribution fee (much lower than the industry standard), which would go down to 10 per cent when a Cagney Productions film grossed more than $800,000. Finally, the production company would be entitled to 100 per cent of the film's profits, while the Cagney brothers would not be liable for any debts incurred by Cagney Productions (Hagopian, 1986, p. 25). With such extremely favourable terms it was obvious that United Artists needed Cagney Productions much more than the other way round.

The first film by Cagney Productions was *Johnny Come Lately* and it did represent a major departure from Cagney's image as it had been shaped by his films for Warner Bros. The star plays a drifter who arrives in a small American town and is persuaded by an elderly newspaper woman to aid her in her battle against town corruption. Although this narrative premise suggests numerous opportunities for action, the film denies Cagney fans such sequences, until at least the final 30 minutes. Instead, the narrative focuses on the relationship between Cagney's character and the elderly woman, which is characterised by a barely disguised strong sexual tension. Furthermore, emphasis is also placed on his relationship with two other older female characters, while the narrative does not develop the obvious romantic storyline between Cagney's character and the newspaperwoman's young niece.

For this reason, when the fighting scenes do eventually appear they come as a surprise and seem to be at odds with the rest of the narrative. This is also reinforced on the level of the film's tone and pace, which were too slow to 'have survived a big studio' (Agee, quoted in Schickel, 1999, p. 130) and which allow the spectator to concentrate on human relationships rather than the hero's quest. In this respect, when the pace picks up it signals a shift in the narrative's emphasis from the nuances of human relationships to the straight-forward question of whether the hero will achieve his goal.

Despite this perceptible change in the star's persona, the film was a modest success for Cagney Productions, grossing $2.4 million at the US box office. Critics, however, had mixed feelings about Cagney's break from tradition, with the majority giving lukewarm reviews and the *New York Post* suggesting that Cagney should return to Warner Bros. and make films such as *Yankee Doodle Dandy* (quoted in McGilligan, 1975, p. 105).

If *Johnny* was Cagney's cinematic declaration of independence, Cagney Productions' second outing, *Blood on the Sun* (1945), could have easily been a Warner Bros. film. In *Blood* Cagney plays a newspaperman who tries to expose a Japanese secret plan to conquer the United States. This time, however, depth of character and human relationships are largely disregarded in favour of an action-driven plot and wartime propaganda. With Cagney's tough-guy persona (accompanied by displays of judo skills) dominating a conventional spy story it seems that the star reneged on his promise to avoid formulaic stories like the ones Warner Bros. used to assign to him. His fans, however, welcomed Cagney's return to form, making *Blood on the Sun* the most commercially successful Cagney Productions film, with a US gross of $3.4 million.

It would take three more years for the company to deliver a third film to United Artists. The film was an adaptation of William Saroyan's Pulitzer Prize-winning play *The Time of Your Life*. The film focuses on people from all walks of life who frequent a saloon in San Francisco. Cagney plays 'Joe ... whose hobby is people', a well-off street philosopher and permanent patron of the saloon who helps the other patrons with their problems, ambitions and desires. The film is organised in a series of episodes that involve Joe and one or more patrons each time, but despite the episodic structure it presents a number of similarities with *Johnny Come Lately*. Specifically, it features Cagney in another role that is radically different from his roles at Warner Bros.; it focuses again on character relationships rather than on any linear development of a hero's quest to achieve an objective; and, interestingly, it also features a final section where Cagney is involved in a fight with the film's villain. And as in *Johnny Come Lately* the fighting sequence is at odds with the rest of the narrative, which here features Cagney permanently sat on a chair drinking champagne and imparting words of wisdom.

The film represents the pinnacle of the star's independence (Figure 1.2). Aside from a stagey aesthetics (a product of a very faithful adaptation that earned the full approval of the playwright) which was against the realist trends of the time, and in direct contrast to the Warner Bros. house style, the film was also as close to a family production and business as possible. Besides James and William Cagney, it featured Jeanne Cagney, the star's sister, in a central role, and Edward Cagney, the star 's other brother, in the role of the assistant production manager.

The film, however, proved a major economic disappointment for both Cagney Productions and United Artists, grossing $1.5 million. With mediocre reviews and with audiences refusing once again to accept a different Cagney persona, *The Time of Your Life* became the last Cagney Productions picture for UA. The company moved back to Warner Bros., which was once again ready to welcome the star back in an independent/unit production arrangement and to grant him terms similar to the ones he enjoyed at UA. Ironically, but certainly not surprisingly, the first Cagney Productions film under this arrangement was *White Heat* (Walsh, 1949), arguably the star's most memorable personification of a gangster. It proved a huge box office success.

Figure 1.2 At the zenith of independence: James Cagney and his sister Jeanne Cagney in a scene from Cagney Productions' *The Time of Your Life* (Potter, 1948).

Conclusion

As in the previous decade, independent production in the 1940s succeeded in keeping American cinema away from the threat of standardisation that the films of the studios potentially represented. More importantly, though, in the second phase of mature oligopoly independent production ensured that American cinema would be free permanently from such a threat as it helped strip the major studios of their distinct identities. In this sense, top-rank independent production in the 1940s achieved something much greater than introducing a marginal 'alternative' cinema or film culture. It laid the foundations for a filmmaker's cinema. Whether these foundations proved solid or not will be one of the subjects of Part II of this book.

Notes

1 Quoted in Schatz, 1999, p. 341.
2 Gomery, 1986, p. 9.
3 Some accounts have claimed that the Patents Company was formed by 11 members (Hampton, 1970, p. 66).
4 Bowser, 1994, pp. 4 and 6.
5 Hampton, 1970, p. 67. For the agreement between MPPC and Eastman Kodak see Bowser, 1994, p. 30.
6 Jenkins, quoted in Izod, 1988, pp. 18–19.
7 Hampton, 1970, p. 67.
8 Aberdeen, 2000, p. 25.
9 Quoted in Bowser, 1994, p. 81.
10 For instance, independent exchanges chose also to supply theatres with entire programmes rather than just individual films, a practice introduced by the General Film Company (Izod, 1988, p. 29).
11 Bowser, 1994, p. 108.
12 According to Izod, 1988, p. 36, *Queen Elizabeth* did not prove successful as a road-show prestige-level film, though Zukor made profits from the exploitation of the film in the states rights market.
13 According to Tino Balio, 1976, p. 10, block booking was used in the industry before Paramount's emergence but never as effectively and swiftly as Zukor used it.
14 Hampton, 1970, p. 172.
15 Balio, 1976, p. 11.
16 Lewis, quoted in Koszarski, 1994, p. 73.
17 Balio, 1976, p. 13. This statement was originally signed by Chaplin, Pickford, Fairbanks, Griffith and William S. Hart. By the time the company was incorporated in April 1919, Hart had pulled out.
18 Balio, 1976, pp. xiv–xv.
19 Schatz, 1996, p. 11.
20 Quoted in Balio, 1995, pp. 179–80.
21 For a discussion of prestige-level pictures in the 1930s, see Balio, 1995, pp. 179–211.

22 This description applies to producers like Goldwyn, Selznick and Wanger but does not apply to Chaplin or Pickford, who were producing films irregularly.

23 Izod, 1988, p. 126.

24 Gomery, 1986, p. 173.

25 The figures are taken from Koszarski, 1994, p. 9, Crafton 1999, p. 258 and Balio, 1995, p. 7.

26 Gomery, 1986, p. 13.

27 Balio, 1976, p. 66. The term 'rentals' refers to the money returned to the distributor after theatres deduct a percentage of the box office and distributors deduct their distribution fee and the print and advertising costs (see Chapter X).

28 Table 1.1 was compiled with data in Balio, 1976, pp. 246–52.

29 The remaining 44 were produced by non-American – especially British – production companies.

30 According to Balio, United Artists picked up distribution for 25 films of dubious quality between 1928 and 1933 in order to increase the number of its yearly releases, which nevertheless remained well below the industry average throughout the 1926–39 period (Balio, 1976, p. 132).

31 Some of these problems included: the studios' battles over which sound system would be adopted by the industry; the upgrading of their production facilities; and the wiring of the theatres for sound.

32 The film was Goldwyn's *Two Lovers* (Niblo), released on 2 August 1928. *The Jazz Singer* opened on 6 October 1927 (Crafton, 1999, p. 211).

33 Schatz, 1996, p. 125.

34 The figure is taken from Gomery, 1986, p. 125.

35 Schatz, 1996, p. 127.

36 According to Matthew Bernstein, Paramount was the first one to initiate unit production, in 1926–7, as a response to the growing success of Loew's (MGM), which had started outperforming Paramount (Bernstein, 1993, p. 43).

37 The figures are taken from Schatz, 1996, p. 159.

38 The figure is taken from Schatz, 1996, p. 159.

39 For an elaboration of the benefits of the shift from central producer to the producer-unit system, see Bernstein, 1994, pp. 95–6, and Balio, 1995, pp. 75–6.

40 Some of these producers who were heading, for various periods of time, their own studio units were Frank Capra at Columbia; Busby Berkeley, Mervyn LeRoy and Henry Blanke (together with director William Dieterle) at Warner Bros.; and Ernst Lubitsch, Joseph Von Sternberg and Cecil B. DeMille at Paramount.

41 Bernstein, 1993, p. 44.

42 Bernstein, 1993, p. 44.

43 For an account of the JayPay Productions, see Bernstein, 1994, pp. 93–113. For details about the problems that *The President Vanishes* encountered with Paramount and the Production Code Administration, see Bernstein, 1994, pp. 97–102.

44 Bernstein, 1993, p. 47.

45 Having lost one of its most active producers (and president of the company), Joe Schenck, whose production outfit 20th Century Pictures merged with Fox in 1935, and despite signing David O. Selznick and Alexander Korda, United Artists was still in desperate need of quality product. Walter Wanger, who had huge experience both as an in-house independent and as a unit producer, was a very appealing solution to provide the three to five additional films per year the distributor needed, which explains why that venture was financed by United Artists (see Bernstein, 1994, p. 115, and Balio, 1976, pp. 138–40).

46 Balio, 1995, p. 105.
47 Finler, 2003, p. 364.
48 Crafton, 1999, p. 190.
49 Balio, 1995, p. 15.
50 Bernstein, 1993, p. 45.
51 According to Balio, despite its relatively marginal position in the industry, United Artists ranked third in terms of the companies that distributed the most prestige pictures in the 1930s (Balio, 1995, p. 205).
52 According to Aberdeen, 2000, p. 69, top-rank independent producers considered the double bill to be 'the stepchild of block booking'.
53 Schatz, 1996, p. 406.
54 Balio, 1995, p. 107.
55 Bordwell et al., 1985, p. 5.
56 The only studio not to open its gates to independent producers in the 1940s was MGM.
57 The figure of $20 million is taken from Balio, 1995, p. 211. According to Joel Finler, 2003, p. 356, the film recorded approximately $31 million in rentals, which means that its gross was in the region of $60 million.
58 The figures are taken from Gomery, 1986, pp. 34 and 52.
59 The figures are taken from Finler, 2003, p. 364.
60 Schatz, 1996, p. 187, Balio, 1976, p. 112.
61 Schatz, 1999, p. 48.
62 The figure is taken from Aberdeen, 2000, p. 62.
63 Staiger, 1983, p. 70.
64 Schatz, 1999, p. 46.
65 Schatz, 1999, p. 27.
66 For further figures and statistics about employment and salary averages during the war period, see Schatz, 1999, pp. 134–5.
67 Finler, 2003, p. 364.
68 *Sergeant York* and *The Bells of St Mary's* were the number one box office hits in their respective years of release. See Finler, 2003, p. 357.
69 For a detailed discussion of this method of financing see Sanders, 1955, pp. 380–389.
70 Sanders, 1955, p. 381.
71 Schatz, 1999, p. 181.
72 Hagopian, 1986, p. 22.
73 Quoted in Aberdeen, 2000, p. 133.
74 Schatz, 1999, p. 182.
75 Schatz, 1999, p. 346.
76 The figures are taken from Balio, 1976, p. 188.
77 Balio, 1976, p. 174.
78 In 1944 the company showed $0.3 million net losses while during 1942, 1943 and 1945 it recorded meagre profits, never exceeding the $1 million mark (Gomery, 1986, p. 175).
79 Schatz, 1999, p. 56.
80 Schatz, 1999, p. 82.

2

Independent filmmaking in the studio era: the Poverty Row studios and beyond (1930s to 1950s)

> Not everybody likes to eat cake. Some people like bread, and even a certain
> number of people like stale bread than fresh bread.
> Steven Broidy, chairman of Monogram Pictures[1]

Introduction

The above statement by the once president and chief executive officer of Poverty Row outfit Monogram Pictures represents an appropriate introduction to a different form of independent filmmaking during the studio years: low-end independent production, which, in Broidy's analogy, is represented by the phrase 'stale bread'. The analogy seems apt. If one accepts that the films of top-rank independent producers and the studio prestige productions represent American cinema's 'cake', and the standard studio film production corresponds to its 'bread', then films from studios like Monogram, Republic, Grand National, Producers Releasing Corporation (PRC) and a large number of other smaller companies operating in the margins of the industry certainly represent American cinema's 'stale bread'. In other words, they represent film production of a particularly low quality and cheap look that could never be confused with the top-rank product examined in the previous chapter. For instance, according to film historian Wheeler Dixon, the key features of Monogram films were 'shoddy sets, dim lighting restricted mostly to simple key spots, non-existent camerawork and extremely poor sound recording', elements far removed from prestige-level independent production or studio filmmaking.[2] Even the most successful financially and 'artistically' Poverty Row studio in the 1930s and 1940s, Republic Pictures, was widely known by industry practitioners as 'Repulsive Pictures'.[3]

Despite the lack of quality and the absence of production values, however, low-end independent production represents a less controversial form of independent filmmaking. This is because the ties with the major studios that top-rank independents such as Selznick International Pictures enjoyed did not exist for companies like Grand National and Producers Releasing Corporation. Indeed, these companies operated completely 'independently' from the majors, producing their films in their own studios (or in hired sound-stages), releasing them through self-owned distribution networks (or through the states rights system) and exhibiting them in small independent theatres located mainly in the neighbourhoods of big cities, small towns and rural areas. With the majors concentrating on servicing primarily the lucrative first- and second-run theatre market in the large metropolitan cities, a large number of independently owned theatres, which could not afford to buy the majors' films, found themselves in need of product.[4] As these theatres traditionally supplied only a fraction of the industry's box office revenues, the studios could afford to leave them to the competition. In other words, these independent companies operated in the shadow of the studios but outside their sphere of influence and, as Flynn and McCarthy put it, '[they] stepped in to garner the miniscule profits that the majors shunned'.[5]

As in the case of top-rank independent filmmaking, the history of low-end independent filmmaking during the time of the domination of the film industry by the studios can be divided into two distinct periods. The first one covers the years of the Great Depression, particularly from late 1930 to 1939. During this period, low-end independent production was actively encouraged by the industry as the introduction of the double bill created far greater demand for product than the major studios could handle. Companies like Monogram, Republic and Grand National were formed to exploit those buoyant conditions and, along with the studios' B units, supplied theatres with cheaply made films, mainly for the bottom half of double bills. The second period covers the 1940s and the early years of the 1950s. During these times, the studios gradually phased out their B-film production, to the extent that the Poverty Row companies (as the low-end independents were also known) became the sole providers of low-cost films to US theatres.[6] As the market for low-budget productions started declining in the mid-1940s, a small number of companies like Monogram and Republic ventured into A-class and prestige-level production, with Republic even scoring a major Academy Award for one of its productions – an Oscar for Best Direction for John Ford's *The Quiet Man* (1951).

Besides the films produced and distributed by the Poverty Row studios, low-end independent production was also characterised by a significant number of films made for various ethnic audiences. This type of film production was practised completely outside the purview of the American film industry and was exemplified by artisanal productions that cost just a few thousand dollars to produce, with money raised directly from private investors or from the members of the ethnic communities the films targeted. The final section of this chapter discusses the phenomenon of the ethnic film.

The first period (1930–9)

Although low-end independent production existed in the periphery of the film industry from the days of the Patents Company, it nevertheless represented a far too marginal phenomenon to merit detailed examination. With companies being formed and dissolved almost overnight, sometimes making only one film before slipping into obscurity, and with the vast majority of these second-rate films lost forever, the field of low-end independent production prior to the introduction of sound is akin to a vast cemetery with a huge number of short-lived production companies and films buried inside.

In many respects it was the introduction of sound that proved to be the catalyst in shaping the field of low-end independent production. As all these companies were small and under-capitalised, very few of them were in a position to afford the substantial costs of the transition to sound. Even those companies that attempted the transition had to utilise 'inferior "bootleg" sound equipment', which meant that their films paled in comparison with the superior sound of the films made by major studios and top-rank independents.[7] As a result, these films were booked only in small, grind-house circuits and returned a very modest profit to their production companies, if any at all. Still, a small number of such companies managed to survive and become an integral part of the American film industry after the introduction of sound, despite the adverse economic climate created by the Great Depression.

Perhaps the key factor that explains the survival and relative longevity of companies like Monogram and Republic in an era otherwise dominated by the Big Five and the Little Three is the introduction of the double bill in US theatres in late 1930. That scheme, which had been in operation in the subsequent-run market as early as 1915 and which entailed the presentation of two cheaply made films (normally westerns) for the price of one, was introduced to the more upmarket theatres as a measure against decreasing cinema audiences.[8] In its new guise, the post-1930 double bill still entailed the presentation of two films for the price of one, but this time the two films were of a different description. On the one hand, there was the main attraction, the film that received top billing. This was normally a well-made, standard studio production or (on some occasions) a prestige-level studio or independent film. Because of its position on the billing, this type of film became known as the A film. On the other hand, there was the film that received the bottom billing. This was normally a low-budget picture made by specific studio units specialising in efficient, no-frills production or a low-budget film made by an independent company with no corporate ties to the studios. This type of film was known as the B film. In other words, the labels A and B were attached to films because of their position in the billing and not because of their quality, despite the fact that on most occasions B films were of a lesser quality than the A films.[9]

The success of the scheme was instant. By mid-1932, a year and a half after its introduction, 6,000 houses (approximately 40 per cent of the nation's theatres) had adopted the double bill, while many exhibitors went as far as showing triple bills. By 1935 it was estimated that about 85 per cent of US theatres made regular use of double features.[10] This overwhelming success created a staggering demand for films, which the studios were in no position to meet, especially at a time when they had to cut down their own production schedules as the Depression had started hitting the industry in late 1931. Equally, the handful of top-rank independents that existed in the early 1930s could contribute only a fraction of the extra product needed. Not surprisingly, then, the early 1930s witnessed the birth of an impressive number – for a Depression-ridden industry – of film companies, formed to exploit these specific conditions. Additionally, a number of small companies that had been formed in the mid- and late 1920s and had been struggling financially ever since found a new *raison d'être* in the early 1930s. According to Lary May between 1929 and 1934, the number of (low-end) independents almost doubled (from 51 to 92).[11] Besides Republic and Monogram, the two best-known independents, which were formed in 1931 and 1935 respectively (and which are discussed below), other such companies included Tiffany-Stahl, Mascot, Syndicate Pictures, Majestic Pictures, Supreme Pictures, Invincible Pictures and many others.

As none of these companies had the capitalisation of the studios, they could never pose individually any real threat to the established forces in the film market.[12] Together, however, they were responsible for a substantial percentage of the product that serviced the lower part of the double bills, especially in small towns and rural areas. In order to prevent further penetration of the market by those new independent companies, the studios, with the support of top-rank independents, decided to take certain measures. The most important one was their attempt to put an end to the inflated demand for films that the double bill had created, by making the scheme illegal. The opportunity to achieve that formally was presented in the form of the Code of Fair Competition for the Motion Picture Industry that the MPPDA drafted on behalf of the studios as part of President Roosevelt's National Recovery Act (NRA) of 1933. Upon the studios' request, the MPPDA used the Code to outlaw the exhibition practice of the double bill and therefore bring the demand for films down to 'normal' levels.

The low-end independents, however, fought hard against the measure, which would not only drive them out of business but also a large number of small exhibitors that depended on the double bill to survive. Although these exhibitors became an important ally to the independents, it was the cinema-going public, which was overwhelmingly in favour of retaining the three-hour, two-movies-for-the-price-of-one-admission programme during the worst years of the Depression that proved to be the catalyst. Thus, in August 1934 the NRA's Code Authority proceeded to legalise the double bill by ruling that the major studio-distributors could not stipulate contractually the terms of exhibition for their films.

The news had far-reaching consequences. Liberated from the pressure of the studios, the vast majority of independent exhibitors embarked on a programme of full implementation of the double-bill practice. This resulted in the creation of stable conditions for the market in low-budget films and the Poverty Row studios were ready to exploit these conditions fully. Only two months after the legalisation of the double bill, Monogram announced that it was looking into ways of increasing its output from 20 to 36 features and from 8 to 16 westerns for the following year (an increase of 85 per cent), while other companies were exploring similar options.[13]

Monogram Pictures

By 1935, Monogram Pictures had emerged as a clear leader in the sector, with an output of 32 films in 1932–3 (16 features and 16 westerns), 36 films in 1933–4 (28 features and 8 John Wayne westerns) and 28 films in 1934–5 (20 features and 8 John Wayne westerns).[14] The company was the latest incarnation in a series of production-distribution outfits established by W. Ray Johnston and Trem Carr, starting with Rayart in 1924 and continuing with Continental Talking Pictures and Syndicate Film Exchange before finally establishing Monogram in 1931.[15] In the early months of that year Johnston and several states rights film exchange owners formed a cooperative organisation, not unlike the one created by First National in 1917.

As franchise holders in Monogram, each exchange owner would buy stock in the company and contribute proportionally to the production costs of each Monogram film. In return, they would participate in the small but seemingly certain profits the company would make, especially as its distribution network was expanding outside the US (where the company was represented in 39 key territories) to cover Britain (through a deal with Pathé) and Canada (through a deal with Empire). With production funds increasing from $1 million in 1932–3 to $3 million in 1933–4 (an average of approximately $100,000 per film), Monogram quickly found itself ahead of the competition when most of its rivals were producing at most 10 films per year.[16] Monogram's main advantage over the other low-end independents was its distribution arm, which enabled the company to retain a larger part of its film rentals than its competitors. In order to sustain the costs of maintaining a distribution apparatus, Monogram had to produce a large number of films per year (around 30 or more), which resulted in the company's quick establishment in the low-end independent market.

As early as April 1933, Monogram executives had already been planning to exploit the company's position in the market by proceeding to the consolidation of a small number of independent companies 'into one organisation large enough to challenge the biggest of existing producing and distributing organisations'.[17] With the question of the legality of the double bill still not settled, however, Monogram decided to put these plans on hold. When the NRA legalised the scheme, Monogram was ready to play the corporate game. By that time, though, other companies had seen the potential for profits from the low-budget market and were moving in from outside the sector, while existing Poverty Row companies, including Monogram, had started feeling the effects of the Depression themselves, which made them much more open to the idea of potential mergers with and takeovers by other companies.

Republic Pictures

Consolidated Film Industries was one of the companies that moved in from outside the sector. Owned by Herbert R. Yates, Consolidated had been (under various names) the largest film developing and printing company in Hollywood since the late 1910s. It had functioned also as a lender to many film production companies, which allowed Consolidated to control their printing contracts. In March 1935, Consolidated foreclosed on loans to small independents like Chesterfield Motion Pictures and Majestic Pictures; it then merged those two and named the resulting company Republic Pictures. Immediately after, Republic proceeded to a merger with Liberty Pictures, Mascot Pictures and Monogram (which was happy to take a back seat, despite its leadership in the market).[18] The new company, which retained the name Republic Pictures, combined the individual strengths of the companies from which it was created and immediately found itself in pole position for dominating the low-end independent market. Specifically, it combined Monogram's established nationwide distribution network and its expertise in the production of westerns (a staple of the low-budget market, as the majors did not produce westerns for most of the 1930s) and Mascot's reputation for quality and its

Figure 2.1 The Singing Cowboy: Gene Autry's popularity helped Republic Pictures establish a dominant position in the low-end independent market.

leadership in the market for chapter plays (serials), where it was competing on an equal level with Universal.

The new company made its mark immediately. In September 1935, it released *Tumbling Tumbleweeds*, a 'singing cowboy western' featuring recording artist Gene Autry (Figure 2.1) in one of his first roles. Made on a miniscule budget of $18,000, the film proved massively successful, grossing in excess of $1 million at the US box office.[19] More importantly, *Tumbling Tumbleweeds* became the first in a large number of such films (starring Autry and, later, Roy Rogers), which proved extremely popular with small-town and rural audiences and contributed substantially to the company's profits throughout the years. Republic also continued Mascot's tradition by releasing quality serials, which cost between $50,000 and $100,000 but which could potentially return more than $600,000 as each of the serial's 12 chapters was sold for $5 a time in more than 10,000 theatres.[20]

Republic's auspicious start, however, was shadowed by management problems. Within two years of its establishment, four of its top executives had resigned, including W. Ray Johnston, who revived Monogram after attracting new franchise holders in a new cooperative, and M. H. Hoffman, who revived Liberty Pictures.[21] Despite the resignations and the extra competition it faced from its former executives, Republic continued to dominate the low-end independent production field for the rest of the decade with allocated production funds reaching the $9 million mark in 1940 and a release schedule of 60 films per year, which was comparable to the schedules of companies like Universal and Columbia.[22] One could only wonder whether Republic Pictures would have been in a position to eventually give the majors a serious challenge, had the merger been successful.

The re-emergence of Liberty and Monogram clearly demonstrates the existence of a substantial market for this type of production. As an increasing number of theatres were adopting the double bill, independent companies started producing more and more films while new companies entered the low-budget film arena. Along with Republic and Monogram, the other key independent in the second part of the 1930s was Grand National Films (GN). Despite its short life span and its origin in Poverty Row, GN attempted to transcend its status and compete aggressively with the major studios.

Grand National Films

The company was established as an independent distributor by Edward L. Alperson, an ex-film exchange manager, in the spring of 1936. Modelled on United Artists but with some production funds available from Pathé and a private investment firm, Grand National was to distribute independently produced films that it would co-finance with the individual films' producers. Within seven months from its inception, GN had already released 10 films, most low-budget productions aimed at the bottom half of double bills. However, the company's potential for growth did not remain unnoticed in Hollywood, especially when rumours surfaced that Dupont (one of the richest corporations in the US) was Grand National's secret bankroller.[23]

The major studios' fears that GN had the potential to become the sixth fully vertically integrated major and therefore challenge openly the status quo seemed to take shape when the company signed James Cagney after one of his frequent walkouts from Warner Bros. due to contract disputes (see Chapter 1). With no studio or top-rank independent willing to poach him for fear of breaking diplomatic relations with Warner Bros., Grand National, which operated outside the studio system, stepped in. The company offered Cagney a one-picture-a-year deal, an agreement vastly different from the one he had at Warner Bros., where the star was making three to four pictures per year. Cagney's presence at GN gave the company a different, more upmarket status, as no big stars were ever allowed to work for low-end independents (the studios believed that participation in such films would degrade irrevocably the value of their performers). Cagney's first film with GN, *Great Guy* (Blystone, 1936), was relatively successful but did not do the business GN had hoped for. Besides the fact that it was a poor imitation of the pictures Cagney was making at Warner Bros., the film's commercial potential was further damaged by poor distribution, perhaps the product of informal collusion by the studios, which were in a position to make their first-run theatres unavailable for the film.[24]

Although the next film GN was planning with Cagney was *Angels with Dirty Faces*, Alperson decided on a different project, a musical comedy with the title *Something to Sing About* (Schertzinger, 1937). The film represented a huge financial gamble for the company, as it was budgeted at $900,000 and anchored all the other GN releases for the 1937–8 season. The production was plagued with problems, which resulted in further costs that the company had trouble covering. The film, which, according to Patrick McGilligan, was an 'attack by Cagney on Hollywood, "show people" and the entire movie star syndrome', lacked again in terms of production values and look.[25] Furthermore, like *Great Guy*, *Something to Sing About* also encountered problems with distribution. This time, however, GN had invested far too much capital to make a profit or even recoup its investment. The company recorded a hefty loss, from which it never managed to recover, especially after Cagney left independent production and returned to Warner Bros. before plans for a third film materialised. Ironically, his first film after his return to the major was the massively successful *Angels with Dirty Faces* (Curtiz, 1938) the rights for which Warner Bros. had purchased when GN dropped its plans to make it with Cagney. With the star gone, GN scaled down production (to the region of 20 low-budget films per year) but continued to experience economic problems. A year later, the company merged with Educational Films, a producer of short subjects (including animated shorts starring Felix the Cat), but a few months later went bankrupt.

Grand National's failed experiment to compete with the established powers, along with Republic's unsuccessful attempt to shun its Poverty Row image, clearly demonstrate that low-end independent production was a completely different concept from top-rank independent or studio production. One could argue, then, that Poverty Row outfits were responsible for a type of cinematic practice, characterised primarily by a cheap-looking aesthetic, which was markedly different from the practice of mainstream, studio-produced cinema. Although such an argument has substantial merit, what complicates matters is that the studios themselves had specific production units that also specialised in quick, efficient and cheap film production, mainly destined for the bottom half of double bills. As a result, a large number of these studio films were produced on a similar economic basis and for the same reason as the films made by Poverty Row studios. Consequently, the studio-produced B films might share a similar aesthetic with films from Republic, Monogram and the rest, a position that would suggest that the films from the Poverty Row studios were 'independent' only because they were produced outside the studio system and not because of any formal differences from B studio production.

Independent B films vs studio B films

The labels 'B' and 'Poverty Row' are not synonymous. According to Brian Taves, B films were of such a wide variety that grouping them under one extremely large category and assuming that all films included were of a similar budget or of a similar aesthetic would be to oversimplify a particularly complex phenomenon. He explains:

> Conceptions of the B movie varied widely. Even among the majors the budget for B pictures often diverged by $100,000 or more. There is no budget or production schedule typical of all B's because of the wide variations among the different companies … [t]he same schedule and budget that resulted in a high-quality B at Paramount or MGM might approximate the investment for an A at Columbia and Universal.[26]

If the B film was practised by different companies in different ways, it could be argued that the Poverty Row studios (which produced only B films during the 1930s) practised this type of filmmaking in a different manner from the studios. Indeed, Taves proposes four different categories of B film, presented in descending order of prestige:

1 major studio 'programmers';
2 major studio Bs;
3 smaller company Bs;
4 the quickies of Poverty Row.[27]

Although Taves here reserves the term 'Poverty Row' for truly low-budget companies like Astor and Weiss (in his chapter 'The B Film: Hollywood's Other Half' he uses the term 'Poverty Row' to refer to companies in both categories 3 and 4),[28] what becomes obvious from his taxonomy is that before any important qualitative differences come into play, B films are divided between the more prestigious, studio-produced Bs (categories 1 and 2) and the considerably less prestigious, often disreputable, non-studio/independently produced ones (categories 3 and 4).

What differentiates the above two broader categories is the level of prestige attached to the films and, less obviously but equally importantly, the audience that is associated with each category. In terms of the first difference, studio programmers and studio Bs mobilised substantial resources and capital as they represented the majors' efforts to reduce overhead costs by utilising the large numbers of actors, staff and crew who were on their payrolls on long-term contracts. For instance, Fox's B unit spent approximately $6 million per year on the production of 24 films (typically $150,000–$200,000 per film).[29] Furthermore, the studios were not in a position to take the production of their B programme lightly, as their reputation depended on both the A and the B films they released.[30] Additionally, the studio Bs and programmers were chosen sometimes for the top half of double bills (depending on the type of theatre they were exhibited in), which made them the main attractions for cinema-goers and therefore films expected to be of unquestionable quality. For all these reasons and despite the lower budgets and the relative lack of glamour in comparison with the A films, studio-produced B films were still visibly mainstream Hollywood pictures, refined productions that their makers could be proud of.

Poverty Row firms, however, produced only B films (at least in the 1930s), with no pretension to quality. Although there were film productions on which companies like Monogram and Republic spent more money than they did on other types of films, the budgets rarely exceeded the $100,000 mark, even for their most 'prestigious' productions. Filmmakers in Poverty Row studios certainly desired the creation of solid films; their filmmaking practice, however, obeyed some very specific and incontestable rules, where quality and aesthetic ratification were not on the list of priorities. These rules included:

1 Completing the film within inflexible shooting schedules, which often did not exceed a working week (six days) and which could entail up to 80 camera set-ups per working day.
2 Bringing the film in on a miniscule budget that often did not allow for more than one take per shot, regardless of the take's quality. For companies whose profit was usually a few thousand dollars per film, going over budget (or over schedule) might have made the difference between profit and loss.
3 Developing stories from inside the company (as purchasing rights to pre-sold properties would drive production costs up); on rare occasions

when rights were cheap and/or were in the public domain, Poverty Row studios would proceed in such deals.

4   Producing a very large number of outdoor pictures (especially westerns), as they required minimal studio work, which meant that they could be produced on extremely low budgets.[31]

In the final analysis, John Tuska argues, '[t]here were two very distinct ways of approaching a motion picture, one where all questions and problems and all energies answered first and last to the budget, the other where the final product itself, the motion picture, took precedence'.[32] Poverty Row studios in the 1930s approached filmmaking only in the first way.

Besides their difference in terms of the prestige they carried, studio Bs and Poverty Row films were further differentiated in terms of the audiences for which they were made. This is arguably a fundamental difference for a position that sees films from the Poverty Row outfits as part of an alternative type of cinema to the mainstream studio product. Specifically, studio Bs were channelled by their respective distributors to first- and second-run, studio-owned and affiliated theatre circuits, aiming therefore at reaching the widest possible audience that – by definition – the studio A films were produced for. As these theatres were concentrated in large metropolitan areas, studio As and Bs were aimed primarily at adult urban audiences, who were considered more sophisticated than the audiences in small towns and rural areas.[33] As a result, and despite their differences from A films, studio programmers and studio Bs generally did not stray too far from the rules of classical narrative construction (cause–effect logic, character motivation and so on) that had exemplified studio production since the mid-1910s.[34]

On the other hand, the Bs of Poverty Row were distributed to a large number of independent exhibitors, which, according to Steven Broidy (Johnston's successor at Monogram), were 'receptive' to the type of product Monogram and the other Poverty Row studios offered.[35] In these theatres, the low-end independents had the opportunity to target audiences which were different from the urban, middle-class cinema-goers who patronised the first-and second-run theatres. These audiences included smaller demographic groups, such as lower classes and ethnic immigrants as well as children and juveniles for Saturday matinée shows.[36] Furthermore, the independents tapped into a largely previously unidentified urban audience in the American Southern states, who visited cinemas primarily on Saturday nights in search of singing cowboy westerns with country music stars.[37]

One common element to all those demographic groups was that they were not interested in the 'classically structured' narratives that characterised studio films. Instead, they were interested in action, thrills, pace, adventure, spectacle, stunts and any other exciting element that could contribute to an 'emotional rollercoaster' type of film entertainment. As a result, and despite their very limited resources, Poverty Row studios tended to emphasise these elements, often to the detriment of classical cinema staples such as 'coherence, mood and characterisation' that exemplified studio-produced As and the majority of Bs.[38] This is particularly noticeable in comparisons between serials (particular types of pictures for the very specific audience of matinées) made by Republic/ Mascot and its rival Universal. According to Jon Tuska, on the one hand, the serials produced by Mascot were characterised by relentless action (as much as possible per episode), while not being very 'long on [narrative] logic'. On the other hand, Tuska argues, Universal's chapter plays 'tended to stress story as much as action', making them more suitable for a more sophisticated audience who could appreciate narrative pleasures as well as thrills.[39]

Wheeler Dixon reaches a similar conclusion in his discussion of the films by Producers Releasing Corporation when he argues that in Poverty Row 'everything is immediate, vicious, do-or-die. All dialogue is reduced to motivation, rather than speculative analysis by the characters ... films are work of the moment, operating on the level of the protagonists, *of* their world'.[40] Finally, Case study 2.1 demonstrates that the Charlie Chan series made at Monogram (1944–9) was indeed characterised by a cheap look and an emphasis on immediacy, pace and thrills, while the Charlie Chan series made as Bs at 20th Century Fox (1931–42) were characterised by a comparatively lavish production design and with a primary stress on story construction.

One could argue, then, that Poverty Row films represented an alternative practice that went against the mainstream classical cinema of the studio system. Although this was particularly evident in the films by the smaller independents (category 4 in Taves's taxonomy), which 'offer[ed] an aesthetic problem in the paradigms of classical Hollywood cinema',[41] it also permeated the films of larger Poverty Row outfits. This type of independent cinema performed an extremely significant social function: it promoted a more accessible and, ultimately, more inclusive American cinema, which embraced audiences from the lower strata of society (and, as we see in the last section of this chapter, from different races and ethnicities), whose limited consumer power had placed them at the bottom of the studios' customer list. In departing from the rules of classical filmmaking, low-end, non-studio production presented a cinema that was less bound by established rules, which justifies the term 'independent', in the same way that the production of films outside the studio system lends itself to that label.

Case study 2.1 Low-end independence at Poverty Row: Monogram and the Charlie Chan film series

> *Charlie Chan in the Chinese Cat* (Phil Rosen, 1944, 65 min.), produced and distributed by Monogram Pictures.

Charlie Chan is a Chinese-American detective who was introduced to the literary world in January 1925 by author Earl Derr Biggers in his novel *The House Without A Key*, published in instalments in the *Saturday Evening Post* (1925). Following the success of this novel Biggers wrote five further novels before he died of a heart attack on 5 April 1933.

Only a year after its publication, Pathé adapted *The House Without a Key* as a 10-chapter serial with Japanese George Kuwa in the eponymous role. This was followed by a Universal film of the second Biggers novel, *The Chinese Parrot*, in 1927, this time with Japanese Kamiyama Sojin in the role of Chan. Although neither project was particularly successful, the Fox Film Corporation decided to adapt the third novel, *Behind that Curtain*, as a vehicle for one of its stars, Warner Baxter. The film was released in 1929 with the British E. L. Park in the role of the detective. Besides the fact that on all three occasions Chan was played by a non-Chinese actor, what was interesting in all three productions was that Chan was a secondary, even marginal, character, especially in the Fox film, where he appears only at the end.

These three early entries did not connote any particular cinematic future for Biggers' literary creation. However, in 1931 Fox purchased the rights to the next two Chan novels, *The Black Camel* (1929) and *Charlie Chan Carries On* (1930). By that time the studio had started responding to the needs of the double-bill market, and developing long-lasting series was perceived as a particularly efficient way of producing cheap product. Biggers' novels represented the possibility of a potentially successful series as they were pre-sold properties and had clear generic qualities. For the role of Chan, the Fox producers cast Warner Oland, a white actor who had nevertheless played 'oriental' characters in a large number of 'yellow peril' films before the 1930s (including playing the role of evil Dr Fu Manchu in three films made at Paramount).

As with the previous offers, *Charlie Chan Carries On* (McFadden, 1931) featured the eponymous character once again in a small role. However, Oland's warm portrayal of the detective made him a hit with audiences. For its second Charlie Chan offering, *The Black Camel* (McFadden, 1931), Fox therefore put Chan at the centre of the narrative and that change became the cornerstone of a formula which would last for 10 years.

The Charlie Chan films at Fox were B films but were produced in a relatively lavish style. For instance, *The Black Camel* was shot on location in Honolulu, while *Charlie Chan at the Opera* (Humberstone, 1936) featured an original short piece of opera composed specifically for the film. Furthermore, it was not unusual for Fox to cast famous character actors in major or minor roles, such as Boris Karloff and Ray Milland, who, of course, cost more money than less-known studio contractees. The budgets for the Fox films were in the region of $200,000 per film (Hanke, 1989, p. 169) and the shooting schedules fluctuated between three weeks and a month.

Fox's attention to the production of the series certainly paid off, as certain Chan films grossed more than $1 million each, a sum normally associated with the box office performance of A films (Taves, 1995, p. 317). This means that despite their status as Fox programmers or Bs, the films drew A-film audiences. For that reason, Chan films were exhibited in the first- and second-run theatres, where they had the opportunity to record grosses of that level. Furthermore, unlike other Fox films made by its B unit, the Chan films were distributed on a percentage basis (rather than a flat fee), which meant that Fox could capitalise on their popularity (Taves, 1995, p. 337). Until 1934, Fox released on average two Chan films per year. From 1935 onwards (as the double bill was legalised and the series had taken off) Fox upped its releases to three films per year, until Oland's death in 1938.

Sidney Toler, another white actor, was selected to replace Oland as Chan. One key difference from the films of his predecessor was that Toler's performance tended to bring about more humour from the situations Chan found himself in, while also developing a slightly more sarcastic approach in his conversations with his children and with potential suspects in the cases he investigated. The series was changing direction, privileging scenes with comic potential over a tightly structured plot. This was also reflected in the speed with which Chan films appeared in the market. At that time Fox was producing the series at a much faster pace, averaging four Chan films per year for 1939 and 1940 (though the shooting schedules remained in the region of three weeks). However, despite the effort to retain quality, the series started losing its popularity. Fox reduced the number of films, offering two in 1941 and one in 1942, before dropping the series after 11 years and 27 films.

On hearing the news that the studio had decided to discontinue the series, Toler, who had bought the rights to the character of Charlie Chan, approached Monogram. The low-end independent had just started making cautious steps towards a slightly more upmarket production and agreed to revive the series. James S. Burkett and Philip N. Krasne, unit producers for the company, undertook the production of the series. Director Philip Rosen and screenwriter George Callahan completed the unit which would produce the first five Chan films for Monogram, starting with *Charlie Chan in the Secret Service* in February 1944.

The differences between the Fox and Monogram Chan films were marked. With budgets dropping from $200,000 to $75,000 per film (Hanke, 1989, p. 169) and production schedules shortened from around a month to a week (*Charlie Chan in the Chinese Cat* was produced between 11 and 19 January 1944), Monogram's approach to the production of the series proves that there was a huge difference between a studio B film and a film from even one of the better-known and better capitalised Poverty Row outfits.

The Monogram look of 'shoddy sets, dim lighting and non-existent camera work' is clearly evident in *Charlie Chan in the Chinese Cat*. In the film, there are at least three instances of perceptible, that is, obtrusive, camerawork and editing that are certainly not motivated by the narrative (the most obvious of these takes place in the scene that introduces the hideaway of the gang of thieves, where a dissolve that consists of a fadeout and two different shots that fade in simultaneously confuses the spectator). Furthermore, there are (supposedly) exterior scenes that are covered in thick fog to hide the sparse setting, while a number of scenes take place in a dark warehouse that requires minimal lighting and no props.

Despite all these 'flaws', however, there is one occasion when the film transcends its cheap look and presents a particularly unusual, and admittedly beautiful, composition. In the scene where Chan and his assistants Tommy Chan and Birmingham Brown go to the dark warehouse to look for Deacon, they are faced with his dead body, half hidden in the darkness. A few moments later the film cuts from a shot of Chan to a shot of the three men's silhouettes against the wall. The shot is not motivated by anything in the narrative and does not resemble any other shots in the film. Equally, it should not be seen as an auteurist statement, as Phil Rosen has not employed any similar shots in other Charlie Chan films. A plausible explanation would be that the shot was created to hide the sparseness of the set (we tend to see the characters in medium shots, which means that we see only the walls of the set). As more shots like this would certainly distract from the story, it stands alone as an artistically motivated shot that was nevertheless inspired by a pragmatic and practical necessity, the lack of setting.

Besides its problems with visual style, the film presents major 'flaws' in the narrative. The main flaw revolves around the book written about the murder of Thomas Manning, in which the author supports that Manning was murdered by his wife and that the detective handling the case withheld evidence because he was having an affair with the step-daughter of the deceased. This claim constitutes the main turning point in the narrative, as it is the imminent publication of the book that motivates Leah Manning to ask for Charlie Chan's help. This creates several problems in terms of the film's narrative logic. Why don't the members of the family of the deceased try to solve the case before any book about their private lives comes into play? Why are they prepared to accept a libellous story about them? Why don't they try to prevent the book from being published?

This and other 'holes' in the narrative are filled by a fast pace and a considerable amount of action (especially in the last 20 minutes of the film) that do not allow the spectator time to question motivation or notice gaps in the story. With 73 scenes and a total duration of 65 minutes, the film switches from scene to scene every 55 seconds, on average.

Another area where the Monogram films were different from Fox's was in the even stronger emphasis the former placed on comedy than the latter. This was largely due to the addition of Birmingham Brown (Mantan Moreland) as Chan's unofficial sidekick in his investigations, who brings comedy value with 'funny' one-liners that tend to emphasise his (stereotypical) cowardice in potentially dangerous situations (*Charlie Chan in the Chinese Cat* contains at least 11 such one-liners). As the series progressed, the part of Birmingham Brown started growing in stature, to the extent that he became as important as the character of Chan. In this way, Monogram attempted to capture two audiences, the Chan fans and the African American audiences, as Moreland was one of the most popular black actors of the 1940s, with credits in more than 100 films for the decade.

Perhaps the most important difference between the Monogram and Fox films was the representation of race (mainly Chinese Americans and later African Americans). With the role of Chan played consistently by whites in the films of both companies (when Toler died, Monogram replaced him with yet another white actor, Roland Winters), the problem of representation was certainly a thorny one. Despite his portrayal by white actors, however, Charlie Chan is one of the most positive representations of non-whites in Hollywood cinema, especially when the most recent representations of 'oriental' characters before Chan had been in 'yellow peril' films and exemplified by villains like Fu Manchu. In the Fox series Chan becomes a model of a 'cultured immigrant' trying to assimilate into American culture (Taves, 1995, p. 336), with his language betraying a good education and his manners an upbringing that satisfied western 'standards'.

In the Monogram films, though, the character becomes gradually more abrasive, more condescending, more critical of his sons and often offensive to several (white) characters that surround him. Consider his patronising attitude to ex-lieutenant Dennis when he wants to give him the credit for solving the Manning murder – 'and this is how you did it' – or his contemptuous response to Dr Recknick's expertise in criminology – 'expert is merely man who make[s] quick decision – and is sometimes right'. The Monogram Charlie Chan, then, signifies a force as progressive as that of the Fox Chan but also a stronger one, as Monogram gradually disperses with the (stereotypical) image of the subservient Other (at least when it comes to Asian Americans), while also highlighting a more resistant and often threatening 'yellowface'. As Ken Hanke put it: 'That they [the Monogram films] are different from the Fox films is undeniable. That this difference is altogether undesirable is questionable' (1989, p. 179).

The second period (1940 to early 1950s)

The second period of low-end independent film production during the studio era is characterised by three significant factors that contributed to the persistence of the low-budget film market. These factors were: (1) the continuation of the double-bill scheme in the 1940s, despite the end of the Depression, which had provided the rationale for its introduction in 1930; (2) the impact of the consent decree of 1940, which affected the low-end independents in a different way than their top-rank counterparts and the studios; and (3) the effects of World War II, which were beneficial for the film industry as a whole. The 1940s became a 'golden era' for the established Poverty Row studios like Monogram and Republic, while new production-distribution companies like Producers Releasing Corporation (PRC; 1939) and Screen Guild (1945) entered the market to exploit these conditions.

By the late 1930s the effects of the Great Depression had started subsiding. Although the country would have to wait a few more years to experience prosperity, economic recovery was well underway by 1937–8, and this was nowhere else more obvious than in the American film industry. The big studios, the majority of which had been experiencing heavy losses or had been in receivership during the mid-1930s, were bouncing back with increased revenues and healthy profits in 1937.[42] Equally, top-rank independents were finding a growing number of avenues open to them as prestige-level films by Selznick, Goldwyn, Wanger and Disney were doing spectacular box office business and studios like RKO started emulating United Artists' model of distributing independently produced films. Despite these rosy conditions, however, the film industry was reluctant to abandon the double-bill strategy, which had helped all involved parties (producers, distributors, exhibitors) during the Depression's hardest times.

The most important reason behind this reluctance was that the double feature presentation had stabilised the market not only for the low-end independents but also for the studios. Irrespective of the studios' complaints about the scheme, the double bill had allowed the major production and distribution companies to operate smoothly as the B films they produced inexpensively represented sure-fire profits, which meant that the studios could afford to take financial risks with their A product. Add to this the public's persistent support of the scheme and it is obvious that it would have been extremely difficult for the industry to justify the discontinuation of its practice.

With the double bill in place for the following decade, the market for B films seemed to be guaranteed. The consent decree of 1940, however, ensured that Monogram, Republic and a few other small outfits would be the rulers of that market as it signalled the beginning of the end for the studios' B production. As noted in the previous chapter, the decree meant that the studios agreed to limit block booking to five films per block and to screen their films in advance in various trade showings. To ensure that exhibitors would be interested in all five films, studios had to raise the production values (and the budgets) of their B films, to the extent that the A/B distinction became increasingly blurred for studio films.

The repercussion of this move by the studios was that the decidedly B films of the Poverty Row firms were the only contenders for the bottom half of double bills. Even when the discontinuation of B production occurred gradually, companies such as Republic and Monogram tried immediately to capitalise by producing and distributing at capacity levels, with Republic announcing 62 films for the 1940–1 season, 66 for the 1941–2 season and 68 films for the 1943–4 and 1944–5 seasons.[43] Finally, to complete the auspicious picture for the low-end independents, the US Justice Department's antitrust lawsuit of 1938 left out the larger Poverty Row companies, despite the fact that Monogram and Republic traditionally block booked their pictures. This was because neither company had ever been involved in the exhibition business or had ever colluded with the major studios (unlike United Artists, which was included in the lawsuit). Monogram, Republic and PRC were allowed to continue their trade practices in the subsequent-run theatre market without any constraints from the government.

Besides the positive effects of the persistence of the double bill and of the consent decree of 1940, the low-end independents stood also to benefit, along with the rest of the film industry, from the surge in theatre attendance that was noted during the pre-war and war years. Between 1939 and 1946, exhibitors saw approximately 25 million new customers added to the 75 million existing ones who flocked to the theatres every week.[44] The new customers were mainly internal migrants who had moved to the big cities from rural areas to work in the factories for the country's defence build-up and, later, war effort. To accommodate the workers' shifts, theatres were staying open around the clock, while the absence of other leisure alternatives made cinema the main recreation choice.[45] Indeed, business was so exceptional that Republic and Monogram saw an impressive increase in their revenues and profits. In particular, Republic's profits exceeded the $1 million mark in 1946, still lacking

Table 2.1 Gross revenues and net profit/loss for Monogram and Republic, 1938–48

Year	Monogram		Republic	
	Gross revenues	Net profit/loss	Gross revenues	Net profit/loss
1938	1,494,402	(180,817)	7,373,972	n/a
1939	947,565	41,642	7,960,000	n/a
1940	1,945,879	(179,656)	7,235,335	590,031
1941	2,030,459	10,897	6,256,335	513,451
1942	2,186,092	157,103	6,700,358	504,351
1943	2,567,186	99,144	9,465,338	578,339
1944	4,300,627	177,833	11,137,125	561,719
1945	4,807,446	165,161	10,016,142	572,040
1946	n/a	n/a	24,315,593	1,097,940
1947	8,100,205	375,895	29,581,911	570,200
1948	9,030,906	(497,696)	27,072,636	(349,990)

substantially in comparison to the profits of a major such as MGM (over $12 million profit in the same year) but in relative proximity to a smaller studio like Columbia ($3.4 million profit in 1946).[46] Table 2.1 presents the financial performance of the two key Poverty Row studios from 1938 to 1948 (the figures in parentheses signify net losses).[47]

Producers Releasing Corporation

With Monogram and Republic consistently profitable (especially after 1941) it was no surprise that new companies would attempt to enter the – now sizeable – low-budget market. The most significant was Producers Releasing Corporation. Like Grand National, PRC (whose original name was Producers Distributing Corporation) was set up as a distribution company in 1939, by Ben Judell, an exchange owner who had recently ventured into production. Like Monogram, the company came together as a cooperative of franchise holders with the main objective of producing and distributing ultra-low-budget films, mainly westerns.[48] Immediately it announced three series of westerns (eight per series) and soon after a programme of 60 features for a total investment of $1 million.[49]

To produce the films, the company hired six associate producers. A few months later, however, Judell found himself in financial trouble, while the company did not seem to have the resources to deliver enough films to sustain its distribution network. In the face of bankruptcy and only a year after its formation, the company was taken over by its creditors, one of which was Sigmund Neufeld Productions, and was renamed Producers Releasing Corporation. Under Neufeld, PRC managed to stabilise operations and become a steady supplier of cheap product to subsequent-run theatres. This became particularly evident during the 1942–8 period, when the company released on average 40 films a year.

According to critics, the PRC product was so cheap – even for Poverty Row standards – that it represented 'the nadir of independent filmmaking'.[50] Filmmakers such as Edgar G. Ulmer, Sam Newfield and Joseph H. Lewis who produced films for the company achieved fame (or notoriety) for making feature films in five days (with some westerns allegedly shot in two days) with ultra-low budgets.[51] In an interview with Peter Bogdanovich, Ulmer revealed that he was not allowed to work with more than 15,000 feet of film, which was the equivalent of two hours of film duration. From this the filmmaker had to deliver a film between 55 and 65 minutes long, which did not allow any margins for mistakes.[52] But for PRC, quality was never an issue. As Wheeler Dixon argued: '[At PRC] no one cared about what was "in the can" as long as you had at least fifty-four minutes of programming.'[53]

It was this kind of indifference towards the content of its films, in combination with the ultra-low budgets and the ultra-short shooting schedules, however, that enabled filmmakers like Ulmer and Newfield to experiment with narrative and style while trying to find solutions to the logistical problems that this type of filmmaking created, and to achieve critical fame that was unexpected for filmmakers working in the low-budget market.[54] Some of Ulmer 's films in particular have attracted considerable critical interest retrospectively, as Case study 2.2 demonstrates.

Case study 2.2 A Poverty Row masterpiece: *Detour*, Edgar G. Ulmer and PRC

> *Detour* (Edgar G. Ulmer, 1945, 63 min.), produced by Leon Fromkess, distributed by PRC.

Edgar G. Ulmer is one of the very few filmmakers primarily associated with Poverty Row studios (and the ethnic film market) to have achieved critical prominence. Having emigrated to Hollywood from Europe at the same time as F. W. Murnau, Ernst Lubitsch, Fritz Lang and Max Reinhardt, Ulmer did not manage to secure a long-term career in a studio, despite a short stint at Universal for which he made *The Black Cat* (1934), one of the company's definitive horror films. Following his exit from Universal, Ulmer accepted work in the ethnic film market and between the mid-1930s and early 1940s made films in Yiddish, Ukrainian and Spanish, while also making one picture for African American audiences. In 1942 he made the film *Tomorrow We Live* for PRC which became the first in a series of 10 pictures he made for the Poverty Row distributor until it was taken over by Eagle-Lion in 1948.

At PRC Ulmer was given unlimited freedom to make any type of film he desired, so long as his films came within the extremely low budgets that the company was notorious for allocating to its productions. Having been used to work for even less money than standard PRC production budgets in the ethnic film market, Ulmer managed to use B-film production as a vehicle for the creation of often distinctive motion pictures, of films that transcended their status as Poverty Row product and became emblems of quality where quality was the last thing expected. Indeed, while at that company, Ulmer was known as 'the [Frank] Capra of PRC' (in Bogdanovich, 1975, p. 397), a label that signifies both the creative freedom he enjoyed and the fact that his films were deemed significantly more artistic than the rest of the company's output.

Detour is Ulmer and PRC's most famous film. With a budget estimated between $30,000 and $66,000 and a production duration estimated between three and six days (Williams III, 1988), the film is located within the third category of B films that Taves proposes (even though the duration of the shooting could also suggest that it flirts with the fourth category, of the 'quickies'). Furthermore, the fact that the majority of the film's scenes were shot in a car over (a very noticeable) back projection of streets and landscapes clearly indicates the film's humble origins at a Poverty Row studio.

Detour is about one man's descent to a life of crime as a result of fate when he decides to hitchhike from New York to Los Angeles on his way to a reunion with his ex-girlfriend. Starting with the seemingly accidental death of David Haskell, a rich-looking bookmaker, who offers him a lift from Arizona to Los Angeles, Al Roberts believes that he will be charged with murder and therefore decides to cover up Haskell's death and steal his money and identity. As he continues his trip to Los Angeles he picks up Vera, a woman who had previously ridden with Haskell and who accuses Roberts of killing him and stealing his car. Afraid that Vera will go to the police, Roberts agrees to help her make as much money as possible by selling Haskell's car but Vera wants him to present himself as the long lost son of Haskell's father, whose imminent death presents an additional opportunity for easy money. Refusing to go that far, Roberts challenges Vera to call the police but ends up killing her in what seems again to be another accident. The film finishes with Roberts hitchhiking and expecting to be caught by the police while cursing fate and what it can do to innocent people for no reason.

Although the film demonstrates a number of characteristics associated with film noir (a narrative unfolded in flashbacks, the protagonist's voice-over, a hero being betrayed by a dangerous woman), it nevertheless does not fit entirely into the noir mould, as it opts for what Dana Polan calls a 'washed out look' that is different to the play of light and dark that characterises noir films (Polan, 2002). This washed out look, however, which is clearly a product of PRC's ultra-low-budget filmmaking policy, dovetails perfectly with the bleak, nightmarish world that the film depicts, while the narrative, organised around three flashbacks, presents a number of instances when the lack of production resources and the rushed manner of the shooting of the film seem to comment on the world the characters live in (Morris, 2001). At the same time it also presents several opportunities for visual excess that Ulmer fully exploits.

During the first flashback sequence, Al and his girlfriend, Sue Drake, walk together from the nightclub they work at to Sue's house. Throughout their walk, which is presented over five short scenes, thick fog covers everything, to the extent that it is impossible to see the setting (only the road signs are visible), while in some instances even the characters are barely discernible. Although the excessive thickness of the fog seems to be determined by the production's effort to disguise the cheapness of the setting (and the fact that the walk did not take place over a long stretch of street, which would have required significant technical resources), it also becomes a comment on the characters' suffocation and entrapment within their miserable lives, a statement about their inability to see ahead (in this case literally) and realise whether there is a future ahead for them or not.

A few scenes later and during the same flashback sequence Al is imagining a bright future for him and his girl. Sue is seen in a medium shot singing their favourite song, 'I Can't Believe That You're In Love With Me', accompanied by three musicians who are nevertheless seen only in shadow projected against the wall behind her. Although the large projected shadows create an unusual image that implies glamour, it is nevertheless obvious that the image was constructed in such a way exactly because it was impossible for the limited resources of the production to portray glamour. But like the function of the fog in the earlier scenes, Al's imagination of a bright future is certainly determined (and limited) by the film's budget and mode of production. There are several other such instances in the film (especially the constant use of back projection of monotonous landscapes and empty roads during the scenes in the car, which create a sense of bleakness that fits in perfectly with the impasse that characterises the protagonists' lives) which make this type of relationship between minimal production values and depicted events prominent in the film.

Although the style that characterises *Detour* could not have been replicated by a major studio (or even arguably by a studio's B unit) the film transcends its Poverty Row status by avoiding stressing only action and thrills, and by paying particular attention to elements such as mood and narrative coherence – traditionally characteristics of A films. Despite such an emphasis, however, the narrative presents a number of gaps or problems. For instance, during the first of the film's three flashbacks Roberts's voice-over informs the spectator that, despite the drabness of his job in a second-class nightclub, his relationship to Sue made life heaven. This statement, however, is followed by a short scene where a very cynical Roberts refuses Sue's affection and proclaims that he will never become the pianist he always wanted to be. Not surprisingly, Sue leaves him in search of a better future in Los Angeles. Similarly, during the second flashback Roberts's voice-over insists that the money he took from Haskell when he assumed his identity was money he would 'rather not have'. The image that supports his words, however, portrays him counting the money and putting it in his pocket without a trace of regret or disgust in his face.

Although in Ulmer's hands these problematic matches between narration and narrative highlight the unreliability of the part of the narration that is presented through Al Roberts's voice-over (to the extent that the spectator cannot help but believe that neither death in the film was accidental), they nevertheless do not cease to be also holes in a story constructed over a shooting period of less than a week. This limitation, however, in this case works in the film's favour, as it adds a further layer of paranoia that makes the world it represents even more nightmarish than it really is. It is this aspect that makes *Detour* a key example of film noir, despite its issues with visual style, and highlights Ulmer's skill as a filmmaker who could make such an artistically interesting film in spite of the limited resources available to him at PRC.

For a longer discussion of Ulmer's work at PRC, see Tzioumakis, 2008.)

Upgrading the product

Republic, Monogram and PRC were the most successful low-end independents in the 1940s. Driven by the possibilities that the 1940 decree and the surge in attendances promised, and while PRC was still trying to establish itself in the market, Monogram and Republic started taking their first, very cautious, steps in A-film production. Republic, in particular, found itself in a very favourable position. First, because its films had always targeted American audiences they proved to be particularly popular during the war years. Second, a large section of the audience for its films had moved from small towns to large metropolitan areas, which meant that Republic films broke into urban theatres, which always produced larger profits. Finally, the company maintained its popularity in rural America, providing a particularly large number of theatres with product. According to *Variety*, by the end of 1941 Republic was servicing more than 8,500 theatres,[55] while Gene Autry, the company's premier singing cowboy star, broke into the top 10 of the most popular male stars for 1940–1, which clearly suggests that Republic's westerns were big business for the company.

With all this success Republic had started replacing its 'cheap Poverty Row aesthetic' with a new look. As Don Miller observed:

> [W]ith the commencing of the 1941–42 season, the Republic schedule took on a new look; the product seemed more firmly entrenched in definite categories, polarized in magnitude but not in quality ... [t]he bulk of the schedule, B pictures all, seemed to have lost that almost indefinable aura of cheapness evident in even the best of them heretofore. Still inexpensive to make, they had become technically polished to a high degree.[56]

If the bulk of Republic's schedule continued to be (more polished) B pictures, the company soon ventured to A-film territory. Its 1943 film *In Old Oklahoma* (Rogell) with John Wayne boasted the studio's longest ever shooting schedule (63 days). By that time Republic was in a position to allocate $17 million for its production slate of 66 pictures (corresponding to $257,000 per film on average).[57] And with many of its western films costing as little as $30,000 to $50,000, Republic was in a position to invest more than $500,000 in specific productions, known as 'Deluxes'.[58] By 1945 the company was spending more than $1.5 million on one or two prestigious productions per year, such as *Flame of Barbary Coast* (Kane, 1945), and was making production deals with top-rank independent filmmakers such as Frank Borzage, who made *Concerto* (1945), the first Technicolor film for Republic, with a budget that exceeded $1.5 million.[59]

Monogram was following suit, 'making swift increase in stature, not only in the quality of its production but in the breadth of its distribution'.[60] In 1943 Monogram released its first A picture, *Silver Skates* (Goodwins), with ice-skating star Belita, which proved a big success. Furthermore, the company announced a policy of fewer films so that it could pay more attention to production values and therefore push for better returns from the theatres. Still refusing to allocate production funds on a par with Republic, Monogram soon became the pioneer of 'exploitation' pictures, 'films with some timely or currently controversial subject which [could] be exploited, capitalized on in publicity or advertising'.[61] The company produced most of these films on high budgets as A films and pushed them in the marketplace with sensationalised advertising. A particularly successful example of such a film was *Women in Bondage* (Sekely, 1943), the story of which revolved around the enslavement of women in a 'fascist' Germany, accompanied by the tagline: 'BLUEPRINT FOR SHAME … womanhood's most sacred ideals and rights … stripped away in a reign of uncurbed fearfulness'. But despite the occasional A films, Monogram, like Republic, continued to make cheap productions in the early 1940s.

By the mid-1940s, however, Monogram was also venturing to $1 million productions and making deals with expensive, ex-studio filmmakers like Roy Del Ruth, whose *It Happened on 5th Avenue* (1947) cost Monogram more than $1.5 million to produce.[62] This was mainly the product of a new company policy articulated by its newly elected president, Steven Broidy, who envisaged Monogram as a major studio.[63] With the company already servicing 7,500 theatres and enjoying massive success with another exploitation film, *Dillinger* (Nosseck, 1945), Monogram seemed to be heading in that direction. In November 1946, the company established a subsidiary, Allied Artists, to handle exclusively the distribution of high-budget films, with *It Happened on 5th Avenue* as its first release.

The decline of the B-film market

With Monogram and Republic focusing their attention increasingly on A pictures during the second half of the 1940s (and attracting distinguished top-rank talent such as Walter Wanger, John Ford, Orson Welles and screenwriter Ben Hecht, who were among several producers to release films through Republic), it became clear that the low-budget market had started losing its appeal as a reliable provider of small, but guaranteed, profits. The main problem was that the cost of the B films had become substantially higher than in the 1930s, while the rentals exhibitors paid to distributors (and producers) had not risen proportionally. This was because exhibitors had established a ceiling on the box office grosses of B pictures and therefore allowed only a specific amount of money to return to the distributor, irrespective of a film's box office performance. As a result, production companies with a specialisation in B films kept increasing their budgets but not their profit margins.[64]

More importantly, however, the B film had started slowly losing its usefulness and therefore its value in the American film market. Despite an initial increase in B-film production in the post-war era (especially the 1947–8 period) to counter rising costs and falling attendances,[65] this category of filmmaking was reaching the end of its cycle. As early as June 1946, Republic had been studying reports which called for 'the elimination of the lesser-budgeted pictures', while at the same time increasing the annual number of its expensive Deluxe productions from two to 10.[66] Furthermore, after the end of the war, a large percentage of the audience began deserting the major cities (and the large number of cinemas that were located in them) for the suburbs and started seeking 'more sophisticated leisure activities' than 'the simplistic entertainment' that the B films had been providing them with since the early 1930s.[67] Add to all this the impact of television, which started taking off in 1948–9 and quickly became the main outlet for simplistic entertainment, and it is easy to see why the B film was losing its *raison d'être*. Although its eventual demise would not be for a few more years (early to mid-1950s), the producers of B films – which by that time were only ex-Poverty Row outfits – felt the pressure of a shrinking market.

Monogram and Republic's ventures in the A-film market, however, were not particularly successful, with the exception of a few titles. By 1948, both companies were experiencing net losses, while PRC had also been in financial trouble, in spite of its refusal to enter the A-film market. During the same year (1948) PRC was taken over by Eagle-Lion, a production-distribution company formed by American billionaire Robert Young and British film entrepreneur J. Arthur Rank. Republic continued to operate with a small profit in the 1950s until two disastrous years (1957 and 1958) brought the company on the verge of bankruptcy before it re-emerged as a television producer. Monogram ceased to exist in 1952, when it was consumed by its own subsidiary, Allied Artists. The company continued producing films in the following decades with an emphasis on the exploitation market, while in the 1970s it had a few big successes, for instance *Cabaret* (Fosse, 1972) and *The Man Who Would Be King* (Huston, 1975).

The trajectory of the low-end independents in the 1940s demonstrates clearly that their existence was intricately linked with the presence of the B-film market, which in its own turn depended mainly on the persistence of the double-bill scheme. Once the B-film market started shrinking and it became apparent that television would develop into the main provider of cheaply made 'simplistic entertainment', the ex-Poverty Row companies did not have any other alternative but to try to raise the stakes. Despite their foray into high-budget production, however, their lack of a solid economic basis, their difficulty in securing exhibition in the first- and second-run theatres and, finally, their inability to release truly competitive product ensured that they would remain marginal players. Not surprisingly, both Monogram and Republic were among the first to enter television production in 1950, while Monogram became the first film company to lease its films to syndicated television in 1951.[68]

Conclusion

If the filmmaking practice by low-end independents in the 1930s represented an alternative cinema that was characterised by 'an air of flatness and unreality'[69] and was defined against the dominant – classical – cinema of the studios, this continued to be the case in the 1940s. Exemplified primarily by the ultra-low-budget films produced and distributed by PRC as well as by a significant number of films by Monogram and Republic (see Case studies 2.1 and 2.2), low-end independents continued to prize action and pace to the detriment of character motivation and narrative coherence. From the mid-1940s, however, the two most significant Poverty Row studios stopped making exclusively B pictures and gradually entered the A-film market. This meant that their films – produced mainly by ex-studio filmmakers such as Borzage for Republic and Del Ruth for Monogram – started embracing the classical narrative and style more readily than before and therefore becoming part of mainstream American cinema. Despite this evolution, however, which occurred towards the end of the studio period, the films of the Poverty Row studios represent historically a type of cinema that differed from the mainstream in both economic and aesthetic terms and therefore deserve the label 'independent', perhaps more so than their top-rank counterparts.

Beyond Poverty Row: ethnic films

Another important part of the low-end independent film market was the ethnic film market, which was established in the mid-1910s but which also reached a peak in the 1930s and 1940s. The term 'ethnic' here does not only refer to films aimed at American audiences of specific ethnicities; rather, it is used as an umbrella term under which one can group several defining audience character-istics, including race, religion and nationality.[70] Thus, under the label 'ethnic', one can bring together films that were made for Jewish audiences (Yiddish pictures), Cantonese-speaking audiences, Hispanic audiences, African American audiences and so on. The unifying element for all these productions was that they were defined against the mainstream films that were made by the studios in English and for the benefit of a white, English-speaking audience.

Ethnic films share a number of similarities with films produced by Poverty Row companies. First, a large number of these films were also produced by very small, thinly capitalised companies which often folded after one or two productions. Second, producers of ethnic films used the states rights market for distribution, in particular territories where a significant ethnic audience existed. Third, such films were aimed at very specific audiences, distinguished on the basis of language, race, religion and nationality (in various combinations) and therefore did not target the mainstream, English-speaking audience, which was serviced primarily by studio-produced films. Finally, like the majority of Poverty Row films, ethnic films were characterised by a cheap look, which, in tandem with a number of other elements, often signified an aesthetic that had few points of contact with the classical aesthetic associated with Hollywood films.

On the other hand, ethnic film production also presented major differences from production at Poverty Row. Arguably, the most important one was that this kind of independent film production did not transpire because of the demand for films that the double-bill scheme instigated. As ethnic films played in specialised theatres, they benefited from the existence of a small but steady audience who actively sought these types of films and as a result was not discouraged by the absence of a second feature in the theatre programme. This particular factor was responsible for another significant difference between ethnic and other low-end independent productions. Because ethnic films were made for specific audiences, they tended to prize narratives and subjects familiar to the individual ethnic groups the films targeted and therefore often avoided the use of established film genres, such as the western, extremely popular with Poverty Row companies. Finally, a large proportion of all ethnic films were produced away from Hollywood and California, the hubs of American cinema, but instead on the East Coast, in places such as New York and New Jersey.

Although ethnic pictures, especially race films aimed at non-white audiences, were available before the introduction of sound, it was the new technology that provided the impetus for the production of films that could 'speak' to specific ethnic groups. Almost immediately after the first 'talkies', a number of production companies formed specifically to serve the various ethnic audiences, who represented a substantial part of the American population but who were ignored by studio productions. Such companies included Judea Films, which was established in 1929 and produced 11 films in Yiddish in the following five years, while smaller outfits like Eron Pictures and Gloria Films contributed the remaining 15 of the total of 26 features that were produced in Yiddish in the 1930s.[71] Furthermore, a number of small distributors (such as the Sphinx Film Corporation) started importing films in Yiddish from abroad, thus creating a small but vibrant Yiddish film market at the time of the Depression.

Other ethnic groups were serviced in a comparable manner. Star Film Company, a distributor of Polish films, released approximately 20 films in the US between 1935 and 1939. Frank Norton (another small distributor) imported Greek films for the ethnic Greek market throughout the 1930s. As Douglas Gomery noted, by the end of the 1930s, the ethnic market had been thoroughly established, to the extent that in New York City alone there were 25 exhibition sites that played films in nine languages: French, German, Polish, Italian, Russian, Yiddish, Greek, Hungarian and Chinese.[72]

The films for the ethnic markets were made on extremely low budgets, often as little as $3,000. Edgar G. Ulmer, a filmmaker who worked for both a Poverty Row company and for an ethnic film production company (see Case study 2.2), admitted that working for the former was 'big time'. If he was allowed only 15,000 feet of film for his pictures at PRC, Ulmer was given 'short ends', leftovers of unexposed film from reels used in other films, to shoot his ethnic films. In other words, he never had a full reel to shoot a scene for his film *Moon Over Harlem* (1939), which was aimed at the African American market. As he put it in an interview: 'It was one of the most pitiful things I ever did'.[73] With most of these films financed by members of specific ethnic communities – Ulmer's *Natalka Potavka* (1937), a film for Ukrainian audiences, was financed by a window-washers union[74] – it is not surprising that the profits for the investors in the ethnic markets were, at best, minimal.

A large number of ethnic films tended to privilege stories about the customs and traditions of the ethnic group they addressed, which suggests that they spoke to their audience as non-Americans with distinct cultural identities. As Thomas Cripps suggests, ethnic films focused on portraying 'a sense of a common past, a setting forth of issues, a lightly sweetened nostalgia and an anatomy of a group's interior life ... to cultivate a warm cultural chauvinism'.[75] In this respect, they were completely the opposite of mainstream American films, which were promoting ethnic assimilation through particularly constructed narratives that effaced specific characteristics of ethnicity. Instead, as Taves suggested (speaking about Yiddish films), 'they supported and perpetuated their respective heritage of customs and cultural identities, offering audiences one of the few opportunities to feel a wholly satisfying cinematic experience in unique rapport with their own people'.[76] Other types of ethnic films, however, especially the ones made for African American audiences, like the cycle of black singing cowboy westerns in the late 1930s, were more assimilatory, inviting 'black Americans to see black men as fully vested American citizens and as righteous heroes'.[77]

The most prominent type of ethnic film production was the race film, especially those produced for African American audiences. As early as 1915, black-owned production companies such as the Peter P. Jones Film Company and Ebony Pictures were producing all-black cast features in Chicago, a city that had experienced an exponential growth of its African American population in the early twentieth century. The following year, Noble Johnson and his brother George established the Lincoln Motion Picture Company, which produced a small number of films aimed at black audiences. Before the end of the decade Oscar Micheaux, the most famous black independent filmmaker, had established his own production company, through which he would produce 41 films in 30 years (1919–49). New companies continued to appear in the 1920s, such as Norman Black-Cast Films, which made films for segregated theatres in the American South (from Texas to Alabama) and Colored Players in Philadelphia. The latter was established by white investors, although it made only black-cast pictures, four in total. Its most memorable production was *The Scar of Shame* (Peregini, 1927), a film that adopted 'a black point of view in its portrayal of class conflict in [the] African American community'.[78]

With few exceptions (among which were the various companies under which Micheaux produced his films) most of these outfits did not survive the introduction of sound. Thus in the 1930s there were only a handful of companies that supplied product to the 400 theatres that served approximately 12 million African Americans.[79] With the exception of Micheaux's companies, however, these firms could not lease studio space and use the new sound systems that the studio-produced films had access to.[80] As a result, a long time after the introduction of sound, certain companies continued to make silent films for theatres that could not afford the costs of wiring.[81] Despite the problems, the market for race talkies developed gradually in the 1930s, from 23 black feature films made between 1930 and 1936 to over 50 made between 1937 and 1940. Partly responsible for such an outburst in the productivity of films for the African American audience were Million Dollar Productions, a company established in 1936, and International Road Shows, a company that produced a number of films in 1939–40.

Unlike the films that were aimed at people of specific ethnicities and therefore utilised particularly constructed narratives that were appealing to such audiences, films by Million Dollar Productions such as *Dark Manhattan* (Fraser, 1937) were gangster films that generally followed Hollywood film conventions. However, these pictures were differentiated from mainstream films by the emphasis they placed on black musical performance in the narratives, on the problems and anxieties entailed in the African American migration from the South to the North in the early twentieth century, and on the positive representations of the black female characters.[82] As a result, they claimed a particular place in independent film production that is similar to the Poverty Row films (using studio genres and narratives but breaking away from the rules of classical filmmaking for ideological reasons). On the other hand,

Micheaux was producing films that tackled the subject of racial oppression. For this reason, his work was placed in greater opposition to mainstream cinema than the films of Million Dollar Productions.

One could argue, then, that there were two distinct articulations of black independent cinema in the 1930s. The first, characterised by the films of Micheaux, was explicitly about tackling racial issues – often in a sensationalised manner – and educating black audiences about the nature of their oppression. This strand of black filmmaking was characterised by a particular 'home-grown' aesthetic which, as Jane Gaines argued, followed but 'was not bound by' the classical style, while also flirting with the avant-garde.[83] The second, characterised by the films of Million Dollar Productions and other independent outfits, emphasised a particular type of entertainment that was modelled on the studio films, even though certain elements were appropriated for the purposes of creating a film production for minority audiences. As Taves suggests, 'there was no trace of the homegrown aesthetic associated with Micheaux; Million Dollar films were … on a par with the contemporary product of Monogram and Republic'.[84]

Black independent film production continued in the 1940s and also benefited from the surge in attendance during World War II. The participation of African Americans in the war effort made them a particularly viable audience and companies like Sack Amusement Enterprises, one of the most important states rights market distributors, entered black film production in the early 1940s. Although the market continued to be buoyant during the decade, the increasing integration of African Americans, which was marked by the improved visibility of characters of that origin in Hollywood productions of the late 1940s and 1950s, made the rationale for the existence of such a 'segregated' market obsolete. As a type of independent cinema, ethnic films are restricted to the years of the studios' domination in the 1930s and 1940s.

Notes

1 Quoted in Strawn, 1975a, p. 275.
2 Dixon, 1986, p. vii.
3 Taves, 1995, p. 322.
4 Some sources from the period put the number of these theatres as high as 11,000. See 'Mute Major', in *Time*, 20 March 1942.
5 Flynn and McCarthy, 1975a, p. 17.
6 Contrary to popular belief, the nickname 'Poverty Row' was not given to companies like Monogram and Republic because they were inadequately capitalised or because they were making very cheap films. According to Merritt (2000, p. 63), the term signifies a small geographical area in central Hollywood where 'various fly-by-night producers' established their companies to make ultra-low-budget films.

7 Gomery, 1986, p. 180.

8 Crafton, 1999, p. 262.

9 For instance, MGM's B films were certainly not made on a low budget, while in terms of quality and production values they were on a par with other studios' A product (especially RKO and Warner Bros.' A films). Also there are many examples of films which were produced with limited resources for the lower half of the double bill but became successful and popular enough to be boosted to A status, for example, *The Payoff* (Florey, 1935; Warner), *A Man to Remember* (Canin, 1938; RKO) and *Penitentiary* (Brahm, 1938; Columbia). See Taves, 1995, p. 315.

10 The figures for 1932 appear in Balio, 1995, pp. 29–30. The figures for 1935 are cited in Flynn and McCarthy, 1975a, p. 15.

11 May, 2000, p. 61.

12 Republic was the only such company with profits comparable to the profits of the Little Three.

13 Yeaman, 1934.

14 'Monogram To Do 32 Movies', 1932; 'Single Movie Billing Plans Bring Attack', 1933; and 'Studio Chief Returns from Indie Meeting', 1934.

15 Miller, 1988, p. 25.

16 The figures for Monogram's yearly budgets are taken from 'Monogram Film Plans Disclosed', 1933.

17 See 'Independents Head East', 1933.

18 For more information on the details of the merger, see Tuska, 1982, p. 183.

19 The figures are taken from Taves, 1995, p. 322.

20 Tuska, 1982, p. 87.

21 Cleary, 1940.

22 Hanna, 1941.

23 See Hagopian, 1986, p. 20.

24 McCabe, 1998, p. 158.

25 McGilligan, 1975, pp. 68–70.

26 Taves, 1995, pp. 316–17 (see also note 9).

27 Taves, 1995, p. 317.

28 Taves, 1995, p. 320.

29 Taves, 1995, p. 318.

30 Taves, 1995, p. 318.

31 For the rules of filmmaking on Poverty Row, see Hanna, 1941; for more on the number of camera set-ups per day, see Bogdanovich, 1975, p. 387.

32 Tuska, 1982, p. 120.

33 See Schatz, 1999, p. 36.

34 Of course there were exceptions to this rule, like Warner Bros.' *The Florentine Dagger* (Florey, 1935), which, according to Taves (1995, p. 339), 'provides a forceful example of the adaptation and integration of expressionist and avant-garde styles into the American feature through the B'.

35 Quoted in Strawn, 1975a, p. 275.

36 Taves, 1995, p. 326.

37 Stanfield, 1998, p. 102.

38 Taves, 1995, p. 334.

39 Tuska, 1982, p. 16.

40 Dixon, 1986, p. ix (original italics).

41 Taves, 1995, p. 338.

42 See Gomery, 1986, pp. 77 and 102.

43 'Rep Plows Back Profits for Record Production Sked…', 1941; 'Republic Stepping High', 1943; '$17 Million Budget for 68 Rep Pix', 1944.

44 See Flynn and McCarthy, 1975a, p. 16.

45 See Izod, 1988, p. 113.

46 The figures for MGM and Columbia are taken from Gomery, 1986, pp. 52 and 162.

47 The figures for Monogram are taken from Quigley, 1950, p. 949. The figures for Republic are taken from Hurst, 1979, p. 7 (with the exception of the data for 1938 and 1939, which are taken from Quigley, 1950, p. 953).

48 Okuda, 1989, p. 32.

49 Fernett, 1973, p. 100.

50 Okuda, 1989, p. 31.

51 Dixon, 1986, p. viii.

52 Bogdanovich, 1975, p. 387.

53 Dixon, 1986, p. viii.

54 For elaborate discussions of how Edgar G. Ulmer and Joseph H. Lewis achieved distinction while working as low-end independents see Tzioumakis, 2008, and Tzioumakis, 2012b, respectively.

55 *Daily Variety*, 29 October 1941.

56 Miller, 1988, p. 258.

57 *Daily Variety*, 29 October 1943.

58 See Gomery, 1986, p. 184.

59 'Republic Pictures Celebrates Its Tenth Anniversary', 1945.

60 'Monogram Marching On', 1943.

61 Quoted in Schatz, 1999, p. 175.

62 Brady, 1946.

63 'New Studio Chief Tells Expansion Plan', 1945.

64 'Broidy Asks Lower Pay Scale on "B" Films to Insure Profit', 1947.

65 See Schatz, 1999, pp. 292 and 331.

66 'Republic Will Release 58 at Cost of $25,000,000', 1946.

67 Flynn and McCarthy, 1975a, p. 42.

68 See 'Monogram Going Into Telepix: 1st Studio to Make Decision', 1950; 'Getting $1,000,000 for 7-Yr License', 1951.

69 Flynn and McCarthy, 1975a, p. 22.

70 This definition is used by Brian Taves (1995, p. 342) in his discussion of B films between 1930 and 1939.

71 The number of Yiddish films in the 1930s is cited in Taves, 1995, p. 343.

72 Quoted in Merritt, 2000, p. 82.

73 All the quotes from Ulmer here are from Bogdanovich, 1975, pp. 374–5.

74 See Isenberg, 2004, p. 11.

75 Cripps, 1997, pp. 130–1.

76 Taves, 1995, p. 343.

77 See Leyda, 2002, p. 61.

78 Gaines, 2003, p. 2.

79 Balio, 1995, p. 2.

80 Crafton, 1999, p. 413.

81 Taves (1995, p. 344) cites the example of Harlem-based Paragon Films as one of the companies that continued to make silent films in the sound era.
82 See Simpson II, 2003, p. 2.
83 Quoted in Regester, 1996, p. 163.
84 Taves, 1995, p. 34.

Part II

American independent cinema in the post-studio era (late 1940s to late 1960s)

3

Independence by force: the effects of the Paramount decree on independent film production

I have to know which [rules] I must abide by in order to safely break other ones…. The trick is to be creative in how one abides by the rules.
Stanley Kramer, filmmaker[1]

It's great to be left alone when you're making a movie, but not when you're finished with it!
James B. Harris, producer[2]

Introduction

The second period in the history of American independent cinema commences with the Paramount decree of 1948, signed by the Big Five and Little Three studios when the US Supreme Court found them guilty of applying monopolistic practices that restrained trade and eliminated competition. The decision had a seismic impact on the structure of the American film industry, as it forced the studios to divest themselves of their theatre chains and therefore lose control of exhibition, one of the three foundations upon which their vertical integration depended. Although the studios found alternative ways to retain control of the film industry, the Paramount decree became instrumental in gradually dismantling the studio system of production, which had been in place since the late 1910s. Instead, the new system privileged a format of independent production that had its origins in the top-rank independent production model of the hyphenate filmmakers, which had started gaining momentum during the 1940–8 period (see Chapter 1), though with some important differences. It could be argued that the Paramount decree formalised the industry-wide shift to independent production that began in 1940 and therefore ushered in American cinema's post-studio era.

To a certain extent, this development, which became particularly evident from the 1950s onwards, continues today. For the purposes of this book, however, we will adopt the position that the second phase of American independent cinema starts in 1948 and finishes in 1967, a year that film historian Paul Monaco calls 'a watershed year ' for the film industry.[3] During that time, a number of factors – including changes in the constitution of the audience and in movie-going habits in general, the conglomeration of the film industry (already underway from the mid-1960s) and the socio-cultural upheaval that the country experienced throughout the decade (represented mainly by an increased protest/anti-Vietnam sentiment and the growing visibility of the civil rights movement) – laid the foundations for new directions in independent filmmaking that we will discuss in detail in Parts III and IV.

With independent production replacing studio production and becoming the dominant approach in planning and executing filmmaking, the discourse of post-1948 independent cinema expanded greatly, to include all films that were financed and distributed by the ex-studios but which were physically produced by a different production entity. The expansion of the discourse brought an unavoidable identity crisis for independent film production. By 1956, over half of the films (53 per cent) distributed by the ex-studios were deemed by the trade press of the time 'independent', as the major Hollywood companies were not physically involved in any aspect of those films' production process. Three years later the figure was as high as 70 per cent, signalling the overwhelming success of this model of film production.[4]

With such a massive proportion of filmmaking in the US deemed as independent, it is clear that the distinctions between mainstream (as exemplified by studio-produced films) and independent production (as exemplified by films produced by top-rank production entities without corporate ties to the majors) that applied during the pre-1948 era were no longer valid. Instead, it was independent filmmaking – with the full endorsement of the studios – that came to represent mainstream Hollywood cinema in this period, while physical production by the studios became marginalised as the studios gradually contributed fewer and fewer films. To complete this picture of the transformation of the American film industry, United Artists, the smallest of the eight main powers and a key distributor of top-rank independents in the studio era, became by the mid-1960s the most successful distribution company in the country, surpassing the other majors in revenues and profits. In the period between the late 1940s and the late 1960s, the terms 'top-rank independent' and 'mainstream Hollywood' filmmaking became virtually interchangeable.

The Paramount decree

The consent decree of 29 October 1940, in which the studios agreed to reduce the number of block-booked films to five and replace blind biding with trade showing (for details see Part I), certainly created more opportunities for independent producers but it did not achieve the main objectives of the US Justice Department: the elimination of illegal trade practices and the divorcement of exhibition from production and distribution. With America at war between 1941 and 1945, trust-busting campaigns had become less persistent and considerably less focused, with only one significant antitrust decision during the period.[5] Immediately after the end of the war, however, the Justice Department, under new attorney general, Tom Clarke, reopened the case against the eight dominant film companies. The New York federal district court that examined the case ruled that the studios had indeed conspired to impose a set of illegal trade practices (price fixing, block booking, favourable agreements with affiliated circuits, zoning and clearance) but, significantly, failed to see that it was the studios' organisation as vertically integrated companies that gave them the power to impose those practices.

Although the federal district court's decision was certainly a victory for the Justice Department, this time the attorney general wanted both objectives fulfilled. After a series of appeals, the US Supreme Court granted the case a hearing, while at the same time smaller antitrust lawsuits mainly brought by independent exhibitors against the studios and their affiliated circuits were being upheld by courts around the country. The hearings took place in 1948 and on 3 May of the same year, the Supreme Court reached its unanimous verdict, which this time identified correctly the studios' control of all three aspects of the film business (production, distribution and exhibition) as the source of their power. Specifically, the Court upheld the federal district court's original decision that had found block booking, price fixing, zoning and clearance, and other studio practices, illegal restraints on trade, and recommended divorcement of exhibition from the other two branches of filmmaking that the eight defendants controlled.

Although studios like 20th Century Fox and, especially, MGM would fight the decision for almost a decade (MGM did not sell its last theatres until 1957),[6] the Supreme Court's decision did not leave the studios any space for compromise. For that reason, when RKO and Paramount became the first two of the eight studios to sign the new decree, in 1948 and 1949 respectively, the terms were unequivocal. Apart from putting an end to all practices that constrained trade and mobilising the divorcement of exhibition from production and distribution, the decree also forced the studios to break off their ties with affiliated theatre circuits, especially in 'closed towns' where one such exhibitor had an absolute monopoly.[7]

The provisions of the Paramount decree (as the Supreme Court's decision became known) seemed to signal an outright victory for top-rank independent producers. Among the key issues that the Society for Independent Motion Picture Producers (the collective bargaining tool for top-rank independents) had lobbied for after the district court's decision were the end of block booking and the divestiture of theatres, both addressed specifically by the Supreme Court's decision.[8] The future seemed bright for these independents as they would be in a position to compete with the studios on an equal basis for access to the best theatres. And as their reputation for producing quality pictures was already in place from the pre-1948 period, the Paramount decree came to represent for them more freedom from the constraints of the studio system as well as greater profits from improved access to the first-run theatres.

The independents' optimism proved false, however, as a cluster of factors – well underway before the 1948 decree – changed the rosy economic conditions that had brought record profits to the American film industry during the war years and presented a much darker picture for both the studios and the independents than what they both had envisaged. Increased production costs, union and labour problems, the introduction of protective quotas in foreign markets, investigation by the House Un-American Activities Committee of communist infiltration of the film industry and, especially, a drop in theatre attendance from 1947 that continued throughout the 1950s and 1960s, changed dramatically the landscape of American cinema. In this new reality, independent production struggled for the first few years after the decree, before becoming the dominant method of film production in Hollywood in the mid-1950s and 1960s.

The post-war recession

Although 1946 was the peak year for Hollywood, with the eight studios' combined profits soaring to a record $122 million (up a remarkable 85 per cent from $66 million in 1945), this turned out to be the last time profits climbed for a very long period, thus marking the beginning of a recession. Only a year later, in 1947, profits were down 27 per cent, to $89 million, while by 1949 they had dropped to $37 million, an alarming 70 per cent down from the 1946 milestone.[9] During the same period the gross revenues of the eight studios' films went down only slightly (14 per cent), however, which suggests clearly that one of the reasons studio profits were slashed was because of a significant increase in production costs. While in the 1930s and early 1940s budgets of

$1 million and over were allocated mainly to a few prestige-level pictures, by 1950 the studios' average negative cost per film was well over that figure ($1.14 million for Paramount; $1.63 million for 20th Century Fox), with the independents following closely ($0.8 million).[10] For this reason, profit margins kept shrinking, especially as grosses remained stagnant.

The drop in theatre attendance (and the ensuing recession) caught the industry by surprise as it invalidated all positive projections by industry analysts, who were arguing that the immediate future of the film industry was secure because returning soldiers could only boost attendances further; increases in salaries and disposable income and decreases in working hours would drive more people to the theatres more often; and resumption of film distribution outside the US (discontinued during the war years) would bring pure profits as the studios had a backlog of unreleased films from as early as 1939.[11]

The reality, however, proved very different. A large number of ex-soldiers who returned from service chose to go into adult education, which minimised their leisure time.[12] A boom in marriages and a sharp increase in birth rates created a huge number of new families who had little time to visit the cinema, especially as they started migrating to newly built homes in the suburbs of large cities, often miles away from the closest theatre (by 1950 it was estimated that 40–50 million Americans had moved to the suburbs).[13] The increase in disposable income (22 per cent up from 1946 to 1949) did not make Americans visit the theatres more frequently.[14] Instead, it allowed them to explore an ever-increasing array of leisure and recreation options giving cinema-going (one of the very few leisure options during the war) fierce competition: attending performances of travelling theatre companies presenting Broadway shows; attending professional sports games; listening to the radio; boating; bowling; golf; amateur photography; recreational driving; and, of course, watching television, especially from 1950 onwards.[15] Finally, immediately after World War II, major European countries (and film markets) like Britain, France, Italy and Germany introduced protective measures against and quotas on the importation of US films to help resurrect their national film industries. One of these measures was the retaining of a large percentage of film rentals by US films in the host country, thus allowing only a fraction of profits back to the hands of the studios. This meant that the studios' profits from their hitherto unreleased films were severely dented, while returns from the distribution of new films were also substandard, as some of these films had to end their runs quickly, to make way for a percentage of home-produced films.

In the wake of recession and with the Paramount decree removing their most significant source of income, their (first-run) theatres, the studios responded with a number of measures that were geared mainly towards cutting operating costs. Having lost their theatres, and therefore no longer being guaranteed exhibition for their films, it made little economic sense for the studios to keep above- and below-the-line talent and crew under contract. Gradually they started releasing their stars, directors, writers and technical personnel from their long-term agreements, which of course had an immediate positive impact on the size of their payrolls. More importantly, in order for the studios to maintain an operational release schedule (and cover the costs of maintaining worldwide distribution networks) they started aggressively recruiting independent producers to supply them with the necessary product.

Although it seems that the independent producers had found themselves at last in a position of power against the studios, which could not function properly anymore as production companies, the truth is that the independents had their own set of pressing problems to deal with. The recession had hit them even harder than the studios and the majority of the top-rank independent production companies were struggling to remain solvent. Writing in 1948 (before the Supreme Court decision), George Yousling, an executive in Security First National Bank, had remarked:

> The growth in independent production reached a peak in 1947. In the latter half of the year the amount of new credit available to independent producers, particularly 'second money', diminished as lenders became more cautious in the face of rising costs and declining returns both in the domestic and foreign markets. At the present time – March 1948 – many independents are unable to obtain sufficient financing to start new productions, and the volume of independently produced films going into production is below the high levels of recent years.[16]

The trade publications concurred. In an article entitled aptly 'Bell Tolls for Indie Producers' that appeared in *Variety* in May 1948, it was reported that with the exception of a handful of extremely well established independents (Disney, Goldwyn, Chaplin and Selznick, who, incidentally, were also experiencing some difficulties in obtaining production funds), financing was simply not available for independent producers.[17] Indeed, in the previous year a large number of independently produced films had failed miserably at the box office, to the extent that they could not even recoup 60 per cent of their costs from theatrical rentals.[18] Banks responded by foreclosing on loans to such companies while hoping to get part of their investment back from the films' foreign box office receipts. From that point on, banks would be ready to loan funds only to companies with tangible assets, like the studios, while if they were to make production funds available to a handful of established producers, they would charge more interest than they would charge the studios and participate actively in the production process.[19]

Perhaps the most characteristic example of the impact of the recession on American cinema in the post-war period was the fate of United Artists.

The company had been experiencing economic difficulties from inception, struggling constantly to keep its position in the film market and competing against immensely better-capitalised, vertically integrated companies. Its financial problems, however, had been increasing during the 1940s, when the rest of the studios opened their gates to independent producers and provided UA with fierce competition. Even in 1946, Hollywood's golden year, United Artists' profit was a petty $0.4 million out of the $122 million the eight companies earned in total.[20]

A great share of responsibility for United Artists' inability to capitalise on the war boom lay with its management regimes and especially the owners' interference in the running of the company, who never allowed the specialised distributor to follow trends in Hollywood cinema. In the immediate post-war period, these problems were greatly amplified, while the company's perennial lack of working capital certainly did not make things easier. By 1948, UA was losing money at an alarming rate and the banks, already unwilling to finance independent production, refused to support producers who were contracted to release through the company, as they considered the distributor 'a poor risk'.[21]

In early 1949, United Artists had only four pictures ready for release, two more in production and no plans for future production. Banks and other creditors had started applying great pressure to secure at least some return on their investment, while in the six months to June 1949 the company had lost already $400,000.[22] Various attempts at restructuring failed to produce any results. By early 1951, UA was losing $100,000 a week and was heading for bankruptcy,[23] until two lawyers with experience in the workings of the film industry, Arthur Krim and Robert Benjamin, took the company over and managed to reverse its fortune. Their success depended to a great extent on their decision to sponsor a particular brand of independent film production and on their efforts to forge a distinct type of relationship between independent producers and the distribution company. Within a few years, United Artists became the most successful distributor in American cinema, while its film distribution and production policies became the blueprint for the ex-studios.

Identity crisis

With United Artists virtually out of the picture until the early 1950s and with the banks taking very few risks after 1947, it comes as no surprise that most of the top-rank independent producers who had established their own companies in the early 1940s returned to the studios, setting up semi-autonomous units. Despite initiatives by independent theatre owners to form a company that could finance top-rank independent production (in the steps of First National – see

Chapter 1) and the formation of Motion Picture Capital Corporation by two former RKO producers to supply funds to independents,[24] even the most stalwart representatives of independent production of the previous years (like Frank Capra, Leo McCarey and James Cagney) signed distribution deals with the studios to secure the future of their companies.

The independents needed the studios to raise finance (because of their tangible assets, the studios were in a position to guarantee bank loans) and to distribute their films worldwide (after the drop in domestic attendance, for films to break even such distribution was an absolute necessity). In their turn, the studios needed the independents to provide them with the necessary product (at a time when they had started firing their personnel and reducing their production schedules) and to cut overhead costs by making independent production companies rent space on their backlots. Before the end of the 1940s, then, studios and independents had already become strong allies. For that reason, when the Paramount decree gave independent producers the opportunity to compete with the studios on an equal basis, not only were the independents in no position to take up the challenge but, had they taken it up, they would have had to go against the hand that fed them, the institutions that allowed them to exist.

But even if independent producers had had the funds to make films away from the studios and the means to distribute them, a major shift in the political climate of the country during the same period would probably have ensured that their films would not stray too far from the mainstream. The hearings of the House Un-American Activities Committee (HUAC) in 1947 and sporadically in the following few years until 1953, which sought to cleanse the film industry of communist infiltration, created a climate of political paranoia under which it became extremely difficult for liberal independent filmmakers to present alternative world-views in their films. As Peter Lev argued, in the early 1950s there were many quality American films, but they were all made 'within socially and aesthetically conservative parameters' as the filmmakers who were not blacklisted by HUAC and continued to work in Hollywood could not afford to take any risks whatsoever.[25] This meant that any form of independent cinema would have to cooperate with Hollywood, especially as the heads of the studio-distributors publicly endorsed HUAC's objectives and terminated the employment of over 350 industry workers who had been 'blacklisted' by HUAC as communists or communist sympathisers.

Besides the political climate of paranoia, industrial and economic conditions did not seem to improve as the new decade came in. Between 1950 and 1953 (the first year when box office receipts climbed slightly since 1946),[26] 3,000 theatres closed, while attendance and profits continued to slide. In 1954 it was estimated that less than one-third of all US theatres were financially viable, while production of films had dropped to 300 from 425 pictures in 1946 (down 30 per cent).[27] By far the biggest contributing factor in the continuation of the slump in the new decade was television, which offered free entertainment in the comfort of one's own home. The proliferation of television sets between 1948 and 1950 was astounding. In 1948 there were a mere 172,000 television sets in the whole of the US. In 1949 the number had increased to 1,000,000 and a year later to 16,000,000. Equally, the number of commercial television stations climbed from 98 in 1950 to 233 in 1953, providing a staggering amount of additional product to the offerings of the three national networks, NBC, CBS and ABC.[28] According to a federal government survey in 1950, families who owned a television set had reduced their movie-going attendance by an alarming 72 per cent, while their children's visits to the theatre were reduced by an equally problematic 42 per cent.[29]

In the face of this protracted economic downturn, independent production – now any form of film production by any company other than majors – became the dominant method of production in Hollywood cinema and can be credited with securing Hollywood's future. Although in many ways independent production in the 1950s and 1960s substantially resembled top-rank independent production of the pre-1948 period, the main difference was in the relationship between the production and the distribution company, a relationship that saw the two parties more as partners, rather than as the former working for the latter. This type of arrangement was to a certain extent reminiscent of the relationship between United Artists and its independent producers in the 1930s and 1940s. What was different, though, was that, this time, the distributor would provide complete production finance in exchange for worldwide distribution rights, therefore asking the independent producer to do only what he or she could do best: produce the film without worrying about raising production funds or marketing the product. Appropriately, the distribution company that first foresaw the benefits of this arrangement and put it into practice was none other than United Artists. According to Tino Balio, United Artists' policies transformed the company 'into a pacesetter of the industry and started a revolution in the motion picture business'.[30]

United Artists' revival

Before moving to United Artists, Arthur Krim and Robert Benjamin managed Eagle-Lion Films, the American-British company that had taken over low-end independent PRC. At Eagle-Lion, Krim and Benjamin initiated a hybrid brand of independent production whereby their company would provide film producers with 'a patchwork of financing consisting of second money, studio credits and completion bonds to supplement conventional bank loans.[31] Although the company had some success and managed to attract a small number of top-rank independent producers (Walter Wanger, Brian Foy and Edward Small), interference from Robert R. Young (the company's owner) in Eagle-Lion's decision-making as well as financial problems forced Krim to resign in May 1949 and seek other opportunities in the film industry.

Krim and Benjamin approached United Artists in January 1951. After demonstrating to the two remaining shareholders, Mary Pickford and Charlie Chaplin, that the company was only a step away from bankruptcy, they convinced the two owners to allow them to manage the company as trustees for their combined stock for a period of 10 years. If United Artists showed any profit at the end of any of the first three financial years under their management, Krim and Benjamin would be invited to acquire 50 per cent of the company's stock for just $8,000.[32] With the two remaining owners finally agreeing to stay away from the day-to-day operations of the company, Krim and Benjamin commenced the battle to save UA from liquidation and potentially become co-owners with Pickford and Chaplin.

After purchasing Eagle-Lion's library of titles, which gave UA some films for immediate distribution and, consequently, some much-needed income, Krim and Benjamin sought to secure distribution rights for independent productions. Among others they obtained the rights for Romulus-Horizon's *The African Queen* (Huston, 1951) (Romulus-Horizon was the second of the two companies owned by Sam Spiegel and John Huston) and for Stanley Kramer Productions' *Cyrano de Bergerac* (Gordon, 1951). With both films proving substantial hits, UA started gradually stabilising operations. By the end of 1951, the company had distributed 45 films and had achieved what only a few months before seemed unthinkable, a $313,000 net profit.[33]

With Krim and Benjamin now co-owners, United Artists continued its revival over the next few years. In 1952, it released 31 films, including the extremely successful Stanley Kramer Productions' *High Noon* (Zinnemann, 1952), a film that grossed $12 million worldwide and gave Gary Cooper his second Oscar. More importantly, UA started projecting to the rest of the industry and to financial institutions a picture of a rationally managed film distribution company, gradually erasing the memories of mismanagement from its recent past. As a result, it started attracting again independent filmmakers like writer-director-producer Ben Hecht, who signed a deal in 1952. In 1953 United Artists upped its releases to 45, including John Huston's *Moulin Rouge* (1953), and lured one of 20th Century Fox's top filmmakers, Otto Preminger, to independent production.

Preminger's first film for UA under the banner of his company Carlyle Productions was the controversial *The Moon Is Blue* (1953), which the distributor released without PCA approval after resigning from the Motion Picture Association of America. The film proved a solid success, grossing $4 million, and initiated a heated debate about the future of the Production Code, which in the 1950s started to look outdated. Furthermore, and as all the majors were exploring new exhibition technologies (various forms of widescreen, 3-D and so on) to battle the effects of television, United Artists decided not to stay behind, investing in 3-D. In 1953, the company released *Bwana Devil* (Oboler, 1953), the distribution rights for which it had secured for $1.75 million. UA lost some money on the film but got great publicity from its involvement with exhibition technologies, which further enhanced its position in the industry.[34]

By 1955 United Artists' reversal of fortune was complete. In the previous year, Hecht-Lancaster (later Hecht-Hill and Lancaster), a newly formed independent production outfit headed by Hollywood star Burt Lancaster, had signed a multi-picture deal with UA and delivered four films in the 1954–5 period alone, including *Marty* (Mann, 1955), which won the Oscar for Best Picture. Joseph L. Mankiewicz had also switched to UA for the production of *The Barefoot Contessa* (1954), an expensive mystery drama he shot in Italy under his production company Figaro. After a short stint at Columbia,

Table 3.1 Number of films released by United Artists and the production companies behind them, 1951–67

Year	Number of releases	Production companies (including non-American ones)
1951	45	34
1952	31	26
1953	45	34
1954	46	30
1955	33	26
1956	49	34
1957	54	32
1958	43	33
1959	39+1	24+1
1960	28+2	19+2
1961	37+1	19+1
1962	32+4	23+4
1963	20+1	14+1
1964	17+2	13+2
1965	17+2	14+2
1966	19+5	13+5
1967	21+6	16+6
Total	576+24	

In 1959 UA bought Lopert Films and also released its films – numbers given as +.

Stanley Kramer returned to UA in 1955 with *Not as a Stranger* (1955), the first of a series of social dramas that would make him one of the most important producer-directors in Hollywood cinema in the 1950s and 1960s. Kirk Douglas brought his Bryna Productions to UA for his first film as a producer, *The Indian Fighter* (De Toth, 1955), and so did young filmmaker Stanley Kubrick, whose first film as a producer-director with his company Minotaur Productions, *Killer's Kiss* (1955), was released by United Artists.

In February 1955 Chaplin sold his share in United Artists for $1.1 million to Krim and Benjamin, while a year later Pickford sold her own 25 per cent of the stock for $3 million.[35] Five years after taking over the company's management, Arthur Krim and Robert Benjamin had become its sole owners and had succeeded in attracting large numbers of top independent producers. Table 3.1 reports the number of independent production companies that released films through United Artists and the number of films the company distributed between 1951 and 1967 (the figures from 1959 onwards include the releases of Lopert Films, a United Artists' subsidiary, of films produced outside the US, which I shall discuss below).[36]

Independent production the United Artists way

The secret of United Artists' success was the adoption of a particular brand of independent production system that had its foundation in Krim and Benjamin's decision to provide complete production finance to independent producers. Instead of going to the banks or other financial organisations to obtain production funds, especially during a period when banks were unwilling to take risks, independent producers would be financed by United Artists in exchange for worldwide distribution rights of the films they would produce. Although at first sight this arrangement is reminiscent of the agreements some independents made with the major studios in the 1940s (unit production), it nevertheless has a number of characteristics that sets it apart from studio-controlled filmmaking. To identify these characteristics we shall examine the details of a typical distribution agreement between United Artists and independent producer Stanley Kramer's Lomitas Productions, which was signed on 31 December 1957. The contract has two main sections, one that focuses on the details of production and one on the details of distribution.[37]

Production

Under the provisions of the contract, Stanley Kramer's company would produce six films (at least three in which Kramer would be a producer-director while in the rest he would undertake only the role of the producer) for United Artists within the three-year period 31 December 1957 to 31 December 1960. All the films would be prestigious productions (Case study 3.1), either based on pre-sold properties – including *Inherit the Wind* (based on a play by Jerome Lawrence and Robert E. Lee), *On the Beach* (based on a novel by Nevil Shute) and *My Glorious Brothers* (from a novel by Howard Fast) – or they would be premised on original screenplays (with two screenplays already agreed upon by the two parties: *The Defiant Ones* and *Invitation to a Gunfighter*).

As the films' financier, United Artists retained a number of approvals (or check points) which were essential for the signing of the deal and which included the following:

- the literary property or subject matter on which the picture was based;
- the production budget;
- the cast budget;
- the production schedule;
- male and female stars;
- the producer;
- the director;
- the locale or locales of production of each picture, if it was to be produced outside the US.[38]

As can be seen, the distributor did not retain a right of approval of the screenplay (provided of course that it could be filmed within the approved budget), which was a major concession to a creative producer like Kramer and unheard of in studio agreements with independent producers. Furthermore, the contract specified that the producer would not have to submit daily rushes to the distributor, even though the latter would have the right to view a rough cut of any of the six productions before the editing for the final cut took place.[39]

In terms of budget, United Artists would lend the agreed funds to Lomitas Productions or, alternatively, would guarantee bank loans to the production company. The distributor would be also responsible for pre-production advances (cost of literary properties; cost of writing the screenplays; other usual pre-production costs), would provide a weekly salary to Kramer for administering the productions for the duration of the contract, and would guarantee completion money (funds allocated to the production company if the film ran over budget). In other words, United Artists would be the complete financier of Lomitas Productions, from pre-production to completion, but once the agreement (with all the distributor's approvals) was in place, the producer would be in effect free to make the type of picture he or she wanted without any form of interference from the investor/distributor.

Case study 3.1 Post-war top-rank independence: Stanley Kramer's Lomitas Productions' *The Defiant Ones*, *On the Beach* and *Inherit the Wind* at United Artists, 1957–60

> *The Defiant Ones* (Kramer, 1958, 97 min.); *On the Beach* (Kramer, 1959, 134 min.); *Inherit the Wind* (Kramer, 1960, 128 min.), all produced by Lomitas Productions, distributed by United Artists.

Unless otherwise stated all quotes and figures are taken from a number of documents available in the Stanley Kramer Papers (Collection 161), Department of Special Collections, Charles E. Young Research Library, University of California, Los Angeles.

Stanley Kramer is arguably the most significant producer-director of social-problem films during the 1950s and 1960s. Starting from the lowly position of a backlot labourer at MGM in the early 1930s, Kramer moved gradually up the industry hierarchy, finally obtaining the position of executive assistant to independent producer David Loew. In 1948, Kramer signed a distribution contract as an independent producer with United Artists, for which he produced five films in four years: *So This Is New York* (Fleischer, 1948), *Champion* (Robson, 1949), *Home of the Brave* (Robson, 1949), *The Men* (Zinnemann, 1950) and *Cyrano de Bergerac* (Gordon, 1951). From his first pictures, Kramer developed a reputation for tackling bold, difficult or even taboo subjects, which he treated with seriousness and maturity in relatively low-budget films that proved artistically and, especially, commercially successful. For instance, *Champion*, which was shot for under $600,000 in 24 days, dealt with the ugliness and corruption in the world of professional boxing; *Home of the Brave*, which was financed completely by private investors, was one of the first American films to deal openly with race prejudice; and *The Men* dealt with the world of heavily injured World War II veterans and their struggle to adjust to life back home. As he put it in an interview, Kramer wanted to 'use film as a real weapon against discrimination, hatred, prejudice, and excessive power' (quoted in Aberdeen, 2000, p. 152).

After *Cyrano*, Kramer signed an independent deal with Columbia, for which he produced 11 films between 1951 and 1954, including: *Death of a Salesman* (Benedek, 1951), *The Wild One* (Benedek, 1953) and *The Caine Mutiny* (Dmytryk, 1954). By far his most successful film during that period, however, was *High Noon* (Zinnnemann, 1952), which Columbia let him produce for United Artists so that Kramer could fulfil an outstanding contractual obligation. During his four-year spell at Columbia, Kramer, who saw himself as 'a creative moviemaker and not just a business executive', found himself in conflict with the major's boss, Harry Cohn, several times. Not surprisingly, then, when his contract expired Kramer chose to return to United Artists, which by that time had completed its miraculous financial recovery, for a more enhanced form of independent filmmaking.

In this third chapter of his career as a producer Kramer decided to undertake also the role of a director, becoming a hyphenate filmmaker. His first picture in this dual capacity was *Not as a Stranger* (1955), a solid hit that dealt with the trappings of the medical profession for an arrogant doctor who liked to 'play God'. His second film as a producer-director, however, a widescreen period epic entitled *The Pride and the Passion* (1957), was a major box office flop. Cross-collateralised, the two films left United Artists with a loss of $700,000 (Balio, 1987, p. 143). Despite the loss, however, United Artists and the filmmaker proceeded to the signing of a new multi-picture deal on 31 December 1957, under the provisions of which Kramer had to produce six films and direct three of these (see this chapter for details of the deal).

The first of these films was based on an original screenplay by Nathan E. Douglas (pseudonym for blacklisted writer Nedrick Young) and Harold Jacob Smith, called *The Defiant Ones* (*TDO*). The story revolves around the escape from a chain gang of two convicts, one black and one white, who hate each other's race but who have to depend on each other for survival as they are chained together. Having spent a record $75,000 to buy the rights to the property, Kramer invited to the deal Curtleigh Productions as a co-venturer. Curtleigh was an independent production company formed by Tony Curtis and his then wife, Janet Leigh. Curtleigh's participation in the production of *TDO* came as a package with Curtis's agreement to play John 'Joker' Jackson, one of the two main leads. For the second lead, Kramer hired the leading African American actor of the era, Sidney Poitier. With a very low (for the period) budget of $881,904 ($128,196 in total deferred), Kramer completed the shooting in seven weeks, signalling a return to his early days as a producer of low-budget social-problem films that aimed at raising awareness of important social issues.

United Artists' marketing of the film capitalised on Kramer's increasing reputation as a distinctive filmmaker who was 'unafraid to tackle bold and uncompromising themes' and submitted the film to a number of international festivals 'as an unusual example of American motion picture making'. The distributor also stressed the significance and controversy of the picture, highlighting a number of key points, which included an emphasis on the chain gang (hoping to induce protests against the system) and the prominence of chain linking as a powerful symbol.

The film opened in Chicago to great reviews and then to the rest of the country, winning many awards, including two Oscars (Best Screenplay and Best Black and White Cinematography). Perhaps more importantly for Kramer's image as a social-problem filmmaker, the film was awarded the Newspaper Guild of New York Page One Award for Motion Pictures 'for its civilised, adult approach in motion picture terms to one of the profound problems of our time'. Although it garnered a profit of $1 million for United Artists, the film's returns for Lomitas consisted of a paltry $17,324.71 net profit (Curtleigh, which had made a gross income participation deal, made a substantial profit from the film).

Kramer's next film was *On the Beach*, which dealt with another massive social problem, the threat of human extinction from nuclear weapons. The film was based on the best-selling novel by Nevil Shute, which dealt with the aftermath of a nuclear holocaust, represented by the lives of Australians as they wait for radiation to reach their continent, the last place with life on the planet. The production attracted a stellar cast that included Hollywood legends such as Gregory Peck, Ava Gardner and Fred Astaire (unusually, in a dramatic role). Although Kramer deferred both his salaries as a producer-director, Astaire deferred $40,000 from his own salary and Peck accepted only $250,000 against 10 per cent of gross receipts, the film's budget was almost three and a half times the cost of *TDO*, surpassing the $3 million mark. The film's production lasted for more than two and a half months and, like many of Kramer's other films, it faced a battle with the Production Code Administration, as the film seemed to promote euthanasia as an alternative to death from radiation.

In its publicity United Artists orchestrated a concerted effort to proclaim the film to be one of the most important in the history of cinema and to make the premiere day a significant event all over the world. This is evident in the film's taglines, which included: 'Never Before in the History of the Industry Has the World Been Linked Together by One Motion Picture'; 'The First Motion Picture for Everyone All Over the World'; and 'If You Never See Another Motion Picture in Your Life, You Must See *On the Beach*'. The result of this approach to marketing brought an unprecedented simultaneous opening of the film in 18 major cities on all six continents, while the film was also specially screened for 1,200 selected Soviet officials in Moscow and for US president Eisenhower in the White House.

Furthermore, United Artists highlighted Kramer's contribution, stressing his individuality as a filmmaker and especially his tendency to 'ignore' or 'throw out' the rules of picture-making in the US and to 'treat with starkly frank fashion' themes that were deemed 'untouchable' by Hollywood. Despite its critical and commercial success (the film grossed $7,189,915 worldwide), the film's high budget and Peck's agreement for gross participation meant that the film lost $700,000.

Kramer's third film, *Inherit the Wind*, tackled the subject of individual free thinking and how it was put on trial when a high-school biology teacher in a small American South town in the 1920s was charged by Christian fundamentalists with teaching illegally the theory of evolution. The film was adapted from a play by Jerome Lawrence and Robert E. Lee and was based on the 1925 *Tennessee* vs *John Scopes* trial (also known as 'the Monkey Trial'), one of the most famous trials in American legal history. With the screenplay written by the same Oscar-winning writing team of *TDO*, the film attracted another stellar cast, led by Spencer Tracy, Fredric March and Gene Kelly (atypically in an dramatic role – just like Astaire in Kramer's previous film). The production was budgeted at a little more than $2.3 million, with Kramer and Kelly deferring the whole and part of their salaries respectively, while this time there was only one gross participation deal, that of the two playwrights.

Inherit the Wind provoked an epic battle with the PCA. As the film was attacking religious fanaticism it had the potential of striking a new blow to the already weakened Production Code. Although Kramer accepted some of the recommendations by the PCA (especially that the community depicted in the film was 'not representative of the True Christian faith'), the film retained its polemic nature by assuming an educational tone, mainly represented by the monologues spoken by Henry Drummond (Spencer Tracy) exposing the dangers of bigotry and fundamentalism.

Like with the other two Lomitas pictures, United Artists stressed the controversial elements of the film and Kramer's indisputable value as a filmmaker with a conscience. Despite a number of awards and rave reviews, however, the film's combined US and international gross receipts were $1,792,336. With advertising and marketing costs alone surpassing the $1 million mark, the film recorded a heavy loss ($1.7 million), representing a major disappointment for both producer and distributor.

Although the filmmaker's independence in this case is determined by his production deal with United Artists, Stanley Kramer is also a filmmaker with a personal visual style, an aspect of his work that is often ignored by critics. His trademark is a combination of the use of deep-focus cinematography and extremely long takes (often more than two or three minutes in duration, while on certain occasions individual scenes consist of just one long take) that allow dramatic situations to develop gradually and reach a peak at the end of a scene. For instance, each scene in *TDO* lasts about two-and-a-half minutes on average, while in *On the Beach* and in *Inherit the Wind* they last three and four minutes, respectively.

Because of the emphasis of his films on tense dramatic situations, Kramer often uses 180-degree tracking shots (the positions of two characters in a frame switch), which often signify an upcoming dramatic reversal or that one character gains an advantage over another character. This is particularly evident in *TDO* and in *Inherit the Wind*, which contain two antagonists with distinct ideological beliefs. Apart from the aesthetic effects such stylistic choices produce, they make the actors' performance easier, as they allow them to act uninterrupted for a substantial amount of time. Under Kramer's direction, Tracy, Poitier and Curtis were all nominated for an Oscar for Best Actor in a Leading Role, while the same three along with Fredric March and Fred Astaire won other US and international acting awards.

Although Kramer directed and produced three pictures, he nevertheless did not produce the additional three films his agreement with UA specified. Despite the heavy losses of *Inherit the Wind*, UA and Lomitas signed a new distribution deal on 2 February 1960 for three more films which Kramer would direct and produce, while his obligations from the previous contract were transferred to the new agreement. The filmmaker continued to tackle difficult subjects, such as genocide and the Nazi crimes (*Judgment at Nuremberg*, 1961), racism (*Pressure Point*, Cornfield, 1962) and child disabilities (*A Child Is Waiting*, Cassavetes, 1963) before scoring big at the box office with the comedy *It's a Mad, Mad, Mad, Mad World* (1963). After these films Kramer moved to Columbia and in 1967 produced and directed arguably his most famous picture, *Guess Who's Coming to Dinner*.

Stanley Kramer managed to establish a significant career by creating a distinct identity for himself and his films. The downside of this success, however, was that he never managed to make any profits for the various production outfits he had set up. Between 1955 and 1963 Kramer's films lost a staggering $7 million at the box office, a loss that was absorbed by United Artists. The main problem was that Kramer suffered from lack of product differentiation, that is, he produced only one type of picture, the social-problem film. This means that once the appeal of this type of picture started declining, he was in no position to follow trends or produce commercially successful films of other types or genres (Balio, 1987, p. 160). As a result, he made a significant contribution to American cinema with certain very distinct pictures, but failed to establish a solvent self-owned production company.

Figure 3.1 Stanley Kramer directing Ava Gardner in the Lomitas Productions Picture *On the Beach*.

Distribution

From the time a negative print was delivered to the distributor, United Artists had the right 'to examine the material and make recommendations'.[40] This provision, however, was of a consultative nature and could not be forced upon the producer, unless the film was not deemed suitable for exhibition for technical reasons and therefore could not obtain a certificate from the Motion Pictures Association of America (MPAA), which had replaced the MPPDA in 1945 as the main trade organisation that regulated Hollywood cinema. Then United Artists would discuss distribution strategies with a representative of the production company, while retaining, however, controlling judgement of the overall marketing plan. The distributor then would undertake the release of the film worldwide through its global distribution network, or in the areas where UA was not represented through foreign sub-distributors.

United Artists was granted permission by the production company, which was the *copyright holder* of the picture, to exploit the film for a period of 10 years, after which the production company had the right to buy the distributor's interest in the picture for an agreed price. This was another of the unique selling points of United Artists, an exception among the majors, which offered independent producers copyright of their pictures. And if a producer actually owned the rights to the films his or her company produced, then this producer had every reason to lay claim to the label 'independent', despite his or her relationship with one of Hollywood's seven main companies (by 1958 RKO had gone bankrupt, bringing the number of majors down to seven).

Once the film was in release, the distributor was responsible for the accounting of the film's gross receipts, which were defined as follows:

- domestic theatrical gross receipts (from the US and Canada and from other outlets such as the Army, the Navy, hospitals and so on);
- foreign theatrical gross receipts (from foreign markets or outright sales or sub-distribution);
- incidental gross receipts (non-theatrical and television).[41]

After grosses were collected, the distributor would have to deduct certain standard fees (trade association fees, taxes, industry assessment fees and so on) before proceeding to obtain its distribution fee, a percentage of each film's total gross receipts, for the service of releasing a film worldwide. The fee was 30 per cent of the gross receipts in the US and Britain, but it could go as high as 45 per cent of the gross in a number of territories (such as Holland, Greece, Finland, India, Mexico, Portugal, Burma, Afghanistan and Pakistan). For the rest of the world the fee was 40 per cent of the film's gross.[42] Following the deduction of the fee, the distributor was left with the producer's share of gross receipts, from which it would subtract the costs of advertising and marketing, other advances pertaining to the exploitation of each film, as well as any money owed to talent who had made gross-income participation deals.[43] The remaining income (known as the producer's net income) would then be divided as follows, with everything else classed as net profits and divided according to specific agreements with net profit participants:

- United Artists (the production loans with 6 per cent interest);
- United Artists (the pre-production advances);
- Lomitas Productions (for any completion money advanced, if the distributor had not provided this money);
- Lomitas Productions' sales representatives;
- other people (deferred salaries of director-producer and stars).[44]

As this was a multi-picture deal, United Artists and Lomitas agreed also to cross-collateralise profits, that is, to balance profits and losses across the six films for the duration of the contract. In other words, profits from a film could be used to pay for pre-production advances for the next picture, while the final profits for the two parties would be allocated and distributed at the end of the three-year period for which the agreement stood. According to Balio, cross-collateralisation was a protection mechanism for the distributor in case one film by an independent producer made exceptional money while the same producer's next picture proved a disaster at the box office.[45]

The reasons for United Artists' success

United Artists' move to offer independent producers complete production financing, creative control, final cut and a share of the profits differentiated the distribution company from the other majors, which did not find it easy to adapt to the post-studio era. One great advantage UA held over its competitors was that it did not have a studio backlot and therefore no stars or technical personnel under contract and no overhead costs, at a time when studio production started declining and studio employees were turning freelance. Unlike the other majors, which were recruiting independent production units to provide them with product but, equally importantly, to make use of the ex-studios' production facilities and empty soundstages for a fee (a practice that inflated budgets considerably), United Artists was happy for its producers to make their own arrangements for the use of studio space, provided that their choice would not have any impact on the budget. For this reason, it did not attach overhead costs to the budgets of individual films (with the exception of 1 per cent of the final production budget),[46] at a time when top-rank independent producers at Paramount (such as Hitchcock and DeMille) were forced to pay a large overhead charge to the studio in return for financing, technical support, distribution and publicity.[47] Needless to say, that these charges were among the first to be deducted from the gross receipts long before these filmmakers claimed any profits from the producer's net income.

Furthermore, and because it did not possess a studio lot, UA was the first financier/distributor to encourage production outside the US. Like the other distributors, UA had blocked or frozen capital in several European countries, a result of the protective measures these countries had taken to encourage domestic film production. Runaway productions (as American productions made outside the US came to be known) gave an opportunity to a financier/distributor to utilise those frozen funds by reinvesting them in production in the same country, while partnerships with local entrepreneurs, use of local tax loopholes and considerably cheaper (than Hollywood) labour costs could bring budgets down. Very soon the benefits of runaway production were recognised by the rest of the majors. By 1959 there were 32 US pictures being filmed in Italy, 28 in France and 20 in Britain, while in the following year 40 per cent of all films financed by the ex-studios were shot outside the US.[48] It was clear that this type of production would become a mainstay of Hollywood cinema, especially when in the 1960s various countries offered subsidies to Hollywood majors to continue making films there.

But, by far, the most important element in the United Artists' arsenal of advantages was the combination of creative control and profit participation, with little or no financial risk for the independent producer. To keep budgets down and potentially increase profit margins, United Artists invited its filmmakers to become co-venturers in their projects, primarily by asking them to defer their salaries. For instance, Stanley Kramer's salary of $75,000 for his role as a producer for each of the six films and of $125,000 if he acted as a producer-director for each of the three films he would decide to direct would both be deferred. Kramer would be paid only a weekly salary of $1,500 for the administration of Lomitas Productions, while he would have to wait his turn to receive either of his deferred salaries or profits from the producer's net income. The three-year contract guaranteed the filmmaker some $225,000 in salary, whether his films returned profits or not.[49] Additionally, the filmmaker and the distributor would convince the major stars to defer part of their own salaries or accept smaller salaries and make profit participation deals, keeping the budget very low (compared with the rest of the industry). In this way, Kramer's films had at least the potential to return profits, if successful at the box office, although, according to Balio, no film distributed by United Artists between 1951 and 1957 did in fact succeed in returning profit to its producer and the distributor. All the profits UA made in those years were purely from the distribution fee.[50]

United Artists continued its impressive post-1951 march to success. In 1957, the company made a deal with the Mirisch Corporation (consisting of three brothers, Walter, Harold and Marvin), who were previously releasing films through Allied Artists. The Mirisch Corporation represented a new type of independent film company, one that specialised in providing a full range of services to filmmakers, including: negotiating contracts and financing; approaching actors for casting on behalf of the filmmaker; arranging pre-production logistics; and even supervising a film's marketing and merchandising worldwide.[51] It was the company's objective to handle all matters pertaining to the organisation of film production so that the filmmaker could concentrate on simply making the film. This type of company had become a necessity in the new environment of America cinema, where a large number of independent filmmakers had to carry out extensive administration work on top of their production duties.

In many ways, the Mirisch Corporation represented the next step to another recent development, the rise of talent agencies into a central position in the American film industry. With the studios no longer generating production deals, talent agencies found an opportunity to expand their main line of work (representing talent in negotiations for film production deals), putting production deals together, preferably by utilising only their roster of clients. Although the Mirisch brothers were not agents, the services they offered covered several aspects of deal making but significantly extended to cover other areas of production and management.

The foundation of their work was to place a number of commercial directors under contract, believing that they would be able to attract the stars. Through the Mirisch Corporation, United Artists distributed the work of filmmakers such as Billy Wilder, John Sturges, Robert Wise, William Wyler, Blake Edwards and Norman Jewison, responsible for a number of commercial and critical successes such as: *Some Like It Hot* (Wilder, 1959); *The Magnificent Seven* (Sturges, 1960); *West Side Story* (Wise and Robbins, 1961); *The Children's Hour* (Wyler, 1962); *The Pink Panther* (Edwards, 1964); and *In the Heat of the Night* (Jewison, 1967). Between 1958 and 1974, the Mirisch Corporation delivered to United Artists 67 films in total,[52] making this one of the most successful agreements between a distributor and a film company in the history of American cinema.

In the 1960s United Artists launched another extremely successful deal, with British producers Harry Saltzman and Albert 'Cubby' Broccoli, who produced for the American distributor the James Bond series of films, starting with *Dr No* (T. Young) in 1962. Finally, United Artists was first among the majors to tap an increasingly large art-cinema market. Since the success of the French film *And God Created Woman* (Vadim, 1956), which grossed $3 million at the US box office, there was an exponential increase in theatres dedicated to non-US fare (from fewer than 50 in the pre-war era to more than 800 in 1958). Equally, the number of films imported into the US had risen from 93 in 1948 to 532 in 1957, which of course signalled the existence of a distinct audience for art-films.[53] To lay a claim to this market, UA acquired one of the foremost distributors in the field, Lopert Films. Through this subsidiary, UA released a number of films from 1959 onwards, including the very successful, critically and commercially, *Never on Sunday* (Dassin, 1960), as well as a number of other moderately commercial but critically applauded films such as *La Notte* (Antonioni, 1962) and *Persona* (Bergman, 1967). By 1967, the year this second period in the history of American independent cinema closes, United Artists (which had also become a public company in 1957) had transformed into the most successful company in the film industry, ahead of all its competitors.

The triumph of a brand of independent production … and of the majors

By the end of the 1950s all the ex-studios had started following United Artists' example. Independent production was in full swing, with almost 70 per cent of the ex-studios' output being independently produced films, forcing industry officials such as United Artists' vice president, Max E. Youngstein, to talk about 'an independent revolution' that had overthrown 'the one-man studio czar system'.[54] Even MGM, the studio that epitomised best the one-man studio czar system (Louis B. Meyer had stepped down only in 1951, after 27 years as production chief), the only studio that had refused to support any top-rank independents in the 1940s and the last company to divest itself of its theatre chains and fire its personnel, finally saw the benefits of independent production. By 1957 and under Joseph Vogel's regime MGM had arranged distribution deals with 10 independent filmmakers, who collectively produced 24 pictures in 1957–8 and brought in $5 million in profits to the distributor.[55]

The new industrial conditions were helped undoubtedly by the loosening of the conservative political and social mores that had made politically progressive films almost impossible in the early 1950s. Films in the late 1950s were again beginning to connect 'to political, social and cultural issues',[56] while on 11 December 1956 the Production Code was revised to permit the representation of previously taboo subjects like abortion, child birth and drug addiction.

As the 1960s came in, the ex-studios were embedded fully in the structures of independent production or, to see it from the opposite perspective, independent production had become the business of the ex-studios, which were transformed into financiers and distributors of independently produced pictures. If after the Paramount decree they surrendered control of exhibition reluctantly, this time they were more than willing to surrender the next foundation of vertical integration – production – to the independents.

Audience decline in American cinema, however, continued. Although the slide was not as dramatic as in the late 1940s and early 1950s, cinema-going simply stopped being a primary recreation activity for the majority of Americans. From as early as 1958, the seven majors' earnings from abroad were higher than their domestic revenues.[57] In the same year, music record sales in the US represented a $350 million business, a figure that would increase exponentially in the coming decade.[58] But if the film industry would eventually find a way to participate in the profits of the music business when the ex-studios started branching out to other media industries, it could certainly not lay claim to the $1.3 billion of disposable income that Americans were spending on garden products in 1965 for their suburban homes.[59] By 1960 the Hollywood majors were distributing about 200 films per year, while three years later the number of releases went down to 143 and movie attendance reached 21 million per week (less than a quarter of what it had been in 1946).[60]

The low number of releases signalled a new development in American cinema – the distributors' emphasis on fewer but more expensive films which had the potential to return large profits. Up until 1947, there were only four films in the history of American cinema that had achieved rentals of more than $10 million: *The Birth of a Nation* (Griffith, 1914), *Gone with the Wind*, *The Best Years of Our Lives* and *Duel in the Sun*, the last three being top-rank independent productions. During the 1948–67 period, however, there were 41 features that went past that landmark, led by *The Sound of Music* (Wise) in 1965, which achieved the phenomenal-for-the-period record of $72 million in rentals.[61] The emphasis on more expensive films, however, brought with it the potential for greater losses if the films failed at the box office. And with approximately three-quarters of all films released by the majors failing to make a profit,[62] it became obvious that American cinema was heading in a direction where very few expensive films per year had the potential to return the size of profits the ex-studios needed to keep controlling the industry.

More importantly, this development had a significant impact on the types of films that were made (historical spectacles, war films, epics) and, therefore, on the types of films independent filmmakers were forced to produce if they wanted to stay in the game. Between 1951 and 1960, the independents were responsible for seven out of the 10 most financially successful films of the period: *The Ten Commandments* (DeMille, 1956); *Around the World in 80 Days* (Anderson, 1956); *South Pacific* (Logan, 1958); *The Bridge on the River*

Kwai (Lean, 1957); *Spartacus* (Kubrick, 1960); *The Greatest Show on Earth* (DeMille, 1952); and *This Is Cinerama* (Cooper and von Fritsch, 1952). All the above films were shot in colour (which enhanced their spectacular elements such as costumes and locations), while all films with the exception of *The Greatest Show on Earth* were made to exploit the new exhibition technologies in which the US distributors had invested to lure audiences out of their homes and into the theatres. Equally, all seven films can be categorised as spectacles or epics and are virtually indistinguishable aesthetically from two of the studio-produced films that appear in the top 10, *Ben-Hur* (Wyler, 1959) by MGM and *The Robe* (Koster, 1953) by 20th Century Fox, leaving *From Here to Eternity* (Zinnemann, 1953), produced and distributed by Columbia Pictures, as the only film in the decade's top 10 that was shot in black and white and was not spectacle-driven, even though it did contain a number of spectacular elements such as exotic locations in Hawaii and one battle scene.[63]

With the majority of US-produced films failing to find an audience and with the policy of producing fewer but more expensive films carrying a higher financial risk, the ex-studios were in danger of finding themselves in an extremely vulnerable position. For that reason, from the mid-1950s onwards they had started diversifying, mainly towards the broadcasting and the music industries. In this manner they were able to supplement their reduced income from theatrical exhibition with revenues earned in these ancillary markets. The company that pioneered this type of convergence with other media-related industries and revolutionised the film business was a former top-rank independent of the 1930s and 1940s, Walt Disney Productions.

By the early 1950s Disney was ready to exploit other income-generating avenues than just the production of animated films. Perhaps worried that the expansion of television would bring the end of newsreels, cartoon shorts and other forms of theatrical film entertainment,[64] Disney decided to increase animated feature film production, while also branching out into live-action production and the theme park business. After more than a decade distributing through RKO, Disney decided to form its own distribution apparatus at a time when the company's output of feature films had started increasing. Indeed, in 1953 Disney formed Buena Vista and distributed its own films, including the commercially very successful *20,000 Leagues Under the Sea* (Fleischer, 1954). Equally importantly, Disney approached ABC, one of the three US television networks that was lacking in significance and revenues compared with its two competitors, and in 1954 created *Disneyland*, a 60-minute weekly series. The show, which was a big hit for ABC, promoted Disney's businesses – including the company's upcoming productions – to the vast US television audience for free. The success of *Disneyland*, which was broadcast at primetime, brought a second Disney 60-minute weekly series to ABC, the hugely popular *The*

Mickey Mouse Club, which was also in the business of promoting Disney's other ventures (including its famous theme park, opened in 1955), while entertaining the nation's children.

Following these moves, Disney diversified further to exploit cross-promotions in the music industry, the publishing industry and the toy industry, and soon was far away from the marginal position it occupied in the late 1940s. By 1956, it averaged more than $2.5 million in annual profits, while 10 years later that figure had climbed to $16 million, making Disney one of the most successful media companies in the world, with film accounting only for one-third of the company's business.[65] Once again, a top-rank independent producer had shown the way. One by one, the major studios started diversifying, mainly into television and music. By the mid-1960s the majors were earning about one-third of their total revenues from television production,[66] while Balio remarks that a quarter of all United Artists' revenues for 1966 came from its music subsidiary, United Artists Records.[67] For the ex-studios, then, which were gradually becoming diversified media companies rather than film financiers and distributors, filmmaking became only one of their activities, though still the primary source of their income (with the exception of Disney). This trend reached its logical conclusion towards the end of the decade, when one by one the majors were bought out by conglomerates with interests in diverse, non-media-related fields (see Chapter 6).

Under these circumstances it is not surprising that this particular brand of independent production, the main method of production in Hollywood cinema during this period, was locked in the trajectory of the seven major distributors and consequently became synonymous with mainstream filmmaking. Such a development necessarily suggests that the Paramount decree did not succeed in its ultimate objective, to dispossess the eight studios of their control and domination of the US film industry. Adverse industrial and economic conditions, a constellation of political, social and cultural factors but mostly the ex-studios' clever manoeuvring in a period of recession and their emphasis on the power of distribution to control the business even when production was arranged individually and without their direct participation, made independent cinema the business of the majors. A great contributor to the ex-studios' success in retaining their dominant position in the industry as distributors was the massive decline in theatre attendance, which in its turn effected an even larger decline in the number of films released. With the number of film releases reaching as low as 143 in a particular year, there was simply no place for new distribution companies to enter the market and compete directly with the seven Hollywood majors (despite some efforts).[68]

Conclusion

Despite ultimately being controlled by the majors, independent production post-1948 continued the project of the hyphenate filmmakers of the 1940s, who had laid the foundations for a filmmaker's cinema and had gradually stripped the studios of their distinct house styles. By moving from distributor to distributor, arranging individual or multi-picture deals and by constructing film packages that often were sold to the highest bidder, independent filmmakers in the 1950s and 1960s indeed finished the job that the previous generation had started. Thus, even when the credits continued to present films by Paramount, Universal or Warner Bros., the logo did not mean anything specific. Writing about the production of *Spartacus* at Universal one year after the company was taken over by the Music Corporation of America (MCA), a talent agency that grew so powerful in the 1950s that it acquired one of the seven majors, Thomas Schatz noted 'how genuinely independent top-feature production had become even at Universal'. He continued:

> This was an unprecedented production by Universal's standards, and its packaging was equally unconventional ... *Spartacus* was a European co-production put together by an outside producer, Edward Lewis, and directed by maverick free-lancer Stanley Kubrick. Much of the film was shot in Spain and several of its international all-star cast owned a piece of the production ... Universal served as no more than the nominal producer, providing production facilities, personnel and distribution. Thus *Spartacus* was by no means a 'Universal picture' in any traditional sense.[69]

The fact that *Spartacus* was not a 'Universal picture', however, did not mean that it was very different formally and aesthetically from other epics of the time, such as *Cleopatra* (directed by Joseph L. Mankiewicz, produced by Walter Wanger and distributed by 20th Century Fox) or *Ben-Hur* (produced and distributed by MGM). Thus although the distinct identities of the individual studios had disappeared completely, there was also a parallel centripetal tendency throughout the industry towards the tried and tested, which eventually eroded any oppositional-to-the-mainstream attitude and made a progressive cinema very difficult, despite some notable exceptions.[70] It was this tendency that laid the foundations for other brands of independent cinema that are discussed in Parts III and IV, after an examination of the low-budget independent market during the 1948–67 period in the following chapter.

Notes

1 Quoted in Balio, 1987, p. 142.
2 Quoted in Monaco, 2001, p. 26.

3 Monaco, 2001, p. 182.
4 Staiger, 1983, p. 78.
5 Schatz, 1999, p. 323.
6 Tasker, 1996, p. 215, Hillier, 1994, p. 7.
7 Balio, 1985, p. 403.
8 Aberdeen, 2000, p. 158.
9 The figures are taken from Schatz, 1996, p. 435, and Schatz, 1999, pp. 290 and 331.
10 Conant, 1976, p. 352.
11 Balio, 1987, p. 19.
12 Balio, 1985, p. 401.
13 Quart and Auster, 2002, p. 43.
14 Schatz, 1999, p. 295.
15 Cripps, 1997, p. 212, Balio, 1987, p. 124.
16 Quoted in Hagopian, 1986, p. 28.
17 Quoted in Schatz, 1999, p. 346.
18 Lev, 2003, p. 25.
19 Davis, 1997, p. 22.
20 The figures are taken from Gomery, 1986, p. 175.
21 Balio, 1976, p. 216.
22 Balio, 1976, p. 230.
23 Balio, 1976, p. 234.
24 Staiger, 1983, p. 77.
25 Lev, 2003, p. 62.
26 Sklar, 1975, p. 285.
27 The figures are taken from Davis, 1997, p. 30.
28 The figures for the proliferation of TV sets are taken from Balio, 1976, p. 224. The figures for the increase in the number of television stations are taken from Lev, 2003, p. 9.
29 Staiger, 1983, p. 75.
30 Balio, 1987, p. 3.
31 Balio, 1987, p. 25.
32 Balio, 1976, p. 234.
33 Balio, 1987, p. 46.
34 Balio, 1987, p. 51.
35 The figures are taken from Balio, 1976, p. 237.
36 The figures are calculated from 'Appendix 1: United Artists Domestic Releases, 1951–1978 (Including Lopert Releases)', in Balio, 1987, pp. 349–87.
37 The contract is 'UA Corp – Lomitas OTB, ITW, TDO Financing and Distribution Agreement', available in Box 258, Folder 2, Stanley Kramer Papers (Collection 161), Department of Special Collections, Charles E. Young Research Library, University of California, Los Angeles.
38 UA Corp – Lomitas OTB, ITW, TDO Financing and Distribution Agreement, p. 2.
39 UA Corp – Lomitas OTB, ITW, TDO Financing and Distribution Agreement, p. 6.
40 UA Corp – Lomitas OTB, ITW, TDO Financing and Distribution Agreement, p. 40.
41 UA Corp – Lomitas OTB, ITW, TDO Financing and Distribution Agreement, pp. 54–6.
42 UA Corp – Lomitas OTB, ITW, TDO Financing and Distribution Agreement, pp. 57–8.
43 UA Corp – Lomitas OTB, ITW, TDO Financing and Distribution Agreement, p. 20.
44 UA Corp – Lomitas OTB, ITW, TDO Financing and Distribution Agreement, p. 21.
45 Balio, 1990, p. 180.

46 UA Corp – Lomitas OTB, ITW, TDO Financing and Distribution Agreement, p. 10.

47 Lev, 2003, p. 202. Although Lev does not include a figure or a percentage of the budget that this overhead charge reached, Balio (1987, p. 141) stated that fellow major Columbia used to charge independent filmmakers such as Stanley Kramer an overhead as high as 25 per cent of a film's budget. One could assume that Paramount's charges were similar to those charged by Columbia.

48 Davis, 1997, p. 34, Monaco, 2001, p. 14.

49 UA Corp – Lomitas OTB, ITW, TDO Financing and Distribution Agreement, pp. 6 and 11.

50 Balio, 1990, p. 170.

51 Balio, 1987, p. 161.

52 Balio, 1990, p. 170.

53 All the quoted figures about the art-cinema market in the US are taken from Doherty, 1988, p. 32.

54 Youngstein is quoted in Doherty, 1988, p. 22.

55 Lev, 2003, p. 198.

56 Lev, 2003, p. 63.

57 Monaco, 2001, p. 10.

58 Balio, 1987, p. 113.

59 Davies, 1981, p. 121.

60 Monaco, 2001, p. 3, Davis, 1997, p. 62.

61 The number of films that went past the $10 million mark in the 1948–67 period is calculated from the table of box office hits 1914–2002 available in Finler, 2003, pp. 356–9.

62 This estimation is for the year 1961 and is quoted in Monaco, 2001, p. 11.

63 The top 10 is taken from Finler, 2003, p. 358.

64 Segrave, 1999, p. 33.

65 The figures are obtained from Finler, 2003, p. 320 and Balio, 1987, p. 317.

66 Davis, 1997, p. 59.

67 Balio, 1987, p. 114.

68 Of course there were several new distribution companies in the art-house cinema field and in the low-budget/exploitation fields, but like in the studio period, these distributors were marginal and in no position to compete in the same arena with the main powers.

69 Schatz, 1996, p. 480.

70 For an interesting discussion of how certain top-rank independent filmmakers managed to make a few politically progressive films within this environment see Mann, 2008.

4

An audience for the independents: exploitation films for the nation's youth

The independent filmmaker [in the 1960s] was a little bit like a guerrilla fighter – he could move fast and flexibly and react immediately to the change in circumstances – whereas a large army was like a large studio that had to have a bureaucracy to keep it all together and that would slow down its response time.
Roger Corman, filmmaker[1]

Producers have always wanted to make 'dignified' pictures. That's not a good word for it. They wanted to make 'nice' pictures. They wanted to make pictures for their mothers and their wives, and their friends. And, damn it, their mothers and their friends don't go to pictures anymore!
Samuel Z. Arkoff, producer and distributor[2]

Introduction

While the major studios were trying to cope with the effects of the Paramount decree, but mostly with the impact of the economic recession, the Poverty Row studios had to deal only with the latter. The US Justice Department had concentrated its efforts strictly on the Big Five and the Little Three, leaving all other companies out of the lawsuit as their position in the industry was marginal and their collusion with the Big Five minimal. The recession, however, hit companies like Allied Artists (formerly Monogram Pictures), Republic Pictures and other smaller outfits in a more forceful manner than the studios. Not only did the Poverty Row studios not possess adequate resources to cope with dwindling audiences, declining profits and the rise of the big-budget film, they also had to deal with the end of the double bill as a dominant exhibition practice and the closure of hundreds of small, neighbourhood theatres that traditionally were the Poverty Row firms' best customers. More importantly, these low-budget companies faced fierce competition from television, which in those early years became a vehicle for action-oriented, cheaply made shows that were modelled on the B film.[3] If the majors tried to battle with this emergent competitor with investment in new exhibition technologies such as widescreen and 3-D and with extremely expensive epics and spectacles that could be appreciated only on the big screen, the Poverty Row studios were in no position to invest either in technology or in blockbusters, despite their occasional attempts to finance films with budgets that reached the $1.5 million mark in the late 1940s (see Chapter 2).

Although all these effects on the low-budget film market did not become manifest overnight, it could be argued that this category of independent filmmaking entered a new era during the late 1940s and early 1950s. That era was marked by three key elements: new distribution rules (the end of the double bill, at least as it had been established in the 1930s and 1940s); an overwhelming emphasis on 'exploitation' as a distribution strategy, as a way of constructing an audience and as a type of motion picture;[4] and, finally, a conscious effort by the low-budget companies to cater for a youth audience, a particularly strong demographic that emerged in the 1950s but was ignored initially by the majors and top-rank independents. These three factors allowed companies such as Allied Artists and Republic to survive the recession, while a number of newcomers, such as Lippert Pictures, Embassy Pictures, William Castle Productions, Roger Corman (through a number of production companies and his own distribution company, the Filmgroup) and American International Pictures, tried to lay their own claim to the market.

Low-end independent filmmaking continued in this guise in a relatively stable manner until the late 1960s, when a new, heavier recession led the ex-studios to adopt partly the low-budget independent mode of filmmaking and create a new brand of independent cinema, which is discussed in Chapter 5. For the purposes of this chapter, the second phase in the history of low-end independent filmmaking stretches from the early 1950s to the end of the 1960s, and mirrors the duration – though not the central features – of the second phase of top-rank independent film production.

The emergence of the teenager and the rise of the youth audience

The most important development in low-budget independent filmmaking and, arguably, its salvation during the period of recession was the emergence of a particular audience demographic loosely labelled the 'youth' audience. This demographic, which, according to Barry Keith Grant, covered all people from the age of 10 to 35, included three main subcategories: children, teenagers (a newly coined age group that included young individuals between the ages of 12 and 19) and post-adolescents or young adults (between the ages of 20 and 35).[5] The last two categories together represented between 70 and 80 per cent of the total film audience during the 1950s,[6] but, until the middle of the decade, young adults and especially teenagers had yet to see pictures specifically geared to them.

The most important of these three categories for the low-end independents was the second category, teenagers. As a distinct sociological entity the teenager was a direct product of American society and culture of the 1950s. While teenagers as a distinct group first appeared in the 1940s, when a large number of adults were away on military service and therefore certain industries started acknowledging younger people as a new potential demographic,[7] their emergence became more noticeable in the following decade, in conditions of economic prosperity and with various cultural changes. 'What lent 1950s teenagers a sense of group identity both peculiarly intense and historically new', Thomas Doherty argues, 'was that their generational status, their social position *as teenagers*, was carefully nurtured and vigorously reinforced by adult institutions around them'. This suggests that for the first time teenagers were actually identified by adult groups as a 'special like-minded community bound together by age and rank', while their 'psychological and physical development was accorded a dramatically public recognition'.[8] As a result, the lifestyle and habits of teenagers became central subjects in public discourse and it was only a matter of time before teenage life became the subject of media representation.

Perhaps the most important effect of the emergence of the teenager in US society – at least from the point of view of the cultural industries – was their inclination to spend a substantial part of their disposable income (approximately 15 per cent, or $1.5 billion a year) on leisure activities and cultural products, mainly films, music records and leisure magazines.[9]

Unlike the rest of the potential film audience, who were deserting movie-going for other forms of cultural and recreational activities, teenagers emerged as the most frequent cinema-goers, refusing to follow the trends established by older generations. More importantly, teenagers emerged as the group that led forward a consumer-based US economy, increasingly becoming opinion leaders for the rest of American culture and mobilising a vast array of advertising resources for the selling of cultural products.[10]

With the teenage-led youth audience in place, one would have thought that it would be only a matter of time before the majors moved in and captured that market. This did not prove the case, at least not until the mid-1950s. The majors distributed only a handful of films with a teenage interest, notably Stanley Kramer and Columbia's *The Wild One* (Benedek, 1953 – originally entitled

Hot Blood), MGM's *Blackboard Jungle* (Brooks, 1955) and Warner Bros.' *Rebel Without a Cause* (Ray, 1955).[11] All three films, however, were characterised by an adult perspective and seemed to emphasise juvenile delinquency as a social problem rather than targeting an audience of a particular mentality and trying to 'speak' to it from a perspective that did not carry with it any judgement.

While the majors were reluctant to address the teenage demographic, the top-rank independents (who by that time had become an integral part of the studio machine) were also unwilling or unable to undertake the task. The reason for this was simple: most of the successful top-rank independent producers were either established movie stars well over the age of 30, or hyphenates who had graduated from the studio system and were even older than the former group. In the words of Peter Lev, 'the film industry's structure and the aging personnel circa 1950 were ill-equipped to make such [youth] films',[12] while one should also not forget that those were very conservative times and consequently the production of films about social problems (including juvenile delinquency) was a delicate and potentially dangerous matter.

With the majors and top-rank independents out of the picture, the road for low-end independents was wide open. Recognising early on that teenage audiences in particular want to see films about their own generation, their own problems, their own music, their own style and with their own stars and idols, low-budget independent producers provided them with exactly these elements. This move towards catering specifically for the youth audiences by meeting their demand for a particular type of filmed entertainment signalled the emergence of the 'teenpic', a particular type of exploitation picture that took several forms and ushered these independents to a new era of low-budget filmmaking.

From Poverty Row to exploitation and showmanship

Although the phenomenon of exploitation pictures was as old as cinema itself, the low-budget exploitation films of the 1950s and 1960s represented a drastically different approach to film content from previous forms of exploitation (though this was not the case when it came to questions of advertising and publicity). In previous decades, exploitation films dealt specifically with 'the gratification of forbidden curiosity', more often than not under the pretence of educating the audience.[13] Ostracised from the content of films made by the majors, top-rank independents and Poverty Row studios, taboo subjects such as venereal diseases, miscegenation, homosexuality, drug use, sexual relations outside wedlock, abortion and childbirth found their way into a number of films that were made strictly outside the American film industry, distributed through the states rights market and screened at any place a distributor could get (including tents and warehouses that were transformed into exhibition sites overnight). From the first cycle of sex hygiene films in the late 1910s to the classic exploitation pictures of the 1930s such as *The Cocaine Fiends* (O'Connor, 1935), *Reefer Madness* (Gasnier, 1936) and *Assassin of Youth* (Clifton, 1937) to the phenomenally successful *Mom and Dad* (Beaudine, 1945), these types of pictures were never a part of the official US film industry.

As a large number of Poverty Row outfits also used the states rights market to distribute their films, they soon realised that they could stir interest in their own films by emulating the outspoken manner in which exploitation films were publicised. For instance, in Chapter 2 we saw how even the bigger Poverty Row studios, like Monogram, made use of exploitation tactics to advertise *Women in Bondage* (1943), a film with a highly exploitable title that dealt with the enslavement of women in Nazi Germany. The use of exploitation techniques in film distribution quickly paved the way for the emergence of a new brand of exploitation film, which this time was made within the structures of the film industry (though still away from the major powers) and which was not disreputable in the same way that the 1930s exploitation films were. As Steven Broidy, president of Monogram Pictures, proudly announced in 1946: 'We make stories which lend themselves to exploitation. Give us a headline and we can give you a completed picture in 60 days. No major studio can compete with us when we turn them out in a hurry.'[14] Indeed, by that time Monogram was doing outstanding business with two low-budget exploitation films, *Dillinger* (Nosseck, 1945), a film about the famous gangster, and the self-explanatory *Black Market Babies* (Beaudine, 1945), made by the director of *Mom and Dad*.

Broidy's description of Monogram's approach to filmmaking gives a clear idea about the main characteristics of this type of exploitation film:

- it is based on a newspaper headline, with a title as outspoken or controversial as the headline itself;
- it covers a number of subjects, often in the form of an exposé that throws light on various forms of illegal activities;
- it promises – but almost never delivers – controversial or titillating visual material;
- it is produced cheaply and quickly while the subject it is set to exploit is still in public discourse (and therefore is still marketable).

Obviously, the success of this type of film depends heavily on its 'exploitation' during the distribution and exhibition stages, which are designed in such a way as to attract maximum public awareness for the lowest possible amount of expenditure on the part of the distributor. The topicality of the subject, trend or fad that most of these films deal with guarantees them a certain amount of publicity (non-paid advertising), and distributors and exhibitors are ready to exploit any available means to attract paying customers, including exaggerated or even outright false advertising about the extent of the presence of controversial elements in the picture. As Mike Ripps, producer of *Bayou* (Daniels, 1957), a film with the tagline 'Somewhere, a 15-year-old girl may be a teenager … in the Cajun country, she's a woman full-grown! … and every Bayou man knows it!', remarked: '[Audiences] don't come to see a picture, they come to see a show'.[15] And the distributors of low-budget independent films were in the business of ensuring that the show would be memorable, even if the picture almost never was. From that moment on, the concept of 'showmanship' became of utmost importance for producers, distributors and exhibitors of exploitation films, prompting various players in the low-budget market to adopt it as the *modus operandi* of their companies (for instance, Broidy christened Monogram 'the showmanship company', while the official slogan of American International Pictures was 'dedicated to showmanship').[16]

The exploitation picture and the strong showmanship with which it was marketed found the perfect audience in the emerging teenage demographic of the 1950s. The increased visibility of teenagers in public discourse (and in newspaper headlines) made them appropriate material for the subject of a large number of exploitation films. And as those films dealt with issues relevant to teenagers, they specifically targeted them as their main audience, often to the point of excluding other potential audiences. Equipped with a new type of picture for a distinct audience demographic, the low-budget independents were ready to shun their Poverty Row image and adopt the exploitation label. A new type of exhibition site that specialised in showing exploitation teenpics and in attracting youth audiences completed the picture, the drive-in theatre.

The era of the drive-in theatres

Although a small number of drive-in theatres had existed in the US since 1933, this type of exhibition site did not become popular until after World War II.[17] The Depression and war years, the inadequate sound technology and, of course, the limited number of automobiles and shortages in petrol (especially during the war years) ensured that the drive-in remained a marginal exhibition site throughout the 1930s. In 1941, the year when in-car speakers were developed, there were 41 drive-in theatres in the country. That number grew to 300 in 1946 and from then on it started increasing exponentially: 548 in 1947; 820 in 1948; 1,203 in 1949; and 2,202 in 1950.[18]

In many respects, the staggering rise in the number of drive-in theatres was a direct result of the population migration to the suburbs in the late 1940s, the expanding automobile culture that accompanied it and, significantly, the absence of a number of socialising patterns that were available to people in other western countries, especially the European ones. With most of the first-run theatres located in the centres of large metropolitan areas, often many miles away from the suburbs, drive-ins gave suburbanites an opportunity to maintain their movie-going habit, while at the same time making use of their cars. Furthermore, drive-ins offered considerably cheaper entertainment than indoor theatres. During the late 1940s and early 1950s, drive-ins charged admission per automobile, as opposed to 'hardtop' or indoor movie theatres, which charged admission per individual. This meant that a family of six could in fact enjoy a night out for as little as $1.50 or $2.[19] Finally, as Andrew Horton argues, the lack of cultivation of 'European' socialising patterns (such as cafés and strolls in the park or a town's central square) in US towns and cities gradually turned the drive-in into a very significant hub for social interaction, especially among the younger generations.[20]

The drive-in 'craze' became even stronger in the 1950s, forcing the industry's trade publications to acknowledge that it was 'the decade's greatest development from the standpoint of exhibition'.[21] By 1956, the number of 'ozoners' (an alternative label for drive-ins) had exploded to 4,700, on the way to a peak of 6,000 two years later (a number that represented approximately a third of all US theatres).[22] The dramatic increase in drive-in theatres coincided with the equally dramatic decrease in indoor theatres during the same period, as between 1948 and 1954 the number of hardtop theatres declined by slightly over 3,000 sites, while the number of drive-ins increased by almost 3,000.[23]

Although from the industry's perspective drive-ins were not adequate replacements for traditional theatres (at least in terms of audience capacity),[24] they nevertheless gave the ailing industry a much-needed life injection. During their peak, in the late 1950s, drive-in theatres accounted for over 25 per cent of theatre rentals, which was certainly not a negligible figure.[25] What is important for the purposes of this chapter, however, was that drive-ins became the main exhibition sites for the low-budget independents, which quickly realised that the main patrons of such theatres were young people, primarily teenagers. Perceived as places where they could consume alcohol without being caught and where young couples could spend time away from the public eye, drive-in theatres became particularly attractive and cheap leisure options for teenagers.

As the drive-in represented a new trend in exhibition, it is not surprising that it was accompanied by a number of novel exhibition practices. The most important one was the 'teenpic double bill'.[26] Unlike the 'classic' double feature presentation of the 1930s and 1940s, in which an A film was paired with a B film, the new practice involved the pairing of two films which were similar in budget, duration and, usually, in genre and which targeted specifically the youth audience. The rationale behind this practice was that it allowed the distributor to claim considerably higher rentals from the theatres than for single-film bookings. This was because low-budget independently produced films normally ended up at the bottom half of a double bill, which meant that the distributor received only a flat fee for the film (as opposed to a percentage of the gross for the top billing). By distributing a pair of similar films, however, the distinction between A and B collapsed, while a low-end distribution company could see both its films as the main attractions and therefore collect a healthy box office percentage, if the films were successful. One of the first such pairings was *Day the World Ended* (Corman, 1956) and *The Phantom From 10,000 Leagues* (Milner, 1956), both distributed by American International Pictures, which proved very profitable for all parties involved.[27]

The success of the practice made this version of the double bill a staple of drive-in theatres. Soon, distributors started experimenting with the scheme, sometimes offering a combination in which the second film was the sequel of the first, while often pairing a current release with an older film (thus recycling their product and exploiting further the lifespan of their films). Other variations of this practice included a double feature where the first film targeted a male audience and the second film a female one, triple or quadruple bills, and even dusk-till-dawn multiple shows.[28] Exhibitors were happy to endorse the practice as it meant good business, especially for their concession stands, the profits of which jumped from $15 million in 1949 to $108 million in 1959.[29]

The emergence of the teen audience, the rise of the exploitation teenpic and the explosion of the drive-in laid the foundations for the continuation of low-budget independent filmmaking. It could then be argued that the B film survived in the 1950s and 1960s despite the end of the classic double bill. It simply metamorphosed into the exploitation film, which was designed to cash in on any fad, trend, development or topical news that could deliver a young audience.

It is now time to explore how industrial and economic conditions shaped the low-end independent filmmaking arena during the 1950s and 1960s and to see which new players emerged during this period.

Low-end independents against television

While the decline of the B-film market was first noted in the post-World War II years, the practice of the double feature presentation lasted well into the 1950s. Even as late as 1954, approximately 70 per cent of all US theatres continued to play double bills in a desperate effort to attract a sharply declining audience.[30] But while in the 1930s this particular exhibition strategy had paid off by attracting a large percentage of the Depression-hit, starving-for-cheap-entertainment American public, in the 1950s the coming of television put an end to this attraction. This was because television offered entertainment for free in the comfort of one's own home. Thus, while the double bill continued in the first years of the 1950s, its effectiveness as an exhibition strategy was severely tested as audiences stayed away or, when visiting the cinemas, opted instead for the expensive widescreen spectacles that could not be enjoyed on television and which normally played as single bookings in the old first-run theatres.

If television was perceived as a major threat for the ex-studios, it was a life-threatening competitor for the low-end independents. This was mainly because television made unprofitable the cheap 'bread and butter' movies (especially westerns and adventure films) that defined the business of Poverty Row studios. By emulating their cheap production methods and by copying their action-oriented content, early television programmes were shorter versions of B films. For instance, Gene Autry, the phenomenally popular singing cowboy of the Republic westerns, started making pictures directly for television and therefore provided television audiences with content similar, if not identical, to his Republic fare.[31] Pretty soon the old B films actually became television programmes (after being re-edited down to 48 minutes per episode to allow for commercials). Realising that this type of programming was successful with the ever-expanding television audiences, Republic and Monogram sold parts of their libraries of film titles to television and earned some profits at a time when the future of their feature production was uncertain.

Not surprisingly, the theatrical exhibitors opposed vehemently the Poverty Row companies' decision to make their films available to television and for a while they boycotted Republic's product. With sharply declining theatre attendances, the smaller exhibitors, which depended on cheap fare, held the view that the repeat appearances of stars (like Autry) on television would decrease their star value.[32] At a time of industry recession, however, leasing their films to television was perhaps the only solution for the low-end independents which managed to stay solvent in the mid-1950s, largely thanks to the lifeline offered by television.

With B films now readily available on television, rentals from the theatrical market for the ex-Poverty Row studios dropped to such low levels that distributors were finding it difficult to recoup the costs of print and advertising, never mind the costs of production.[33] It could be argued, then, that television turned low-end independents and theatre exhibitors against each other at a time when they needed one another more than ever. But as theatrical exhibitors suddenly found themselves to have become a secondary source of profit and exhibition outlet – behind television – for low-end independent producers and distributors, it was they (the exhibitors) that were hurt the most. This is an additional reason (besides the industry recession) why more than 3,000 theatres closed between 1948 and 1954.

But even during the difficult days of the early 1950s, low-budget independents had a number of opportunities to attract production funds, arguably more than their top-rank counterparts. 'Because the Hollywood industry had suffered economic reverses due to anti-trust decisions and the popularity of television', Peter Lev argued, 'smaller studios and independent production companies found it easier to raise financing for relatively small budget projects'.[34] For instance, important financial institutions like Morris were willing to provide first money for projects such as Lippert's *Treasure of Monte Cristo* (Berke, 1949) 'in way of an experiment ... to an expansion of motion picture financing activities in [the] lower budget field'.[35]

Other options available were the creation of companies through investment from franchise holders (the way Monogram was set up). Companies like Screen Guild (later Lippert Pictures) and American Releasing Corporation (later American International Pictures) were established in this manner. Finally, and as the market kept shrinking, there was also the option of mergers between small companies in the hope of establishing a more stable basis of operations that could attract production investment from major lending institutions (similar to the way Republic was established). As *Variety* noted, the point behind the trend for consolidation was that it was 'uneconomic for these minor distribs to compete for the same customers – most of them small exhibs who pay minimum rentals'.[36] However, despite a merger between Eagle-Lion and Screen Classics and negotiations between several companies for a number of merger deals (including one between Monogram and Lippert in the summer of 1950) the consolidation of the low-budget film sector did not materialise.

The exploitation teenpic and the companies behind it

Sam Katzman

The low-budget independent market started blossoming in 1956, when the first exploitation pictures that targeted specifically teenage audiences proved box office hits. The producer and film that were credited with launching the wave of exploitation teenpics which were to flood American cinema for at least the following decade were Sam Katzman and his *Rock Around the Clock* (Sears, 1956). With almost 200 films behind him as a producer or executive producer for Monogram, Columbia and his own Victory Pictures banner between 1934 and 1956, and with a vast experience in all aspects of the film business, Katzman was one of the few veteran producers in American cinema who 'managed to move comfortably from genre to genre with equal aplomb, giving the same care and attention to every film'.[37] Furthermore, he was one of the most, if not the most, prolific producers in the industry (with producer credits in a staggering 37 films during the three-year period 1954–6), aiming to 'entertain the masses with simple, up-to-the-minute, topical, fast moving fare'.[38]

After the success of *Blackboard Jungle*, Katzman was the first person to realise the potential of rock'n'roll as a new trend that was worth exploiting. As 'Rock Around the Clock', the song that was heard during the credits of *Blackboard Jungle*, had become an enormous chart hit, Katzman signed Bill Haley and His Comets, the band that sang the song, to appear in a film. Taking on the title of the song itself, the film *Rock Around the Clock* proved also a big hit. Immediately Katzman started planning a new production based on the latest craze. Eight months after the release of *Rock Around the Clock* (March 1956) and after six other films Katzman produced in between, he had out in the cinemas *Don't Knock the Rock* (Sears, 1956), 'the Real Story Behind The World-Wide Rock 'N' Roll Headlines!', as the film's tagline promised. In the next five years Katzman would produce three more music films, with the final one, *Don't Knock the Twist* (Rudolph, 1962), trying to capitalise on a different teenage craze, the twist dance.

The success of Katzman's first film, which was produced under his Clover Productions and released through Columbia Pictures, made other independent producers and major and independent distributors jump on the bandwagon of the exploitation teenpic, starting with the music film itself. As film critic Thomas Wiener argued, 'the problem with Katzman's films was that they were so widely successful that they spawned endless variations of the formula,'[39] as some of the titles clearly illustrate: *Shake Rattle and Rock!* (Cahn, 1956); *Rock, Rock, Rock* (Price, 1956); *Rock, Pretty Baby* (Bartlett, 1956); and *Jailhouse Rock* (Thorpe, 1957).

American International Pictures

With the teenage market proving large enough to sustain music films and many other types of films with a teenage appeal, the low-budget independents found a new *raison d'être*, catering – in some cases almost exclusively – to this new audience which was ignored by the established powers. This was particularly true for American Releasing Corporation (ARC), a small independent distributor that had been established in 1954 and that had been releasing, to that time, 'old-style' B films. By 1956, ARC had changed its name to American International Pictures (AIP) and was in the business of serving exclusively the youth audience. According to Richard Staehling, AIP, Sam Katzman and Albert Zugsmith (another producer who specialised in exploitation films) were responsible for almost half of the output of teenpics between 1955 and 1969.[40]

ARC was formed by Samuel Z. Arkoff, a lawyer and former television producer, and James H. Nicholson, a former theatre manager. With a small investment (rumours have it in the region of $3,000), 20 per cent of which was provided by small exhibitors who were getting increasingly desperate for product,[41] Arkoff and Nicholson entered the film business at an extremely difficult time for low-end independent film companies. But despite the bad financial state of Poverty Row market leaders such as Republic and Allied Artists, Arkoff and Nicholson believed that conditions would soon improve. Their optimism lay in the belief that the gradual phasing out of the studios' B films would soon create a product shortage in the low-budget film market, which ARC would be ready to exploit.

The co-founders of ARC were not wrong. By the mid-1950s, exhibitors were getting so desperate for product that they were 'willing to deal with any moviemaker carrying a 35mm print'.[42] In November 1955, ARC announced plans to expand its release schedule to one film per month, starting from April 1956. One month before the implementation of the new schedule, the company had changed its name to AIP and had five independent production units under contract (one of them headed by filmmaker Roger Corman), which would deliver the number of films per year the distributor promised.[43]

The first releases under the AIP banner were two juvenile delinquency films that clearly targeted a youth audience, *Hot Rod Girl* (Martinson, 1956) and *Girls in Prison* (Cahn, 1956). By October 1956 the company had out the first successful imitation of Katzman's *Rock Around the Clock*, *Shake, Rattle and Rock!*, while the rest of its films for the year included other teenpics such as *Runaway Daughters* (Cahn) and two science fiction films, *The She-Creature* (Cahn) and *It Conquered the World* (Corman). The company's science fiction films were also in the process of being 'juvenilised' so that they could become more appealing to the new teenage audience. As Garry Morris has argued, irrespective of the genre to which they belonged, AIP's 1950s films focused specifically 'on teenagers and other socially unempowered groups and their inability to assimilate into a society whose conventions (conformity, ambition) they ridiculed and rejected'.[44] This meant that teenagers were consciously placed in the foreground, primarily as narrative agents, while their way of life, style and problems were also brought centre stage.

Equally importantly, the company made a conscious decision to minimise the participation of older adults or other 'figures of authority' in its films, making even more explicit its intention to focus exclusively on teenagers and young adults.[45] Thus, despite the fact that trade publications such as the *Hollywood Reporter* repeatedly described AIP pictures as 'badly-written, sloppily-edited, poorly-directed low-budget film[s]', the company's target audience did not care.[46] The classical model of American filmmaking (as exemplified by the technical perfection of studio films) that was important for adult audiences was not important for teenagers, as it was not for immigrants, children, ethnic and rural audiences who enjoyed the B films and the Poverty Row 'quickies' in the previous decades. Apart from sharing a strong lineage with the old-style B films, then, the exploitation-inspired independent filmmaking of the 1950s and 1960s can also claim to have performed the social function that low-end independents during the studio era had performed, that is, catering for the audiences excluded by mainstream cinema.

Although the financial success of AIP was minor compared with the profits of the majors, the company quickly established itself in the low-budget market as a leader. By 1958, its five independent units had already produced 58 features, while AIP became the first new exploitation company to release its films in hardtop and drive-in theatres at the same time (no small feat, as indoor theatres normally refused to play a film at the same time as a drive-in theatre).[47] Working quickly and efficiently, AIP provided financing to its contracted producers, who would make films on a budget as low as $100,000–$150,000 within two to three six-day weeks. However, AIP's total investment in its films was much higher than this figure (closer to the region of $250,000 per film) as it spent wildly on the advertising of its product.[48] Much more than for its actual films, which, according to Staehling, were characterised by a style 'as distinct and as identifiable as that of Orson Welles',[49] AIP became famous for its approach to distribution and publicity, areas in which the company excelled.

The foundation for an AIP film was a sensational or topical premise around which the company's marketing campaign could be built. Arkoff and Nicholson admitted unapologetically that their starting point for the production of a picture was a catchy and exploitable title before they moved to secondary questions such as writing a script for the film.[50] A typical example of this process can be seen in the production history of *The Wild Angels* (Corman, 1966), which spearheaded the cycle of biker films, a production trend that continued well into the 1970s.

After a frustrating time at Columbia, Roger Corman was approached by Arkoff and Nicholson to discuss the possibility of a new film for AIP that would be produced in the spring of 1966 and exhibited during the summer drive-in season. After discussing extensively 'what was going on in the country at the time',[51] Corman suggested a film about the Hell's Angels, an idea he had got from a picture of a Hell's Angel's funeral that he saw in *Life* magazine.[52] As this was the time when the Hell's Angels phenomenon was coming to prominence, Arkoff and Nicholson found the concept highly exploitable and immediately greenlit the film. Corman then visited a number of Hell's Angels hangouts to

Figure 4.1 'Their credo is violence': Peter Fonda and other Hell's Angels are ready for trouble in Roger Corman's *The Wild Angels*.

research the screenplay but also to try to persuade the Angels to appear in the film, which would provide the picture with immense free publicity. The Angels shared with Corman a number of stories, some of which the filmmaker used in the film as distinct plot lines, while they also agreed to participate in the production. Not surprisingly, according to McGee and Robertson, the film 'emerged as more of a series of anecdotes than a cohesive story', but it carried a stamp of authenticity that did not exist in similarly themed films.[53]

Although the participation of the Angels in the film did give the project great publicity, AIP and Corman did not stop there. The film was advertised with the controversial tagline 'Their Credo Is Violence, Their God Is Hate … and They Call Themselves the Wild Angels', while further advertising referred to it as 'the most terrifying film of our time', promising a shocking spectacle that would unsettle audiences. The accompanying poster featured the leather-clad Peter Fonda and Nancy Sinatra while giant flames and a bikers' parade were featured in the background. With a number of theatre owners refusing to book the picture after its preview, the film generated 'a storm of controversy unequalled in the genre [of juvenile delinquent films] since the days of *Blackboard Jungle*'.[54] The outrage and controversy, however, did not discourage audiences; on the contrary, the box office performance of the film justified fully AIP's and Corman's exploitation approach. The picture grossed more than $5 million during the first month of its release, becoming AIP's highest-grossing title to that date.

Although *The Wild Angels* was produced and released towards the end of the second era in low-end independent filmmaking, it nevertheless demonstrates clearly AIP's expertise in low-budget films which were based on exploitable subjects. Throughout the years, the company became such an expert in this type of filmmaking that it created a number of production cycles and trends that other independents (and often major studios) followed, while also maximising the exploitation of cycles started by other companies. Since its inception and until the late 1960s, AIP virtually created:

- the low-budget science fiction/horror trend;
- the 'sand and spear ' cycle (which even though it was started by Embassy Pictures became another of AIP's specialties);
- the classic horror cycle (mainly Corman-produced films based on Edgar Alan Poe's short stories);
- the beach films, launched with the extremely successful *Beach Party* (Asher, 1963)
- the biker/protest film (*The Wild Angels* spawned a large number of imitations and variations, at least 12 of which produced by AIP).[55]

Besides Arkoff and Nicholson's ability to read the teenage market and establish trends, the company's success was undoubtedly founded on its '"state-of-the-art" marketing campaigns',[56] which exploited every possible outlet that could publicise their films. Table 4.1[57] offers a codification of the principles

Table 4.1 American International Pictures' approach to marketing and audience

The formula for success	The Peter Pan syndrome
OBSERVE trends and emerging tastes	a younger child will watch anything an older child will watch;
KNOW as much as possible about your audience	an older child will not watch anything a younger child will watch;
ANTICIPATE how you will sell your chosen subject	a girl will watch anything a boy will watch;
PRODUCE with prudence, avoiding expense for what won't show on the screen	a boy will not watch anything a girl will watch;
	therefore
SELL with showmanship in advertising and publicity	to catch your greatest audience you zero in on the 19-year old male
USE imagination	
HAVE good luck: even if you do everything else right, you'll still need it	

behind AIP's approach to marketing (the formula for success) and the rationale for choosing to cater for the teenage audience (the Peter Pan syndrome).

Another important reason for AIP's success was that its co-founders and senior executives understood from the very beginning that the company operated firmly within the exploitation market and therefore had no pretences about making art (unlike the majors and the top-rank independents). This realisation allowed the AIP officials to place an unabashed emphasis on the commercial aspects of their pictures, being neither afraid nor ashamed of creating a coarse image for their company during the 1950s and 1960s, which was far removed from the dignified image of the majors.[58]

The success of AIP in the exploitation arena mobilised other low-end independents. By the late 1950s and early 1960s the company was facing great competition from a number of imitators, which had one advantage over AIP, namely, they could produce exploitation pictures for the youth audience even more cheaply than AIP. According to Arkoff, as early as 1959 AIP was in no position to continue with its teenpic double bills as such combinations by other companies had flooded the drive-in market, making a serious dent in AIP's profit margins.[59] The threat of imitators overtaking the innovator was permanent for AIP, forcing its founders to look constantly for the new fad that would create the new trend or cycle, which would place the company ahead of competition once again. Two of AIP's biggest competitors at the beginning of the 1960s were Joseph E. Levine's Embassy Pictures and William Castle Productions.

Embassy Pictures

Joseph E. Levine was another great believer in the importance of showmanship, even though he was firstly interested in good scripts and secondly in whether the stories in these scripts were 'promotable'.[60] Originally a small exhibitor based in New Haven, Connecticut, Levine set up a regional distribution company, Embassy Pictures, to release foreign art-films, especially Italian neo-realist successes such as *Bicycle Thieves* (De Sica, 1948) in the New England territory. As interest in foreign films increased during the 1950s, Embassy was not in a position to compete with Lopert Films (see Chapter 3) or other distributors of art-house films that operated nationally. Still, the company was successful enough to expand its operation along the East Coast of the US. In 1956, Embassy scored a substantial commercial success with a dubbed version of *Godzilla, King of the Monsters!* (Honda, 1954; extensively re-edited by Terry O. Morse), which it distributed in the Eastern states.

Swapping the foreign art-film for more popular, action-oriented non-US films was a major coup for Embassy. In 1958, Levine bought the US distribution rights for an Italian production based on the legend of Hercules under the title *Le Fatiche di Ercole* (Francisci, 1958) for $125,000. After changing the film's title to *Hercules* and dubbing it into English, Levine spent almost 10 times the acquisition fee in promotion and advertising ($1,156,000), while also saturating the market with 600 prints. The film grossed $15 million and established Embassy as a very promising new distribution outfit.[61] During the 1950s and 1960s, however, Embassy remained first and foremost a distributor of imported art-films and popular European films, while only occasionally venturing into the finance, production and distribution of American films, exploitation or otherwise. Thus Embassy Pictures was the financer and distributor of the prestigious film adaptation of Eugene O'Neill's masterpiece *Long Day's Journey into Night* (Lumet, 1962) with Katharine Hepburn and Ralph Richardson, while also distributing low-budget exploitation films such as *Village of the Giants* (Gordon, 1965). Embassy became a major player in the American market after 1967, when it distributed *The Graduate* (Nichols, 1967), one of the key films of the next phase in the history of American independent cinema.

William Castle Productions

Unlike AIP and Embassy, William Castle Productions was just a production outfit with no stakes in distribution. Operating under the rule that a producer is as responsible as the distributor for publicising his or her pictures, William Castle, the head of the company, brought this rule to the extreme. Castle had been working for Columbia as a director of B films from 1943 until the mid-1950s, often directing Sam Katzman productions. In 1958 he established his own production company, which in a way was a throwback to the studio times, as all creative personnel were under contract to Castle. Like the other exploitation companies in the low-budget arena, Castle realised that he had to make films that were tailored to a young audience. Unlike his competitors, however, Castle did not only concentrate exclusively on the teenage and the young adult demographics. He also aggressively targeted children as young as nine years, creating a core audience (spanning from nine- to sixteen-year-olds) for his low-budget horror films.[62] Furthermore, and unlike any of his competitors, he made himself a well-known public figure by making cameo appearances in his own films as a narrator, often talking directly to the camera, providing prologues and epilogues to the stories his films told or introducing his latest gimmick, which more often than not was the main attraction for the audience of his films. From the very beginning he placed his name on the marquee advertising his films, while the phrase 'William Castle Presents' always preceded every other title in the opening credits (see Case study 4.1).[63]

Case study 4.1 The emergence of the exploitation gimmick: William Castle and *Macabre*

> *Macabre* (Castle, 1958, 80 min.), produced by William Castle Productions, distributed by Allied Artists.

William Castle was an alumni of the B units of Columbia Pictures, specialising in directing rather than producing. From 1943 to 1948 Castle averaged three or four films per year, all low-budget adventure and mystery films, along with the occasional western. A film that stands out during that period was *When Strangers Meet* (1944), a low-budget thriller, which is now recognised as a fine example of the emergent noir style that would characterise a large number of films during the post-war period and which featured a very young Robert Mitchum in his first major part (Farber, 1975, pp. 46–7). Castle then moved to Universal, where for the next four years he continued making 'programmers' (see Chapter 2) for the ex-studio, only to return to Columbia in 1953. During his second stint there Castle made more westerns, while on a few occasions he worked for fellow low-end independent producer Sam Katzman, through his Esskay Pictures. Still based at Columbia when the first wave of teenage exploitation films occurred, Castle decided that the time was ripe to try film producing, moving up from the lowly status of an in-house B-film director to the more promising rank of an independent producer-director of exploitation films.

William Castle Productions – also known as Susina Associates (Hefferman, 2004, p. 96) – was established in the form of a filmmaking unit in 1957. Rather than recruiting freelance talent for the duration of a production, Castle set up his company, in partnership with screenwriter Robb White, in the style of Walter Wanger Productions or Selznick International Pictures, whereby a small number of creative individuals (such as cinematographer Carl E. Guthrie and music composer Von Dexter) were under contract to Castle and therefore contributed to many of his independent films (Castle, quoted in Strawn, 1975c, p. 293).

The company's first production was a horror film entitled *Macabre*. Although low-budget horror films were at their peak in the mid/late 1950s, what set *Macabre* apart from the films of the period (such as the ones produced by Roger Corman and distributed by AIP) was that it did not feature any monsters or beasts, which were the attraction of films such as *War of the Colossal Beast* (Gordon, 1958) or *Monster from Green Hell* (Crane, 1958) and could be exploited imaginatively in advertising. Instead, Castle's film, under the considerably more subtle and not particularly exploitable title *Macabre*, was a return to a more classic horror (without the science fiction element), in some ways reminiscent of the RKO cycle of B films in the 1940s that were produced by Val Lewton. In this respect, in order to compete with the youth-oriented horror/sci-fi films of the time Castle had to invent different exploitation strategies.

Produced during a two-week period in the summer of 1957, the negative cost of *Macabre* was very low, even for exploitation standards, at $80,000

(Doherty, 1988, p. 168). To raise interest in a film that did not seem to have any clear assets that could attract the youth audience, Castle orchestrated an advertising and publicity campaign that made his film one of the most commercially successful exploitation titles of the year. At the centre of this campaign was the gimmick of buying life insurance from Lloyd's of London and offering $1,000 to the families of any cinema patrons who died of fright (McGee, 1989, p. 23). This 'offer' featured centrally on the film's poster, which depicted three images of the same terrified woman in close-up, in one of which she is attacked by a skeleton.

Expressing verbally the hypothetical effects of his films on his audience was always a strong point in Castle's bag of tricks. Among the advertising taglines he used, alongside the insurance offer, one could find wildly imaginative invitations to cinema-goers, all ending inevitably in exclamation marks: 'See it with someone who can carry you home!' 'If it frightens you to death, you'll be buried free of charge!' 'As blood-chilling as being buried alive!' 'There will be a sharp penalty for anyone who reveals the ending!' and 'We hung [*sic*] the cameraman to keep him from disclosing the terrifying surprises!' (All taglines are available on the film's page on IMDb.) Finally, to maintain hype even after people had seen the film, Castle printed small badges that read 'I am no chicken. I saw *Macabre*' and asked exhibitors to distribute them to audiences on their way out of the theatres (Grindhouse Cinema Database, no date). Despite all the ballyhoo, the offer of life insurance was by far the main attraction to the film and Castle's main contribution to exploitative advertising.

The film itself opens without any credits. As a close-up of a clock hung against the wall becomes the first image of the film, an extra-diegetic narrator (Castle) begins addressing the audience:

> Ladies and gentlemen, for the next 1 hour and 15 minutes you will be shown things so terrifying that the management of this theatre is deeply concerned for your welfare. Therefore we request that each of you assume the responsibility of taking care of your neighbour. If anybody near you becomes uncontrollably frightened, would you please notify the management so that medical attention can be rushed to their aid? Please set your watches. It is 6:45 in the evening in a town called Porton.

Castle returns after the narrative resolution and announces:

> Ladies and gentlemen, please do not, I repeat, do not reveal the ending of this picture to your friends as it will spoil their enjoyment of it.

Although the use of extra-diegetic narrators and of direct address to the audience is not rare by any standards in Hollywood cinema, what distinguishes Castle's introduction and conclusion are: (1) the nature of his announcements – warming up the audience for the scary content of the film asking them to keep the film's end to themselves (although the introduction also takes the more conventional role of introducing the setting and time of the narrative); and (2) the fact that the film's producer himself has taken the role of the narrator. Furthermore, the hyping of the film by its own producer-director in the introductory segment signals the integration of marketing and publicity with the narrative, a union of elements that becomes much more notable in Castle's later films (especially *The Tingler* [1959] and *13 Ghosts* [1960]), while it precedes by more than 20 years the emergence of the high-concept film, a type of filmmaking where the integration of narrative with advertising comes to define the film's aesthetics.

In between these two announcements, the story revolves around the efforts of a small-town doctor and a group friends and relatives to save the doctor's young daughter from being buried alive. The narrative is organised in a rather complex structure. On the one hand, the story moves forward, with a very clear deadline (the doctor has five hours to find his daughter before she dies) and occasional shots of a clock revealing how much time is left. On the other hand, the film offers two flashbacks, where it packs together a number of events that occurred before the spectator's entry to the narrative, aiming at revealing motivations and explaining the relations between the various characters. Not surprisingly, the story presents several holes or unanswered questions (such as who placed the dead body of the graveyard watchman in the Tylos' family grave?).

More importantly, it contains a number of scenes that exist almost purely for shock value, without adding anything to the narrative. For instance, in the first scene at the graveyard, a hand comes out from behind a grave and scares Polly (and the spectators), only for it to be revealed that the hand belongs to the doctor's father-in-law, who had come to help find his grand-daughter. Equally, in the funeral parlour, the characters spend approximately five minutes of screen time looking inside various coffins for the little girl as the sound of breathing is heard coming from somewhere in the room. After many speculative comments it is revealed that the breathing noise is being made by an archaic ventilation system installed in the parlour.

But these narrative problems do not detract from the pleasures *Macabre* offers. For a film advertised as being able to cause death by fright, narrative structure is of secondary importance. Instead, it is the ability to frighten the audience by any means possible that is foregrounded, with the scenes in the graveyard (approximately one-third of the film's duration) providing an environment where fright can come at any time, from any direction. In many respects then *Macabre* represents a return to the classic B film, which was not consumed for the narrative pleasures it provided but for its action, fast pace and adherence to various formulae. And as many such B films contained excessive moments that transcended the limitations of their production (see Chapter 2), so did *Macabre*, which contains one particularly distinctive scene in terms of visual style. As the doctor and his friends push a coffin out of the parlour, Castle uses a tracking shot that is intercut with a number of close-ups of the various characters exchanging glances for approximately one minute of screen time. The editing and camera movement are certainly reminiscent of the famous staircase sequence in Hitchcock's *Notorious* (1946), perhaps an homage to the famous filmmaker, whom Castle tried to emulate by becoming as well known as his films and by making appearances in them. On the other hand, it has been suggested that Hitchcock borrowed the rule of 'strictly no admittance to the theatre after the feature has begun' for his film *Psycho* (1960) from Castle, allegedly returning the homage (Ebert, 1998).

Castle's exploitation tricks proved extremely successful. The film grossed approximately $1.2 million in the US (Doherty, 1988, p. 168) and kick-started an era of outrageous gimmickry, during which Castle was the undoubted king. The profits from *Macabre* enabled the filmmaker to invest in unusual devices that offered an unforgettable experience to audiences, especially those who did not go to the theatre for the film but for the show.

Castle's panache for introducing often very elaborate gimmicks to increase ticket sales of his films has been unequalled in the US film industry and has brought him, not unjustifiably, the label 'King of the Gimmicks'.[64] For his first film under the banner William Castle Productions (besides being a producer Castle also doubled up as the director of his films), *Macabre* (1958) (Case study 4.1), he took an insurance policy with Lloyd's of London for each ticket-buying customer, in case someone died from fright during the run of the film. For his second film, *House on Haunted Hill* (1959), Castle came up with 'emergo', a black box installed close to the screen of theatres, out of which a 12-foot plastic skeleton would emerge to scare audiences at a specific time during the film. The production of the film cost Castle $150,000, but the creation of 'emergo' proved a much more expensive investment, in the region of $250,000.[65]

The gimmick enabled Castle to enhance the audience's experience of *House on Haunted Hill*, creating a show that was more memorable than the film itself, while at the same time building up a very young clientele who clearly did not visit the cinema in order to obtain pleasure from the narratives of his films. As filmmaker John Waters remarked:

> Emergo was perfected and installed in theatres all over the country. The kids went wild. They screamed. They hugged their girlfriends. They threw popcorn boxes at the skeleton. Most important, they spent their allowance and made the film a huge hit.[66]

The great success of *House on Haunted Hill* (the film grossed over $3 million) encouraged Castle to come up with progressively more outrageous gimmicks, which broke many of the rules of classical filmmaking by becoming integral parts of the film narratives themselves, calling attention to the artifice of filmmaking. For his third film, *The Tingler* (1959), the filmmaker made use of 'percepto', a device that sent slight electric shocks to a number of theatre seats at a specific point in the film – when the narrative was interrupted by

Castle's voice asking the audience to scream – causing spectators to jump off their seats in fear. Next came 'Illusion-O', a sort of ghost viewfinder that was handed to viewers upon entrance to the cinema, which allowed them to see at specific times one or more of the film's *13 Ghosts* (1960). While the narrative was being unravelled, the phrase 'look through your ghost-viewer ' appeared at the bottom of the screen several times, cueing the audience (and attracting attention away from a thinly plotted story) to expect the appearance of ghosts which could only be seen through the device.

For his fifth film, *Homicidal* (1961), Castle introduced the 'Fright Break'. Once again the narrative was interrupted and Castle's voice was heard saying: 'This is a Fright Break. You hear that sound? The sound of a heart-beat? It will beat for another 65 seconds to allow anyone who is too frightened to see the end of the picture to leave the theatre. You will get your full admission refunded.' To ensure that a minimum of cinema patrons would ask for their money back, Castle came up with 'Coward's Corner', whereby if a person wanted to leave the auditorium and ask for a refund, they would be humiliated in front of the entire cinema audience by having to follow yellow footsteps up the aisle, past written messages that read 'Cowards Keep Walking', and under the sound of a recording that shouted 'Watch the chicken! Watch him shiver in Coward's Corner!'[67]

For his next feature, *Mr Sardonicus* (1961), the filmmaker allowed the audience to determine the end of the narrative by inviting them to fill in polling cards with which they would decide the fate of the film's villain. For that reason he prepared prints with two endings, letting spectators decide which ending would be screened. By the time of *13 Frightened Girls* (1963) and *Straight-Jacket* (1964), the course of the extreme gimmick had reached its end. Taking on board the reviewers' criticisms that he could not produce a successful film without gimmicks, Castle moved into more conventional filmmaking. He did manage to prove his critics wrong, however, as a few years later William Castle Productions became responsible for seminal horror film *Rosemary's Baby* (Polanski, 1968), which was produced for approximately $3 million and grossed more than $30 million at the US box office.[68]

Roger Corman and the Filmgroup

Although both Embassy and William Castle Productions were important exploitation companies throughout the period, they nevertheless did not directly compete with AIP, opting instead to concentrate their efforts on different segments of the youth audience (young adults and young children, respectively), thus leaving the bulk of this audience, the teenagers, to AIP's exploitation fare. Ironically, one of the most important competitors of AIP was one of the company's producers, Roger Corman. Arguably as prolific as

Katzman, Corman made low-budget teenpics at such a fast pace that he was distributing them theatrically through three different companies, AIP, Allied Artists and his own small distribution outfit, the Filmgroup, while occasionally making pictures for other distributors such as the Woolner Brothers Pictures and Howco International Pictures. Because of his long-term association with AIP (1954–69) as a producer-director, it is easy to overlook his contribution to the rise of the various forms of exploitation teenpics in the mid-1950s, giving the credit instead to the distributor. However, Corman's impact on the field of low-budget teenpics and his methods of exploitation were as important as Arkoff and Nicholson's, if not more so. For instance, film historian Wheeler Dixon maintains that 'outside of William Castle no other director used as much gimmickry as Corman did'.[69] For all these reasons, Roger Corman deserves as much credit for AIP's success as its co-founders.

Corman started his career in the late 1940s as a messenger and later story analyst at 20th Century Fox, but quickly got disillusioned with the cumbersome manner in which filmmaking took place within the major. After a short stint in Europe, he came back to the US to write, direct and/or produce low-budget films, but almost immediately dropped the writing to concentrate on the other two roles. Between 1954 and 1959 Corman produced and directed 23 films, while taking the producer credit in 10 additional pictures that were directed by others. According to Peter Lev, it was Corman who recognised first the emergence of the teenage audience,[70] but as he was mainly working within the science fiction/horror genre he did not initially participate in the outburst of music films in the mid-1950s that have been recognised as the first wave of exploitation teenpics. Instead, he worked actively in shaping the conventions of the science fiction/horror cycle (the films of which are often called 'weirdies'), making it also appealing to a younger audience and in the process 'setting in granite the teenpic exploitation style'.[71]

Corman's approach to filmmaking was very similar to Arkoff and Nicholson's. According to Dixon, 'the Corman formula' consisted of four main elements:

- spend no money;
- play up the basest, most sensationalistic angle;
- exaggerate wildly in the advertising;
- book each film in as many theatres at once as possible to forestall negative word of mouth.[72]

Despite the emphasis on exploitation, Corman's extremely speedy and efficient way of filmmaking, which often involved only one day of pre-production per film,[73] allowed him to experiment with the formal elements of filmmaking, repeatedly transcending the boundaries of his chosen genres and the limitations of his cheap productions. His filmmaking practices and the emphasis he placed on topical issues, even within the 'weirdie' movie framework, allowed him (and some other exploitation filmmakers) 'to achieve a particular topicality and cutting edge social relevance which the mainstream industry could not match'.[74] This was particularly evident in his science fiction films, which have been interpreted as allegories for the anxieties about nuclear destruction during the 1950s and 1960s, as well as in his ultra-low-budget, black comedy feature *The Little Shop of Horrors* (Corman, 1960), which shows the dark face of the consumer revolution of the 1950s.[75] Whether Corman's success was through 'accidental incompetence' and/or 'deliberate subversion of industrial codes', as David E. James speculates,[76] his films left an indelible stamp on the 1950s and 1960s. Furthermore, during the mid-1960s Corman attempted to bridge his exploitation film techniques with influences from the European art-cinema (particularly evident in *The Wild Angels*) in the hope of having his films played at both art-houses and drive-ins.[77] The result was a new style of filmmaking that was recuperated by the ex-studios and became one of the precursors of what film historians have called the Hollywood Renaissance (see Chapters 5 and 6).

Finally, Corman also ventured into film distribution through the establishment of the Filmgroup, a very small releasing company operating with a skeletal staff and a few booking exchanges. Although the Filmgroup's distribution output remained very limited (20 titles in five years) and the company recorded minimal profits (between $1,500 and $3,000 a year),[78] it nevertheless proved a very important stepping stone for Corman in terms of learning the distribution business. Thus, in 1970 and after a falling-out with AIP over the release of *Gas-s-s-s* (Corman, 1970), the filmmaker was ready to take much bigger steps in the field of film distribution. He established a new production/distribution company, New World Pictures, which became very successful in the exploitation sector.

Corman, Levine and Castle were only the tip of the iceberg in the low-end independent production/production-distribution market. Throughout the 1950s and 1960s and as the youth audience continued to embrace exploitation pictures, a very large number of producers and distributors were set up to 'exploit' the opportunities offered by the teenpic. Most distributors, however, enjoyed a rather short lifespan, releasing only a small number of films before eventually going out of business.

The majors and the low-budget exploitation market

Besides the volatile conditions of the low-budget exploitation market, the main reason for the inability of new distributors to establish themselves was the majors' presence in that same market, after the mid-1950s. Universal and

Columbia in particular became key players in the finance and distribution of exploitation films. Having been important producers and distributors of B films during the 1930s and 1940s, Universal and Columbia moved also to the teenage market when they saw the low-end independents' success in the mid-1950s. Not having the power of the Big Five to invest in new exhibition technologies or the foresight of United Artists to redefine the rules of top-rank independent production, the two majors came to depend on the success of exploitation films, while also playing cautiously in the mainstream market.

Specifically, Columbia depended on the success of the low-budget productions of Sam Katzman in order to invest in bigger pictures for adult audiences, such as *Picnic* (Logan, 1955) and Stanley Kramer productions such as *The Caine Mutiny* (Dmytryk, 1954) Equally, Universal counted on the success of films such as *The Creature Walks Among Us* (Sherwood, 1956) and the Zugsmith-produced exploitation pictures such as *The Incredible Shrinking Man* (Arnold, 1957) to be able to invest in films such as *Written on the Wind* and *The Tarnished Angels* (Sirk, 1956 and 1958, respectively), both of which were also produced by Zugsmith. Soon, companies like MGM, Warner Bros. and Paramount also entered the game, with the first distributing another film made by Albert Zugsmith Productions, *High School Confidential!* (Arnold, 1958); the second releasing the Devonshire Productions' *Untamed Youth* (Koch, 1957); and the third distributing Aurora Productions' *Mister Rock and Roll* (Dubin, 1957).

Although of course the majors did not desert their core adult audience, they nevertheless claimed more than substantial profits from the youth market until the end of the 1960s. For that reason, it was impossible for the low-budget independent market to sustain more than a handful of distributors, which partly explains why only one such company, American International Pictures, made a name for itself and is best remembered as the main representative of exploitation filmmaking that targeted teenage audiences during the period.

Conclusion

Despite the lack of a real challenge to the power of the majors, low-end independents in the 1950s and 1960s were considerably more successful than their Poverty Row predecessors in the previous decades. Their shift to exploitation strategies and, especially, their conscious targeting of the teenage audience took them away from subsequent-run theatres (even if the drive-ins were perceived as the new subsequent-run exhibition sites) and put them at the centre of developments in American cinema, at a time when no firm direction for its future was apparent.[79] While the majors were in a deadlock trying in vain to rediscover the mass audience of the war and pre-war years, for the low-end independents one particular segment of the audience was large enough to keep them in business.

Away from the shadow of the majors, these low-end independents did not have to adhere to tested formulas and subject matters that originated during the studio years. From its very nature, the concept of the exploitation picture depends on the dramatisation of topical issues (rock'n'roll; juvenile delinquency; motorcycle culture; surfing culture; and so on), the novelty of which often attracted new cinematic approaches. Of course, once one exploitation picture was successful, then it provided a sacred formula for an often large number of imitations. But unlike the films of the majors, which operated clearly within genre frameworks that had existed for decades, the films by the low-end independents operated in cycles that were never longer than a period of a few years (beach party films) and sometimes shorter than a year (calypso music films). This means that potentially all formulas were renewed every time a new trend arose, apart from some written-in-stone elements such as the low-budget, the wild exploitation and the target audience.

This process allowed a number of filmmakers to experiment not only with issues revolving around the dramatisation of a novel subject, but also with formal elements of filmmaking in a way that studio filmmakers or top-rank independents would never be allowed. From the use of narrative as a thinly disguised vehicle for rock 'n' roll performances in *Rock Around the Clock*, to the integration of exploitation gimmicks in the unravelling of stories in William Castle's films, to the introduction of art-cinema techniques (jerky camera movement, rapid pans, extreme long shots) and rock soundtrack as non-diegetic accompaniment in *The Wild Angels*, low-end independents certainly helped expand film language in American cinema. They also taught the majors a lesson about where the audience for motion pictures was. In the late 1960s, the majors finally moved forcefully to the low-budget arena to find solutions to problems that had started 20 years earlier with the disintegration of the studio system and had continued ever since. American independent cinema was about to enter a new phase in its history.

Notes

1 Quoted in Shiel, 2003.
2 Quoted in Strawn, 1975b, p. 260.
3 Ebert, 1975, p. 137.
4 For definitions of the three examples of exploitation in American cinema, see Doherty, 1988, p. 3.
5 Grant, 1985, p. 199.

6 Strawn, 1975c, p. 291, Davis, 1997, p. 43.
7 McGee and Robertson, 1982, p. 11.
8 Doherty, 1988, p. 46.
9 Doherty, 1988, p. 54.
10 Doherty, 1988, p. 54.
11 One should also include here 20th Century Fox's film *Love Me Tender* (Webb, 1956), which starred Elvis Presley, the biggest youth star of the 1950s.
12 Lev, 2003, p. 63.
13 Chute, 1986, p. 32.
14 Quoted in 'Salesman', 1946.
15 Quoted in Chute, 1986, p. 39.
16 Broidy is quoted in 'Monogram Marching On: Company Shows Swift Increase in Stature', 1943; the slogan for AIP is quoted in Staehling, 1975, p. 224.
17 Horton, 1976, p. 234.
18 Schatz, 1999, p. 293.
19 Horton, 1976, p. 235.
20 Horton, 1976, p. 238.
21 Quoted in Doherty, 1988, p. 113.
22 Monaco, 2001, p. 46.
23 Horton, 1976, p. 235.
24 Monaco, 2001, p. 46.
25 Davis, 1997, p. 47.
26 Doherty, 1988, p. 113.
27 Corman and Jerome, 1998, p. 31.
28 Doherty, 1988, p. 152.
29 Doherty, 1988, p. 115.
30 Doherty, 1988, p. 30.
31 'Rep Studio Open to Indie TV Prod'n; Rogers' TV-1st Run, 30G; Autry, 20G', 1951.
32 'Republic Okays Old Films for Tele; Editing, Rescoring to Fit TV Needs', 1951.
33 Arkoff, quoted in Strawn, 1975b, p. 256.
34 Lev, 2003, p. 173.
35 'Lippert Gets First Financing Morris Plan Ever Made Films', 1949.
36 'Monogram, Lippert Co May Merge; Negotiations Now in Progress', 1950.
37 Quoted in McGee and Robertson, 1982, p. 45.
38 Quoted in Doherty, 1988, p. 73.
39 Wiener, 1975, p. 27.
40 Staehling, 1975, p. 225.
41 Osgerby, 2003, p. 100.
42 Doherty, 1988, p. 35.
43 'Nicholson Forms New Distrib Unit', 1956.
44 Morris, 1993, p. 4.
45 Quoted in Osgerby, 2003, p. 105.
46 The *Hollywood Reporter* description is quoted in McGee and Robertson, 1982, p. 60.
47 Strawn, 1975b, p. 262.
48 The figures for AIP's budgets are taken from Scheuer, 1958.
49 Staehling, 1975, p. 225.
50 *Los Angeles Times*, 21 September 1958.
51 Mason, 1976, p. 264.

52 McGee and Robertson, 1982, p. 118.
53 McGee and Robertson, 1982, p. 118.
54 McGee and Robertson, 1982, p. 119.
55 Osgerby, 2003, p. 98.
56 Jancovich, 1996, p. 198.
57 The 'formula for success' is taken from Nicholson, 1970. 'The Peter Pan syndrome' is taken from Doherty, 1988, p. 157.
58 Arkoff has been quoted as stating explicitly that film is no art and that 'Once we open a vein, like a miner, we continue mining until the vein runs out of ore'. Getze, 1974.
59 Strawn, 1975b, p. 264.
60 Powers, 1979, p. 43.
61 All the figures relating to *Hercules* are taken from Powers, 1979, pp. 39 and 45.
62 Strawn, 1975c, p. 292.
63 Strawn, 1975c, p. 295.
64 Waters, 1983, p. 56.
65 The figures for the cost of the film and of the device are taken from Doherty, 1988, p. 169.
66 Waters, 1983, p. 56.
67 Waters, 1983, p. 57.
68 The figures are taken from http://www.imdb.com/title/tt0063522/business.
69 Dixon, 1976, p. 13.
70 Lev, 2003, p. 173.
71 Doherty, 1988, p. 150.
72 Dixon, 1976, p. 11.
73 Davis, 1997, p. 49.
74 Shiel, 2003.
75 In this respect Corman's work is very reminiscent of Edgar G. Ulmer's films, which also managed to transcend their Poverty Row status. See Chapter 2 for more details.
76 James, 1989, p. 144.
77 Mason, 1976, p. 267.
78 Flynn and McCarthy, 1975b, p. 305.
79 Monaco, 2001, p. 3.

Part III

American independent cinema and the 'New Hollywood' (late 1960s to late 1970s)

5

The New Hollywood and the independent Hollywood

We've gotta save the movie industry, man. We've gotta save it, or it's all over for the movies.
Dennis Hopper, filmmaker[1]

Introduction

If the Paramount decree and the post-World War II recession ushered independent filmmaking in the US towards its second major phase, the factors that led to its further evolution in the late 1960s were once again economic, though changes in American society and culture played also a significant part. The end of the 1960s was one of the most volatile periods in the history of the country, characterised by: civil unrest in the streets of major American metropoles like New York and Chicago; assassinations of extremely influential political figures such as Robert Kennedy, Martin Luther King and Malcolm X; the escalation of the war in Vietnam (and the intensification of the country's commitment to it); the continuation of the Cold War with the Soviet Union; and the increased visibility and activism of formerly marginalised social groups in terms of race and sexuality (such as African American, gay and lesbian people) or age (young adults and college students). All these factors contributed to a remarkable change in attitudes and mores in American culture which, reflected in the films of the period, make even the most liberal films of the late 1950s and early 1960s (such as the social-problem films by Stanley Kramer) look like fake Hollywood constructions with naive ideological messages.

While the country was in social and cultural upheaval, the American film industry had to face its own set of severe problems as well as keep up with the transformations in the American social and cultural fabric. These problems included: the financial overexposure of the majors (manifested mainly in the production of a large number of expensive family films that increasingly started to falter at the box office, and in the efforts of many majors towards diversification); the continual audience decline, which reached an ultimate low of 15.8 million people a week in early 1971);[2] the decrease in the number of theatres; the entrance of the television networks into the theatrical market, which increased competition and contributed to a glut of product; and an extremely outdated (despite substantial revisions) Production Code, which the industry was still trying to enforce at a time of sweeping changes in sexual mores. Grouped together with the larger social and political problems the country was experiencing, they represented another life-threatening set of obstacles for the film industry, which had only recently started stabilising after the impact of the Paramount decree.[3]

Facing a new, more severe recession that was going to make its presence particularly felt between 1969 and 1971, the industry looked for help or leadership in every direction. To the rescue came a form of a relatively low-budget independent production by (mostly) hyphenate filmmakers that quickly became the model for mainstream Hollywood filmmaking for a short period (c. 1967–76), a period often labelled the 'New Hollywood' or the 'Hollywood Renaissance'. Combining a mixture of exploitation strategies, art-house filmmaking techniques and an emphasis on distinctly American themes within not always clear-cut generic frameworks, the Hollywood Renaissance films can be seen as the product of a new marriage between independent film production and the majors. The main difference between the New Hollywood and the previous eras was that during this short period of time the majors allowed filmmakers an unprecedented degree of creative control in the filmmaking process. As a result, American cinema entered a phase characterised by the production of many stylistically diverse and narratively challenging films that were much more tuned into the social and political climate of the time than the films made for the majors by top-rank independents in previous decades.

One of the consequences of the emergence of this type of film was the further muddling of what could constitute American independent cinema. As films like *The Graduate* (Nichols, 1967; produced by Embassy and Lawrence Turman and distributed by Embassy) and *Easy Rider* (Hopper, 1969; produced by Pando Company and Raybert Productions and distributed by Columbia) were radically different aesthetically from the big-budget, in-dependently produced films of the period, they laid a stronger claim to the label 'independent' than their top-rank counterparts. For instance, although, strictly speaking, films like *Easy Rider* and *The Secret of Santa Vittoria* (Kramer, 1969; produced by Stanley Kramer Productions and distributed by United Artists) have an equally valid claim to be termed 'independent' (both were produced by one or more companies other than the ex-studios but both were distributed by major releasing corporations) the two films could not have been more different in terms of everything else.

The former was a biker/social protest/road film with a particularly distinctive film style that went against well-established stylistic and narrative norms. It was shot for approximately $500,000 and was written, produced and directed by actors Dennis Hopper and Peter Fonda, who had no prior experience in filmmaking. On the other hand, the latter was a very expensive ($6.3 million budget) period comedy drama that was very 'Hollywood' in its look. It was produced and directed by a famous top-rank independent producer and starred Oscar-winners Anthony Quinn and Anna Magnani.[4] Even without any additional information about their production history, one would be immediately inclined to think of the former as an amateurish production created away from the influence of the majors, while perceiving the latter as the personification of the expensive Hollywood picture that the majority of top-rank independents were producing under the sponsorship of the majors in the 1950s and 1960s.

This means that the discourse of American independent cinema expanded once again to include the type of picture that films such as *Easy Rider* represented, while top-rank independent production started occupying a much more marginal position in the discourse. While prior to 1967 this new type of independent film would normally be classed as low-budget exploitation with some artistic pretence, during the years of the Hollywood Renaissance it gradually also became an integral part of the mainstream (supported by the majors). This does not mean, however, that all exploitation films became automatically part of the mainstream. The vast majority of exploitation films continued to be made away from the majors, with Roger Corman and American International Pictures still leading the way (see Chapter 6).

To make things even more confusing, a different brand of very low-budget independent filmmaking that had emerged a few years before the New Hollywood and that has been labelled by critics the 'New American Cinema' (1959–63) became another, particularly strong, contender for appropriating the label 'independent'. Although its emergence falls chronologically under the period covered in Part II of this book, its influence on commercial American independent cinema became particularly evident in the low-budget films of the late 1960s. For this reason, it is discussed in this chapter.

The New American Cinema

In the late 1950s/early 1960s, a group of filmmakers that among others included John Cassavetes, brothers Jonas and Adolfas Mekas, Shirley Clarke,

Edward Bland, Alfred Leslie, Lionel Rogosin and Robert Frank was brought together by its distinctly anti-Hollywood approach to filmmaking. Bearing a strong kinship to movements in various European countries such as the Nouvelle Vague in France, the Free Cinema in Britain and similar attempts for an alternative cinema in Italy, Poland and the Soviet Union, this American filmmaking movement attempted a radical break from the 'official' American cinema as it was represented by the films of the majors and of the independents (top-rank and low-end).

For these filmmakers, independence meant producing and distributing ultra-low-budget films entirely outside the structure and influence of the US film industry. Writing in *Film Culture*, a journal dedicated to this mode of filmmaking, in 1959, film critic and filmmaker Jonas Mekas explained that the New American Cinema filmmakers sought to 'free themselves from the over-professionalism and over-technicality that usually handicap the inspiration and spontaneity of the official [Hollywood] cinema, guiding themselves more by intuition and improvisation than by discipline.'[5]

Driven by their commitment to these principles, the above filmmakers (minus Cassavetes) formed the New American Cinema Group, an organisation established to support formally all those new voices in American cinema. Perhaps the most important development within the Group was the formation of the Film-Makers' Cooperative, a distribution organisation dedicated to the marketing and releasing of New American films, in April 1962. Prior to the establishment of the Cooperative, the key films of the New American Cinema were either self-distributed or released marginally by small distributors, such as British Lion International Films, which released *Shadows* (Cassavetes, 1959). The Film-Makers' Cooperative was run by the filmmakers themselves, who every year elected an executive committee to supervise the organisation. In distributing a film, the Cooperative retained 25 per cent of the film's gross, returning the remaining 75 per cent to the filmmaker. Furthermore, it was open to distributing any type of independently made film regardless of length, subject matter, budget or width (from 16mm to 70mm).[6]

Although the Cooperative distributed a number of independent films, these were mostly non-commercial, short subjects which could not sustain financially a releasing organisation, even a non-profit one. One had to wait until 1964 to see the first features released by the Cooperative: Jonas Mekas's *Guns of the Trees* and Jerome Hill's *Open the Door and See All the People*. By the mid-1960s it was obvious that the Cooperative had to open up to mainstream exhibition sites and therefore take a more commercial direction. For that reason, the members of the Group created a subdivision, the Film-Makers' Distribution Center, which undertook the task of handling the more commercial films and 'expand[ing] the theatrical distribution of independent cinema across the country.'[7]

With the Distribution Center designed to promote commercial features, the original Cooperative was usurped by experimental or non-narrative filmmakers who in the meantime had joined forces with the New American Cinema filmmakers as advocates of an alternative cinema. Very quickly, the Group, *Film Culture* and a number of the original independents led by Jonas Mekas shifted almost entirely their focus towards the avant-garde and the experimental, therefore dispensing with any concerns about commercial narrative cinema. From the mid-1960s, the filmmakers most commonly associated with the movement were Stan Brakhage, Gregory Markopoulos, Kenneth Anger, Michael Snow, Jack Smith, Robert Breer and James Broughton, all experimental filmmakers, while Andy Warhol, another important independent filmmaker, had only a tentative relationship with the Group.

Although the phenomenon of the New American Cinema was extremely short-lived (film critic P. Adams Sitney called it 'an illusion' that started with the first films of a small group of filmmakers and 'ended abruptly when they had completed them and were seeking distribution for them and financing for further projects'),[8] it nevertheless exerted immense influence on the New Hollywood, and more generally on one of the routes that post-1970 American independent cinema took. The main reason for this was John Cassavetes, whose films, especially his first feature, *Shadows*, influenced the development of a low-budget 'quality' independent cinema in the 1970s, which would become even more evident in the following decade with the emergence of what became known as 'contemporary American independent cinema' (see Part IV). Cassavetes and his approach to filmmaking became also responsible for creating the very powerful and romantic ideology of the lone and uncompromised auteur who works with a dedicated circle of friends and who goes to great lengths to see his distinct vision on the screen. This ideology became particularly influential in more recent iterations of independent filmmaking in the US.

The influence of John Cassavetes

The son of Greek immigrants, John Cassavetes started his career in American cinema as an actor, achieving a certain degree of fame as a youth rebel in *Crime in the Streets* (Siegel, 1956) and as a hard-pressed airport worker in *Edge of the City* (Ritt, 1957). However, it was his role as jazz-musician-by-day-turned-private-investigator-by-night Johnny Staccato, in the NBC show *Johnny Staccato* in 1959–60 that made him a familiar figure to the wider public. Since 1957, Cassavetes had established in New York the Variety Arts Studio, an actors' workshop, with the objective of developing theatrical skills through the means of improvisation. In an appearance on *Night People,* a late-night radio show, the 27-year-old actor stunned the show's presenter and audience by claiming that *Edge of the City* (the film he was promoting) was not a good film and that he could make a better film for a fraction of the cost. In what became arguably the first instance of crowdfunding in American cinema, he went on to ask the listeners to send money so that he would make 'a movie about people'.[9] Over the next few days, the radio station was inundated with letters containing small bills (approximately $2,000 in total) while other film industry figures also proceeded to donate various sums. With a final figure of $40,000 and a 16mm camera, Cassavetes went on to film an improvisation experiment that originated in his workshop. The result was *Shadows,* the film that kick-started the New American Cinema and which, for film scholar Geoff King, 'stands as a bridge between the alternative American cinemas of the 1950s and 1960s and the later independent film movement'.[10]

The film (see Case study 5.1) introduced a particularly distinct approach to narrative filmmaking, but perhaps more importantly established Cassavetes

Figure 5.1 John Cassavetes's unique visual style: an emphatic close-up of Lelia Goldoni and Anthony Ray in *Shadows.*

Case study 5.1 'Not actors acting but characters living': John Cassavetes's *Shadows*

> *Shadows* (John Cassavetes, 1959, 85 min.), produced by Maurice McEndree, distributed by British Lion International Films.

The roots of *Shadows* can be located in the radio show 'Night People', where Hollywood actor John Cassavetes claimed that he could make a more real film than the Hollywood productions he participated in as an actor. Even though rumours have it that he was not actually serious about breaking into filmmaking, the overwhelming response of the show's listeners made Cassavetes take on the task immediately.

With a budget of $40,000, a 16mm camera, free sound equipment he obtained through his connections and no professional technical crew, Cassavetes gathered a small group of unemployed actors from the Variety Arts Studio, the acting workshop he had established with Burt Lane in 1957 to develop acting skills through improvisation exercises, to make the film. Already familiar with his improvisation exercises, one of which involved Cassavetes asking his students to create a situation about two light-skinned black siblings, a sister and a brother, and the sister's white boyfriend, who discovers she is black (reminiscent of one of the plot lines in *Shadows*), the actors worked on specific character sketches provided by Cassavetes. One of the main sketches included the following information:

> BENNIE: He is driven by the uncertainty of his color to beg acceptance in this white man's world. Unlike his brother Hugh or Janet [Note: the sister became Lelia after this was written], he has no outlet for his emotions. He has been spending his time trying to decide what color he is. Now that he has chosen the white race as his people, his problem remains acceptance. This is difficult, knowing that he is in a sense betraying his own. His life is an aimless struggle to prove something abstract, his everyday living has no outlet. (Carney, 1994, p. 35, note in original)

With other character profiles specified in a similar manner, the filmmaker and his actors developed a number of situations revolving primarily around three siblings, Hugh, the eldest of the three and the one whose skin colour is unequivocally black, and Ben and Lelia, whose light skin colour allows them to pass as whites. Without scripting any concrete details of the dramatic situations created, Cassavetes, who undertook the task of operating the hand-held camera, and his amateur crew spent most of 1957 and the first months of 1958 shooting the film on location in New York. After a substantial editing period, the film premiered in the autumn of 1958 and was immediately embraced by the New York independent and avant-garde communities. In January 1959, *Shadows* became the recipient of *Film Culture*'s 'First Independent Film Award', as 'more than any other film, [it] presented contemporary reality in a fresh and unconventional manner … was able to break out of conventional molds and traps and retains original freshness' (Carney, 1985, p. 34).

The filmmaker, however, was not happy with the film, the formal attributes of which (especially editing and camerawork) had taken precedence over narrative concerns and characterisation. In a move that broke his association with and endorsement by *Film Culture*, Cassavetes proceeded to re-shoot several scenes and re-edit the film so that he would be able to explore more intensely 'the situations and emotional lives of particular characters locked into a time-bound narrative form' (Carney, 1985, p. 34). The result was a different version of the film, which was released commercially a year later (November 1959) and which brought Cassavetes's work closer to mainstream cinema (this second version is the one that is commercially available and will be discussed in the following paragraphs).

Despite its unquestionable dependence on narrative, *Shadows* is characterised by an aesthetic that is remarkably different from the dominant (classical) Hollywood one. The location shooting, the grainy black and white cinematography, the technical imperfections, the prominent jazz soundtrack and especially the improvised acting, which creates a very strong feeling that the film's characters are 'real' people whose lives happen to be documented by Cassavetes' camera, make the film look more like a record of the time rather than a fictional tale about three siblings and their racial identities.

This 'reality' is further reinforced by the absence of melodramatic plot mechanisms, which allows spectators a particularly distanced position in relation to the events portrayed. Thus, even in the scene where Tony (the boyfriend) finds out that Lelia is black, the matter is handled subtly, with few traces of the emotional outbursts that Hollywood films have made spectators so used to. As Cassavetes himself put it, he tried to express the 'small feelings' which are normally suppressed or ignored in the grand melodramatic plots of Hollywood films (Carney, 1994, p. 33). Although the film does deal with the impact of racism on the lives of two brothers and a sister, this does not constitute the major plot line of the film. Instead, the film is more interested in showing how the siblings fit into the urban bohemian environment of late 1950s New York, where racism is just a part of everyday reality. This makes questions of racism and of racial identity incidental, one more issue the characters have to deal with in their everyday lives, rather than the central problem of the film. Cassavetes achieves this effect in three major ways.

Firstly, he structures a narrative that is particularly episodic and loose. The film consists of 33 scenes that are connected either through dissolves or, more prominently, through a large number of long fade-to-black pauses which separate one scene from another rather than bridging them in a smooth manner. Specifically, Cassavetes uses this technique on nine occasions, while employing straight cuts to link scenes only on six occasions (the rest of the scenes are linked with dissolves). Secondly, although Hugh, Lelia and Ben are seen in a few scenes together, they are first and foremost characters in their own stories within the film. Thus Hugh tries to deal with his failures as a musician in the New York jazz scene; Lelia tries to find love in an environment where casual sex seems to be the norm; while Ben tries to deal with an empty life moving from café to bar for the duration of the narrative. It is obvious none of the siblings has any established goals (in the classical narrative sense), which explains why there is a lack of psychological motivation and an absence of clear cause-and-effect logic. Finally, Cassavetes avoids the use of almost any direct references to the problem of racism in the film's dialogue. Instead, he allows his actors to register their feelings and concerns about the issue through performance (gesture, exchange of gazes, body language) with his camera ready to pick up the slightest detail. This approach creates a considerably more understated treatment of the problem, allowing it to be part of the bigger picture, part of life, and not just something that was afforded prominence because of its undoubted (melo)dramatic value.

The film closes with the line THE FILM YOU HAVE JUST SEEN WAS AN IMPROVISATION, which clearly sets it within an amateur/experimental context as opposed to the professional context of Hollywood filmmaking. Despite such a status (sufficient to prevent any commercial aspirations), the film enjoyed unexpected box office success, especially after winning the BAFTA award for Best Picture in 1960, and two BAFTA acting awards for Lelia Goldoni and Tony Ray.

as 'the outsider ', 'the maverick', 'the pioneer ', the filmmaker who started a trend and paved the way for other talented individuals who wanted to use the medium of cinema for personal expression. For future generations of filmmakers, Cassavetes represented the American auteur in its most pure and unadulterated form: the filmmaker who writes their own scripts, arranges their own financing, organises the whole project on their own, works with a small circle of dedicated friends who are willing to work for very little or even for nothing, edits their own work, arranges distribution after the film is completed and, in the case of Cassavetes, even 'writes his own press pack and does the layouts for many of the posters and newspaper ads'.[11]

More importantly, this type of auteur remains faithful to their artistic vision and demonstrates a certain aversion to mainstream cinema, which is dismissed as pure entertainment or escapism. With Charles Chaplin in the 1920s and 1930s and Orson Welles in the 1940s and 1950s acting as luminaries and previous points of reference for such filmmakers, Cassavetes took this form of filmmaking many steps further, by building a consistent body of work that spanned almost three decades and by demonstrating that a successful filmmaking career away from the influence of the majors was indeed possible. For film critics, Cassavetes' film output stands 'as a monument in the independent canon'.[12] For filmmakers of later generations, Cassavetes stands as a powerful symbol. As Martin Scorsese put it:

> Whenever I meet a young director who is looking for guidance and advice,
> I tell him to look at the example of John Cassavetes, a source of the greatest
> strength. John made it possible for me to think that I could actually make a
> movie.[13]

After *Shadows* Cassavetes made two films in Hollywood – breaking thus his association with the Group: *Too Late Blues* (1961) for Paramount and *A Child Is Waiting* (1963) for Stanley Kramer Productions (distributed by United Artists). Of particular interest was the latter, where Cassavetes was hired to direct a top-rank independent production with major stars (Burt Lancaster and Judy Garland). A series of disagreements between him and Kramer, however, forced Cassavetes to leave the picture during post-production and Kramer to take over the supervision of the film's editing. As a result, Cassavetes denounced the final film, labelling it an 'overly sentimental' Hollywood creation,[14] and decided never to return to commercial filmmaking as exemplified by both studio and top-rank independent film production. Cassavetes' experience with these two films clearly proves that top-rank independent production had been completely assimilated into the structures and processes of Hollywood production, therefore pointing to low-budget arrangements as perhaps the only ones distanced from the ex-studios' influence. The need for a different type of independent production as an alternative to the mainstream (apart from pure exploitation) was absolutely critical at that time, and the films of the Hollywood Renaissance came to fill the gap.

Cassavetes returned triumphantly to his low-budget/aesthetically challenging filmmaking roots with *Faces* (1968), a film he financed from a number of acting jobs he took in studio productions. The critical success of the film, which was commercially released by the small independent Continental Distributing, established Cassavetes as a major force in independent filmmaking and was widely perceived as the first film of the 'Cassavetes canon'.[15] It was followed by films such as *Husbands* (1970; distributed by Columbia), *Minnie and Moskowitz* (1971; distributed by Universal), *A Woman Under the Influence* (1974; distributed by Faces International – a company established by Cassavetes himself when national distributors showed no interest in his film), *The Killing of a Chinese Bookie* (1976; distributed by Faces International); *Opening Night* (1977; distributed by Faces International); *Gloria* (1980; distributed by Columbia) and *Love Streams* (1984; distributed by Cannon Films).[16]

Although some of these films, like *A Woman Under the Influence* and, especially, *Gloria* became relative commercial successes and despite the names of Columbia and Universal as the distributors of three of his pictures, Cassavetes' cinema remained stylistically and narratively challenging, with films that often explored 'uncharted territory' and with a film output so diverse that makes him in the eyes of film critics 'America's most idiosyncratic and least categorizable filmmaker '.[17]

The New Hollywood

During the late 1960s, the American film industry presented an unusual picture. On the one hand, it had reached a respectable level of stability after the Paramount decree had changed the organisational structure of the industry and the rise of television had made American cinema a secondary leisure activity. An increasing number of big-budget productions, either produced and distributed by the majors, or produced independently but still released by the majors, had started reaching large audiences, sometimes returning rentals of extremely sizeable proportions (seven films released in the 1960s recorded rentals of over $26 million).[18] Big-budget epics and spectacles that targeted mainly a family audience seemed to provide some answers to the industry's acute financial problems. Even the number of releases increased from just over 140 in 1963 to 230 by the end of the 1960s.[19]

This picture of the industry, however, revealed only half the truth. The success of these films was more often than not offset by the size of their budget and marketing costs and by the various profit participation schemes that shifted a significant percentage of the films' rentals to the talent. Furthermore, the success of *The Sound of Music* (Wise, 1965), *Doctor Zhivago* (Lean, 1965), *Mary Poppins* (Stevenson, 1964), *My Fair Lady* (Cukor, 1964), *Thunderball* (T. Young, 1965) and *Cleopatra* (Mankiewicz, 1963), in short six out of the 10 biggest box office champions in the history of American cinema till 1969, represented a particularly successful two-year period mid-decade, and therefore cannot be deemed as representative of the whole decade. During the late 1960s, an increasing number of such big-budget productions bombed at the box office: *Dr Dolittle* (Fleischer, 1967), *Star!* (Wise, 1968) and *Hello Dolly!* (Kelly, 1969), all films distributed by Fox and designed to emulate the success of *The Sound of Music*, recorded dismal grosses. All the other majors witnessed similar results: *Camelot* (Logan, 1967) failed for Warner Bros.; *Chitty Chitty Bang Bang* (Hughes, 1968) for United Artists; *Sweet Charity* (Fosse, 1969) for Universal; and *Paint Your Wagon* (Logan, 1969) for Paramount. *Cleopatra*, another Fox picture, despite its position in the top 10 of box office champions, had cost excessively to produce and market and therefore should also be included on the list of films that underperformed at the box office.

Although there were a handful of exceptions, such as *Funny Girl* (Wyler, 1968) and Disney's *Love Bug* (Stevenson, 1969), which proved successful with the family audience, great, sometimes spectacular, success at the US box office in the late 1960s was found mostly by low-budget, independently produced films: *The Graduate* ($43.1 million in rentals); *Bonnie and Clyde* (Penn, 1967; produced by actor-producer Warren Beatty and distributed by Warner Bros. – $22 million); *Easy Rider* ($16.9 million); *Midnight Cowboy* (Schlesinger, 1969; produced by Jerome Hellman Productions and Florin Productions and distributed by United Artists – $16.3 million); and *Goodbye, Columbus* (Peerce, 1969; produced by Willow Tree and distributed by Paramount – $10.5 million).[20]

Besides their status as independent productions, the above group of films shared a large number of other characteristics, the most important of which were their conscious targeting of a young audience and their emphasis on questioning established traditions, in terms of both the types of stories they presented and the manner in which the presentation of the stories occurred on screen. These films set new trends in their treatment of controversial material such as the representation of violence (*Bonnie and Clyde*); sex (*Midnight Cowboy* and *The Graduate*); and drugs (*Easy Rider*) and struck the final blow to the already weakened Production Code, which was replaced in 1968 with the ratings classification system.

What becomes especially important with this category of independent filmmaking is not so much the fact that film production was arranged by companies other than the Hollywood majors (although this of course is a starting point in any approach to American independent cinema), but that a large number of independent producers consciously assaulted the codes and conventions of mainstream American filmmaking, the majority which had been established firmly for almost half a century. Furthermore, as American society was also in the process of questioning its very foundations, burying forever 'the optimism that dominated American life and spirit since the Second World War',[21] the above films, along with many other less financially successful ones, were perceived as considerably more sensitive to the sweeping cultural changes of the period. They were perceived as representative of the counterculture, an alternative culture developed around the differences in attitudes, mores and style between American youth and the older generations, who continued to represent the official culture, the establishment.

With the ex-studios and top-rank independents clearly representing the establishment in American cinema, it was no surprise that the new, low-budget independent cinema was automatically deemed as the cinema of counterculture, a cinema geared specifically towards the youth generation and firmly endorsed by it. Perhaps the most vocal example of this characteristic was the tagline for *Where It's At* (Kanin, 1969), which made no attempt to hide the fact that it targeted only one particular demographic: 'Where it's at for you, Dad, isn't necessarily where it's at for me'.[22]

As the established cinema had its own codes and conventions, grammar and syntax, the young filmmakers of the new independent cinema had to create their own language. In a short span of time, a large number of cinematic techniques, mainly associated with art-house filmmaking in Europe and Japan, were imported to American cinema. These included, among many others, improvisational acting, repeated actions, camera zooms, jump-cuts, freeze frames, telephoto shooting, hand-held camerawork, split screen, more frequent use of extreme close-ups and extreme long shots and image–sound mismatches. As film style in mainstream American cinema had been obeying the rules of classicism and, for that reason, had largely remained unobtrusive, subordinate to the needs of a causally driven narrative, the sudden appearance of these new cinematic techniques and their infusion with existing staples of Hollywood style changed dramatically the 'look' of American films.

Even the causally driven narrative with its psychologically motivated protagonist who has to fight a number of obstacles before reaching a clearly set goal had to lose some of its force in the presence of a film style that often drew attention away from narrative and to itself. Coherence and clarity, the key characteristics of the classical narrative, gave way to what Robin Wood called 'the incoherent narrative' of the 1970s cinema, a narrative 'where the drive toward the ordering of experience [was] visibly defeated'.[23] And if narrative became considerably less classical in its structure, film genres underwent such radical transformations that they almost ceased to perform the supremely important ideological function of keeping the spectators' expectations constant. Instead, genres were perceived by independent filmmakers as sets of conventions and rules that could be explored, questioned and very often subverted, resulting in the unsettling of the spectators' expectations. For instance, Sam Peckinpah's *The Wild Bunch* (1969; co-produced by Phil Feldman Productions and Warner Bros.) clearly subverts the codes of the western genre when it mixes modern iconography (automobiles, machine guns) with a more traditional one, but mostly by refusing to distinguish between heroes and villains, one of the most fundamental points of departure from the genre.

Although the changes in American film during the late 1960s and early 1970s were particularly notable, leading a number of film critics and cultural interpreters to talk about a post-classical or post-modern Hollywood cinema,[24] there was still continuity with the previous dominant aesthetic system. Despite evidence of 'a breakdown of classical storytelling conventions, a merger of previously separated genres, a fragmentation of linear narrative, a privileging of spectacle over causality [and] the odd juxtaposition of previously distinct emotional tones and aesthetic materials',[25] American cinema continued to operate as a narrative cinema where all the above elements of a potentially new aesthetic system were assimilated gradually into the powerful classical aesthetic. This was mainly because, as David Cook argued, the directors of the New Hollywood 'were not modernists who sought to demolish primary forms like representation and narrative. Rather, they concentrated their attack on secondary forms – most notably individual genres',[26] while also making extensive use of techniques that were normally associated with art-house cinema. For that reason, Hollywood cinema did not entirely lose the identity that had characterised it in the previous decades, despite the fact that some of the changes that occurred were radical.

The new state of American cinema that the Hollywood Renaissance effected was considerably more tuned into the state of American culture during the 1967–76 period. The changing attitudes and mores in lifestyle that the counterculture had brought in were not only the subject of many films of the period, such as *Easy Rider*, *Midnight Cowboy* and *Alice's Restaurant* (Penn, 1969). They were also reflected in the stylistic and narrative experimentation that young filmmakers such as Brian De Palma, Francis Ford Coppola, Martin Scorsese, Paul Schrader, Dennis Hopper and many others were practising. One could argue that changing America and changing American cinema became objectives that for a short period coincided as the younger generations set out to discover their own culture, while a number of young filmmakers were setting out to create part of this culture for them, in this case to discover their own approach to cinema. And if, according to John Belton, the main difference between the establishment and counterculture was 'just plain "style"',[27] it was obvious that many battles of the war of the new independents against mainstream Hollywood would take place on the level of visual style, by assaulting the aesthetic norms of the classical style upon which the established Hollywood cinema was founded.

The war of the new independents against mainstream cinema, however, was not limited to the field of film aesthetics. The Hollywood Renaissance was driven by the overly ambitious objective of putting an end to the domination of the majors and their preferred mode of filmmaking, which by that time was top-rank independent production. By borrowing a model of filmmaking again from European art-house cinema, whereby filmmakers were able to produce and distribute commercially successful films without the institutional support of a national distributor, and by subscribing fully to the auteur theory, which placed the filmmaker at the centre of the creative process, the independents attempted to bring about these fundamental changes in the structure of the American film industry.

Film distribution, however, became the insurmountable obstacle for any independent that wanted to apply fully the art-house filmmaking model in America. As this branch of the business of filmmaking remained firmly under the control of the ex-studios and of a small number of minor releasing companies, it was impossible for any structural changes to take place. Even the low-budget independent films needed national distribution to become profitable and enable the young filmmakers to find financing for their next projects. As there was no other avenue for national (and international) distribution besides self-distribution, which required the filmmakers' time and effort in touring the country with a print, filmmakers were forced to accept the importance of the established major distributors. On the other hand, though, the majors had to accept the necessity of supporting the new independent movement as the expensive genre films they financed and produced increasingly had problems with finding an audience large enough to render them profitable. Thus when *The Graduate*, a film produced and distributed by Embassy, was pronounced the box office champion of 1967 and the second most successful film in terms of rentals for the whole decade, the majors had no seconds thoughts about supporting the independent producers who sought to destroy them.

Allowing young filmmakers an unprecedented degree of creative control (which meant allowing the assault on the aesthetic of the 'official' cinema) was a small price to pay for the majors. For, despite the fact that the management of the majors for the first time in their history were in no position to predict what kinds of films the audiences wanted to see, and therefore know what kinds of films they should finance, betting on the low-budget independents represented only a small financial risk. With films like *Easy Rider* produced for a fraction of the cost of top-rank independent pictures like *The Secret of Santa Vittoria*, the road to profitability was considerably easier at a time when expensive, star-studded genre films proved time after time to be box office poison. Furthermore, a large number of these films had their financing arranged from outside sources, a development that reduced the majors' financial stake. More importantly, because the new independent filmmakers had embraced the counterculture, they were the only category of filmmaker with the potential to deliver to the majors the most important demographic: the youth audience. As one MPAA survey in 1968 revealed, 16–24-year-olds were responsible for almost half (48 per cent) of all ticket sales,[28] which made it clear that reaching this one particular age group made the difference between profitability and financial failure.

Although the majors had no idea about what types of film the young generation wanted to see, they were nevertheless the only organisations with the means to reach this audience, to inform it about the existence of films that were made for them. Despite the fact that the majors' marketing staff were more accustomed to promoting expensive films that targeted a family audience, their coverage of the US market, their presence in all major international markets and their relationship with major exhibitors were essential for the adequate commercial exploitation of any film. This means that the success of the stylistically and narratively challenging New Hollywood films was to a large extent due to companies such as Columbia, United Artists and Warner Bros., which made films like *Easy Rider*, *Midnight Cowboy* and *Bonnie and Clyde*, respectively, readily available in large cinemas in and outside the US. Writing specifically about *Easy Rider*, a film that was originally to be produced by Roger Corman and distributed by American International Pictures, Teresa Grimes highlights the significance of major distributors:

> With the distributing power of Columbia behind it, what could have been just another Corman-produced biker film made it through the conventional distribution/exhibition channels to reach a mass audience. Whether *Easy Rider* would have been the massive success it was had it been made and distributed by AIP is of course questionable.[29]

If the price the majors paid for endorsing the new independent movement was small, the price the new independents had to pay for having their films distributed and exhibited nationally and internationally was considerably higher. Their 'dependence' on the old studios for marketing and distribution automatically signalled the failure of their attempt 'to overthrow the studio system' or 'to democratize filmmaking'.[30] Yet the same 'dependence' ensured the emergence of some of the most idiosyncratic voices in American cinema and the unexpected success of some truly individualistic films that normally would have struggled to find an audience had the majors not been behind them (an issue that would be noted again in more recent years, when the majors through their specialty film divisions supported a very substantial faction of contemporary independent filmmaking – see Chapters 8 and 9). As Biskind put it: 'although individual revolutionaries succeeded, the revolution failed'.[31] This was particularly evident in the fate of many independent production companies like BBS – producer of characteristic New Hollywood films, including *Five Easy Pieces* (Rafelson, 1970), *The Last Picture Show* (Bogdanovich, 1971), *The King of Marvin Gardens* (Rafelson, 1972) and *Hearts and Minds* (Davis, 1974) and the Directors Company (set up by Francis Ford Coppola, Peter Bogdanovich and William Friedkin), which collapsed once the industry came out of recession and moved firmly into the blockbuster business in the mid-1970s.

Conclusion

Although the Hollywood Renaissance lasted less than a decade and the expensive, independently or studio-produced film made a thunderous comeback in 1975 with *Jaws* (Spielberg), the low-budget independent films of the 1967–76 period changed the landscape of American cinema forever. Besides the importation of a large number of film techniques and practices that enriched immensely the formal attributes of American cinema, and in addition to their ability to capture the spirit and mood of a nation in turmoil, the new independent films proved that there was space for a 'cinema about people'. This type of cinema offered often uncompromising views of contemporary America which were far removed from the safe representations and harmless entertainment associated with mainstream Hollywood cinema, but which were welcomed by a young generation that was disillusioned with the state of things.

What is of greater significance, however, is that the New Hollywood films succeeded – some of them spectacularly – in spite of the oppositional stance they adopted against the norms and values of Hollywood cinema. This success inspired a number of filmmakers, who would constitute the nucleus of the next independent film movement (John Sayles, Jim Jarmusch, Spike Lee, Susan Seidelman, Wayne Wang) to make their first film away from the influence of the ex-studios. It also gave a number of disenfranchised groups, who historically had been misrepresented or neglected by mainstream cinema, concrete hopes for developing their own brand of independent filmmaking and therefore taking control of their own representations. In this respect, the New Hollywood influenced and became the precursor of a more clearly defined brand of independent filmmaking that will be examined primarily in Part IV of this book.

Case study 5.2 'The end of American cinema as we know it': *The Last Movie*

> *The Last Movie* (Dennis Hopper, 1971, 108 min.), produced by Alta-Light Productions, distributed by Universal.

The staggering success of *Easy Rider* in 1969 had made Dennis Hopper, the film's co-screenwriter and director, a hot property in the US film industry. Despite anecdotes about his wild drug- and alcohol-fuelled shenanigans during the production of *Easy Rider*, and a reputation for being impossible to work for or with, the major distributors were focusing on his apparent ability to produce films that engaged with the elusive youth audience and therefore were more than interested in seeing what his follow-up picture would be. One such major, Universal, was looking for an opportunity to finance and distribute a 'hip' film that could prove a crossover hit. For that reason it had created a new unit headed by executive Ned Tanen with the purpose of financing and distributing challenging, offbeat films. Tanen's first deal was with Hopper for *The Last Movie*, while the unit was also involved in the financing of other important New Hollywood films, including *Minnie and Moskowitz* (Cassavetes, 1971) and *American Graffiti* (Lucas, 1973).

The idea for *The Last Movie* had preceded *Easy Rider* and was Hopper's personal project. As early as 1965, Hopper had tried to produce the film with financing from successful music producer Phil Spector but the lack of interest from major distributors had made Spector withdraw his support. After *Easy Rider*, however, Hopper found himself in the pleasant position of being able to fulfil his dream project. Despite the fact that both BBS (as a production company) and Columbia (as a distributor) passed on the project in fear of having to deal with the filmmaker's inflated ego, Tanen had no reservations and brought the project to Universal.

The film's story revolves around a stuntman who decides to stay behind in a small village and develop it as a resort for western film productions after the movie production for which he originally worked had used the village. The deal for the film afforded Hopper the opportunity to materialise his vision free from the distributor's control. Specifically, Universal gave Hopper a budget of approximately $900,000 and complete creative control, including final cut, provided that the filmmaker would not go over budget. As an extra measure, the distributor made Hopper a co-venturer in the project as he was asked to forfeit his fee for his job as a director, star, editor and producer of the film for a hefty percentage of the gross (50 per cent).

Principal cinematography took place in a remote village and a small town in Peru, Chinchero and Cuzco, respectively. From the very beginning of the shoot, the US media afforded the film great publicity, focusing primarily on the consumption of alcohol and drugs and on the sexual appetite of the filmmaker and several members of the cast. Furthermore, the production had to deal with the Catholic Church as well as the oppressive political climate that the military dictatorship had created in Peru. Despite these problems and incessant rumours and reports about an out-of-control production headed by 'a sullen renegade who talks revolution, settles arguments with karate, goes to bed in groups and has taken trips on everything you can swallow or shoot' (quoted in Hoberman, 1988, p. 21), Hopper managed to exert admirable control over the production. Having shot and exposed approximately 40 hours of material, he managed to finish the shoot slightly under budget and on schedule.

The post-production of the film, however, proved an extremely laborious process that would take 16 months to complete. Although the filmmaker had the footage he needed, he wanted to experiment and create different versions of the film. Together with two other editors, for one of whom *The Last Movie* was his first editing assignment, they spent endless hours using 'the Peru footage in every conceivable way, varying the story, changing the ending, introducing sub-plots, making sociological comments about the plights of the Indians and the tyranny of the Peruvian junta' (Rodriguez, 1988, p. 86).

When the film was eventually ready for release in the autumn of 1971, the omens were not auspicious. Despite the film's triumph at the Venice Film Festival, where it won the award for Best Picture, test screenings in the US had indicated that audiences disliked it. Furthermore, the film received an overwhelmingly hostile reception from both critics and public. The major critics called it 'hateful', 'pure fiasco', 'disaster ', 'pitiful', 'lowest rating', 'an embarrassment … endless, chaotic, suffocating, acid-soaked' (Hoberman, 1988, p. 21). The public did not respond favourably. Only two weeks after its opening, Universal withdrew the film from the cinemas, writing off almost all the film's production and marketing costs.

Arguably, the main reason behind the film's complete failure was its devastating assault on almost all conventions of mainstream American cinema, which alienated all segments of the audience, even the one that was associated with counterculture and had embraced the experimentation of *Easy Rider*. But while *Easy Rider* looked as amateurish as *The Last Movie*, the former nevertheless benefited from a clear narrative structure and a recognisable realist *mise-en-scène*, despite the absence of clear-cut goals or psychological motivation for the main characters and the many instances of discontinuous editing and obtrusive camerawork.

The Last Movie, on the other hand, retains only a schematic narrative structure, which, as the film enters in its final third, gives way to a form of representation that dispenses with questions of narrative. Equally, film style is used particularly liberally, often without any concern for highlighting the directions the story is taking and with such blatantly anti-Hollywood stylistic choices as intertitles explaining that scenes are missing, deliberately scratched parts of the print, the sound of the rolling camera audible, Hopper and other actors going in and out of their roles and acknowledging the presence of the camera, the appearance of the director 's credit superimposed on a shot 13 minutes into the film and its title presented in the same way almost 26 minutes after the opening shot.

Even though the narrative does deal with the efforts of a stuntman to develop an area as a potential setting for western movies, this is only one story, perhaps the most obvious, amidst a number of other sub-plots that take place before and after the stuntman's decision. Hopper edits these stories in a non-linear manner, interrupting scenes with inserts of events that are taking place earlier or later in the story and with shots that are repeated. Gradually another strong storyline emerges: the people of the town who witnessed the making of a Hollywood western decide to re-enact it as a ritual, complete with real shootings and killings as they cannot understand that violence in films is faked for the cameras. Through this storyline Hopper tries to offer a critique of Hollywood, its films and American society in general, while also exploring questions about the nature of cinema and of cinematic reality in particular. These elements bring him close to modernist filmmakers of the era, such as Jean-Luc Godard, Ingmar Bergman, Akira Kurosawa and Michelangelo Antonioni, and take him far from the Hollywood mode of filmmaking.

The almost overwhelming defeat of classical narrative, especially in the last 30 minutes of the film, proved one step too far for audiences. Unlike genre and film style, which were amenable to change and to the infusion of new ideas, attacking the dominant (narrative) mode of representation itself was something that was a particularly advanced proposal for audiences of commercial cinema, mainstream and independent.

After the failure of his film, Hopper's directorial career was all but terminated (his next film, *Out of the Blue*, came out almost 10 years later, in 1980, and he worked only occasionally as an actor in small independent films until the 1990s, when he reinvented himself and staged an extremely successful comeback. Despite its almost universal critical panning at the time, *The Last Movie* remains one of the most daring examples of experimental filmmaking in the history of American cinema.

Notes

1 Quoted in Shiel, 2003.
2 Cook, 2000, p. 22.
3 According to Balio (1987, p. 126), the industry started showing signs of recovery and stabilisation only after 1964 and responsible for that was the success of the blockbuster trend which had started accelerating.
4 The figures for the films' budgets are taken from Biskind, 1998, p. 74 (*Easy Rider*), and Balio, 1987, p. 146 (*The Secret of Santa Vittoria*).
5 Mekas, 2000, p. 74.
6 'Film-Makers' Cooperative', 1966, p. 46.
7 'Film-Makers' Cooperative', 1966, p. 46.
8 Adams Sitney, 2000, p. 71.
9 Carney, 1994, p. 29.
10 King, 2005, p. 71.
11 Carney, 1994, p. 28.
12 Levy, 1999, p. 102.
13 Scorsese is quoted in Boorman and Donohue, 1997, pp. 90–1.
14 Jacobs, 1980, p. 39.
15 Margulies, 1998, pp. 286–7.
16 Cassavetes is also credited as the director of *Big Trouble* (1986; distributed by Columbia).
17 Levy, 1999, pp. 103–4.
18 Balio, 1987, p. 126.
19 Monaco, 2001, p. 39.
20 The rental figures are taken from Finler, 2003, p. 359.
21 Quart and Auster, 2002, p. 67.
22 Stein, 1969, p. 16.
23 Wood, 1984, p. 47.
24 See Krämer, 1998, pp. 289–309.
25 Jenkins, 1995, p. 113.
26 Cook, 2000, p. 161.
27 Belton, 1994, p. 275.
28 Cook, 2000, p. 67.
29 Grimes, 1986, p. 57.
30 Biskind, 1998, p. 17.
31 Biskind, 1998, p. 434.

6

American independent cinema in the age of the conglomerates

Introduction

As the phenomenon of the Hollywood Renaissance was underway in the late 1960s, a very different development had been taking place in the American film industry at approximately the same time. After almost 50 years of self-ownership, almost all major ex-studios were in the process of becoming subsidiaries of conglomerates, 'diversified companies with major interests in several unrelated fields',[1] or in the process of becoming conglomerates themselves, through a programme of aggressive diversification. Starting with Paramount, which was bought out in 1966 by Gulf & Western (a company that held interests in such fields as automobile bumpers, sugar, real estate, fertiliser, cigars and zinc), other majors were taken over by similarly diversified conglomerates: United Artists by Transamerica (1967), Warner Bros. by Kinney National Service (1969), MGM by Las Vegas hotelier and finance mogul Kirk Kerkorian (1969), while Columbia and Fox adopted the conglomerate model by diversifying further themselves, before being taken over in the 1980s by the Coca-Cola Company and Rupert Murdoch's News Corp., respectively.[2]

The repercussions of this development were far-reaching not only for the ex-studios but also for producers and distributors across the independent film spectrum. Top-rank independent production, already the majors' preferred method of production since the 1950s, kept its hegemonic position in the conglomerate-run Hollywood cinema, especially as the 'countercultural' low-budget films of the New Hollywood that had met with great success in the early 1970s started faltering at the box office. The main difference between top-rank independent production pre- and post-conglomeration was a renewed emphasis on the potential of the 'event film' (the blockbuster) to return stratospheric profits not only from the theatrical market but also from many other profit centres that were controlled by other divisions of the same conglomerate.[3] Led by the stunning profits of *Jaws* (Spielberg, 1975; produced by Zanuck/Brown Productions and Universal) and especially *Star Wars* (Lucas, 1977; produced by Lucasfilm and distributed by Fox), this type of independent production became representative of mainstream cinema and has remained as such to date (see Chapter 8).

Low-end independents, on the other hand, were affected by the conglomeration of the industry in more complex ways. The majors' move to the production and financing of even fewer event films created enormous gaps in the US film market which existing and new independent producers and distributors rushed to exploit. As a result, the first years of the 1970s were a particularly prolific period for low-budget, exploitation filmmaking. New production/distribution companies such as New World Pictures, Dimension Pictures, Crown International, New Line Cinema and a large number of smaller production and distribution outfits, some of which specialised in hardcore pornography, achieved what seemed to be particularly strong footholds in that sector of the industry. With the number of releases from the majors reaching extremely low levels (culminating in the all-time low of 78 pictures by seven majors in 1977) and with film product becoming scarce, the future of low-budget independents seemed to be secure and not only in the short term.[4]

These conditions, however, were reversed in the second half of the 1970s, once the majors' blockbusters moved onto exploitation turf, in terms of content and target audience (science fiction and monster films targeting young audiences) and in terms of the sites where they were physically exhibited (the drive-in theatres). As a result, exploitation companies had to reconfigure and renegotiate their place in the industry, which in effect meant increasing their budgets and improving the production values of their own films so that they could compete with the far glossier studio productions. But as the independent companies were far less capitalised than the conglomerated majors, their effort was doomed to failure from the start. Only the lifeline presented by the advent of video and cable towards the end of the 1970s saved them from extinction, as these technologies created a new space for low-budget exploitation product away from the theatrical exhibition market.

The conglomeration of the US film industry seemed to make the distinction between mainstream and independent filmmaking slightly easier. Any film company that was not owned by a conglomerate had a very good reason to label itself 'independent', as it was the conglomerates that were now seen as the agents of mainstream cinema, the controllers of what was once a distinct film industry run by a handful of ex-studios. Additionally, this definition of 'independence' had the benefit of carrying a somewhat charged meaning, as the conglomerates were perceived widely as impersonal corporate forces that had moved in from 'the outside' and had replaced 'movie people' with 'businessmen who were interested only in money'.[5] In this respect, they were the enemy of the 'real' film companies which were still run by people with creative input.

Although this definition of independent filmmaking has certain advantages (it neatly divides American film production and distribution into conglomerate-owned or not; it makes independence a political matter), it is nevertheless extremely problematic. On the one hand, it means that companies like Columbia or 20th Century Fox could also lay claim to the label, despite the fact that they were modelling themselves on the same corporate entities that had bought out the other majors, and they had represented mainstream cinema for more than 50 years. After all, and until fully diversified in the mid-1970s, the main source of income for Columbia and Fox was from their film production and distribution, much like American International Pictures and Roger Corman's various film ventures, companies with a long history of 'independence', albeit in the low end of the market. On the other hand, this definition could also mean that a previously independent company like Embassy Pictures stopped being independent after its takeover by AVCO, a huge conglomerate with interest in finance and aeronautics, in 1968.

Such distinctions, however, are never absolute. For instance, under the aegis of its new parent company, Embassy continued its selective distribution programme of foreign imports with the occasional prestige production such as *The Lion in the Winter* (Harvey, 1968) and Hollywood Renaissance picture *Carnal Knowledge* (Nichols, 1971). In other words, Embassy continued to function in much the same way as before its takeover by AVCO. And if Embassy was simply an exception, what about United Artists, whose extremely successful, 16-year-strong management team was left intact to operate under the auspices of parent company Transamerica? Are United Artists and Embassy less 'independent' than Fox and Columbia because their logo is accompanied by the logo of the parent company?

It comes as no surprise then that the discourse of American independent cinema became even more expansive (and complicated) in the 1970s, especially as the conglomeration of the film industry was taking place at the same time as the Hollywood Renaissance. It was not until the late 1970s that yet another format of low-budget filmmaking came to dominate the discourse of independent cinema and consequently push other forms of independent filmmaking to the sidelines. This new format would establish a clearly alternative American cinema with no links to the majors (conglomerated and non-), at least to start with, and therefore carry the label 'independent' without any ambiguity.

The present chapter will discuss the effects of the conglomeration of the film industry on independent filmmaking. As Chapter 5 has already explored the particular brand of filmmaking that came to represent the Hollywood Renaissance, the main emphasis here is on low-end, exploitation filmmaking. Furthermore, this chapter will chart the birth of the late 1970s independent film movement, which in many ways was a response to the increasing power of the conglomerated majors. First, however, the reasons for the conglomeration of the film industry are briefly discussed, along with the key changes the new owners of the majors implemented in the industry as a whole.

Raising the stakes

Although by the mid-1960s all the majors had diversified to other media-related fields (television production and distribution, music licensing, publishing and so on), film distribution and production had certainly remained their main sources of income (with the exception of Disney, which had had several profit centres since the 1950s). When in the late 1960s some of the majors' expensive films started faltering at the box office and the losses brought down the value of their stock, these companies became ripe targets for corporate takeovers. Apart from their real-estate holdings, what made the majors important corporate acquisitions were their film libraries, which could be exploited perpetually in a number of existing and future ancillary markets.[6] Within a short period of time (1966–9) the landscape of American cinema had been transformed radically, even though the names Paramount, MGM and Warner Bros. continued to exist.

Among the changes the conglomerates brought to the American film industry, four present the most interest in terms of their impact on low-end independent production and distribution. First, conglomerates shielded the majors from the vicissitudes of an unpredictable film market as their extremely broad economic basis allowed them to absorb much more easily than a single corporation the increasingly large losses during periods of box office drought. The ex-studios therefore found themselves in a position where they could afford to take expensive gambles with the potential for huge payoffs. This meant that they could concentrate strictly on the production and finance/distribution of a few blockbuster films per year.

Second, and largely as a consequence of the first repercussion, the average film budget started increasing exponentially. While negative costs had certainly increased throughout the years (from slightly over $1 million in 1950 to $1.75 million in 1971) the increase was never too far from national inflation rates. However, during the eight years 1972–9 negative costs multiplied five-fold (from $2 million to approximately $10 million).[7] This increase limited even more the number of films financed by the majors.

Third, conglomerates installed new management regimes, which tried to rationalise the conduct of the film business. Besides emphasising further the production of blockbusters, the university-trained management teams put in place various scientific audience research mechanisms to measure tastes, preferences, viewing habits and so on. This information was subsequently fed back to decisions about production, which became increasingly dependent on research reports, charts and data and, not surprisingly, films became more formulaic and uniform. These practices seemed justified when the rentals from theatrical exhibition of some of these films (*Jaws* $133.4 million and *Star Wars* $188.1 million) reached unprecedented levels.[8]

Finally, as experts in matters of corporate diversification, conglomerates recognised the importance of opening up to new markets and creating more outlets for the commercial exploitation of the product their subsidiaries produced and distributed. For that reason, they actively encouraged the expansion of the majors to media- and leisure-related fields with an eye to creating new profit centres for a commodity that was already produced and therefore in need of only additional marketing and advertising costs. This development became particularly notable from the mid-1970s onwards, when new technologies such as video and cable presented great possibilities for extending the commercial life of a film, to the extent that some of the conglomerates dispensed with many of their non-media-related subsidiaries and concentrated solely on media acquisitions.

These developments were instrumental for low-budget independent cinema. Specifically, the renewed emphasis of the majors on the production of a small number of blockbusters created even bigger gaps in the film market which independent producers and distributors exploited. With the yearly releases by the majors dropping from 145 in 1972 to 78 in 1977 (before bouncing back to an average of 100 for the rest of the decade),[9] the perennial problem of access to exhibition seemed to be all but resolved. This was especially so when the number of screens increased (from 13,800 in 1970 to 16,500 in 1977)[10] and when weekly attendance, which had reached an all-time low of 16 million in 1971, started increasing again, reaching 22 million visitors by the decade's end.[11] Not surprisingly, then, a large number of independents flooded the market with low-budget product, while even the kings of exploitation, American International Pictures, shifted gears and produced considerably more refined pictures than in the 1950s and 1960s.

The end result of all these developments was the gradual polarisation of the US film market, with the conglomerate subsidiaries/diversified corporations and their expensive films occupying one side of it, and the rest of the film companies – 'the independents' – with their much cheaper productions occupying the other. It was at this point when the discourse of American independent cinema started privileging more firmly low-budget filmmakers over top-rank ones, especially when a critical mass of 'quality' (as opposed to exploitation) low-budget films started to emerge in the late 1970s.

Economic opportunities in the low-budget independent sector (late 1960s to 1974)

As the majors were struggling financially during the economic recession of 1969–71, and the New Hollywood independents were trying to secure a place in mainstream cinema, the independents in the low-budget, exploitation sector had been having an altogether different experience. Unlike the majors, which were still searching for their audience, these independents knew exactly which segment of the population their target audience was. For this reason, they continued successfully to supply youth audiences with cheap, generic product, exhibited primarily at the approximately 6,000 drive-in theatres of the country. As a matter of fact, conditions were so good for these independents that, at a time when 20th Century Fox was recording losses of $80 million in one year (1970),[12] a small company like American International Pictures was enjoying its most successful year yet, with a profit of $632,000.[13]

AIP was not alone in feeling that these were good times for low-end independents. Crown Pictures, a distribution company that had been releasing a handful of low-budget films per year for a number of years, was ready to expand in terms of both distribution business volume and producing its own films (after 1972).[14] Roger Corman chose 1970 as the year to establish his own production/distribution organisation, New World Pictures, after his lengthy and particularly successful association with AIP. Only a year later, former New World Pictures employees Charles Swartz and Stephanie Rothman and veteran independent producer Lawrence Woolner established Dimension Pictures to compete directly with New World Pictures for the same market. Finally, after six years on the market 'for "special events" on college campuses', New Line Cinema established a national distribution apparatus in 1973 to release low-budget 'arty and freak' films.[15]

All these production/distribution companies had several common characteristics. First – with the exception of AIP, which went public in 1970 – they were limited companies that were owned and run by their founders and not by a board of directors.

Second, their operation and initial success were based on the distribution of a large quantity of cheap films which were designed to fill in the increasing number of available playdates in the nation's theatres, hardtop and drive-in.[16] For instance, when in 1972 the seven majors released just 145 films, it was

Table 6.1 Taglines from exploitation films of the early 1970s

Distributor	Film	Tagline
American International Pictures	*Pick Up on 101* (Florea)	'Anybody's back seat will do so long as he's going her way'
New World Pictures	*Private Duty Nurses* (Armitage)	'The mouth to mouth they give is not CPR!'
Dimension Pictures	*Sweet Georgia* (Boles)	'She made plowboys into playboys'
Crown International	*The Stepmother* (Avedis)	'She forced her husband's son to commit the ultimate sin!'

these independents that supplied the majority of the remaining of the 315 films released by US distributors that year,[17] and therefore prevented the threat of product shortage from materialising.

Third, their films tended to exploit the new freedom in representation of sex and violence made possible by the introduction of the ratings system in 1968. According to Ed Lowry, who wrote specifically on Dimension Pictures, films from such independents belonged almost exclusively to mostly 'R-rated sub-genres (the softcore nurse/teacher/stewardess film, the women's prison picture, the graphic/erotic horror movie, the imported kung-fu actioner, and the whole range of blaxploitation)'.[18] Table 6.1 compares for instance the taglines from one film each from AIP, NWP, Dimension and Crown, all released in 1972. The differences seem to lie only in the inspiration of the marketing departments of each company.

Fourth, as exploitation companies, they were watching closely trends and cycles in American cinema, trying to cash in on the latest fad or craze. Although business analysts and trade publications like *Variety* were proclaiming at the peak of the industry recession 'that the only current trend was no trend at all',[19] low-end independent producers never stopped looking for winning formulas. Some, in fact, were very successful, like New World Pictures with its nurses cycle, which was sustained for five films: *The Student Nurses* (Rothman, 1970); *Night Call Nurses* (Kaplan, 1972); *Private Duty Nurses* (Armitage, 1972); *The Young Nurses* (Kimbrough, 1973); and *Candy Stripe Nurses* (Holleb, 1974).

Finally, these companies allowed filmmakers a substantial degree of creative control during the production process. This freedom was sometimes translated into the making of innovative films, especially in terms of the use of film style and the representation of political issues. For instance, even the softcore sex films of the *Nurses* cycle often featured narratives that revolved around such political matters as 'abortion, ecological issues, black disadvantage and alternative education',[20] issues rarely tackled by the majors in the early 1970s. Although independent companies often gave filmmakers such freedom consciously, claiming that this practice differentiated them from the majors, film historian Jim Hillier has argued that such freedom was 'inherent' in the production practices these companies followed. Writing specifically on New World Pictures he argued:

> freedom was inherent in the ways the films were produced. Expectations tended to be low for a number of reasons: the films would have no aspirations to critical acclaim (as a rule, they would not be press shown), the budgets were extremely low, and producers would generally be absent and more concerned with selling the product than with actually making it – Corman, would certainly absent himself from the start of the shooting until it was more or less finished.[21]

AIP, New World, Crown and Dimension were only the tip of the iceberg, the best-known of a large number of low-end independent film producers and distributors, some of which also enjoyed commercial successes with low-budget films that have remained cult favourites throughout the years. These included Bryanston Distributing Company, which released *The Texas Chainsaw Massacre* (Hooper, 1974), and Fanfare Films, which released the extremely successful *Born Losers* (Laughlin, 1967; co-distributed with AIP), the first film in which the character of Billy Jack appears. In 1971, Tom Laughlin wrote, directed, produced and starred in *Billy Jack*, a film that became a commercial triumph ($32,500,000 in rentals on a less than $1 million budget), after Laughlin and Warner Bros. distributed it with the method of 'four-walling'.[22]

The blossoming of the exploitation sector in the early 1970s continued the project of the Poverty Row studios and of the low-end independents of the 1950s and 1960s (targeting audiences the majors excluded, working with genres the majors shunned, filling in playdates, especially in the drive-in theatres, and so on). One could go as far as to argue that the period between the late 1960s and the mid-1970s is reminiscent of the 'classic years' of the Poverty Row studios in the 1930s and 1940s. This is because the number of important distributors, the volume of their business, the freedom they granted filmmakers (provided they would stay within specific budget and genre constraints), the distributors' association with a particular type of exhibition site (then the subsequent-run theatre, now the drive-in theatre) and the emphasis on showmanship (Crown executives invented the term 'Crownmanship' to distinguish their own brand of film promotion) suggest that the exploitation independents of the 1970s had found their own niche market, just like their predecessors during the studio years.[23]

The end of exploitation as we know it

The runaway success of *Billy Jack* in 1971–2 represents, arguably, the zenith of low-end independent cinema in the early 1970s and made the retrenched majors question once again their knowledge of the film market. Once the majors came out from the heavy recession of 1969–71 and the effects of conglomeration (a renewed emphasis on blockbusters, scientific audience research and new marketing techniques, aggressive diversification, and so on) were becoming apparent, it became clear to them that, first, the exploitation market was too important to be overlooked and, second, the youth audience for that market was too large to be ignored.[24] Not surprisingly, the majors decided to move onto exploitation turf and 'upgrade' the normally extremely cheap independent product by throwing their millions of dollars on monster, science fiction and car chase films such as *Jaws*, *Star Wars* and *Smokey and the Bandit* (Needham, 1977).

The majors' move to the low-end independent market was initiated during 1974–7 and went into a full effect from the late 1970s onwards. A significant factor in that move was the phenomenon of 'blaxploitation' (see Case study 6.1), the mass production and distribution of films geared to African American audiences who in the early 1970s had appeared to be a significant demographic. Between 1970 and 1972 alone there were more than 50 films aimed specifically at the African American cinema-going community, while the trend increased further in the following two years before it started declining in 1975.[25]

Some of these films became very successful financially – for instance, *Shaft* (Parks Jr, 1971) recorded rentals of more than $7 million on a $1 million budget – to the extent that blaxploitation films were considered significant contributors in leading Hollywood out of the 1969–71 recession.[26]

This means that besides the low-end independents, which, expectedly, jumped immediately on the blaxploitation bandwagon, the majors were also heavily involved in the perpetuation of the trend until the mid-1970s. For instance, Warner Bros. backed, among others, *Superfly* (Parks Jr, 1972); MGM financed and distributed, among others, *Black Mama, White Mama* (Romero, 1972) and a number of successful films produced by Roger Corman's brother, Gene Corman, including *Cool Breeze* (Pollack, 1972); and Paramount distributed *The Legend of Nigger Charley* (Goldman, 1972).

The majors' involvement with a type of film that was traditionally associated with exploitation filmmaking demonstrates clearly that by the mid-1970s the rulers of the industry were in the process of adopting and appropriating practices 'from the industry's margins'.[27] With the blaxploitation 'experiment' paying off handsomely at a time of retrenchment, the majors started realising that the low-end independent sector had a lot more to offer. As the success of their glossy exploitation films, especially of *Jaws*, made clear that their future lay in such types of production, the majors rushed to adopt more practices associated with exploitation cinema. Soon they were employing strategies such as sensational advertising and saturation bookings, while also targeting drive-in theatres for exhibiting their films. In doing so, the majors not only managed to regain their position of almost absolute control of the American film market, but they also eliminated the competition that these independents provided until the mid-1970s. By the end of the decade, the majors were back controlling approximately 90 per cent of the theatrical market (a figure that in the early 1970s was estimated closer to 70 per cent),[28] a degree of control comparable to the one the same companies enjoyed during the studio years.

Figure 6.1 Pam Grier is Foxy Brown: Grier became an international star after her appearance in leading parts in a number of films that targeted an African American audience.

Case study 6.1 Blaxploitation, the AIP way: *Foxy Brown*

> *Foxy Brown* (Jack Hill, 1974, 90 min.), produced and distributed by American International Pictures.

In 1971, an extremely low-budget film, which was financed by private investors and distributed by the tiny Cinemation Industries, became a huge commercial success: $10 million gross on a $500,000 budget (Guerrero, 1993, p. 86). The film was *Sweet Sweetback's Baadasssss Song*, written, directed, produced, edited by and starring black artist Melvin Van Peebles. Its spectacular commercial success proved to majors and exploitation independents alike that there was a significant African American audience who had remained untapped. That audience wanted to see dynamic representations of black people, which would not follow old Hollywood stereotypes that promoted subservience and/or assimilation to white dominant groups. Instead, they would advocate opposition or resistance to the historical oppression of the black population by white individuals and institutions. With estimates bringing this potential audience to approximately 30 per cent of the ticket-buying public in major cities (Guerrero, 1993, p. 83), it was clear that African American theatre-goers could provide film companies with much-needed new revenues. Thus a type of film that was labelled by trade publications as 'blaxploitation' (exploitation films for black audiences) was born.

Never late to capitalise on a fad, craze or trend, AIP jumped immediately on the blaxploitation bandwagon and offered as early as January 1972 a very successful film in the cycle, *Black Mama, White Mama* (Romero, starring Pam Grier). A few months later, AIP was experimenting with black content within existing genre frameworks such as horror, with *Blacula* (Crain, 1972), and the gangster film, with *Black Caesar* (Cohen, 1973). By that time, however, almost every company in Hollywood was making blaxploitation pictures, thus creating congestion in the film market.

To differentiate its product, AIP initiated a cycle of pictures that featured a strong female character played by Pam Grier, who was under a five-year contract to the company (1971–6). Although the idea of a strong female protagonist also runs through *Cleopatra Jones* (Starrett, 1973) and *Cleopatra Jones and the Casino of Gold* (Bail, 1975), both starring Tamara Dobson and financed and distributed by Warner Bros., AIP developed a fully fledged cycle that lasted three years (1973–5) and four films: *Coffy* (Hill, 1973), *Foxy Brown* (Hill, 1974), *Friday Forster* (Marks, 1975) and *Sheba, Baby* (Girdler, 1975). Naturally, AIP continued the production of other types of blaxploitation pictures such as *Truck Turner* (Kaplan, 1974) and *Bucktown* (Marks, 1975) in case its Pam Grier films failed to attract black male audiences.

Despite the fact that *Coffy* became the most commercially successful film of that AIP cycle, *Foxy Brown* is, arguably, a more useful example for an understanding of the company's approach to this particular group of films. Originally intended as a sequel to *Coffy* under the title *Burn, Coffy, Burn*, with the same above-the-line talent, the film became *Foxy Brown* when Arkoff noticed that sequels had stopped performing as well at the US box office. Rather than releasing a new *Coffy* film, which could underperform in an increasingly competitive marketplace, the company's president decided on the production of a 'new' picture with a different heroine in the mould of *Coffy*. This gave the company's official policy of exploiting a proven formula a new twist. While *Burn, Coffy, Burn* would have been a pre-sold title in little need of substantial advertising costs, given the success of the original film, by opting for a new film (with a brand new advertising campaign), AIP demonstrated its commitment to distinguishing itself from the other exploitation companies. It also sent a signal to the majors, which were moving onto exploitation turf, that AIP was a serious company that did not depend on sequels.

Although *Foxy Brown* was marketed as a 'new' blaxploitation picture with Grier, the film certainly uses most of the successful ingredients that were introduced in *Coffy*: the revenge plot line; the problem of drugs in the black community; the protagonist's use of her sexuality to achieve her objectives; sex and violence (and sexual violence); and a fast, upbeat music soundtrack produced by Motown legend Willie Hutch. Even the poster and tagline that are used to advertise the films present similarities. The poster for *Coffy* features a large picture of a scantily clad Grier holding a shotgun, while around this image there are a number of smaller pictures, mostly of fights and of Coffy in a bikini. The tagline of the film makes a reference to *The Godfather* (then the most commercially successful film of all time) and reads: 'She's the GODMOTHER of them all … the baddest One-Chick, Hit-Squad that ever hit town'. Similarly, the poster for *Foxy Brown* features another large picture of Grier, this time in an evening dress and in a suggestive position reaching for her gun. Again, smaller pictures of fights (this time mostly between scantily clad women) accompany the main image. The film's tagline is reminiscent of that for *Coffy* but also pays tribute to Grier, who, in the meantime, had become one of blaxploitation's main stars: 'Don't mess aroun' with Foxy Brown; She's the meanest chick in town! She's brown sugar and spice but if you don't treat her nice she'll put you on ice! Pam Grier as "FOXY BROWN."'

Not surprisingly, *Foxy Brown* is not very different stylistically from *Coffy* either. The pace is fast and becomes faster when fight or chase scenes occur. In such scenes editing becomes of primary significance (both films were edited by Chuck McLelland) as the quick cuts increase the pace while at the same time hiding the absence of production values and lack of elaborate camera set-ups. The camera often lingers on Grier's body, especially her breasts (more often and for longer than in *Coffy*). Even in unsuspecting scenes like the one where Foxy is giving a passionate speech about the need for action against the problems of the black race, Grier is stooping for the duration of the scene, allowing the camera to fixate on her bosom for a protracted period. Finally, as AIP was committed to producing and distributing PG-certificate films, most of the violent scenes were sanitised (the camera tilts, pans or cuts away before a controversial representation and returns to show the aftermath, especially when it comes to murder and rape).

By the time *Foxy Brown* was released, *Coffy* and *Cleopatra Jones* had already innovated in terms of gender representations by offering black women active roles in both narratives. For that reason, *Foxy Brown* was not allowed enough space for innovations of an aesthetic or political nature. Still, there are a few instances in which the film transcends its low-end exploitation status and offers interesting representations. An example of a use of film technique not normally expected at this level of filmmaking occurs approximately 37 minutes into the film, when Foxy visits the home of the female crime boss and her male lover. The scene, which lasts two minutes, makes extensive use of tracking shots, eye-line matches and point-of-view cutting, off-screen sound and deep-focus cinematography, to present a purely visual comment on the power relations between the three characters (ultimately highlighting Foxy's power over the other two, despite the fact that she is in the most disadvantageous position for the duration of her visit).

An example of an interesting gender representation occurs a couple of scenes earlier, when Foxy confronts her brother after finding out that he betrayed her. Foxy enters his apartment and like a raging bull destroys everything in front of her. She injures him and makes him give her important information and proclaims that his days in the city are over. Throughout the scene the male sibling is represented as a very weak man who is repeatedly humiliated by his sister, in front of his white lover. The reason why this reversal of gender representations works so well is because this is one scene where Foxy is not portrayed as an erotic spectacle. The camera stays away from her breasts or other parts of her body and focuses primarily on her face, while the low camera angles employed make Foxy look menacing but without objectifying her. Thus Foxy's domination over her brother is not undermined by a simultaneous eroticisation of her own image, which is not the case in the majority of the film's scenes.

Like *Coffy*, *Foxy Brown* was a big hit for AIP in 1974. In the same year, the company released more blaxploitation titles, such as *Sugar Hill* (another film with a black female protagonist) and *Truck Turner*, before the cycle started slowing down in late 1975.

The one practice the majors adopted that, arguably, proved the most harmful for the low-end independents was their move to the drive-in theatres, the one type of exhibition site that the independents had had almost total control of since the 1950s. With the number of drive-ins already in decline in the early 1970s (as the value of the land on which they operated had been increasing steadily), the independents had already started feeling the pressure. For that reason, when the majors started using the drive-in theatres as exhibition sites for their own brand of exploitation productions and claimed the remaining youth audience who patronised mainly this type of theatre, the independents were faced with nothing less than extinction.

On one level, the majors were forced to move to the drive-ins. Their adoption of the saturation release method dictated the use of a massive number of theatres which would all play the same film on the same dates. With Universal's *Jaws* opening in more than 400 theatres in 1975, De Laurentiis and Paramount's *King Kong* (Guillermin) in 961 theatres in 1976, and Columbia's *The Deep* (Yates) in 800 in 1977 (2.6, 6.5 and 5.3 per cent of all the nation's screens, respectively),[29] using the drive-in theatre as a first-run exhibition site became a necessity for all the majors. On a different level, however, the majors' physical move to the drive-ins was strategic, designed to reduce the number of playdates for the independents and therefore kill off the already weakened competition.

These developments placed the low-end independents in an impossible situation. The smallest and least capitalised ones exited the market *en masse* and immediately: Fanfare Films in 1974; Cinemation Industries, Bryanston Distributing and Manson Distributing in 1975; American Film Distributing Corporation in 1976; and Monarch Releasing Corporation, responsible for the hugely controversial *Snuff* (Findlay and Findlay, 1976), in 1977. The larger exploitation independents (AIP and New World Pictures) along with the smaller Crown and Dimension had no choice but to fight back by producing and distributing considerably more expensive productions which would have a chance of competing with the studio fare both in the drive-ins and, very importantly, in the multi-screen theatres that had been mushrooming in the US since the mid-1960s and especially the 1970s. The response of American International Pictures to this situation is a particularly interesting example.

The gradual rise and rapid fall of American International Pictures

Like the other exploitation companies, AIP experienced a particularly successful period until the mid-1970s, achieving an impressive increase in both its profits and its revenues (see Table 6.2).[30]

By 1975, the company was in such good shape that Samuel Z. Arkoff, AIP's co-founder, was not afraid to choose competition with the majors over retrenchment in a changing film marketplace. Even though AIP's capitalisation was considerably larger than that of the other low-end independents, its financial basis was nevertheless still minimal compared with the conglomerate-owned majors. For instance, at the time when Universal was investing $12 million in *Jaws* for production costs alone, AIP's credit line (funds the company could borrow from the banks to use for production costs) for the whole of 1975 was $11 million.[31] Despite this inequality, AIP proceeded in the financing and

Table 6.2 American International Pictures' net profits, 1970–6

Year	Net profit (US$)	Revenues (US$)
1970	632,000	21,000,000
1971	n/a	n/a
1972	270,521	20,800,000
1973	744,400	24,500,000
1974	931,400	32,516,000
1975	2,853,000	46,930,000
1976	2,883,000	51,044,000

distribution of very expensive pictures by the company's standards, such as Vincente Minnelli's *A Matter of Time* (1976), starring Ingrid Bergman, Charles Boyer and Liza Minnelli, which was budgeted at $5 million.[32]

Although the company's first steps towards expansion were successful, its march towards the industry's major league was severely curtailed in the final months of 1976, when the US Treasury Department repealed the federal income tax shelters that the Nixon administration had created in 1971 to stimulate film production after the recession.[33] These credits allowed corporations significant write-offs in their income tax bills, should they invest part of their corporate income in film production.[34] This meant that a corporation could reduce its income tax bill and stand to gain profits as well, should the film it invested in become profitable. Despite their unquestionable contribution to the regeneration of the film industry (it was estimated that tax shelters became responsible for an influx of more than $100 million of outside investment in film production during the first half of the 1970s), tax credits were placed under pressure when strong allegations that they were used for the financing of pornographic films surfaced in the mid-1970s.[35] The Tax Reform Act of 1976 eliminated the shelters and closed this important revenue of film financing to the independents.

As the conglomerated majors had by that time fully bounced back from the recession, the elimination of tax credits hit mostly the low-end independents, even the most successful ones, like AIP. To continue operating efficiently at a time when the company's product was becoming increasingly expensive in terms of both production and, especially, distribution costs, Arkoff sought tax shelters and subsidies outside the US, in particular in Germany, Canada and Australia.[36] This move became especially important as AIP's marketing costs had reached unprecedented levels and the company needed to keep production expenditure as low as possible.[37]

Despite the efforts to keep costs down while competing with the conglomerated majors, AIP had already become a prisoner in the industry's irrevocable course towards star-studded films with inflated budgets. By the last month of 1977, the company was – reluctantly – prepared to finance $7–$8 million pictures such as *Force 10 from Navarone* (Hamilton, 1978, with Harrison Ford) and *Meteor* (Neame, 1979; with Sean Connery), which ended up costing $17 million).[38] To meet these demands, AIP negotiated a considerably larger line of credit from American banks (from $11 million in 1975 to $35 million in 1978).[39] The company's financial results, however, hardly justified such a move. Both its profits and its revenues remained stagnant in 1977 and 1978, while in 1979 AIP recorded a net loss for the first time in its history ($1.5 million).[40]

Not surprisingly, AIP immediately became a target for a corporate merger or takeover. Filmways, a former television production company that had successfully diversified with interests in the fields of insurance, publishing, manufacturing of electronics and television and film finance, had been following AIP's slump since the final months of 1978. Although Arkoff had treasured his independence for almost a quarter of a century and had taken in the past measures to shield AIP from hostile takeovers, this time he was ready to succumb to the need for a conglomerate parent. As he put it in October 1978, several months before the merger between AIP and Filmways:

> Responsible management must weigh the prospects of a much heavier debt burden against the better alternative of operating on a broader financial foundation. The concept of affiliation with Filmways seems to offer the more desirable option.[41]

The merger, which was valued at approximately $25 million, created a stronger AIP, as banks could now take into consideration Filmways' assets when arranging production loans. According to the terms of the deal, Arkoff remained AIP's chairman but he now had to report to the Filmways executive board of directors.[42] Only a few months later, however, Filmways executives accused Arkoff of having overstated AIP's assets before the merger and forced him to resign. Less than a year after the merger, Filmways retired the name American International and replaced it with Filmways.[43]

From the theatrical to the video market

If AIP 'disappeared' in 1980 after playing the majors' game, the other smaller exploitation companies met different destinies. Dimension Pictures also made an effort to upgrade its product. In the 1977–8 season, the company allocated production funds in the region of $15 million and enjoyed the noteworthy success of *Ruby* (Harrington, 1977), which grossed $16 million. Following this, Dimension tried to shift from quantity to quality, producing and releasing only a few films, with budgets around $3 million each. The company's slim capitalisation, however, did not allow this to happen, especially when in the first months of 1979 Dimension faced a series of lawsuits brought against it by a number of producers releasing through it. Soon the company found itself on the verge of bankruptcy, for which it officially filed in February 1981.[44]

New World Pictures also moved towards 'respectability' in the late 1970s. From large quantities of exploitation pictures earlier in the decade (budgeted at around \$125,000–\$200,000) the company shifted to the production of a smaller number of releases by the decade's end, which included a few expensive films, including \$2 million for *Avalanche* (Allen, 1978) and \$3 million for *Battle Beyond the Stars* (Murakami, 1980).[45] Corman quickly realised that face-to-face competition with the majors was destined to fail so he kept distributing low-budget films, while trying to test the market with a few expensive productions. As a result he managed to survive the pressure of the majors, especially when he started utilising the new exhibition technologies that video and cable television represented. In 1983 Corman sold New World Pictures for \$16.5 million and started a new venture, this time focusing primarily on the lucrative home video market.[46]

Crown International Pictures continued its selective distribution policies and the small programme of production it had initiated since 1972. Although Crown also increased its budgets substantially (by 1978 it was allocating \$20 million alone in production costs),[47] it nevertheless avoided an AIP/Dimension-type expansion. Like Corman, Crown executives recognised very early on the significance of video and cable, especially as these technologies were developing outside the US. More than any other exploitation company, Crown focused on the international home video and television market, becoming a reliable supplier of exploitation product and surviving also the squeeze of the late 1970s.

Although extremely low-budget exploitation filmmaking by a large number of tiny independent companies continued during these developments, this type of cinema became gradually associated with the home video market. With both the majors and the larger independents resorting to saturation releases, ultra-low-budget independents found video to be the only exhibition outlet available to them. With the penetration of the VCR increasing exponentially in the 1980s (see Chapter 7), exploitation cinema found what seemed to be a permanent home in the home video market.

A new hope: the birth of the new American independent cinema

With the top-rank independents engulfed in the structures of the major conglomerates and with low-budget exploitation producers out of necessity moving out of the theatrical and to the home video market, independent filmmaking was all but dead in the late 1970s. The repealing of tax credits, and especially the industry's obsession with the production of blockbusters, which made almost all newcomers to independent production ally themselves to a major distributor in order to finance expensive productions with the potential for handsome payoffs, made the practice of independent production (production with no ties to the majors) a virtual impossibility.[48]

At the same time, American culture and politics had been feeling the impact of a conservative movement that was associated with the rise of the New Right. By 1978, the New Right had become a major force in the country, advocating 'a politics of return' to 'pre-New Deal, pre-social welfare economics, to the traditional male-supremacist family, to fundamentalist religious values and to a time when United States was the most powerful military nation on earth'.[49] Reacting especially against the politics of the counterculture, this conservative movement (the outcome of which was the sweeping victory of Ronald Reagan in the 1980 presidential election) found expression in a large number of popular films of the period, especially films made by or for the majors, and spearheaded a return to a 'simpler ', more affirming Hollywood cinema.

One of the effects of this shift was the majors' gradual closing of doors to creative filmmakers or to filmmakers with dissenting political views, in short the individuals who were an integral part of the Hollywood Renaissance. Coppola, Scorsese, Schrader, Bogdanovich, Hopper and Friedkin among others gradually became marginal filmmakers in the 1980s. The final straw had come in 1980 when Michael Cimino's *Heaven's Gate*, a $44 million (production and marketing costs) epic that is often referred to as the last great auteurist film of the 1970s, sank without a trace at the US box office, recording an unbelievably poor $12,032.61 gross in its first theatre run.[50] The unprecedented commercial failure of the film precipitated the end of the most successful major of post-World War II Hollywood cinema, United Artists. In 1982 Transamerica sold United Artists to Kirk Kerkorian, already owner of MGM, who retained the rights to the company's library of titles and dismantled its distribution network. UA went out of the film finance and distribution business and re-emerged in the mid-1990s as a small specialty distributor (see Chapter 8).

The above conditions clearly suggest that American cinema was once again in the claws of monopolisation, this time those of a decreasing number of conglomerated majors, while the force of the conservative movement was also threatening to turn the diverse, thought-provoking and stylistically and narratively challenging cinema of the late 1960s and early 1970s into harmless entertainment. In these circumstances, it is not surprising that the new breed of independent films that emerged in the late 1970s and early 1980s were extremely low-budget, made completely away from the majors (or their numerous subsidiaries), were markedly different aesthetically and/or politically from mainstream films and occupied themselves with subjects that the majors' films avoided. In other words, as Peter Biskind put it, 'they were anything Hollywood was not'.[51]

Although, arguably, the key independent film of that time, *Return of the Secaucus 7* (Sayles, 1980), was financed by the filmmaker's savings and with loans from family members, many of these independents were supported by funding from various non-profit sources and organisations, including:

- federal government grants (allocated primarily through the National Endowment for the Arts and the National Endowment for the Humanities);
- local government grants (allocated primarily through municipal or state film bureaus, most of which were established after 1976);[52]
- public television – the Corporation for Public Broadcasting (CPB) and its main programming outlet, Public Broadcasting Service (PBS), which was established in 1969.

The entrance of public television into the financing of independent filmmaking was orchestrated by the US Congress, which in 1978 mandated that 'public television should use substantial amounts of independently produced programming in pursuing its broad programme issues'.[53] Established as an alternative to commercial television 'to provide diversity of viewpoint and vision, reflective of the diversity of [the American] nation',[54] PBS (through its 'American Playhouse' series) quickly became one of the key financers of this new breed of independent filmmakers who produced films such as *Alambrista!* (R. Young, 1978; financed in part by PBS), *Northern Lights* (Nilsson and Hanson, 1978; financed in part by PBS) and *Heartland* (Pearce, 1980) (financed in part by the NEA).

What is of particular importance here is that the ethos of public service broadcasting became a defining factor (at least initially) for the articulation of this new independent cinema. At a time when the mainstream film industry was moving towards the era of ancillary profits (video, cable and pay-TV in particular), this brand of independent filmmaking was occupied with voicing alternative views, representing minorities, examining social problems, uncovering 'hidden histories', in short dealing with subject matter that commercial television and (largely) film avoided. This is the point when American independent feature filmmaking became widely perceived as a vehicle for the articulation of alternative voices and political positions and therefore clearly different from other forms or brands of independent filmmaking, such as top-rank and exploitation cinema.

The first new independent films were released theatrically either by existing art-film distributors, such as New Yorker Films, distributor of *My*

Dinner with Andre (Malle, 1981), which treated them as 'American art-house' pictures (giving them limited release and booking them to specialty theatres), or by other small distributors in search for any type of product during the cut-throat environment of the late 1970s (such as Levitt-Pickman, distributor of *Heartland*). Almost immediately, however, a new infrastructure in support of this type of filmmaking started emerging, especially after the commercial success of *Return of the Secaucus 7* in 1980 (which grossed $2 million on a $60,000 budget – see Case study 6.2). New distributors such as the Samuel Goldwyn Company (established in 1978 by Samuel Goldwyn Jr., son of the legendary independent producer and once part-owner of United Artists), Island Pictures (established in 1982 and re-labelled Island/Alive in 1983), Castle Hill Productions (established in 1980) and Cinecom (established in 1982), all formed within a few years of each other, were dedicated specifically to releasing this type of film while occasionally also distributing successful non-US films (Chapter 8 gives more on the institutional support for independent films).

With an institutional apparatus in the making, the new American independent cinema started demonstrating some commercial potential: *My Dinner with Andre* ($1.9 million gross); *Chan Is Missing* (Wang, 1982; distributed by New Yorker Films – $1 million); *Eating Raoul* (Bartel, 1982; co-distributed by Quartet Films and 20th Century Fox-International Classics – $4.7 million); *El Norte* (Nava, 1984; distributed by Island/Alive – $2.2 million); *Stranger Than Paradise* (Jarmusch, 1984; distributed by the Samuel Goldwyn Company – $2.5 million); *Blood Simple* (Coen and Coen, 1984; distributed by Circle Films – $2.1 million); and *She's Gotta Have It* (Spike Lee, 1986; distributed by Island Pictures – $7.1 million).[55] As Peter Biskind put it:

> where before there had been a trickle of poorly funded documentaries, supplemented by the occasional underfinanced grainy feature, there was now a comparative flood of slick, reasonably well produced theatrical pictures … suddenly there seemed to be an indie *movement* … the hope was that these home-grown filmmakers would generate the energy, excitement and box office that Ingmar Bergman, the Italians and the French New Wave had enjoyed in the 1960s.[56]

Despite the fast emergence of an institutional framework dedicated to it, the new independent cinema of the late 1970s and early 1980s was clearly a cinema of filmmakers and especially of directors (often writer-directors). While in the low-budget exploitation sector during the previous decades it was the distributor or the production-distribution company that was primarily defining the film (Republic, Monogram, AIP, New World Pictures – with filmmakers like Edgar G. Ulmer, William Castle and Roger Corman being the exceptions), in the landscape of the new American independent cinema a film like *Return of the Secaucus 7* was an 'independent film' and 'a John Sayles' film but not 'a Libra/Specialty [the film's co-distributors] film'. In this respect, this type of cinema was certainly reminiscent of the cinema of John Cassavetes, whose personal approach to filmmaking became one of the key influences on this wave of independents. On the other hand, it was also reminiscent of the Hollywood Renaissance, another brand of independent cinema revolving around the filmmaker and often embracing oppositional values. The main differences between the two were: the Hollywood Renaissance filmmakers were allowed to work within the majors, while the new independents were not; and even though the Hollywood Renaissance filmmakers made relatively low-budget films, their budgets were large compared with the miniscule budgets of the new independents.

Conclusion

The emergence and relative commercial success of the first new independent films of the late 1970s and early 1980s once again demonstrated that the oligopolisation of American cinema – this time by the infinitely-more-powerful-than-the-studios conglomerates – was impossible. Commercial independent filmmaking persisted in spite of the squeezing of the exploitation sector, the total appropriation of top-rank independent production by the conglomerated majors, and the absence of any serious source of funding. It transmogrified into ultra-low-budget, quality film production that took place away from the influence of the majors, while a distinct institutional apparatus that would eventually support and define it was emerging. Independent production became the province of the individual filmmaker, who was no longer in need of the (until then necessary) backing of a large national distributor to finance, market and release his or her film.

The independent film movement of the late 1970s and early 1980s assumed a central position within the discourse of American independent cinema, as it was different from mainstream filmmaking both in terms of production-distribution and in terms of aesthetics, while it was also far removed from the disreputable exploitation filmmaking. As such, it laid a particularly strong claim to the label, while the success of some of the films ensured that the word 'independent' would enter public discourse, signifying a very particular type of film as the decades progressed.

Case study 6.2 The godfather of contemporary American independent cinema: John Sayles and *Return of the Secaucus 7*

> *Return of the Secaucus 7* (John Sayles, 1980, 110 min.), produced by Salsipuedes Productions; distributed by Libra/Specialty.

Perhaps because of its unexpected commercial success and John Sayles's distinguished later career, which continues into the 2010s, *Return of the Secaucus 7 (Secaucus)* is often seen as a point of departure for contemporary American independent cinema, while the filmmaker's name is always included on the list of the most influential filmmakers of the sector. Financed by Sayles himself, who wrote, directed, edited and played a small part in the film, and released by two tiny distributors, Specialty Films and Libra Films, *Secaucus* is in many ways a paradigmatic film for independent cinema in the late 1970s and early 1980s in the US.

After a successful early career as a fiction writer, Sayles quickly moved to screenwriting with a job at New World Pictures. There he scripted a number of successful exploitation films, including *Piranha* (Dante, 1978), *Alligator* (Teague, 1980) and *The Howling* (Dante, 1981). It was during the early days of his apprenticeship at Corman's company when Sayles decided to make his own film. By March 1978, he had already finished the screenplay for *Secaucus*, a story about the reunion of seven friends who used to be politically active during their college years at the height of counterculture. With savings from three screenwriting jobs and the income from the publication of his fiction, Sayles put together $40,000 out of $125,000 necessary for the production of the film. Securing an extra $20,000 from further screenwriting work and by deferring the rest of the budget, Sayles was able to start production with no external financing (Rosen, 1990, p. 183). As a matter of fact, he declined an offer of investment in his film by Roger Corman in order to maintain complete control over every aspect of the film (Molyneaux, 2000, p. 23).

During the principal cinematography stage, which lasted five weeks, Sayles took a number of creative decisions that were determined by budgetary constraints. He took out of the script elaborate – and therefore expensive – camera movements; he employed non-union actors, who were paid much less than the Screen Actors Guild normally specified; he shot the film in and around a ski resort which he had rented off-season for a fraction of the normal price; he used a 16mm camera; and he used his experience at penny-pinching New World Pictures to come up with ways to keep production costs low. Following the end of the shooting, Sayles and Maggie Renzi (the film's producer and Sayles's life partner) hired an editing table and taught themselves how to edit the film.

The film was selected for Filmex, the Los Angeles Film Festival, in 1979. It was received well by the public and attracted the interest of three distributors, United Artists Classics, Libra Films and Specialty Films. Sayles decided to make a deal with Specialty Films, a very small, Seattle-based releasing company, which was established by the owner of a West Coast art-house film exhibition chain to ensure constant product supply to these theatres. Furthermore, Sayles and Specialty brought Libra Films in on the deal as a subcontractor to handle distribution in the East Coast, a region where Specialty did not feel it knew the market well.

Lacking the resources and financial muscle of a national theatrical distributor, Specialty and Libra devised what is known as a grassroots approach to the film's distribution. They concentrated on a small number of important film markets (New York, Chicago, Seattle, San Francisco, Los Angeles, Boston and Washington, DC) and tried to reach their target audience (the 1960s generation) on a personal level, with strategies such as direct mailing, advertising in local communities, pre-screenings for influential local people (film critics, community leaders and so on) and other word-of-mouth promotional activities. As the film's release coincided with the disastrous opening of *Heaven's Gate*, the distributors used this to promote Sayles's film as the anti-*Heaven's Gate*, a picture of modest origins with a good script, compared with the $44 million fiasco of the conglomerate-owned United Artists, which was panned universally. Furthermore, the marketing campaign also focused on Sayles and his transition from writer to filmmaker.

Despite a poor opening in New York and San Francisco, the release of the film in the other regional markets was very successful. Fuelled with an award from the Society of Los Angeles Film Critics to Sayles for Best Original Screenplay and with the film's inclusion in many '10 best' lists around the country, the film reopened in New York. Accompanied by the clever ad line, 'the film everyone's missed' (Rosen, 1990, p. 193), the film became a success, playing in one Manhattan theatre for 22 weeks and opening elsewhere in New York. The film eventually grossed more than $2 million from its first theatrical run.

What is immediately evident from the first shots of the film is that this is not a glossy Hollywood production. Sayles's realistic dialogue and location shooting provide the film with a sense of verisimilitude that is absent from the big-budget productions of the time. As the story revolves around a reunion of seven friends with a common political past, the film's emphasis is placed heavily on their interaction, especially their verbal exchanges (as one large group or in smaller units). Throughout the film the spectator gradually discovers their secrets, their political views, their romantic/sexual inclinations, the ties that bind them together and their relation to each other and to the group as a whole.

As a result, the film's narrative is structured in a loose manner, driven by small incidents that occur to individual members of the group during the reunion (how will Jeff react to the news that his partner, Maura, slept with J.T.? Will Frances succumb to Ron's sexual advances?) or by larger enigmas that turn out to be irrelevant to the unfolding of the story (will Chip, the only outsider and the audience's surrogate, be accepted by the rest of the group?). The absence of a heavily structured narrative trajectory allows the question of how these people have coped in the real world after their activist years – the real subject of the film – to be explored without the help of the usual narrative tricks (suspense, deadlines and the pursuit of clear-cut goals).

To avoid a theatrical aesthetic of 'filmed conversations' Sayles interjects a couple of 'action' sequences. In one sequence, the male characters play basketball and Sayles, the editor, gradually speeds up the editing pattern of the scene as the spectator expects that Jeff (who has just found out that J.T. has slept with his partner) will hurt J.T. Although the aesthetic of the scene is somewhat at odds with the rest of the film, it nevertheless stands as the closest thing to a climactic narrative sequence, as, in the end, Jeff does instigate an injury (only a slight one) on J.T. In the second action scene, the male characters dive repeatedly into a river while the female characters admire their (the male characters') naked bodies. Apart from presenting an opportunity for action in beautiful scenery, the scene raises the question of women's (and the spectator's) visual pleasure from the male naked body, reversing an extremely strong tradition in American cinema where the spectator's visual pleasure is almost entirely associated with looking at the female body. Although both scenes add pace in the film, *Secaucus* remains a dialogue-driven exploration of the death of political radicalism and a comment on the destiny of the 1960s generation under the threat of the New Right.

After *Secaucus*, Sayles established a consistent career in the independent sector, with the exception of *Baby, It's You* (1983), which he made for Paramount. With a body of 18 feature films in 36 years, including the commercially successful *The Secret of Roan Inish* (1994) and *Lone Star* (1996), Sayles has remained an influential voice in American independent cinema, especially as his films continue to tackle social and political issues that major film productions and newer independents rarely do: civic corruption and its effects on small town politics (*City of Hope*, 1991); corporate capitalism (*Sunshine State*, 2001); racism (*The Brother from Another Planet*, 1984, and *Lone Star* 1996); change of sexual identity (*Lianna*, 1983); disability (*Passion Fish*, 1992); the labour movement (*Matewan*, 1987)]; and so on.

Notes

1　Balio, 1987, p. 303.
2　Decca Records, the controlling company of Universal, had already been bought by MCA, a talent agency with interest in television production, in 1962. In order for the takeover to be allowed by the US Justice Department MCA had to divest itself of its talent agency holdings.
3　In 1977, it was estimated that the top six grossing films of the year were responsible for approximately one-third of all income generated from the 199 releases of the year (Davis, 1997, p. 116).
4　The figure is taken from Finler, 2003, p. 366.
5　Biskind, 1998, p. 402.

6 Balio, 1987, p. 303.

7 Cook, 2000, pp. 99 and 133.

8 Finler, 2003, pp. 359–60. For a fascinating account of audience research and how its results informed the production of *Star Wars*, see Earnest, 1985, pp. 1–18.

9 Finler, 2003, p. 366.

10 Finler, 2003, p. 379.

11 Both figures for audience attendance are taken from Finler, 2003, p 379.

12 Monaco, 2001, p. 37.

13 'AIP Announces Biggest Product Line-Up History', 1970, pp. 1 and 3.

14 Barron, 1978, p. 1.

15 Wyatt, 1998a, p. 76.

16 Crown is an exception here as it distributed only 6–10 films per year.

17 The figures are taken from Finler, 2003, pp. 366–7.

18 Lowry, 2005, p. 43.

19 'In Times Like These, Film Fare Trend Should Be Escapist, AIP Reasons', 1970.

20 Hillier, 1994, p. 47.

21 Hillier, 1994, p. 47.

22 For more information on the distribution history of the film, see Wyatt, 1998b, pp. 74–5.

23 'Crown Int'l to Celebrate 15th Anniversary in '74', 1973.

24 According to an MPAA-commissioned survey in 1977, 57 per cent of all tickets were bought by people who were under 25 years old (Cook, 2000, p. 23).

25 Davis, 1997, p. 111.

26 Cook, 2000, p. 262.

27 Cook, 2000, p. 257.

28 The figures are taken from Cook, 2000, p. 335.

29 The figures are taken from Cook, 2000, p. 16.

30 The figures in Table 6.2 are taken from: Isenberg, 1970, pp. 1 and 17; Getze, 1974; 'Record Profits Gross for AIP as 20th Year Winds', 1974, pp. 1 and 18; and '$2.9 Mil A.I. Profits for Fiscal 1976 on Record Gross Income', 1976, pp. 1 and 4.

31 The figure for *Jaws*' budget is taken from Cook, 2000, p. 41. The figure for AIP's credit line is taken from 'AIP Free of Debt, Bank Loan Repaid', 1975.

32 The figure is quoted in McBride, 1976, pp. 1 and 4.

33 Cook, 2000, pp. 11–12.

34 Cook, 2000, pp. 12 and 312.

35 Segers, 1975, pp. 3 and 38.

36 'American International Draws Lotsa Exhibs to N.Y. "Advance"', 1977.

37 'AIP Orders 3835 Prints for Six Summer Releases', 1977.

38 Levin, Gerry, 1977; 'AIP-Filmways Merger Dropped, Says Arkoff', 1978.

39 'Major Revolving Credit Pact Finalized by AIP', 1977; 'American International Pictures, Filmways Inc. Terminate Merger Plan', 1978.

40 'Tax Credits Substantial Factor in AIP's Fiscal Year Profits', 1977; 'Legal Steps Re Filmways-AIP "Conditions" Unstated; Don March's Future Influence Awaits Clarity', 1979.

41 Murphy, 1978.

42 For a brief account of the deal, see 'AIP – Filmways Nuptial Contract: Arkoff's Working, and Exit, Pay; Answers Only to Richard Block', 1979, pp. 4 and 32.

43 Lewis, 1995, p. 35. The company had already dropped 'Pictures' from its name in the early 1970s, having become American International.

44 Lowry, 2005, pp. 48–9.
45 The figures are taken from Hillier, 1986, p. 51.
46 The figure is taken from Hillier, 1986, p. 53.
47 Barron, 1978, p. 1.
48 Schreger, 1978, pp. 1 and 6.
49 Ryan and Kellner, 1990, p. 11.
50 Balio, 1987, p. 341.
51 Biskind, 2005, p. 19.
52 Edgerton, 1986, p. 41.
53 Daressa, 1986, p. 56.
54 Richter, 1986, p. 22.
55 The figures are taken from Biskind, 2005, p. 17.
56 Biskind, 2005, p. 17, original italics.

Part IV

Contemporary American independent cinema (1980s to date)

7

Mini-majors and major independents

Introduction

As the conglomeration of the film industry was in full swing in the late 1970s, the development of new technologies such as cable and pay-cable television, home video and (during the 1980s) satellite television created new lucrative markets for the exploitation of the feature film. Gradually, the theatrical run became only one – though still extremely important – avenue for the commercial exploitation of a film, before it found its way to the ancillary markets. With the commodity already produced, the only expenses involved included new marketing campaigns tailor-made for the particular demographics the new exhibition technologies served, and the cost of the transfer to the new format (such as the production of video cassettes). Realising that the ancillary markets could exponentially increase the profits from film production, the conglomerate owners of the majors moved to control all those markets.

This move became particularly evident in the early and mid-1980s, when the conglomerates started downsizing their interests in other areas, concentrating instead on expanding their holdings in the entertainment and leisure fields. The result of this process was that the conglomerates evolved gradually into fully diversified entertainment corporations. This evolution was characterised by a wave of mergers and takeovers in which the parent companies of the former studios acquired or established a large number of entertainment-related divisions to accompany their film-producing and film-distributing subsidiaries. The main consequence of this development was the creation of a horizontal industrial structure whereby all the divisions of the conglomerate were in the business of distributing and promoting different formats and versions of the same product, a feature film that was originally financed and distributed by the majors. This 'interdependency of cultural production and distribution', which is often referred to as 'synergy', influenced immensely the trajectory of mainstream American cinema, as these companies increasingly privileged the production of properties that could be easily exploited in ancillary markets. In other words, they privileged the production of films that could attract repeat viewings (because of the stars they featured, the special effects they contained, the music that accompanied them and so on).[1]

The introduction of all these distribution technologies signalled the creation of new exhibition outlets, all of which needed sufficient product to operate cost-effectively. At a time when the majors were distributing just over 100 films a year on average, it was clear that demand for films would be staggering. Exploiting their existing film libraries (licensing their old films for exhibition in the cable and video markets) was one of the main measures the majors took, but the demand was mainly for new product. This became particularly evident in the mid-1980s, when the home video market showed a tremendous growth (from 1,850,000 VCR sets in 78,000,000 households [2.4 per cent penetration] in 1980, the number reached 32,000,000 in 87,400,000 households [37.2 per cent penetration] in 1986, on the way to 67.6 per cent penetration three years later).[2] With pay-cable subscriptions exceeding slightly the number of VCRs in 1986 (32,500,000 subscriptions),[3] it was clear that any film producer stood a chance of having their film released in one or more of the non-theatrical markets, regardless of the film's quality and often regardless of whether the film received theatrical distribution. This was particularly good news for the exploitation independents who survived the cut-throat environment of the theatrical market in the late 1970s. Companies like New World Pictures and Crown International moved almost exclusively to the home video market and took their place next to newcomers (Vestron, Vidmark, Full Moon and many others) established to exploit specifically these highly unusual circumstances.

These circumstances, however, were not auspicious only for the exploitation companies. As those low-end independents exited the theatrical market they created new gaps that larger companies like Filmways (the rebranded American International Pictures) were in no position to fill on their own. Existing theatrical distributors such as New Line Cinema and Cannon started reducing their number of imports in the early 1980s, focusing instead on the financing and distribution of American films that could be exploited more easily in the ancillary markets. Furthermore, the theatrical market saw the establishment of a number of new companies, both in the distribution business (Miramax Films) and in the production business (the De Laurentiis Entertainment Group and Orion Pictures, both of which later entered theatrical distribution). Although these companies would also feel the pressure of the majors, they would nevertheless try to survive first by feeding the many distribution pipelines of the majors before exploiting the option of branching out to ancillary markets themselves, and perhaps competing directly with the entertainment conglomerates.

These companies have been labelled – often interchangeably – 'mini-majors' or 'major independents' and represent a new development in the independent sector. Although a concrete definition for both terms is still largely elusive, Justin Wyatt and Jim Hillier have offered some useful suggestions. On the one hand, Wyatt argues that major independents are the hybrid production and distribution companies that were allowed a large degree of creative autonomy after they were taken over by a conglomerate parent.[4] This makes New Line Cinema and Miramax major independents after their respective takeovers by Turner Broadcasting System in 1994 and the Disney Corporation in 1993, respectively. On the other hand, Hillier suggests that a mini-major is an adequately capitalised independent production and distribution company that 'operate[s] – or tried to operate – outside the orbit of the majors', but which has set itself up as a smaller version of a major.[5] This definition makes pre-1994 New Line Cinema and a company such as Orion Pictures mini-majors. Although such definitions are somewhat problematic (the first one uses the term 'independent' when a company is a subsidiary of a conglomerate; the second presents the companies simply as smaller majors and does not allow space for qualitative differences between majors and mini-majors), they nevertheless provide a platform from which one can explore this relatively new phenomenon in the independent sector in some detail.

Whether labelled mini-majors or major independents, Orion, Miramax, New Line and a few others were responsible for the production, finance and/ or release of a very large percentage of US films during the 1980s, 1990s and 2000s. As they were not owned by a conglomerate parent company (at least until 1993 for Miramax and 1994 for New Line), but mainly because they worked with much lower budgets and with more unusual film material than the majors, these companies became part of the discourse of American independent cinema. Very soon each company had found its own niche in the American film market: Orion became known for the production of mid-budget, quality films; New Line became particularly associated with low-budget horror films, such as the *Nightmare on Elm Street* series in the 1980s and with the very successful *Teenage Mutant Ninja Turtles* franchise in the early 1990s; while Miramax, originally specialising in the marketing and distribution of controversial films from the UK and the US, eventually took over Orion's place in the industry after moving to the production and distribution of mid-budget quality films with the potential for crossover success.

Together, these 'independents' contributed to the institutionalisation of American independent cinema, as they provided a large part of the infrastructure for the development of a thriving brand of filmmaking that presented several differences from mainstream filmmaking (the blockbusters and star-studded vehicles of the majors). The concept of the institutionalisation of American independent cinema will be discussed in detail in the following chapter. This chapter will concentrate on the phenomenon of mini-majors as particular examples of independent companies within the American film industry in the 1980s. As the subject has been under-researched, the chapter will undertake a thorough examination of one such mini-major, Orion Pictures, and will discuss in detail its organisation, structure, conduct of business and especially its position in the industry. Even though Orion went bankrupt in December 1991, it was widely considered throughout the 1980s as 'a sanctuary for creative filmmakers', who could not make the films they wanted within the conglomerate environment of 1980s Hollywood.[6] For this reason, this chapter will pay particular attention to the measures the company took to avoid the possibility of a corporate takeover and thus retain its independence amidst a small number of fully diversified entertainment conglomerates.

A star is born

Orion came into existence in February 1978, when five top executives left United Artists after disagreeing with the executives of Transamerica, the corporate parent of UA, and formed a new company.[7] The departure of Arthur Krim, Robert Benjamin, Eric Pleskow, Morris 'Mike' Medavoy and William Bernstein sent shockwaves through Hollywood mainly because Krim and Benjamin had been running UA for 27 years but also because of its unprecedented nature. As in UA, Krim became the chairman of the newly founded company with Benjamin acting as co-chairman and Pleskow as president and chief executive officer, whereas Bernstein and Medavoy assumed the positions of executive vice-president of business affairs and of worldwide production, respectively.

The industrial reputation of the Orion executives brought in willing investors immediately after the company's formation. Warner Bros. quickly established a distribution deal with Orion and helped the new company raise $90 million in financing.[8] The deal saw Orion becoming Warner's first satellite film production company, in the same way that Warner's music division had a number of satellite labels (Warner/Reprise, Atlantic, Elektra and Asylum) under its orbit, labels which were autonomous in terms of management and creative decisions, but which had to use Warner's distribution apparatus to place their product in the market. This type of arrangement specified that Warner Bros. and Orion were equal partners in a new company called Orion Ventures Inc. Orion would have complete autonomy and control over the 'number and type of films' made and Warner Bros. would 'market and distribute the films', even though, according to the contract, Orion would be also granted 'the broadest autonomy and control over distribution and advertising'.[9]

Although the model of Orion Ventures Inc. with its substantial financing and its seemingly favourable terms gave the five executives an excellent opportunity to re-enter the film business at a time when the average negative cost for a film was still relatively low, it nevertheless proved to be problematic for both partners. Questions of authority and control over Orion's projects were raised even within the first six months of the partnership.[10] Marketing and distribution, in particular, became a moot point in the two companies' conduct of business, as Warner Bros. had the ultimate say in such matters, despite the above-cited contract clause. Thus Orion-produced films with some box office potential such as *A Little Romance* (Hill, 1979), a love story that featured Laurence Olivier, and, especially, *The Great Santini* (Carlino, 1979), a gritty drama with Robert Duvall, which was released on three different occasions with modified marketing campaigns, did not manage to find an audience partly because of the way they were handled upon their release by the major.

Furthermore, Warner Bros.' foreign distribution offices were empowered to veto the release of Orion's films if they thought that they would not perform well in specific markets, which could deprive Orion of potential profits.[11] Finally, and perhaps more importantly, Orion was not in a position to deliver to Warner Bros. the stratospheric profits that the expensive, effects-laden, action/adventure-oriented films were bringing to the other majors. With Orion's line of credit set at $90 million, it was obvious that the company could not afford to make such films. As a matter of fact, Orion had to pass on *Raiders of the Lost Ark* (Spielberg, 1981) due to its high cost and the principal players' demands from the film's gross. As Medavoy put it:

> the deal was too one-sided, which was the reason why we passed … But basically Lucas, in effect, really was the co-financier, and that becomes the tail that wagged the dog. But at the same time, in effect, really talent is going around saying, 'Hey, we're worth so much and we're willing to throw in our talent in exchange for control and rights'.[12]

Coupled with Warner Bros.' charging Orion a distribution fee which extended from 30 per cent for domestic releases to 40 per cent for worldwide ones, the risks in producing an event film were much higher for Orion in the case of box office flops, as Warner Bros. would be the first party to collect money from the film's gross, in the form of a distribution fee. In other words, Orion was not in a position to follow the signs of the time in the American film industry, signs that were overwhelmingly pointing towards the direction of blockbuster and star-driven high-concept films.

Between 1978 and 1982 Orion produced 23 films for Warner Bros. Of these, only two were big hits, *10* (Edwards, 1981) and *Arthur* (Gordon, 1981), both vehicles for Dudley Moore, with rentals of $37 and $42 million, respectively,[13] six were moderate successes, while the other 15 films lost money at the US box office.[14] With the above results hardly demonstrating a high-flying start for Orion or substantial profits for Warner Bros., both partners in the venture felt that the arrangement was not working out. In fact, shortly after Orion had passed on *Raiders of the Lost Ark*, Krim had sent a memo to his partners in which he explained that the risks in the filmmaking business had become considerably higher for companies that were not in the distribution business, so much so that if a film company did not possess an extensive library of titles, it could not aspire to remain competitive in the long run.[15] Krim's memo essentially mapped Orion's aspirations to become a producer-distributor that would have the power to exploit its films in various ancillary markets, mirroring practices associated with the Hollywood majors. In other words, Krim wanted to turn Orion into a mini-major.

The company decided to venture into the distribution business before its contract with Warner Bros. expired. As its first priority Orion set out to acquire a film library from an existing independent company. After briefly entertaining the possibility of taking over Embassy Pictures (which by that time had shifted its attention to television production) and Allied Artists (which was deemed too small for Orion's plans) Orion targeted Filmways. Despite a few hits in the early 1980s such as *The Amityville Horror* (Rosenberg, 1980) and *Love at First Bite* (Dragoti, 1980), Filmways had been experiencing severe financial difficulties, to the extent that it could not afford the marketing costs for a number of completed films that awaited distribution, including Milos Forman's *Ragtime* and Brian De Palma's *Blow Out*.[16] With its stock at a very attractive price, a partnership of companies fronted by Orion and including, among others, Home Box Office (HBO), a recently formed cable broadcaster, bought out Filmways for $26 million.

Almost immediately the new owners started bringing Filmways around by selling the company's non-media-related subsidiaries. A few months later, on 30 July 1982, the name Orion officially replaced the name Filmways.[17] In order to distribute the two unreleased Filmways films, especially the eagerly anticipated *Ragtime*, Orion established the first of a series of deals with HBO, which mainly revolved around the pre-selling of film rights to the cable channel and the subsequent use of the generated revenue to market and distribute the films theatrically.[18] However, the most important element in the Filmways takeover was that Orion acquired its library of approximately 950 titles. This meant that Orion could enter the distribution business in both theatrical and ancillary markets, at a time when VCRs had started taking the US market by storm. In addition, Orion demonstrated an appetite for competing directly with the established powers in the arena of theatrical distribution by announcing plans to release at least one picture per month and, in the words of Eric Pleskow, 'to be as voluminous a supplier of motion pictures to the world as any other company'.[19]

The new Orion constellation

Orion entered the theatrical distribution business almost fully adhering to its plan to release one film per month for the second half of 1982: *A Midsummer Night's Sex Comedy* (Woody Allen) in July; *Summer Lovers* (Kleiser) in August; *First Blood* (Kotcheff) in October; and *Split Image* (Kotcheff) in November. *First Blood*, in particular, which starred Sylvester Stallone, became by far the most profitable film in that period, grossing more than $45 million at the US box office.[20] Orion had bought the domestic rights from Carolco for $8 million, a substantial price for a company just entering the business, and invested heavily in the marketing of the film. With several millions of pure profit just from *First Blood* in its first year as a distributor, Orion was this time off to a flying start, even though it failed to secure sequel rights in what was destined to become a significant franchise in the 1980s.[21]

In 1983 Orion established a new division, Orion Classics, to handle art-house foreign films in the American market. The decision to create the Classics division saw Orion following a new trend in Hollywood, which marked the majors' attempt to control the specialised art-house film market (see Chapter 8). The formation of Orion Classics became a platform for a second mass departure of executives from United Artists, which by that time did not bear any resemblance to the glorious major company of past decades. Tom Bernard, Donna Gigliotti and Michael Barker, the executive team at United Artist Classics, accepted the invitation to lead the new Orion division and, in a way, continue the policies that had helped UA Classics dominate this niche market for the previous four years. Besides the team's unquestionable savvy in the art-house market, the parent company hoped that they would also lure European talent to Orion at a time when the company enjoyed almost no previously established relations with Hollywood talent.[22]

Distribution of the in-house Orion production slate started in early 1983. The first two films released were *Lone Wolf McQuade* (Carver), with the then extremely popular Chuck Norris, and the Richard Gere vehicle *Breathless* (McBride), a remake of Godard's *À Bout se Souffle* (1959). Both films were moderate successes and the same can be said for Carlos Saura's *Carmen*, which became the first film to be released by the Classics division. For the newly established Orion moderate successes were still successes. As Medavoy stated in *Variety*: 'if every picture on [t]here broke even I'd be very happy', a surprising statement considering the essentially capitalist nature of the film business but, more importantly, a sign of the somewhat different path Orion was willing to follow.[23]

Orion's modest business philosophy opens up the debate on the position of the company within the Hollywood industrial landscape in the 1980s and whether a film company with such a mentality could be included in the club of the majors, even as the smallest of them, as Stephen Prince has suggested.[24] As we will see, Orion drifted between this modest approach articulated by its head of production in 1983 and a more piecemeal attempt to expand to the major league (especially after the success of its 1986–7 film output). The obvious lack of coherence in Orion's business strategies turned out to be a costly mistake, as the company was left behind at a time when the established majors were in the process of achieving full vertical and horizontal integration and moving entirely into the business of making blockbusters in the 1990s.

Immediately after the modest success of its first titles, Orion revealed plans to compete directly with the major studios. For the period between July and December 1983, the company announced plans to release nine films, with another 14 features scheduled for 1984. The lion's share of the 1984 production slate was in the last quarter of the year, when *The Cotton Club* (the new Francis

Figure 7.1 *Back to School*: the Rodney Dangerfield vehicle gave Orion Pictures an unexpected $100 million hit. Only the Oscar-winning *Platoon*, *Dances with Wolves* and *The Silence of the Lambs* proved financially more successful in the company's history.

Ford Coppola film), *Amadeus* (the new Milos Forman film) and *The Terminator* (a science fiction action/adventure film with Arnold Schwarzenegger) were to be released. Most of the films distributed between 1983 and 1984, however, failed at the box office (only *Amadeus*, *The Terminator* and Gene Wilder's *The Woman in Red* returned profits). Despite this drawback, the company persisted with a record 15 features for 1985 and yet again aimed to release them at a steady rate (approximately one film per month) to prove to exhibitors that it was a reliable supplier of film product.

The year 1985 proved to be a very successful one for the company. Films such as *The Terminator, The Woman in Red, Code of Silence* (Davis) and *Desperately Seeking Susan* (Seidelman) performed well at the US box office, whereas *Back to School* (Metter) proved to be the biggest hit of all, approaching the $100 million mark.[25] This success set the foundations for a record 17 pictures scheduled for release in 1986, mostly in-house productions. These 17 films were to be wholly financed by Orion with funds accumulated through deals with HBO.[26] According to *Variety*, only the 1985 deals with HBO brought Orion funds within the region of $50–75 million, bringing up the level of total revenue that the company generated from its partnership with HBO (since 1982) to in excess of $150 million.[27]

The shining star

The success of Orion's films in 1985 and the deals the company made with HBO convinced American banks that Orion was on its way to 'major status' and for that reason they extended its credit line from $100 million to $200 million. With advances from the above deals and from a major pact with RCA/ Columbia, which acquired the foreign home-video rights to Orion's theatrical releases, the company accumulated enough capital to finance every major picture that went into production in the second half of 1985 and 1986 (for release in 1987) with an average cost of $7.5–8 million.[28]

In fact, the only dark moment in Orion's business trajectory at the time was the spectacular failure of *The Cotton Club*, which cost around $46 million and grossed only $25.9 million. However, despite the disappointing box office figures of Coppola's gangster-musical epic, Orion continued to record healthy profits.[29]

Towards the end of 1985 the Orion management struck more deals with foreign distributors for the rights of its theatrical releases. In addition, and with an eye to ancillary markets, Orion negotiated deals with foreign cable television companies in several western European countries.[30] Finally, in December 1985, Orion announced plans to form its own home-video division in order to increase its profits from that particularly lucrative ancillary market. Up to that point, the Orion titles had been distributed by independent video companies such as Vestron and Thorn EMI in the US and by RCA/Columbia in the rest of the world. Since the deals for both the US and abroad were due to expire at the end of 1987, Orion postponed the launch of its home-video subsidiary (Orion Home Entertainment) until December 1987.[31] Additionally, and in the fashion of a diversified company, Orion had commanded a large share of profits from network television with the phenomenally successful series *Cagney and Lacey*, which since 1985 had also started an extremely lucrative career in syndication.

By the end of 1985, Orion seemed to be moving firmly in the same direction the majors had taken since the mid-to late 1970s, namely horizontal integration, with several divisions of the company specialising in different entertainment areas. At the same time, however, Arthur Krim continued to ground the company's production output in the low- to mid-budget region, while explicitly refusing to place Orion in the same league as the majors, which were in the blockbuster business. For the Orion chairman, the company's future would involve minimum-risk investment and more co-financing deals to avoid big financial disasters.[32] This incoherent approach to the filmmaking business exemplified Orion's history in the second half of the 1980s and, as mentioned earlier, proved fatal for the long-term future of the company.

In the short term, however, Krim's philosophy seemed to pay off handsomely. 1986 was the year of *Platoon* (Stone), a $5.4 million, independently financed film about the Vietnam War that had previously been rejected by all major studios. Orion, which bought the film's rights from Hemdale, opened the film on a platform release (opening the film in a small number of screens and waiting for word-of-mouth to build up) and watched it do impressive business. It went on to gross $137 million at the North American box office alone and become the highest money-earner in Orion's history to that point, while also winning four Oscars (including one for Best Picture) in 1987.

The success of *Platoon* convinced Orion that the market for low- to mid-budget films (in the $6–10 million range) was still lucrative and that the company – in the absence of the majors – was in a position to control it. That market, however, was even less stable than the market for blockbusters, mainly because even blockbusters that failed at the box office were still in a better position than mid-budget films to recoup part of their cost from the ancillary profit centres, especially those associated with merchandising. If, on the other hand, a $10 million film failed to find an audience in its theatrical outing, it would be extremely difficult for the distributor to get even a small part of its investment back apart from distribution in cable, video and television, as the film's failure in its theatrical run would largely predetermine its performance in those ancillary markets.

The extraordinary financial success of *Platoon* and of other solid hits such as *Hannah and Her Sisters* (Woody Allen, 1986) pushed Orion for the first three months of 1987 to number one at the US box office.[33] Orion was ready to continue its monthly releases with increasingly expensive films such as *Robocop* (Verhoeven) and *No Way Out* (Donaldson) scheduled for the summer months in direct competition with the summer blockbusters of the majors. With the Classics division also securing record financial results from the distribution of art-house box office champions such as *Jean de Florette* (Berri, 1986), Orion retained its top position at the box office for the following three months of 1987.

Inevitably, the increased rentals brought about plans for further expansion. With the line-up of films for the following season looking strong, especially the comedy *Throw Momma from the Train* (DeVito, 1987), and with the establishment of a home-video subsidiary already arranged for the end of 1987, Orion's executives started exploring the possibility of entering the exhibition arena. After Reagan's *laissez-faire* policies reversed the Paramount decree of 1948, the majors had started re-acquiring theatres, especially in large metropolitan areas. Even though theatre ownership by a production/distribution company in the 1980s did not automatically indicate the same benefits of the vertical integration of the studio era, it nevertheless meant tighter diversification and further control of all exhibition outlets.[34] Although it is debatable whether a company without a corporate parent such as Orion had the financial muscle to expand aggressively in that area, the Orion executives, in theory at least, seemed to be willing to follow the majors' path and invest in theatre acquisition.

Orion's venture into exhibition did not materialise, however. In later interviews, both Pleskow and Medavoy admitted that the company could never afford the purchase of theatre chains, while its plans for expansion to exhibition was part of a rhetoric aiming to demonstrate that Orion was not lagging far behind the majors.[35] By the end of 1987, the company had slipped at the box office to fourth place. The rentals from its successful films such as *Throw Momma from the Train* were offset by the financial failures of films such as *Best Seller* (Flynn, 1987) and *House of Games* (Mamet, 1987), and the company's financial stability was further threatened when in March 1988 its accounts revealed a long-term debt of 64 per cent of capitalisation.[36] Most of the heavy debt had originated from the company's extensive borrowing for the establishment of the home-video arm and the executives' belief that once they released films from the company's library for video exploitation they would be able to record more profits. The ex-AIP library, however, did not exactly consist of major titles with considerable potential in that ancillary market.

More importantly, the differences between Orion and the established majors had started to show as Orion did not have a corporate parent to guarantee the flow of capital under difficult circumstances (such as a series of box office failures) and did not own production facilities or possess any real estate that it could use as collateral to raise funds. From that point on, Orion entered a period of decline which could not have been reversed despite record rentals from such successful releases as *Dances with Wolves* (Costner, 1990) and *The Silence of the Lambs* (Demme, 1991).

The fading star

In order to safeguard the company's independence, Arthur Krim had convinced John Kluge, one of the richest businessmen in the US, to become the largest shareholder in Orion and thus fend off any takeover suitors, if and when they ever appeared. When Viacom, a large cable television operator, which had diversified into all areas of entertainment, made such a move for Orion, Kluge went to extreme lengths to keep the company independent, eventually acquiring himself a controlling interest as large as 72 per cent.[37] This meant that Kluge had made a large investment in Orion and, not surprisingly, expected to see good financial results. If the returns from the late 1987 line-up were disappointing, the 1988 slate looked more promising, with star-studded films such as Ron Shelton's *Bull Durham* (starring Kevin Costner and Susan Sarandon) and Alan Parker's Oscar-targeted *Mississippi Burning* (starring Gene Hackman and Willem Dafoe). Along with the Classics' release of the art-house smash *Camille Claudel* (Nuytten) with Isabelle Adjani and Gerard Depardieu, Orion sought to repeat its 1986–7 triumph.

However, things did not work out this time. Although *Bull Durham*, *Mississippi Burning* and other hits such as *Dirty Rotten Scoundrels* (Oz) and *Colors* (Hopper) returned rentals of approximately $20 million each, the company was not able to recoup its investment, as the above films' budgets and marketing costs were considerably higher than the production and advertising costs of Orion's earlier films. Furthermore, *Mississippi Burning*, with eight Oscar nominations, lost to *Rain Man* (Levinson) in all major categories, while Peter Yates's *The House on Carroll Street* grossed less than $0.5 million, despite positive reviews. Not surprisingly, by the end of 1988, Orion had fallen behind all the majors in terms of its percentage at the US theatrical box office.

The poor performance of the films sent Orion's debt to new heights and the company found itself in a position that did not allow much room for manoeuvre. Under these circumstances, the decision to stick to a release schedule for 15 films in 1989–90 was certainly a gamble, one that was destined to have major repercussions in the next two years, especially when the first 1989 releases were extremely disappointing in terms of their box office gross, with Woody Allen's critically acclaimed *Crimes and Misdemeanours* proving only a modest hit (around $18 million) and with *Bill and Ted's Excellent Adventure* (Herek; approximately $40 million gross) becoming the only solid hit for the company. To make things worse, *Valmont*, Milos Forman's first feature after the multi-Oscar winner *Amadeus*, proved also a major financial disaster, recording a petty $1,132,000 gross in its theatrical run. A very important reason for *Valmont's* cold reception was the fact that less than a year earlier Universal had released the extremely successful and star-studded *Dangerous Liaisons* (Frears, 1987), which, like *Valmont*, was also based on Choderlos de Laclos's novel. For a second consecutive year Orion occupied a position behind all the majors at the US box office, with 4.2 per cent market share.[38]

Orion's survival depended heavily on the production roster of 1989 scheduled for release in the following year. On paper, the line-up looked very impressive: a Robin Williams vehicle (*Cadillac Man*, Donaldson), the new Woody Allen film (*Alice*), Richard Benjamin's *Mermaids* (with Cher), the sequel to *Robocop* (*Robocop 2*, Kershner), an action film with Charlie Sheen (*Navy Seals*, Teague), a film with rising star Alec Baldwin (*Miami Blues*, Armitage), Dennis Hopper's neo-noir *The Hot Spot*, Phil Joanou's mafia picture *State of Grace* and, finally, a $20 million gamble, the revisionist western *Dances with Wolves*, which marked Kevin Costner's directorial debut. Furthermore, the company had some other films mainly as fillers for the a-film-per-month schedule as well as two potentially prestige productions, Alan Rudolph's *Love at Large* and the Arthur Miller-scripted/Karel Reisz-directed *Everybody Wins* with Nick Nolte and Debra Winger. Last but not least, the Classics division had lined up the incredibly successful, in Europe, Jean-Paul Rappeneau's *Cyrano*, which had the potential to surpass the box office record of the previous Orion Classics hit, Pedro Almodovar's *Women on the Verge of a Nervous Breakdown* (1988), which had grossed $7,179,000.

Just before the first 1990 release, however, Orion was hit by its first restructuring at the top management level. Mike Medavoy left Orion for another newly founded company, Tri-Star, a subsidiary of Columbia, HBO and CBS. Medavoy's breaking away from a team of executives who, to that point, had worked closely together for 16 years and had developed a reputation for being extremely loyal to the company and to each other clearly suggested that there were cracks in the working relationship among the Orion management team. His departure, however, coincided with a huge deal that Orion made with Sony in February 1990, according to which Columbia acquired the foreign theatrical distribution rights for the following 50 Orion productions for $175 million.[39] Although the above deal advanced Orion much-needed cash, it also excluded the company from any profits from the lucrative European market. In the very likely event that Orion had a hit, it would be Columbia that would reap the benefits.

The returns from the first films released in 1990 were not particularly encouraging, but they marked a substantial improvement over the previous two years. *Cadillac Man, Mermaids, Madhouse* (Ropelewski, a comedy with Kirstie Alley and John Laroquette) and *Navy Seals* grossed between $20 and $35 million each, proving either modest box office successes (*Navy Seals* and *Madhouse*) or modest failures (*Mermaids* and *Cadillac Man*). The second instalment of *Robocop* was a solid hit (returning $22,317,000 in rentals), as was *Cyrano*, which proved a massive hit in the art-house market, grossing in excess of $15 million and becoming the most successful foreign film release in the history of the North American box office, as well as receiving six Academy Award nominations. However, the company showed dismal results from a series of films, most of them in-house productions, which ended up grossing less than $2 million each: *The Hot Spot; State of Grace; Everybody Wins;* and *Love at Large.* As a consequence, whatever small profits the company made from its hits were easily offset by these box office flops. If *Dances with Wolves,* which was the last film to open, in December 1990, had also failed, Orion would have been in extreme financial trouble.

The last bonfires

The company's release strategy for *Dances with Wolves* was similar to the strategy it followed for *Platoon.* With the latter essentially promoted as the film that depicted 'what really happened in Vietnam', *Dances with Wolves* was promoted as a revisionist western that 'speaks the truth' about the Indian genocide by white people. And as Orion opened *Platoon* in a only few theatres to build word-of-mouth before expanding it in time for the Oscar nominations, so did it release *Dances with Wolves* in only 14 sites, before opening the film wide after an unprecedented public response.[40] With the help of 12 Oscar nominations, the film reached its peak in 1,608 engagements, accumulating an astounding $184,208,842 gross at the North American box office ($81,538,000 in rentals) and a stellar $240,000,000 in the rest of the world. Even these highly unexpected returns from the film were not substantial enough to reverse Orion's overall situation. By the time *Dances with Wolves* was at the peak of its popularity, almost three weeks before the 1990–1 Academy Awards, Orion recorded a $63 million net loss for the same fiscal year.[41]

One very important reason behind Orion's inability to capitalise on the success of *Dances with Wolves* was the fact that the producers of the film had pre-sold foreign theatrical rights to various European distributors to raise funds for the $20 million budget of the film. This of course meant that Orion did not see a single cent from the $240 million gross outside the US and Canada.[42] Still,

Orion could at least count on its share from the $81.5 million rentals from the US market, which would help distribute its 1991 films, especially what turned out to be the company's last hot property, *The Silence of the Lambs*. Released during the least commercial end-of-winter season (13 February 1991) in 1,497 theatres and as *Dances with Wolves* was still running high, the film reached block-buster success levels, grossing $130,726,716 at the US box office ($59,883,000 in rentals) and recording an equal gross in international theatrical markets. This time Orion had not made the mistake of selling the ancillary rights for the film and consequently benefited from its unexpected financial success.[43]

Although both *Dances with Wolves* and *The Silence of the Lambs* dominated the box office for most of 1991, the profits were not enough to reverse the financial results of the company. It was pretty obvious then that by the end of 1991 Orion was well on its way to bankruptcy unless it was sold to a company which had enough capital to guarantee a debt of $500 million.[44]

Unfortunately, the rest of Orion's history had a lot more to do with its attempt to resolve its financial problems than with its contributions to American cinema. *The Silence of the Lambs*, which became only the third film in the history of American cinema to win all five major Academy awards, stood as Orion's swan song.

The fall

In many respects, Orion's decline and eventual bankruptcy in 1991 was precipitated by its persistence in operating independently, especially after it seemed that it had established itself in the theatrical market as a mini-major and had made the decision to compete with the industry powers, the conglomerate-run former studios. As these companies continued their involvement in mergers and takeovers to maximise their exploitation of synergies and to control every possible distribution window, Orion's policy of independence was seen as an anachronism. For industry observers the consensus was that, by the late 1980s/early 1990s, the entertainment industry game had become far too advanced for a company with clear financial limitations such as Orion. Having missed the 'opportunity' to merge in the late 1980s, Orion had no other option but to try to survive on its own, mostly through a series of manoeuvres, which each time provided the company with the necessary means to stay in the game for a short period but never for the long run.

As the company started losing money in 1988, its main shareholder, John Kluge, tried to sell it to a number of interested parties. Despite reports that such a sale would be under the condition that the new owner would respect Krim's management regime,[45] in reality Kluge did not have a clear plan about the future of the company. According to Pleskow, interested buyers such as Canal+ were discouraged by Kluge, who would not agree a price for his controlling interest in Orion, despite protracted negotiations.[46] With Orion's debt increasing steadily in the last years of the decade it became clear, after a point, that nobody wanted to touch the company. Despite the fact that the price of Orion's share had become extremely attractive for a company with a 1,000-strong library of film titles, buyers kept away. The most significant problem with the Orion library, the only real asset of the company, valued at around $300 million, was that most of the titles were cheap exploitation features inherited from AIP (see Chapters 4 and 6), made before 1982, and with little potential in the ancillary markets. Additionally, all the deals the company had made with cable and video companies in the short run had resulted in a long-term mortgaging of its films and the devaluation of its library by at least $200–300 million.[47]

With the company's debt reaching the $1 billion mark and after a major reshuffle at the top level, in which the 81-year-old Arthur Krim was removed from his position as chairman,[48] it was obvious that Orion desperately needed a debt-restructuring plan to become operational again. Proposals by the new management, however, fell through and Orion eventually filed for bankruptcy on 11 December 1991. New efforts to acquire the company by New Line Cinema, Savoy Pictures and even Republic Pictures Corporation (which by that time had become a successful television producer) also failed. Finally, almost a year after filing for bankruptcy and after the remaining original Orion executives (Eric Pleskow and William Bernstein) had resigned, the court approved a restructuring plan. The plan made Orion a distribution company which could only exploit its library of titles and could enter the production business only when fully funded by third parties.[49] Thereafter the company operated in the margins of the industry until 1997, when it became one more part of Kirk Kerkorian's media empire as MGM bought Kluge's film holdings, which included Orion Pictures Entertainment, for $578 million.[50]

Conclusion

Orion's short-lived attempt to compete with the traditional powers taught every company in Hollywood, major or mini-major, independent or semi-independent, a valuable lesson about survival in contemporary American cinema. In a nutshell, Orion's failure beyond any doubt underlined the overwhelming power of corporate capital, which represents the only type of safety net for the extremely precarious nature of the film business. Orion was unfortunate in choosing to pursue independence at a time when the stakes were already too high and the traditional majors had already transformed into global superpowers. Ultimately, Orion was ill-equipped to join the superpowers and its destiny was decided a long time before its petition for bankruptcy protection.

This lesson was best learnt by companies such as Miramax and New Line Cinema, which, to a certain extent, shared Orion's relatively limited financial power. Within a short period of time in 1993 and 1994, these two companies secured their survival (at least for the following two decades) by swapping their independent status for that of the 'major independent'. This move provided them with the opportunity to make films 'parallel to the majors' while also 'stressing art house acquisitions which ha[d] the potential to cross over to a wider market'.[51] In this respect, New Line Cinema and Miramax managed to get the best of both worlds as the success of expensive films such as *The Lord of the Rings* trilogy (Jackson, 2001–3) and *Sex and the City: The Movie* (King, 2008) (New Line Cinema), the *Spy Kids* trilogy (Rodriguez, 2001–3) (Miramax/ Dimension) and *Gangs of New York* (Scorsese, 2002) (Miramax) has shown, while at the same time continuing the distribution of cheaply made, often challenging films such as *Bamboozled* (Spike Lee, 2000), *Storytelling* (Solondz, 2001), both New Line Cinema releases, and *Chasing Amy* (Kevin Smith, 1997) and *Full Frontal* (Soderbergh, 2002), both distributed by Miramax. As we will see in Chapter 9 though, conglomerate ownership was not enough to safeguard their long-term future as in late the 2000s both companies were restructured by their parent companies and were effectively closed as distributors.

On the other hand, the Orion project taught the traditional powers a different lesson, namely that there are still gaps in the now global entertainment market which, when exploited wisely by companies with vision, can undermine the conglomerated majors' oligopoly, even for a short period of time.

Case study 7.1 'That's what you thought you saw': Orion Pictures, Filmhaus Productions, David Mamet and *House of Games*

> *House of Games* (Mamet, 1987, 100 min.), produced by Filmhaus Productions, distributed by Orion Pictures.

David Mamet has been one of the most influential contemporary American playwrights, whose plays such as *Sexual Perversity in Chicago* (1974), *American Buffalo* (1976), *Glengarry Glen Ross* (1984), *Speed-the-Plow* (1988) and *Oleanna* (1992) have been produced around the world, often in record-breaking productions. From 1981, Mamet also started writing screenplays for big-budget films such as MGM/Lorimar's *The Postman Always Rings Twice* (Rafelson, 1981) and Fox's *The Verdict* (Lumet, 1982). His screenwriting experience eventually attracted him to film directing.

Since his first film as a writer-director, *House of Games* in 1987, Mamet has written and directed 10 feature films, the majority of which have been produced and/or distributed by small independent outfits such as Triumph Releasing (*Homicide*, 1991) and the Samuel Goldwyn Company (*Oleanna*, 1994), classics divisions of major companies (*The Spanish Prisoner*, 1997; *The Winslow Boy*, 1998; and *Redbelt*, 2008) – all by Sony Pictures Classics) and even specialty divisions of major independents (*State and Main*, 2000 – distributed by Fine Line Features, New Line Cinema's specialty film distribution arm), while two of his more recent films, *Heist* (2001) and *Spartan* (2004) were financed by a well capitalised independent company, Franchise Pictures, and distributed by Warner Bros. Irrespective of where Mamet gets financing for his films, he has developed a very distinct and personal style of filmmaking that clearly departs from a number of conventions associated with mainstream Hollywood cinema. As a result, he has been widely considered a marginal filmmaker who does not follow Hollywood's commercial trends and therefore an important independent writer-director.

Although there was considerable interest from many parties in *House of Games* (a dense psychological thriller about a female psychologist cheated by a gang of con artists), most envisaged the film as a major production with stars and with Mamet only as the film's screenwriter. Mamet, however, wanted to direct his script himself, so he decided to 'go independent' by approaching producer Michael Hausman. Hausman was a well known figure in the independent film sector as he had been involved in the first wave of the PBS-funded contemporary independent films such as *Alambrista!* and *Heartland* but had also worked in major productions such as *Silkwood* (Nichols, 1983) and *Places in the Heart* (Benton, 1984). In 1986, Hausman approached Orion Pictures with the script for *House of Games*. Always eager to develop new relationships with talent, the distributor agreed to finance the production for approximately $5 million in negative costs and let Mamet produce the film according to his very specific vision. Orion raised the funds by pre-selling the film's rights to HBO and to a number of foreign distributors on an individual basis. With Hausman's company Filmhaus Productions undertaking the administration of the production Mamet found himself in the envious position for an independent filmmaker of being able to concentrate on the creative aspect of the film.

With this unusual amount of creative freedom for a first-time filmmaker, Mamet made a number of decisions that exerted particular influence on the aesthetics of his film. Arguably the most important one was that he brought a number of close collaborators from his career in American theatre to work on the film, despite the fact that some of them – actors included – had no experience in filmmaking and made their debut in *House of Games*. All of them, however, had worked for many years with Mamet in the production of his plays, while most of the actors had been Mamet's students in acting workshops where the playwright had professed a particularly distinct approach to stage (and film) performance.

As a result the filmmaker and his above-the-line crew functioned as an ensemble, an intricately linked group of creative units whose overall contribution to the production and aesthetics of the film surpasses any one individual contribution. This means that the division of labour during the production of the film did not follow the strict hierarchy that has traditionally characterised the mode of production associated with mainstream (classical) filmmaking. This is not to imply that there was no pecking order in the division of labour that informed the production of *House of Games*, or that Mamet, as the film's director, did not have the final say in questions of frame composition or editing. Rather, it means that the creative aspect of the film's production was, more forcefully than is usual, shaped by the dynamics of a tightly knit group of players.

The film's aesthetics is characterised by a particular use of film style that supports a narrative constructed in a very distinct way. Although the film's narrative structure follows, for the most part, the basic principles of classical narrative (causal coherence, continuity and character motivation), on certain occasions it departs radically from those principles and follows a logic of its own. These departures are mainly manifest in several clear breaks from the rules of social and/or cultural verisimilitude which immediately provide the story with a high degree of implausibility compared with a classical narrative (for instance, the long poker-game sequence in the film is so full of actions indicating that it is staged that the spectator is left wondering how the main character manages to miss all of them).

Equally, the film style employed to support such a narrative generally adheres to the rules of continuity and transparency, though, on several occasions, it also breaks those rules and consequently evokes a strong sense of 'artificiality'. These effects are mainly conveyed through the frequent absence of realist conventions in parts of the film's *mise en scène*, including frame composition, camera movement and editing (for instance in several frames the confidential information exchanged by characters should have been heard by others standing close by). For this reason, although film style is at the service of the narrative and visually supports a story that often follows a specific logic, it also comments on the narrative and in many ways breaks the spectator's engagement with the story, something that a classical style would rarely do.

If one adds here the nature of the actors' performances, which follows Mamet's view that acting should be plain and physical and not emotive in order to allow the words of the text 'speak for themselves', *House of Games* represents undeniably an example of independent filmmaking that not only was financed, produced and distributed away from the majors, but also differs aesthetically from mainstream American cinema of the late 1980s. However, without Orion's financial and institutional support *House of Games* could have looked and sounded very different, if it had been made at all. The company did manage not only to provide the full budget for the film with minimum financial risk for itself, but also to secure exhibition both in the US and abroad for a feature with no established director or marketable stars. With global distribution and exhibition secure, the filmmaker was in a position to make the film according to his – very specific – vision and hence avoid potential compromises in creative decisions. This means that the mini-major should be given its due credit for allowing the emergence of a distinct voice in contemporary American independent cinema.

Notes

1 Maltby, 1998, p. 26.
2 The figures are taken from 'The 1980s', 1991, p. 86.
3 'The 1980s', 1991, p. 87.
4 Wyatt, 1998a, pp. 86–7.
5 Hillier, 1994, p. 21.
6 The account of Orion Pictures presented here is a shorter version of an article entitled 'Major Status – Independent Spirit: A History of Orion Pictures (1978–1992),' originally published in *New Review of Film and Television Studies*, vol. 2, no. 1, pp. 78–135 (http://www.tandf.co.uk). For more information on the company's reputation in the industry see Hillier, 1994, p. 21.
7 For details on the resignation of the UA executives and their reasons, see Balio, 1987, pp. 333–9.
8 Thompson, 1987, p. 56.
9 Medavoy, 2002, pp. 96–7.
10 Medavoy, 2002, p. 103.
11 Pleskow, 2005.
12 Medavoy, interview with the author, 15 June 2004, Los Angeles, CA.
13 Unless stated otherwise, all rental figures for Orion films are taken from 'All Time Film Rental Champions', 1991, p. 83.
14 Hanson, 1985, p. 25.
15 Medavoy, 2002, p. 115.
16 Lewis, 1995, pp. 33–7.
17 'Filmways Banner Retired as "New" Orion Pictures Raises Own Flag; Shareholders Double Stock Base', 1982, pp. 3 and 26.
18 Hanson, 1985, p. 25.
19 'HBO & Orion Still Going Steady as Paycabler Picks Up 14 Films; Homevideo's in $50–75 Mil Deal', 1985, p. 44.
20 Medavoy, 2002, p. 127.
21 Medavoy, 2002, pp. 126–7.
22 For a detailed account of Orion Classics see Tzioumakis, 2012a, pp. 65–84.
23 Medavoy was quoted in 'Diverse Orion Slate Readied, with 23 Releases Through 1984', 1983.
24 Prince, 2002, p. 17.
25 Unless stated otherwise, all US box office gross figures for Orion films are taken from the Internet Movie Database (http://www.imdb.com).

26 Thompson, 1987, p. 60.
27 'HBO & Orion Still Going Steady as Paycabler Picks Up 14 Films; Homevideo's in $50–75 Mil Deal', 1985, p. 44.
28 *Best Seller* (Flynn, 1987) was the only production that was not financed completely by Orion (Thompson, 1987, p. 60).
29 'Orion Execs See Increased Credit, Longterm Profits', 1985, p. 31.
30 'Goldschmidt, with 11 Upcoming Pics from Orion, Tempers Intl. Tough Spots with Rosy Market', 1985, p. 13.
31 'Orion to Form Homevid Label for Own Output', 1985, p. 95.
32 'Execs Downplay Losses at Upbeat Orion Annual Meet', 1986, p. 20.
33 'Orion Constellation Growing Brighter While Top Execs Remain Realistic', 1987, p. 32.
34 Maltby, 1998, pp. 39–40.
35 Pleskow, 2005.
36 'Most of the Cards Have Been Dealt', 1988.
37 'A Friend in Need', 1990; 'Orion Pictures: From Hunted to Hunter ', 1990.
38 Hillier, 1994, p. 10.
39 'A Friend in Need',1990, p 39.
40 The film scored an incredible $114,558 average per screen, when an average of $10,000 is considered a marker of a solid performance. The figure is taken from http://www.boxofficeguru.com/d.htm.
41 'Orion Moves to Trim Its Heavy Debt Load', 1991.
42 Pleskow, 2005.
43 Pleskow, 2005.
44 'Sell Orion Pictures Now Or Wait Until It Revamps Its Debt Burden', 1991, p. 5.
45 'A Friend in Need', 1990, p. 39.
46 Email communication with Barbara Pleskow, 15 August 2006.
47 'Sell Orion Pictures Now Or Wait Until It Revamps Its Debt Burden',1991, p. 5.
48 'New Management Takes Over at Orion Pictures', 1991, pp. 3 and 18.
49 'Cash-Starved Orion Trying to Sell Off Pix', 1991, p. 133.
50 Medavoy, 2002, p. 204.
51 Wyatt, 1998a, p. 87.

8

The institutionalisation of American independent cinema

Introduction

Orion's fall and eventual bankruptcy demonstrated to the other independents that economic survival depended heavily on 'cooperation' and 'symbiosis' with the conglomerated majors, the only companies with the power to release a product in every possible exhibition outlet and therefore maximise its profitability. Furthermore, the conglomerates also had the financial muscle to absorb any losses at a time of box office dry spells like the one Orion experienced in the late 1980s and early 1990s. The symbiosis between majors and independents has taken primarily two forms. First, it has taken the form of corporate takeovers, whereby independent companies are bought out by the majors but are left to operate as semi-autonomous units (this was the case with Miramax and New Line Cinema in particular, until they were shuttered in the late 2000s). Second, it has taken the form of distribution contracts, whereby independent production companies become satellite companies for major distributors, much like Orion with Warner Bros. (1978–82) and a number of the so-called 'neo-indies' such as Morgan Creek and Castle Rock.[1] Whatever the form, commercial independent film production and distribution have become increasingly 'dependent' on the entertainment conglomerates, to the extent that the label 'independent' has become even more contentious than in previous decades. Furthermore, and not surprisingly, the discourse of independent cinema has expanded to such an extent that the vast majority of films produced in the US can be considered independent, which makes mapping the independent film sector an increasingly difficult proposition.

The majors, moreover, have not controlled the independent sector only through their close ties with independent producers and distributors. They have also utilised their 'classics' divisions, specialty film subsidiaries that were originally established to distribute non-American films in the US. Starting with United Artists Classics, which, as well as the films of Truffaut, Fassbinder and Schlöndorff, also distributed a few low-budget American-based productions such as *Lianna* (Sayles, 1983) and *Streamers* (Altman, 1984), the classics divisions (such as Orion Classics and 20th Century Fox-International Classics) gradually shifted their interest from acquisitions of non-US films to the distribution of independently produced and financed American films.[2] This shift became particularly evident in the 1990s, when a new breed of specialty film divisions such as Sony Pictures Classics, Fine Line Features (a specialty film arm of major independent New Line Cinema), Paramount Classics and Fox Searchlight entered the market, followed by Focus Features (a division of NBC Universal and now Comcast), Warner Independent Pictures and Picturehouse Entertainment (a specialty film division set up by New Line Cinema and HBO) in the 2000s. As a result, an increasingly large number of (relatively) low-budget independently produced and financed films found their way to theatrical exhibition while more and more of the profits from the commercial exploitation of these films were ending up in the majors' pockets (via their subsidiaries).

With the conglomerates controlling and defining the rules of the game in the independent film sector, companies with no ties to the conglomerates' film distribution divisions (the Hollywood majors, the major independents and the rest of the specialty film divisions) have been pushed to the periphery of the industry, destined for a life of financial struggle that more often than not has led to bankruptcy (see Table 8.2, p. 235). Only a handful of companies, led by 'indie powerhouse' Lions Gate (now Lionsgate),[3] have survived without the support of a conglomerate parent in the 2010s. This demonstrates clearly that American independent cinema has become to a substantial extent a category of filmmaking practised mainly through the support of entertainment conglomerates, a view that has forced critics and filmmakers to suggest that independent film was increasingly 'a euphemism for a small-studio production', especially during the 1990s and 2000s, when the studios introduced their specialty film subsidiaries.[4] In other words, independent film has been seen as an 'industrial category', much like genre and auteurism, which the controllers of the industry have been utilising increasingly to market low-budget films that do not contain any conventional commercial elements (stars, a name-director, special effects, clear genre frameworks, etc.). As a result, the use of the label 'independent' has become increasingly difficult to sustain, and new, more ambiguous labels such as 'indie' (short for independent but also signifying a film that could have been produced and/or distributed by any major independent or specialty film division) and 'indiewood' (a 'grey area' between Hollywood and independent sector)[5] have become staples of the vocabulary used by filmmakers, film critics and industry analysts alike.

The majors' entry to the independent sector, especially after 1989, when the financial success of Steven Soderbergh's *sex, lies, and videotape* demonstrated that – given the right marketing and exploitation – low-budget independently produced films had the potential for extraordinary box office gross, precipitated the establishment of a powerful institutional apparatus that supported a particular brand of independent filmmaking to which the labels 'indie' and 'indiewood' have been attached, often interchangeably.[6] This brand has been characterised by a number of elements associated with mainstream Hollywood cinema, especially its firm grounding in narrative, and a number of alternatives, which, according to Geoff King, include 'the experimental "avant-garde", the more accessible "art" or "quality" cinema, the politically engaged, the low-budget exploitation film and the more generally offbeat or eccentric'.[7]

The eclectic mixture of conventions from all these modes of filmmaking has created a distinct type of (generally low-budget) film that has been labelled 'independent' (and 'indie' and 'indiewood') primarily because of its difference from mainstream American cinema (here associated with effects-driven blockbusters and expensive genre-star vehicles) and very often regardless of whether the film has been financed, produced and/or distributed by an independent company, a specialty film division, a major independent or even a major company. A particularly good example here is *The Life Aquatic with Steve Zissou* (Anderson, 2004), a film that borrows from most of the alternative modes of filmmaking identified by King but that was financed by Disney and released through its distribution arm, Buena Vista (which more recently changed its name to Walt Disney Pictures).

Although the foundations of the institutional apparatus of American independent cinema were put in place in the late 1970s and early 1980s with the establishment of such non-commercial organisations dedicated to supporting independent filmmaking as the Independent Feature Project (1979) and the Sundance Institute (1981), the majors' entry ensured that an increasingly large number of films, often supported by the above organisations and institutions,[8] would find their way to commercial exhibition and box office success. The success of some of these films (such as *sex, lies, and videotape*, which grossed $24.7 million in the US and approximately $30 million in the rest of the world)[9] enhanced the status and prestige of the organisations that nurtured or supported them and increased their visibility both with the public and within the film/entertainment community. Furthermore, the institutional apparatus of American independent cinema benefited from the existence of a small number of independent distributors (see Table 8.2, p. 235), which, despite their generally short lifespan and their eventual marginalisation in recent years, contributed substantially to the success of the above type of filmmaking in the late 1980s and 1990s; these distributors included Cinecom

(1980–90), Skouras Pictures (1985–94) and October Films (1990–7), among others.

With this level of support behind it, this brand of independent filmmaking began to blossom in the late 1980s, to the extent that critics and filmmakers alike started talking about 'an indie film movement', albeit one that has existed in almost perfect harmony with the majors and their overwhelming control of the entertainment industry. This chapter will discuss the emergence of this 'movement' and its contentious relationship to the conglomerated majors. First, however, a brief examination is warranted of the phenomenon of the satellite production company in the post-Orion era, through a discussion of two 'rich' independent companies, Phoenix Pictures and Revolution Studios.

A business of co-dependants

After Orion established the modern incarnation of the satellite production company with Warner Bros. in the late 1970s, one by one the rest of the majors gradually adopted this practice. Such deals generally involved a contract between producer and distributor whereby the latter provided the former with office space in the studio lot, staffing and development funds so that the producer could develop films which the distributor could option. Once a film was greenlit for production, the distributor would then provide the producer with the budget (or guarantee the bank loans) or, as has been the case more recently, ask the producer to secure part or all of the negative costs from outside sources in exchange for distribution in all media.

This type of arrangement between independent producers and major distributors became extremely common in the 1990s and continues to be so, especially as staggering increases in production and marketing costs have made co-financing deals essential. For producers, co-financing is almost always the only solution, as very few production companies can afford the costs of a high-budget or even mid-budget film.[10] For distributors, co-financing has also become extremely significant, as the small number of films each distributor releases every year tends to represent an extremely large investment even for a division of a conglomerate. For this reason distributors have been looking increasingly to reduce their financial exposure in the likely case that their films do not perform according to expectations. Such an approach to filmmaking has started affecting the American film market to the extent that *Screen International* announced in 2001 that 'what we knew previously as studios and independents are all becoming co-dependents' while 'the traditional idea of what constitutes a studio and what constitutes an independent is being eradicated'.[11] Table 8.1[12] presents a list of the production pacts between major

Table 8.1 Pacts between independent producers and majors/major independents and specialty film divisions, November 2004

Distributors	No. of pacts	Key production companies
Majors/major independents		
Disney	23	Jerry Bruckheimer; Live Planet (Ben Affleck and Matt Damon); Boxing Cat (Tim Allen)
Dreamworks	20	Aardman Animations; ImageMovers (Robert Zemeckis); Red Hour (Ben Stiller)
Fox	13	Icon (Mel Gibson); Lightstorm (James Cameron); Scott Free (Ridley and Tony Scott)
MGM/UA	22	Mr Mudd (John Malkovich); Bunyan Tree (Matt Dillon)
Miramax/Dimension	12	View Askew (Kevin Smith and Scott Mosier); Quentin Tarantino; Los Hooligans (Robert Rodriguez)
New Line Cinema	7	Rat (Brett Ratner); Benderspink (Chris Bender and J. C. Spink)
Paramount	28	Cruise/Wagner (Tom Cruise); Darkwoods (Frank Darabont); MTV (Van Toffler; David M. Gale)
Sony	35	Cheyenne (Bruce Willis); Happy Madison (Adam Sandler); Spyglass Entertainment (Roger Birnbaum); Revolution Studios (Joe Roth)
Universal	28	Imagine (Brian Grazer and Ron Howard); Kennedy/Marshall (Kathleen Kennedy and Frank Marshall); Mandalay (Peter Guber); Playtone (Tom Hanks and Gary Goetzman); Tribeca (Robert De Niro and Jane Rosenthal)
Warner Bros.	34	Castle Rock (Martin Shafer); Franchise Pictures (Elie Samaha); Wildwood (Robert Redford); Malpaso (Clint Eastwood); Section Eight (George Clooney and Steven Soderbergh)
Specialty film divisions		
Fox Searchlight	3	Umberto Pasolini; David O. Russell
Focus Features	7	Pretty Pictures (Neil La Bute); This is That (Ted Hope)

and major independent distributors and independent production companies in November 2004. No less than 232 'independent' companies had such deals in place with the majors and their divisions that year.

A characteristic example of such a production company, which after a few years of attachment to a major distributor returned to independence, is Phoenix Pictures. The company was set up in 1995 by former head of production for United Artists and Orion Pictures Mike Medavoy, and his business partner Arnold Messer. Since then, it has produced a number of medium-budget films, such as *The People vs Larry Flynt* (Forman, 1996) and *The Thin Red Line* (Malick, 1998), a small number of high-budget pictures, including *The 6th Day* (Spottiswoode, 2000) and *Shutter Island* (Scorsese, 2010), as well as the indiewood hit *Black Swan* (Aronofsky, 2010). According to Medavoy, once it became clear that it was not possible for his new company to be a producer-distributor but only a producer there were two basic models to follow: (1) obtain finance from non-US entertainment-related companies (a model that other successful independent producers such as Franchise Pictures followed) or (2) set up a partially financed output arrangement with one of the major players.[13] Phoenix Pictures chose the second model and after arranging a distribution deal with Sony/Columbia it joined the growing list of production outfits that became satellite companies for the majors.

To launch its operations Phoenix attracted a number of partners (including Sony) which invested in the company in the form of equity finance. With the size of the original investment reaching $74 million, Phoenix managed to secure approximately $600 million production financing and entered the production business with the intention of catering to the mid-budget market (in the mid-1990s, $25–30 million) with director-driven films.[14] For its first five pictures the necessary funds were raised through a deal that involved Phoenix 'borrowing money from a bank to fund a film and then buying an insurance policy to insure itself against any potential loss'.[15]

Although the scheme created many complications, especially as the first five Phoenix films as a group lost money, which meant that Phoenix sought to receive compensation from the insurance companies,[16] it nevertheless was successful enough to allow the company's establishment in the industry. Since then, Phoenix has financed and produced films with production funds secured from a number of sources, including the majors and their specialty film divisions.[17]

However, a series of developments in the industry, such as the staggering increase in the stars' salaries and an overcrowded marketplace that puts pressure on every film to secure as wide an audience as possible in its opening weekend before a new wave of films is released a week later, made the production of mid-budget films in the late 1990s and 2000s a virtual impossibility. Even if a company managed to secure a star of a smaller calibre at a lower cost, such a film still had fewer chances to find an audience in its opening week than an expensive film featuring a big star. These conditions forced Phoenix to shift from director-driven pictures towards genre/exploitation films, such as the teen horror *Urban Legend* (Blanks, 1998), while also venturing into blockbuster territory, for example with *Stealth* (Cohen, 2005), before returning more recently to director-driven films, including indiewood productions such as *Black Swan*.

In the early 2000s the company broke its pact with Sony/Columbia. Rather than be tied exclusively to one major, Phoenix Pictures has become 'a supplier to all studios', developing properties with its own funds and approaching different distributors for the arrangement of production deals.[18] As the majors also recently have moved towards decreasing the numbers of their pacts with independent production companies, Phoenix found itself on a growing list of companies that, according to *Variety*, have gone 'indie', and 'seem to be thriving despite the lack of studio support'.[19]

Revolution Studios, on the other hand, was attached to Sony/Columbia from its inception in 2000 until the late 2000s, when it switched its focus to other markets. Set up by Joe Roth, former head of production at Disney and Fox and one of the co-founders of Morgan Creek in 1987, Revolution Studios did not concentrate on director-driven, mid-budget films; it focused immediately on star-driven genre pictures like *America's Sweethearts* (Roth, 2001; starring Julia Roberts and Billy Crystal) and the universally panned *Gigli* (Brest, 2003; starring Ben Affleck and Jennifer Lopez), while also making expensive, effects-driven action adventure films such as *Hellboy* (del Toro, 2004). Despite the failure of *Gigli* and of several other titles, Revolution Studios produced a remarkable number of films (47 pictures in the seven years 2001–7) for Sony, prompting *Screen International* to pronounce it as 'far and away the most successful and consistent of the independently financed production labels funnelling movies into the studio system'.[20] And even though the underperformance at the box office of an increasing number of its films forced the company to scale back in 2008 and focus primarily on television production, Revolution Studios has since become a very significant player in licensing its library of titles in a variety of ancillary markets, especially as, over the years, it has built up its library substantially through the acquisition of titles from various competitors.[21]

The success of the company in the 2000s lay both in the type of films it produced and in its structure. Like Phoenix Pictures, Revolution Studios had a number of partners, which contributed proportionally to the negative costs of each film Revolution produced. This arrangement allowed Revolution to capitalise fully on its successes, while experiencing minimal losses when its films failed at the box office. It also allowed its distributor and partner, Sony Pictures, a constant flow of mainstream films for which the major paid only a fraction of the films' negative costs. In this respect, if for a company that specialises in director-driven pictures and produces one or two films per year (like Phoenix) the best business strategy is to become a supplier to all majors, then for a company like Revolution Studios, which produced a high volume of films per year, it was to maintain an affiliation with only one major.

Despite the fact that Revolution was not able to sustain this model for more than a few years, its runaway success in the early 2000s forced the trade press to consider its approach to filmmaking 'the classic new model for an independent in Hollywood',[22] and to incorporate companies like Phoenix and Revolution within the discourse of American independent cinema in the 1990s and 2000s. This part of the discourse, however, has been largely overshadowed by a different group of films and set of production and distribution companies which have laid a much stronger claim to the label 'independent' than the majors' affiliates. The emergence of this 'other' American independent cinema became possible only after a strong institutional apparatus was put into place, with the Hollywood majors also present but under a different guise.

Institutional framework (1): organisations dedicated to supporting independent filmmaking, finance opportunities and independent distributors

Film critics have repeatedly referred to *sex, lies, and videotape* as the film that changed the face of American independent cinema and have labelled 1989, the year of the film's release, a 'watershed' year in the history of the independent film sector.[23] Although the scale of its commercial success and its award of the Palme d'Or at the Cannes Film Festival in 1989 (see Case study 8.1) have been, arguably, the best-known elements of the picture, *sex, lies, and videotape* is also the film that effectively revealed to all aspiring filmmakers the existence of significant available institutional support. For this film, the support came in the form of the Sundance Institute (through the film's participation in the Institute's showcase, the Sundance Film Festival)[24] and the presence of a sizeable industrial infrastructure (in this case, represented by Miramax Films), which could lead a film to unprecedented levels of profitability. Despite the existence of such support and infrastructure for more than a decade, it was only after the success of Soderbergh's film that names such as Sundance and Miramax became widely known.

The Sundance Institute was established in 1981 by star-director Robert Redford as a summer camp for a small number of new filmmakers in the mountains of Utah, where industry professionals would teach them 'how to develop their [the filmmakers'] uneven screenplays into solid, workable properties'.[25] Although the Institute quickly attracted criticisms of attempting to refine alternative aesthetic proposals, it nevertheless became an important training ground for young filmmakers, especially those coming from an ethnic or any other minority background. Starting with just 10 projects in 1981, Sundance developed 325 film projects in its first 20 years, with approximately a third of them making it into production.[26] In 1985, the Sundance Institute took over the rights of the US Film Festival, a showcase for films that were made completely outside the American film industry, which had been experiencing severe financial difficulties. In 1990 the name of the festival changed to the Sundance Film Festival and became the primary exhibition forum for independently produced and financed films.

As the Festival has grown in stature by the year – the number of film submissions increased from 60 in 1987 to 2,000 in 2003 to 12,187 (4057 features) in 2014[27] – it has attracted the attention of independent and major distributors, which attend the screenings in the hope of locating the next breakthrough film. After the success of *sex, lies, and videotape*, which won the Audience Award at the 1989 Festival, and until the digital revolution started changing the rules of the game in the late 2000s, Sundance was known as the 'deal place',[28] the site where distributors would decide which (few) independently produced films will receive theatrical release. The Festival has launched the commercial career of a number of films (and of their respective makers), especially of those that won awards, prompting film critics to call the Sundance the 'engine' that drives independent filmmaking, with the specialty film distributors providing the equally important 'proper marketing push', until the late 2000s, when the sector consolidated following the closure of several of these distributors.[29] Indeed, as early as the mid-1990s the Festival had become so successful that similarly named festivals (like Slamdance and Slumdance) running concurrently with Sundance in Park City, Utah, were launched.

Not surprisingly, the wild success of the Festival overshadowed and, to an extent, overwhelmed the Institute, which had to renegotiate its position within the independent film sector. From a new position of power, the Institute expanded to incorporate other channels for developing filmmaking talent, such as the Screenplay Reading Series in Los Angeles and New York and the Documentary Film Program.[30] Furthermore, Sundance branched out in the entertainment business, providing further institutional support through the Sundance Channel, a commercial cable broadcaster that aspired to connect 'viewers with filmmakers, the creative process, and the world of independent film'.[31] Although the channel operates independently from the non-profit Institute and was established in 1996 with the active participation of the majors (Paramount and Universal), it nevertheless provides a forum on cable television for low-budget films and offers coverage of film festivals as well as discussions about the state of the independent sector. More importantly, for the purposes of this chapter, the Sundance Channel (along with the similarly styled Independent Film Channel) has adopted and presented independent film as an industrial category, a product with a distinct character and identity that is geared to a specific television audience.

Like Sundance, the Independent Filmmaker Project (IFP – formerly the Independent Feature Project) is an organisation established (in 1979) 'on a belief that a truly vital American cinema must include the personal, idiosyncratic, and sometimes controversial voices of filmmakers working outside of the established studio system'.[32] From a small organisation that supported the work of a variety of independent filmmakers, the IFP has grown into a large national association that numbers over 10,000 members and has branches in several US cities.[33] Its main showcase is the Independent Filmmaker Project Film Week (formerly the Independent Film Project Market and earlier the

Independent Feature Film Market), during which filmmaker members can screen their work – complete or in progress – for distributors and/or investors (with recent years also including television, web-based and VR work).[34] Furthermore, various branches of the IFP have been part of an international network of organisations that foster the development of national cinemas, including the Cannes Film Festival and Market, the Berlin International Film Festival, the Rotterdam Film Festival and many others.[35] In this manner, the IFP also has been able to channel its members' films to key international markets, where some American independent films have enjoyed considerable success due to their aesthetic affinities with art-house films.

In addition, IFP/West (by far the largest branch of the organisation) is the body behind the Los Angeles Film Festival, one of the most important festivals for independent filmmaking and a site of various workshops and seminars for existing and aspiring filmmakers. IFP/West, which in 2005 changed its name to Film Independent (FIND), is also the organisation that sponsors and presents the Independent Spirit Awards. According to the organisation's guidelines, the Awards celebrate 'uniqueness of vision', 'original, provocative subject matter', 'economy of means' and 'percentage of financing from independent sources', even though the budget ceiling for such films was increased in the early 2000s to $20 million, a figure far removed even from the relatively expensive $1.2 million that *sex, lies, and videotape* (recipient of the award for Best Feature in 1990) cost.[36]

Like the Independent Feature Project, the Association of Independent Video and Filmmakers (AIVF) was another membership-based organisation (5,000 members by 2005) that since 1973 had striven to support independent film and video-making.[37] Until the mid-1990s, the AIVF administered various small grants provided by the US government through its National Endowment for the Arts (NEA). In 1996, however, the grants to individual filmmakers were discontinued while the NEA's support shifted towards contributing to the organisation's operating costs.[38] Like the IFP, which publishes monthly *The Filmmaker*, the AIVF published its own monthly periodical, *The Independent: A Magazine for Video and Filmmakers*, while its in-house publishing activities extended to a number of books that advised filmmakers on all aspects of the business. However, in 2006 the Association ceased operations after failing to raise sufficient funds to support its objectives.[39] Its periodical publication, however, continued under the title *The Independent Film and Video Monthly* through the support of Independent Media Publications, a non-profit organisation established in 2007 with the explicit intention of continuing to publish the magazine.[40]

The increased public visibility of the Sundance Institute and Festival immediately raised the profile of all the above and other more recently established organisations and convinced filmmakers and the public alike that independent cinema had become a cultural phenomenon with a relatively small but extremely vocal support. Equally importantly, Miramax's (still a small independent distributor in 1989) unprecedented success with *sex, lies, and videotape* whetted the appetite of other established small distributors, which immediately started looking for the next low-budget film with breakthrough potential. These companies, however, had to face fierce competition from a number of new small distributors which entered the theatrical market in 1990, the year following the release of *sex, lies, and videotape* (Greycat Films, Cabriolet Films, Triton Pictures, IRS Media, Rainbow Releasing and October Films, the best-known of the group), hoping to repeat the business of Soderbergh's film with another picture.

As a result, independent film production entered a new, particularly active period, driven by the competition of specialised theatrical distributors, some of which were prepared to offer filmmakers lucrative deals to secure distribution rights for their films. For instance, a film like *Swingers* (Liman, 1996), which was produced for $250,000, was acquired by Miramax for $5 million, while *The Spitfire Grill* (Zlotoff, 1996), winner of the Sundance Film Festival Audience Award in 1996, was acquired by Castle Rock for a staggering $10 million.[41] Table 8.2 contains a list of independent distributors that were particularly active in the 1980s and 1990s. Some of them were established before the boom of the late 1980s and most of them went out of business after only a few years.

Although the presence of major independent and smaller distributors made access to theatrical exhibition a real possibility for hundreds of low-budget, independently produced and financed films, the sector has also been driven by the possibilities for financing from, and distribution in, the ancillary markets: video, cable, satellite television (since the late 1980s), European terrestrial television (in the mid-1990s), DVD (in the 2000s) and streaming (in the 2010s). As each of these markets needed a regular supply of product and as some of these markets competed against each other, companies like Live Entertainment and Vestron (video), HBO and Showtime (cable), BSkyB (satellite), Pro 7 and Channel 4 (Dutch and British television broadcasters, respectively) and Netflix (originally a California-based DVD rental and later film and television streaming company) started (part) financing films in exchange for distribution rights in one or more non-theatrical markets. HBO in particular became one of the main financers of a number of low-budget films, especially in the 1990s and 2000s, some of which, such as *Mi Vida Loca* (Anders, 1993), received theatrical distribution and enjoyed critical and commercial success. Furthermore, and according to *Variety*, the staggering growth of film sales in DVD format in the 2000s certainly raised the level of investment in film production, creating 'the first major paradigm shift since the

Table 8.2 Independent distributors, their lifespan and their key films

Company	Lifespan	Key film
First Run Features	1968 to date	*To Die For* (Van Sant, 1994)
Frameline	1973–2009	*Tongues Untied* (Riggs, 1990)
Atlantic Releasing Corporation	1976–93	*Extremities* (Young, 1986)
Samuel Goldwyn Company	1978–2001	*Wild at Heart* (Lynch, 1990)
Castle Hill Productions	1980–2006	*Someone to Love* (Jaglom, 1987)
Cinecom	1980–90	*Matewan* (Sayles, 1987)
Horizon Films	1981–8	*Variety* (Gordon, 1983)
Island	1983–8	*River's Edge* (Hunter, 1986)
Island/Alive	1983–5	*Kiss of the Spider Woman* (Babenco, 1985)
Cinevista	1983–93	*Liquid Sky* (Tsukerman, 1983)
Trimark Pictures	1983–2002	*The Doom Generation* (Araki, 1995)
Circle Films	1984–91	*Beirut: The Last Home Movie* (Fox, 1987)
Angelika Films	1984–94	*Sweet Lorraine* (Gomer, 1987)
Skouras Pictures	1985–94	*Homer and Eddie* (Konchalovsky, 1989)
Roxie Releasing	1985–2001	*Red Rock West* (Dahl, 1992)
Cineplex-ODEON Films	1986–98	*Serial Mom* (Waters, 1994)
Zeitgeist Films	1986 to date	*Poison* (Haynes, 1991)
Taurus Entertainment Company	1987 to date	*Class of 1999* (Lester, 1990)
Avenue Pictures Productions	1987–91	*Drugstore Cowboy* (Van Sant, 1989)
Silverlight Pictures	1987–9	*Life is Cheap . . . But Toilet Paper Is Expensive* (Wang, 1989)
MCEG Productions	1988–90	*The Chocolate War* (Gordon, 1988)
Aries Films	1989–92	*Bad Lieutenant* (Ferrara, 1992)
Strand Releasing	1989 to date	*Totally Fucked Up* (Araki, 1993)
October Films	1990–2000	*Ruby in Paradise* (Nunez, 1993)
IRS Media	1990–5	*Gas Food Lodging* (Anders, 1992)
Triton Pictures	1990–3	*In the Soup* (Rockwell, 1992)
Cabriolet Films	1990–3	*The Kill-Off* (Greenwald, 1989)
Greycat Films	1990–6	*Henry: Portrait of a Serial Killer* (McNaughton, 1990)
First Look Pictures Releasing	1991–2010	*Guncrazy* (Davis, 1992)
Arrow	1993–2000	*My Life's in Turnaround* (1994, Ward and Schaeffer)

home video boom of the '80s and a total revitalization of the opportunities for independent producers' at that period of time.[42]

The existence of so many potential sources of production finance and the increased revenues from exploitation of film in non-theatrical markets meant that individual filmmakers were in a position to raise funds for their pictures by pre-selling distribution rights piece by piece. In this respect, they could often produce their films with minimum interference and seek theatrical distribution only after completion of production, primarily through participation in one of the key festivals for independent films (see Case study 8.1).

Figure 8.1 *Mi vida loca*: the HBO-financed film featuring Mexican television star Salma Hayek was eventually released by Sony Picture Classics and proved a critical and financial success.

Case study 8.1 The definitive independent film: *sex, lies, and videotape* and the American 'indie' cinema

> *sex, lies, and videotape* (Steven Soderbergh, 1989, 100 min.), produced by Outlaw Productions, distributed by Miramax Films.

'No movie in the sound era has had a greater importance on indie cinema … than *sex, lies, and videotape*' (Merritt, 2000, p. 312); 'It's hard to think of a more influential indie than Soderbergh's first feature, *sex, lies, and videotape* … The film forever changed the public perception of independent movies' (Levy, 1999, p. 94); it [*sex, lies, and videotape*] 'was the paradigmatic independent film' (Biskind, 2005, p. 40); '*sex, lies, and videotape* … remains a milestone in development of the indie sector as we know it today' (King, 2005, p. 261).

Although American independent cinema has had a number of landmark films since the breakthrough success of *sex, lies, and videotape* (*slav*) in 1989 – *The Blair Witch Project* (Myrick and Sanchez, 1999) and *My Big Fat Greek Wedding* (Zwick, 2002), which respectively scored $140.5 million and $241.4 million at the US box office alone, represent unequivocal commercial triumphs for independent cinema – Soderbergh's film is still casting its shadow on the independent film sector, despite changes in the industry, the majors' entry and the overwhelming institutionalisation of this type of cinema in the two decades that followed. This is, arguably, because the film's production background, its rise to the public eye, its marketing and distribution history, its subject matter, several of its narrative and formal dimensions and its wide critical and financial success created an ideal for American independent film, against which future individual films would be judged, at least for most of the 1990s. As *slav* hit all the right notes and was seen by audiences as large as those associated with many Hollywood films, it succeeded in opening the gates for the emergence of more films with similar production/distribution histories, offbeat subject matter, challenging narrative and visual style, and so on.

Prior to *slav*, Steven Soderbergh had little filmmaking experience. After taking filmmaking classes as a teenager and making a small number of short films between 1977 and 1979, he moved from Louisiana to California to break into the industry. For the following eight years he wrote a number of scripts, none of which attracted any interest from a production company, while also making a few more short films and working in a number of film-related jobs. He eventually made a documentary for the rock band Yes, *Yes 9012* (1986), which was nominated for a Grammy Award in the Best Video (Long Form) category. In 1988 Outlaw Productions, a recently established independent production company, optioned one of Soderbergh's screenplays, *Dead from the Neck Up*. Soderbergh, who by that time had returned to Louisiana, decided to drive back to California to develop the script and write the screenplay for another film Outlaw was developing, *Revolver*. On the way to Los Angeles, he drafted a third script, which became the basis for *slav*.

On the basis of the script's strength, Outlaw arranged financing from RCA/Columbia Home Video, which put up $600,000 in exchange for US home-video rights, and Virgin, which put up the rest of the $1.2 million in exchange for all rights outside the US and Canada (Wiese, 1992, p. 143). With the budget secure, Soderbergh shot the film with a group of relatively well known actors (James Spader, Andie McDowell, Peter Gallagher), newcomer Laura San Giacomo and a small production team at his home town of Baton Rouge, Louisiana. The film, which largely revolves around a series of verbal exchanges between four main characters in interior locations, was shot in five weeks within the allocated budget. Soderbergh also assumed editing duties and had the final cut of the film ready for its premiere at the US Film Festival.

Although the film lost the Grand Jury Prize award to *True Love* (Savoca), it won the Audience Award for Best Feature. It attracted the interest of a number of distributors, including some of the majors, which nevertheless balked at the news that home-video rights had been pre-sold (Wiese, 1992, p. 144). At that point US theatrical, pay-TV and syndication rights were the only ones left, which made the possibility of a theatrical distribution deal very difficult. However, Miramax agreed to purchase all remaining rights for $1 million, while also investing an extra $1 million in print and advertising costs.

To start the film's marketing campaign Miramax took *slav* to the 1989 Cannes Film Festival. Although there had been precedent, in that US independent filmmakers had won the Festival's awards in the past (Jim Jarmusch had won the Golden Camera for *Stranger Than Paradise* in 1984, as had Hanson and Nilsson for *Northern Lights* in 1979 and Robert M. Young for *Alambrista!* in 1978, it was extremely rare for an independent film to be accepted in the main competition programme.

Surprisingly, *sex, lies, and videotape* won the Palme d'Or and started a trend whereby three more American independent films won it in the following five years: *Wild at Heart* (Lynch, 1990), *Barton Fink* (Coen and Coen, 1991) and *Pulp Fiction* (Tarantino, 1994). The film became one of the most anticipated films of the year and Miramax carefully designed a marketing strategy before the film's official release in New York and Los Angeles in August 1989.

Miramax's strategy focused primarily on the 'sex' element of the title, pitching the film as an adult comedy about sex. With the poster featuring two couples (one hugging and one about to kiss), Miramax also exploited the (small) star power of the film, especially James Spader, who was relatively well known through a series of roles in teen films in the mid- and late 1980s. The poster also highlighted the film's victory at Cannes, while also featuring recommendations from arguably the three best-known film critics in the US, Vincent Canby (*New York Times*), Roger Ebert (*Chicago-Sun Times*) and Richard Corliss (*Time*). The distributor opened the film at the end of the summer period in only four theatres (in New York and Los Angeles) to build word of mouth further. The results justified Miramax's decision. The film scored $46,220 per theatre and eventually reached a record (for an art-film) of 536 screens and took approximately $25 million at the US box office (the figures are taken from http://www.boxofficeguru.com/s.htm).

If the majority of the audience went to the cinema expecting a provocative film about sex or, more precisely, about scopophilia, the film offered just that but on a different level. Without a single shot of nudity, the film explores four people's attitudes to sex (and love) as they elaborate these in a series of encounters among them. Graham's arrival in Baton Rouge to spend a weekend with his old college friend, John, and his frigid wife, Ann, becomes a catalyst for all parties involved (the above three and Ann's sister, Cynthia, who has been having an affair with John) to reconsider their views on sex and their relationships to each other, and to embrace the possibility of a happier future.

Although both the film's style and narrative structure are relatively conservative (the insertion of video images as flashbacks does not distract from the story, the narration of which follows the rules of continuity editing) and therefore locate the film much closer to mainstream Hollywood than to the other alternatives open to independent filmmaking, the picture stands out in terms of offering a mature and intelligent treatment of sex in contemporary society. Its emphasis on the discourse of sex rather than on the depiction of the act allows the film to place important questions about sex and love under the microscope. As a dialogue-driven film in which not a lot happens, *sex, lies, and videotape* would never have been made as a large-budget, studio-produced film, especially as the 1980s saw mainstream American cinema shifting towards high-concept films and politically regressive action adventure pictures.

> The film's spectacular financial success signalled the existence of a sizeable market for films that differed from Hollywood standard fare. In this respect, it did change the landscape of commercial independent cinema, especially as, in the following years, such films started coming from Hollywood as well as from outside it.

Although the advantages of such an approach to film finance are obvious and throughout the years helped fund thousands of films, the pre-selling of ancillary rights presented also a considerable downside: it prevented distributors from paying high prices to obtain the theatrical rights in the US market, success in which has often determined a film's performance in other markets, at least in the pre-media convergence era (see Chapter 9), while in some cases discouraging distributors from bidding for these rights altogether. This was because the distributor would have to assume the considerable costs of prints and advertising on top of the funds already spent for the acquisition of theatrical rights, while also waiting for the parties that provided the budget for the film to recoup their investment first before receiving any theatrical rentals. Despite the potential problems, however, film finance through the pre-selling of the ancillary rights of a picture became one of the very few avenues open to filmmakers who did not want to work with finance from the majors or the major independents.

Institutional framework (2): the studio specialty film divisions

In the late 1970s, Krim, Benjamin and Pleskow, the top executive team at United Artists, started planning the establishment of a new specialty film division, which would handle a small number of art-films per year. By that time interest in art-house cinema had been minimal in the US and key art-films of the decade such as Bergman's *Cries and Whispers* (1972), Fellini's *Amarcord* (1973) and Kurosawa's *Dersu Uzala* (1975) were released under the unlikely umbrella of Roger Corman's New World Pictures. The executives' exit from UA in 1978, however, put these plans on hold.

United Artists Classics was finally formed in 1979 under a different regime, with the specific mission of acquiring the US distribution rights of art-films. In the five years of the company's lifespan, it distributed films by such art-cinema stalwarts as Jean-Luc Godard (*Passion*, 1983), Rainer Werner Fassbinder (*Lili Marleen*, 1981; *Lola* 1981; *Die Sehnsucht der Veronika Voss* [*Veronika Voss*], 1982) and Andrzej Wajda (*Czlowiek z Zelaza* [*Man of Iron*], 1981). However, it was the success of Truffaut's *Le Dernier Métro* (*The Last Metro*, with rentals of $1.9 million and pay-TV rights of $450,000) in 1980 and especially of Beineix's *Diva* (in excess of $2 million rentals from theatrical distribution alone) in 1981 that demonstrated to the majors that such specialty film subsidiaries had a promising future in the 1980s film market.[43]

Even though the main reason for the formation of UA's Classics division was the exploitation of the names of famous European auteurs, the company also tried to capitalise on the stir created by the first new American independent films of the late 1970s. Starting with Brian De Palma's experimental *Home Movies* (1980), UA Classics also distributed such films as Canadian production *Ticket to Heaven* (Thomas, 1981), *Cutter's Way* (Passer, 1981), *Head over Heels* (Micklin Silver, 1982), John Sayles's follow-up to *Return of the Secaucus 7*, *Lianna* (1983), and Robert Altman's *Streamers* (1984). In a five-year period the company distributed 34 features and demonstrated that it could become a serious player in the art-house cinema market as well as in the emerging American independent film market.[44]

In April 1983, however, and in a move that mirrored the exit of the five United Artists executives in 1978, the top management team of United Artists Classics also resigned from the company. Tom Bernard, Michael Barker and Donna Gigliotti immediately joined Orion and assumed the management of its new division, Orion Classics. Between 1983 and 1992, when the parent company collapsed, Orion Classics became the undisputed leader in the art-film market, while it also distributed a relatively small number of US and Canadian films, including *Strangers Kiss* (Chapman, 1983) and *Slacker* (Linklater, 1991).[45]

The other two companies from the wave of the classics divisions,[46] 20th Century Fox-International Classics and Triumph Films (a company formed by Columbia in collaboration with the French major Gaumont) were also short-lived, distributing only eight and 26 films, respectively, despite the fact that the former co-distributed the commercially successful *Eating Raoul* (Bartel, 1982; $4.7 million US gross).[47] Like the art-film market of the 1960s, the US specialty film market of the 1980s was not sizeable enough to sustain a large number of such distributors. As a matter of fact, the market was so tiny that even Orion Classics, which was consistently successful throughout its lifespan, recorded annual profits in the region of $650,000–700,000, figures that were considered crumbs for a major company in the 1980s.[48]

The level of independence of those divisions from their parent companies was different from division to division. Orion Classics, for instance, operated as an autonomous unit from Orion Pictures and was not affiliated with Orion's domestic sales operations.[49] Having built a relationship with the three heads of the Classics division from their years at United Artists, Orion's management stood clear of interfering with their decisions and distribution practices, and allowed them the freedom to create a subsidiary with a distinct identity. When Orion collapsed in 1992, Bernard, Barker and Marcie Bloom (who took over Gigliotti's position in the company when the latter left in 1984) moved to Sony and took charge of Sony Pictures Classics (SPC). Since then, the company has become the key distributor of art-house films in the US theatrical market while also distributing a number of famous American independent films such as *Amateur* (1995) by Hal Hartley, *Lone Star* (1996) by John Sayles and, more recently *Please Give* (Holofcener, 2010) and *Whiplash* (Chazelle, 2015).

In many respects, Sony Pictures Classics and Fine Line Features (which was formed approximately at the same time as SPC) together with the Disney-owned (since 1993) Miramax represent a second wave of specialty film divisions. This is because they were established or taken over by the majors to exploit the boom in US independent filmmaking in the early 1990s (after *sex, lies, and videotape*). At that time, these divisions were still small distribution companies that specialised in the acquisition and marketing of completed US and non-US films for distribution in the American market (and therefore were similar to the Classics divisions of the 1980s). However, they also started financing and producing films (with Miramax quickly moving to a different league due to the increasingly large budgets it invested in its own films), while Fine Line focused almost exclusively on US cinema, distributing only a handful of non-US films in its 14-year history.[50] In this respect, and as they were constantly evolving in the 1990s, these companies had more to do with the next wave of specialty film subsidiaries by the Hollywood majors, which focused first and foremost on financing and producing increasingly expensive 'indie' and 'indiewood' productions and then on acquisition of independently produced films.

This wave of companies, which commenced with the establishment of Fox Searchlight in 1994, tried clearly to emulate the phenomenal success of Miramax, which with the financial support of Disney behind it had become quickly so influential in the film market that, according to industry analysts, it 'changed the industry's DNA'.[51] For this reason, these companies operated on a different model from Fine Line and SPC, with the latter remaining primarily in the acquisition business throughout its 25-year history.

Fox Searchlight was established in 1994 'as the independent arm of Twentieth Century Fox ... a filmmaker-oriented company, creating distinctive films helmed by world-class auteurs and exciting newcomers'.[52]

Paramount Classics was set up in 1998 to 'seek low-cost pics that [could] generate enough biz on the arthouse circuit to stay in the black', though in later years (mid-2000s) it shifted to films that were 'riskier, more creative and aimed at a younger demo'.[53] In the process it also rebranded and changed its name to

Paramount Vantage. As Sony Pictures Classics specialised in acquisitions, in 1999 Sony restructured an existing division into a second specialty film label under its corporate umbrella, Screen Gems. The subsidiary's mandate was to produce as well as distribute low-budget American films for niche audiences, though despite releasing some quality independent films such as John Sayles's *Limbo* (1999), the company's focus has been primarily on genre films, such as the *Resident Evil* (2002–) and *Underworld* (2003–) film series.

Focus Features was established in 2002 as Universal's specialty film division after a long and complex history of corporate amalgamation. This involved the merger of October Films with Gramercy and USA Home Entertainment and the renaming of the new organisation as USA Films, before Universal acquired it, merged it with in-house division Universal Focus, relabelled it Focus Features, and merged it with independent producer and occasional distributor Good Machine in 2002.[54]

A year later AOL Time Warner set up Warner Independent Pictures with the intention of attracting pictures that 'are adventurous, intimate, personal, taboo-breaking and experimental, and artists who explore the unexamined with courage and insight, and in ways that shed new light to the human condition'.[55]

The last specialty film division to be established by a conglomerated major in the 1990s and 2000s (2005) was Picturehouse, a joint venture between New Line Cinema and HBO, with the intention to 'release 8–10 pictures a year' from a wide-ranging community of independent filmmakers and with projects primarily originating from HBO Films, New Line Cinema, projects jointly funded by HBO and New Line Cinema, and acquisitions.[56] The establishment of Picturehouse signalled the end of Fine Line Features, which ceased operations after 2005. Finally, coming in full circle, United Artists – relabelled United Artists Films – was relaunched as MGM's specialty division in 2002, with plans to craft 'a compelling film slate that reflects its proud heritage of nurturing creativity and autonomy' and to focus 'on producing and acquiring eight pics a year, with budgets of less than $20 million'.[57] However, despite releasing key independent titles such as *Coffee and Cigarettes* (Jarmusch, 2004) and *Capote* (Miller, 2005), UA Films was used as a pawn several times in the corporate battles of its parent company, MGM, while at some point during the late 2000s it was run by Hollywood star Tom Cruise and his producing partner Paula Wagner. Since the release of the Cruise-produced *Valkyrie* (Singer, 2008), UA Films has not distributed any other picture while it co-produced a small number of films distributed by MGM, including *Fame* (Tancharoen 2009) and *Hot Tub Time Machine* (Pink, 2010). As Chapter 9 will discuss in detail, despite their dominance in the independent film market in the 1990s and 2000s, the majority of these divisions were closed by their parent companies in the late

2000s, leaving a highly changed independent film landscape that is still being reshaped as part of a broader post-media convergence ecosystem.

Table 8.3 presents a list of the conglomerated majors' specialty film divisions established since 1980.[58] If one compares the films distributed (and later also financed and produced) by the majors' divisions in Table 8.3 with the films released by the independent distributors (and sometimes producers) in Table 8.2, one would find it extremely difficult to argue that the films in Table 8.3 are different from or 'less independent' than those in Table 8.2 because they were financed and/or distributed by a major's subsidiary. A case in point here is Gregg Araki, one of the key filmmakers of the post-1989 indie film movement.

Araki rose to fame with a trilogy of films he wrote and directed, *Totally Fucked Up* (1993), *The Doom Generation* (1995) and *Nowhere* (1997), which are often referred to as '90210 on acid', because, as Araki himself put it in an interview (speaking specifically about *Nowhere*): 'it is going to be my version of *Beverly Hills 90210* ... beautiful fucked-up kids who talk about being bored, alienated, sexually ambiguous, they take drugs; it's the flipside of the mainstream.'[59] Does the fact that *Nowhere* was released by Fine Line Features, a specialty film division of New Line Cinema, a major independent, make it 'less independent' than *The Doom Generation*, a film that was released by the independent distributor Trimark Pictures (before its takeover by the larger independent Lions Gate, now Lionsgate)? Or are they both 'less independent' than *Totally Fucked Up*, which was distributed by Strand Releasing, a company largely outside the mainstream that specialises in distributing films with gay and lesbian interest?

Table 8.3 Studio specialty film divisions, 1980 to date

Specialty film division	Lifespan	Key American films
United Artists Classics	1980–4	Lianna (Sayles, 1983)
Triumph Films (Columbia-Gaumont)	1982–5	Purple Haze (Burton Morris, 1982)
20th Century Fox-International Classics	1982–4	Eating Raoul (Bartel, 1982) (co-distributed with Quartet)
Universal Classics	1982–4	No American film distributed
Orion Classics	1983–97	Slacker (Linklater, 1991)
Fine Line Features	1992–2005	Short Cuts (Altman, 1993)
Sony Pictures Classics	1992 to date	Safe (Haynes, 1995)
Fox Searchlight	1994 to date	Boys Don't Cry (Peirce, 1999)
Paramount Classics	1998–2008	You Can Count on Me (Lonergan, 2000)
Screen Gems	1999 to date	Adaptation (Jonze, 2002)
United Artists Films	1999–2008	Coffee and Cigarettes (Jarmusch, 2004)
Focus Features	2002 to date	Lost in Translation (S.Coppola, 2003)
Warner Independent Pictures	2003–8	Good Night, and Good Luck (Clooney, 2005)
Picturehouse	2005–8	Factotum (Hamer, 2005)

Perhaps one could argue that Araki 'moved up' with each successful film he made, eventually attracting the attention of a major's specialty film division with *Nowhere*. But if this is the case, as some critics have argued – that independent companies are training grounds for talent before the majors enter and 'steal' them for their own pictures – the fact that Araki went back to independent distributors for his next three films – *Splendor* (1999; Samuel Goldwyn Company), *Mysterious Skin* (2004, Tartan USA) and *Smiley Face* (2007, First Look International) – seems to refute this argument. Equally, Araki's return to conglomerated, but on a much lesser scale, distributors than the ones belonging to the Hollywood majors for his two more recent films, *Kaboom* (2010, IFC Films) and *White Bird in a Blizzard* (2014, Magnolia Pictures), demonstrates that he (and other filmmakers) are able to make their often challenging and personal films in a number of distribution arrangements.[60]

However, there is one particularly significant difference between the Hollywood majors' specialty film divisions and the independent distributors: almost all the ex-studio subsidiaries branched out into film finance and production, especially from the late 1990s onwards, compared with the standalone companies of the late 1980s and early 1990s, which remained primarily in the acquisition and distribution business. As Tom Bernard of Sony Pictures Classics, the one studio division that survived the late 2000s market consolidation and has remained mostly a distribution company, remarked about the companies of the third wave of conglomerate-owned specialty film labels:

> These companies have all turned into another label in the system that feeds the foreign and TV deals and makes a cheaper level of pictures. They become mirror images of what the studio does. Art movie companies have fallen by the wayside.[61]

Indeed, as early as the mid-2000s, companies such as Fox Searchlight could greenlight without permission from the parent company films with budgets up to $15 million,[62] while from inception Focus Features had a budget ceiling of $30 million for its productions (with parent company permission).[63] When a company invests figures like these in individual pictures, however, it certainly expects a proportionate payoff. This means that the films often take increasingly fewer risks with the material they present (and the manner in which they present it). As a *Variety* editorial put it succinctly, 'most specialty divisions that have a media conglom to pay the bills now also have a mandate to make mainstream movies that make money'.[64] This explains why Fox Searchlight has not steered clear of 'genre films', Paramount Classics remained conservative in its choices for the duration of its existence[65] and Focus Features created a sister label, Rogue Pictures (2004–8), to trade in genre films, in the same way that Dimension Films (1994–2005) was the genre label of Miramax Films.

The conglomerated studio subsidiaries' branching out into low- to mid-budget film production has created also another important difference between them and the standalone companies, namely the different release strategies each type of distributor has adopted. Instead of following the 'grassroots marketing' approach which entails the city-by-city, market-by-market platform release pattern, the majors' divisions (and some of the larger independents like Lionsgate) have used saturation releases and other marketing techniques associated with mainstream cinema. For instance, when Fox Searchlight understood that its film *Antwone Fisher* (Washington, 2002) had the potential for substantial commercial success, after a two-week limited release with impressive financial results, it relied on the parent company to supply the extra advertising costs necessary to open the film widely (over 1,000 playdates). Equally, for the genre picture *The Banger Sisters* (Dolman, 2002), 20th Century Fox assisted its subsidiary in opening the film in a massive 2,738 theatres. Tom Rothman, former president of Fox Searchlight and later 20th Century Fox co-chairman, summarised the benefits of being this type of specialty film division in contemporary American cinema:

> It's not just the ability to take pictures wide, like *Antwone Fisher* and *The Banger Sisters*. It's also that there is a globally integrated campaign for movies. We're the only specialty company that doesn't have to go begging territory by territory ... [Fox Searchlight] has the best of both worlds. That is, the risk-taking and flexibility of a specialty label and the power, leverage and scope of a major studio.[66]

The mix of practices associated with the majors with elements associated with independent filmmaking (low to middle-sized budgets, risqué content) has created a hybrid form of cinema (sometimes referred to as 'indiewood' or 'Indiewood') that has laid also a strong claim to the label 'independent'.[67] One of the repercussions of this development is that an increasing number of films that have been deemed as 'independent', especially in the 1990s and the 2000s, originated within the divisions of the major studios, while at the same time these companies decreased the number of pictures they acquired from independent filmmakers working away from the majors. With divisions such as Fox Searchlight and Focus Features achieving impressive financial results, for most of the 2000s, this created a very particular independent film market led by these companies' increasingly expensive and/or star-studded films such as *Lost in Translation, Sideways* (Payne, 2004), *Brokeback Mountain* (Ang Lee, 2005), *Babel* (Iñárritu 2006), *There Will Be Blood* (P.T Anderson, 2007), *Burn After Reading* (Coen and Coen, 2008) and *The Grand Budapest Hotel* (W. Anderson, 2014). (For more on the success of indiewood in the 2000s and 2010s see also Chapter 9.)

Regardless of their corporate association with the conglomerated majors, the majors' specialty film divisions have been instrumental in establishing a much more robust infrastructure for independent filmmaking than in the 1980s. This is because they have provided a solid platform for the finance, production and/or distribution of a particular brand of filmmaking, certain characteristics of which will be discussed in the last section of this chapter. In this respect, it is hardly surprising that both the majors' specialty film divisions and the standalone companies have been considered the main advocates of American independent cinema. In the eyes of several institutions that contribute to definitions of American independent cinema, they represent opposite sides of the same coin.

The aesthetics factor

As the industrial background of a film has become gradually an irrelevant factor in its claim to independence (see also discussion of this background in the post-media convergence era in Chapter 9), questions of aesthetics have assumed an increasingly prominent position in the discourse of contemporary American independent cinema. Film scholars have argued that an inclusive definition of the post-1980 independent cinema must consider not only 'the position of individual films or filmmakers in terms of industrial location' but also 'the kinds of formal/aesthetic strategies they adopt', as well as 'their relationship to the broader social, cultural, political or ideological landscape'.[68] As a matter of fact, even industry practitioners, like the co-founders of Phoenix Pictures, have been accustomed to phrases such as 'independent production style' and distinguish between films that are 'economically independent and artistically independent'.[69] As film critic Emmanuel Levy has observed:

> Two different conceptions of independent film can be found. One is based on the way indies are financed, the other focuses on their spirit or vision. According to the first view, any film financed outside Hollywood is independent. But the second suggests that it is the fresh perspective, innovative spirit and personal vision that are the determining factor.[70]

The emphasis on the personal vision and spirit that the second view prizes makes any effort to examine independent cinema as a form of filmmaking that is characterised by a unified aesthetic impossible. Unlike mainstream Hollywood cinema, which, for a number of film scholars and critics, has been exemplified historically by the relatively unified classical aesthetic, contemporary US independent cinema defies such labels. According to Levy, this is one of the reasons why the term 'independent' has survived: it is a 'sufficiently flexible term to embrace a variety of artistic expressions. Neither ideologically, nor stylistically unified', Levy continues, 'indies have elevated eclectic aestheticism into a principle'.[71]

The paradigms that independents have drawn from are many. As mentioned above, in his examination of contemporary American independent cinema Geoff King has mentioned several: 'the experimental "avant-garde", the more accessible "art" or "quality" cinema, the politically engaged, the low-budget exploitation film', and any other mode of filmmaking that differs from Hollywood cinema. On the other hand, though, very rarely has an independent film eschewed completely the narrative form, the very foundation upon which American cinema was built since the first decade of the twentieth century. This is mainly because the overwhelming majority of such films were made for the purpose of commercial exploitation. This means that before media convergence started changing radically the rules of the game in the late 2000s these films had no option but to adhere to at least the basic rules of narrative representation in order to have a chance of securing exhibition in the screens of multiplex theatres and not be limited to exhibition in the few venues that screen non-commercial films. As a result, independent cinema, especially during the 1990s and 2000s and under labels such as 'indie' and 'indiewood', could be seen as a hybrid form of filmmaking that mixes a number of elements associated with Hollywood filmmaking (especially its grounding in narrative) with a vast number of elements from alternative formal systems.

This feature of post-1980 American independent cinema suggests a degree of kinship with the Hollywood Renaissance films of the late 1960s and early 1970s, the majority of which were produced independently but distributed by the majors. Peter Biskind has suggested that the 'independents' of the post-1980 period were part of the rich legacy left by the New Hollywood, 'a loose collection of spiritual and aesthetic heirs' to filmmakers such as Dennis Hopper, Warren Beatty, Robert Altman, Peter Bogdanovich, Martin Scorsese and many others.[72] If that generation of filmmakers was influenced mostly by European art-cinema and tried to expand the language of American cinema, more recent independents have continued and enhanced this project *ad infinitum*. They have borrowed elements from many more formal paradigms, tackled previously un- or under-explored subjects (especially issues related to minorities) and often offered challenging films at a time when mainstream cinema's emphasis on event films, franchises and remakes has reached unprecedented levels. Arguably the most characteristic example of the ways contemporary independent cinema has moved stylistic, narrative, thematic and cultural boundaries in the 1990s and 2000s, before the digital revolution-influenced media convergence opened up the independent sector to a vast expanse of media-making (and not just filmmaking) in the late 2000s and 2010s is what has come to be known as New Queer Cinema.

Although the commercial independent cinema of the 1980s had provided the platform for the release of a small number of films that dealt with representations of gay and lesbian people, such as *Lianna, Desert Hearts* (Deitch, 1986), *Parting Glances* (Sherwood, 1986) and *Longtime Companion* (René, 1990), in the early 1990s there was an explosion of independently produced films that offered such representations. *My Own Private Idaho* (Van Sant, 1991) *Poison* (Haynes, 1991), *Paris Is Burning* (Livingston, 1991), *Young Soul Rebels* (Julien, 1991), *The Hours and Times* (Munch, 1991), *RSVP* (Lynd, 1991), *Swoon* (Kalin, 1992), *The Living End* (Gregg Araki, 1992) and *Zero Patience* (Greyson, 1992) all sprang from a vibrant independent film festival scene (with the Toronto and Sundance Film Festivals at the forefront). The release of all these films within the 1991–2 period led film critics to approach them as a distinct body of work within the context of contemporary American independent cinema to which B. Ruby Rich attached the label 'New Queer Cinema'.[73] As Julianne Pidduck has argued, the critics' 'reappropriation of the epithet "queer" [was] a conscious political strategy that rhymes with an aesthetic that celebrates the "abject," the criminal, the underworld of queer desire'.[74]

Indeed, compared to their 1980s predecessors, which featured gay and lesbian characters who tried to 'fit in' within the structures of a heterosexual universe (*Parting Glances*) and who had to deal with the 'problems' that their alternative sexuality entailed (*Lianna*) within straightforward narratives, the new films were remarkably different. First, many celebrated homosexuality as a deviant practice in an attempt to shock mainstream audiences and 'challenge more forcefully [their] preconceived notions about gay culture and society'.[75] Not surprisingly, such an approach rendered some of the films (especially *Poison* and *The Living End*) instantly controversial and provided them with notoriety that has increased their cachet as truly representative texts of a particular culture.

Second, and as an extension of the above element, this group of films put forward a political agenda. Although this agenda, which revolves mainly around the problem of homophobia and of the lack of equal rights for the gay community, existed a long time before the appearance of these films, in the 1990s it was reshaped by the sweeping influence of the AIDS pandemic. As a result these films were characterised by a directness of subject that certainly reflects the changes effected by AIDS.[76]

Third, all these films were exemplified by a diversity of narrative and style, which, according to José Arroyo, was a product of the films' struggle 'to represent a new context against the legacies of both dominant cinema and a previous history of gay representation'.[77] From the *cinéma-vérité* style of *The Hours and Times* to the different visual styles Haynes employs for each of the three segments in *Poison*, to the black and white still photography style of

Swoon, to the mock *Beverly Hills 90210* aesthetic of Araki's films (especially *The Doom Generation* and *Nowhere*), the films of New Queer Cinema invented a language of their own (often referred to as 'homo pomo') that made them representative texts of an emerging queer identity.[78] Equally, the emphasis of many of these films' narratives on 'desire, death and criminality' differentiates them from the films of the 1980s and 'illustrates a historical refusal of positive image strategies by new queer film-makers'.[79]

The New Queer Cinema is not the only example of a group of films within the independent film sector that pushed a number of boundaries and provided a voice for a cultural minority group. At approximately the same time, there was another group of films that this time re-invented African American cinema. In 1991 alone, approximately 15 films by black filmmakers (not all independently financed and/or distributed) found their way to the theatres, a number that was higher than the number of such films released in the 1970s and 1980s together.[80] Led by independently financed *Straight Out of Brooklyn* (Rich) and *Hangin' with the Homeboys* (Vasquez) and the Hollywood major-produced and -distributed *Boyz n the Hood* (Singleton) and *New Jack City* (Mario Van Peebles), this new black cinema broke into the mainstream and quickly established itself as a category of filmmaking with its own codes and conventions.

These two categories of American cinema illustrate perfectly the important role aesthetics has played in co-defining contemporary American independent cinema, especially in the 1990s. While all the films associated with the New Queer Cinema were produced, financed and released by independent companies, many of the new black films were produced, financed and/or distributed by the majors or major independents; besides *Boyz n the Hood* and *New Jack City*, which were distributed by Columbia and Warner Bros. respectively, one should also add *Jungle Fever* (Lee; distributed by Universal) and *A Rage in Harlem* (Duke; distributed by Miramax).

Despite their different locations of production, however, in terms of formal and stylistic choices, content, ideological disposition and cultural viewpoint, *Boyz n the Hood*, financed and distributed by Columbia, is much closer to the independently produced and distributed *Hangin' with the Homeboys* than to any of the other films Columbia (or Columbia/TriStar) financed and/or released in 1991, which include such mainstream productions as *Bugsy* (Beatty), *The Doors* (Stone), *Hook* (Spielberg), *Hudson Hawk* (Lehmann), *Mortal Thoughts* (Rudolph), *My Girl* (Zieff), *The Prince of Tides* (Streisand) and *Terminator 2: Judgment Day* (Cameron). Even though this means that the label 'independent' becomes virtually meaningless, it nevertheless describes a particular type of film regardless of its production/finance/distribution background. As James Schamus, producer of a large number of independent films and one of the most vocal advocates of the low-budget independent cinema in the 1990s, remarked, in a speech he gave in 1999, independent films could be 'found both within the studio system, within the mini-majors and major independents, as well as "outside" the system'.[81]

Conclusion

After decades in the margins of the industry and despite the continuing problems of definition, American independent cinema in the 1990s and 2000s finally established itself as a relatively distinct category of filmmaking, both in the global entertainment industry and in public discourse. As a matter of fact, it has become such an integral part of American cinema more broadly that in the IFP/West (later FIND) Independent Cinema Awards ceremony of 1999, James Schamus suggested the disbandment of the IFP. As the organisation was formed to support 'personal, idiosyncratic, and sometimes controversial voices of filmmakers working outside of the established studio system', by the end of the 1990s, Schamus argued, it certainly had 'won its battles'.[82]

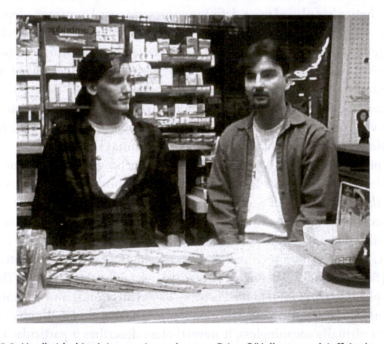

Figure 8.2 Hardly 'clerking': inexperienced actors Brian O'Halloran and Jeff Anderson, who played the two main leads in *Clerks*, contributed substantially to the fresh feel of Kevin Smith's film.

The institutionalisation of American independent cinema has succeeded in making a particular brand of filmmaking marketable at a global level and in effect helped a very large number of personal, idiosyncratic and offbeat films receive theatrical distribution and often find a substantial audience. Despite arguments that see the terms 'independent' and 'institution' as mutually exclusive, the emergence of an institutional framework laid the foundations for a staggering increase in the number of new filmmakers from all kinds of backgrounds in the US. As a result, commercial cinema has gone often to areas that were previously uncharted and American film has come increasingly closer to becoming 'a democratic art'. This development, however, became particularly pronounced from the late 2000s onwards, when the effects of the introduction of digital technology in production, distribution and exhibition started changing American independent cinema in dramatic and radical ways. Chapter 9 discusses American independent cinema in the age of media convergence.

Case study 8.2 'I wanted to be an independent filmmaker. I wanted to work at Miramax': Kevin Smith and *Clerks*

> *Clerks* (1994, 92 min.), produced by View Askew Productions, distributed by Miramax Films.

When Miramax was bought out by Disney in May 1993, industry observers and film critics did not know whether the company would be allowed to continue the distribution policies that had made it so successful in the independent film market (i.e. whether it would become Disney's specialty film division) or whether the conservative Hollywood major would impose on it its own business practices. The release of films such as *Pulp Fiction* and *Clerks* reassured fans of independent cinema that Miramax would continue to operate with the necessary autonomy and release films that its parent company would never be associated with. Although *Pulp Fiction* became the most successful film in Miramax's history till that time, 1994 was also the year of *Clerks*, a $27,000 production, financed by the filmmakers themselves (director Kevin Smith and producer Scott Mosier) and made into a success by Miramax's distribution machine. If *Pulp Fiction* represented glossy independent cinema backed by a large (for low-budget standards) negative costs (approximately $8 million), *Clerks* stood at the exact opposite end of the independent spectrum. It was made for next to nothing, featured no stars and looked like an amateur production.

The film was financed from a number of sources outside the industry. Having read that Robert Townsend had financed *Hollywood Shuffle* (a key independent film of the late 1980s) through credit cards, Smith applied for a number of credit cards, the total limit of which provided him with half the budget. He raised the rest of the necessary funds by selling his comic-book collection, by using part of his college tuition fees (returned to him after dropping out of film school), from his wages from working at a convenience store (the Quick Stop café, where the film was shot) and by deferring salaries and fees for every participant in the film.

After succeeding in raising approximately $27,000, Smith made a number of budget-specific decisions that determined the film's amateur aesthetic: he photographed the film in black and white (as lighting when filming in colour is more expensive); he used one 16mm camera for all the shots in the film; he used a number of long takes and master shots with very little camera movement (as this was the cheapest type of shot he could use); he hired inexperienced actors (who contributed to the fresh feel of the film); he used the shop he was working at as the film's location, filming through the night; and he edited the film himself (with the help of Mosier). The result was a personal film that, despite lacking fluidity of style, was characterised by the energy and freshness of its young makers.

Smith submitted the film to the Independent Feature Film Market (IFFM), one of the major showcases for work by independent filmmakers at the time. Although the film's screening did not attract the interest of any distributor, it nevertheless attracted the attention of a member of the Sundance Advisory Committee, who invited Smith to compete at the Sundance Film Festival in January 1994. The film won one of the main awards, the Filmmaker's Trophy, and was bought by Miramax during the run of the Festival for $227,000. Almost half of this money went to blow up the film to 35mm so that it was suitable for commercial exhibition, while $40,000 went to repay the balance of the credit cards and the interest. The rest (approximately $80,000) went to the production team. By that time Miramax's reputation as the patron saint of independent filmmakers had been thoroughly established, to the extent that for Smith there was no other distributor, as the heading of this Case study indicates (quoted in Biskind, 2005, p. 164). Buying *Clerks*, however, was important for Miramax too, as it sent a clear message to other independent distributors that, despite its new corporate parent, it would continue to select risqué or controversial films (Biskind, 2005, p. 164). *Clerks* was characterised by extremely strong language and made constant references to sexual practice. The film received an NC-17 certificate, which is considered poison for the box office career of any film in the US market. Miramax responded by hiring Alan Dershowitz, an attorney famous for his participation in the O. J. Simpson case, who managed to convince the MPAA to change the rating to an R.

The film's ultra-low budget was exploited in the distribution and marketing of the film, in which Miramax invested substantial funds. As the film passed the $1 million mark in terms of gross, it was advertised as one of the most successful films in the history of cinema (in terms of budget–gross ratio). Its success was also assisted by Miramax's decision to place a trailer for the film in 800 prints of *Pulp Fiction*, targeting a particular youth demographic that was not expected to respond negatively to Smith's use of strong language or the quirky humour of the film's universe. *Clerks* grossed approximately $3 million and established Smith as one of the strongest voices in the independent film sector. In the following years the film achieved cult status and has made handsome profits in the ancillary markets. Besides making the film available in various formats and versions, Smith and his collaborators have created numerous *Clerks*-related tie-ins, including: autographed theatrical posters, a *Clerks* animated series, *Clerks* comic books, *Clerks* T-shirts, *Clerks* 16mm celluloid frames, *Clerks* bumper stickers and a *Clerks* soundtrack, autographed by Smith. In 2004, View Askew, Smith and Mosier's production company, and Miramax distributed the Tenth Anniversary DVD, while in 2006 the film's sequel, *Clerks II*, grossed theatrically over $24 million for standalone distributor the Weinstein Company (http://www.imdb.com/title/tt0424345/business?ref_=tt_dt_bus). In 2016, a second sequel was announced, for release in 2018.

As for Smith, between *Clerks* in 1994 and until 2005, when Bob and Harvey Weinstein left Miramax to start the Weinstein Company, he made all his other films, (with the exception of *Mallrats* (1996, Universal), at the Disney subsidiary, becoming closely associated with the company, so much so that part of the narrative of his 2001 film *Jay and Silent Bob Strike Back* unfolds in a fictional Miramax studio space. Together with Quentin Tarantino they represent the two key independent filmmakers associated with the company at its peak.

Notes

1 According to Hillier (1994, p. 21), a 'neo-indie' is different to a mini-major in that the former establishes close ties with the majors, while the latter – as seen in Chapter 7 – 'operates outside the orbit of the majors'.

2 For a book-length examination of the studios' classics divisions and the rest of the subsidiaries they established to trade in the independent film market in later years, see Tzioumakis, 2012a.

3 DiOrio, 2003, p. 16.

4 Levy, 1999, p. 505.

5 King, 2005, pp. 9–10. King's definition is for 'Indiewood' (with capital 'I') while I use the term with lower case 'i' somewhat differently to King. See note 67 more details.

6 See, for instance, Needham (2010, p. 8), who uses the terms 'indie' and 'indiewood' without distinction to refer to particular developments in American independent cinema.

7 King, 2005, p. 2.

8 In an article entitled 'From Independent to Indie: The Independent Feature Project and the Complex Relationship Between American Independent Cinema and Hollywood in the 1980s', I argue that the Hollywood majors were also present in these non-commercial organisations such as the IFP and the Sundance Institute, contributing funds to the

organisations' operational costs, sponsoring events and of course participating in the markets and festivals these organisations arranged for independent filmmakers. In this respect, the majors were never too far away from the independent film scene, even in the 1980s, when American independent cinema was largely perceived as not associated with the Hollywood mainstream (Tzioumakis, 2017, pp. 233-56).

9   The figures are taken from Biskind, 2005, p. 82.

10   By 1998 the average negative cost for a film had reached $53 million, with blockbuster films costing two or three times that figure. See http://www.filmsite.org/90sintro.html (accessed 15 April 2017).

11   Goodridge, 2001b, p. 1.

12   The data are taken from 'Fact on Pacts', 2004, p. 71.

13   Medavoy, 2004.

14   Medavoy, 2002, pp. 299–300.

15   Medavoy, 2002, p. 296.

16   Medavoy, 2004.

17   Medavoy, 2004.

18   Medavoy, 2002, p. 344.

19   Harris, 2002, pp. 8–9.

20   Kay, 2002.

21   For a brief discussion of Revolution's recent strategy of film acquisitions see Molloy, 2016,.

22   Goodridge, 2001b, pp. 1 and 4.

23   Holmlund, 2005, p. 6, Levy, 1999, p. 94, Biskind, 2005, p. 40, Pierson, 1995, p. 2, King, 2005, p. 261, Merritt, 2000, p. 312.

24   In 1989, when *sex, lies, and videotape* debuted in the Festival, it was still known as the US Film Festival. It changed its name to the Sundance Film Festival in 1990.

25   Peary, 1981, p. 47.

26   The figures are taken from Goodridge, 2001a, pp. 17–18.

27   Merritt, 2000, p. 354, Brown, 2002, p. 10, '30 Years of Sundance Film Festival', 2015.

28   Levy, 1999, p. 40.

29   Merritt, 2000, p. 355.

30   Goodridge, 2001a, pp. 17–18.

31   Fuchs, 2004.

32   See https://www.nypl.org/weblinks/1357 (accessed 16 July 2016).

33   The number of members cited is retrieved from the organisation's website, http://www.ifp.org/about/#.V4QcW5X6s5s (accessed 11 July 2016).

34   Luers, 2016.

35   For a list of IFP's international partnerships and fellowships see the organisation's website, http://www.ifp.org/programs/international/international- fellowships/#.V4YbSJX6s5s (accessed 13 July 2016).

36   For details about how FIND shortlists and selects nominees for an Independent Spirit Award, see the organisation's website, http://www.filmindependent.org/spirit-awards/faq/ (accessed 11 July 2016).

37   For more information about the history of the organisation see Angell, 2006.

38   Loosvelt, 2005, p. 38.

39   Hernandez, 2006.

40   See http://independent-magazine.org/about.

41   The figures for *Swingers* are taken from Levy, 1999, p. 279; the figure for *Spitfire Grill* is taken from Biskind, 2005, p. 228.

42 Dawes, 2003, pp. 13 and 32.

43 The figures are taken from Klain, 1983b, p. 532.

44 For a detailed examination of United Artists Classics see Tzioumakis, 2012a, pp. 23–43.

45 For a detailed examination of Orion Classics see Tzioumakis, 2012a, pp. 65–84.

46 There was also a fifth classics division, established by Universal (Universal Classics), but it distributed only four films between 1982 and 1983, none of which was an American production.

47 Biskind, 2005, p. 16.

48 Medavoy, 2004.

49 Klain, 1983, pp. 3 and 31.

50 For a detailed examination of Fine Line Features and Sony Pictures Classics see Tzioumakis, 2012a, pp. 87–129. For a book-length study of Miramax see Perren, 2012.

51 Harris, 2004, pp. 1 and 15.

52 Quoted in 'Fox Searchlight Acquires Jason Reitman's Debut Feature "THANK YOU FOR SMOKING" from David O. Sacks' Room 9 Entertainment', 2005.

53 McNary, 2004, p. 5.

54 For a detailed examination of Focus Features see Tzioumakis, 2012a, pp. 177–98, Needham, 2010, pp. 8–30, King, 2009, pp 235-277, and King, 2010, pp. 6–30.

55 See Boogarlists, 2011, p. 108.

56 Tzioumakis, 2012a, p. 212.

57 Quoted in United Artists Theaters, online, http://m.shopsmp.com/index.cfm?p=ajaxstore&s=2138816925&fr=ct/2138213578 (accessed 1 December 2016), and Carver, 1999.

58 Although Orion went bankrupt in 1992, under a new management regime its Classics division released a few more films in the following five years, including *Trees Lounge* (Buscemi, 1996), until the company was sold to MGM.

59 Araki is quoted in Chang, 1994, p. 53.

60 For a discussion of the debate over whether contemporary American independent cinema is a training ground for talent, see Levy, 1999, p. 506 and Biskind, 2005, p. 470.

61 Bernard is quoted in Harris, 2003.

62 Rooney, 2004a, pp. 8 and 15.

63 *Variety*, 7 April 2003, pp. 1 and 54.

64 *Variety*, 7 April 2003, pp. 1 and 54.

65 *Variety*, 7 April 2003, p. 55.

66 Mohr, 2005, pp. 1 and 41.

67 Despite being mobilised to discuss very similar developments in American independent cinema, the two terms have also some distinct differences. For King (2009, pp. 1–4), 'Indiewood' is an industrial/institutional phenomenon in the 1990s and 2000s that produced a number of films with particular textual qualities that stem from both the mainstream and the independent sector. For Tzioumakis (2012a, pp. 10–12), 'indiewood' is a period in the history of contemporary American independent cinema that starts from the mid- or late 1990s and continues to a substantial extent to our times, in which the dominant expression of filmmaking is characterised by many of the elements identified by King. See also Note 7.

68 King, 2005, p. 2.

69 Messer, 2004 and Medavoy, 2004.

70 Levy, 1999, p. 3.

71 Levy, 1999, p. 6.

72 Biskind, 2005, p. 1.

73 Rich's article 'New Queer Cinema' originally appeared in *The Village Voice* and was reprinted in *Sight and Sound*, September 1992, pp. 30–4.

74 Pidduck, 2003, p. 279.

75 Allen, 2003, p. 154.

76 Arroyo, 1993, p. 93.

77 Arroyo, 1993, p. 93.

78 The term 'homo pomo' was coined by B. Ruby Rich in her 1992 article.

79 Pidduck, 2003, p. 278.

80 Levy, 1999, p. 415.

81 Schamus, 2002, p. 255.

82 Schamus, 2002, p. 253.

9

American independent cinema in the age of media convergence

Introduction

The institutionalisation of American independent cinema from the late 1980s onwards transformed radically a sector that was originally organised around the quality low-budget, theatrically distributed and exhibited feature-length fiction film. Despite the fact that the industrial and institutional apparatus that helped transform the sector was originally instigated by organisations and companies that had few or no links with the Hollywood majors and were envisaging an American independent cinema that would be markedly different from the cinema associated with the films of the now conglomerated ex-studios, the truth of the matter is that Hollywood was never too far away from the independent sector. For instance, as we saw in Chapter 8, the majors' classics divisions distributed some well known independently produced films in the first half of the early 1980s, even though they stayed away from finance and production. Furthermore, the ex-studios themselves routinely financed and sponsored events in support of the independent film sector and participated in independent film markets and fairs in the hope of identifying films with commercial potential and exploiting that potential by using their marketing and distribution resources. They also underwrote a substantial part of the operating costs of organisations such as the Sundance Institute, while talent (actors, writers, directors and producers) associated with Hollywood cinema was drafted in to contribute to the Institute's programmes right from the start.[1] Indeed, such initiatives often attracted considerable criticism as they were deemed mainstream Hollywood efforts to 'refine' oppositional film practices and use the low-budget quality film sector as a springboard for recruiting the most promising talent for major productions.[2]

However, it was the conglomerated majors' second entry to the independent film market, through the establishment of specialty film subsidiaries or the corporate takeover of standalone companies and their relaunch as 'major independents', that became the lynchpin for a massive investment in that sector in the 1990s. With the majors more willing to use their financial and other resources than in the 1980s, the American independent cinema sector entered its 'indie' cinema phase in the early 1990s, which was characterised by increasingly high budgets, the use of (particular types of) Hollywood stars, the increasingly frequent use of generic frameworks (missing from the majority of the quality independent films of the previous decade) and an emphasis (much more substantial than in the past) on marketing and the use of authorship as a strong selling point for many of these films.[3] These trends continued to determine the sector in the second half of the 1990s, when the conglomerated Hollywood majors and other powerful media and entertainment conglomerates instigated another wave of specialty film divisions. Budgets and marketing costs continued to rise, major Hollywood stars started to appear increasingly in films made by these divisions (often using them as a platform to prove their talent, acquire cultural capital and pursue personal projects), genre became an even stronger staple of this type of filmmaking than in the past, while marketing reigned supreme in terms of which films received a theatrical release and which were noticed in an increasingly congested marketplace.

All this was particularly significant as this last wave of specialty film divisions became increasingly involved in film production (rather than focusing primarily on acquisitions as the companies in the previous waves of such divisions did) with a view to controlling further the commercial potential of their films. With the rest of the companies in the sector that could afford to take risks and expand their operations in order to remain competitive also shifting gears, American independent cinema found itself increasingly defined by 'indiewood' film as the 1990s was coming to a close, a trend that continued and intensified significantly in the following decade. And while Miramax and New Line Cinema had been moving increasingly to big-budget productions and franchised entertainment with titles such as *Gangs of New York* (Scorsese, 2003) and especially *The Lord of the Rings* trilogy (Jackson, 2001–3), respectively, and with only occasional releases of indiewood films, the other divisions of the conglomerated majors rushed to fill in the gap. In this respect, by the mid-2000s Fox Searchlight, Focus Features, Paramount Classics (Paramount Vantage from 2006) and Warner Independent Pictures became the undisputed leaders of an indiewood-defined American independent film market (see Case study 9.1).

This trend seemed to be reaching its apex in the mid- and late 2000s with the critical and commercial success of such indiewood productions as *Babel* (2006, Iñárritu, Paramount Classics), *Juno* (Reitman, 2007, Fox Searchlight), *Burn After Reading* (Coen and Coen, 2008, Focus Features) and several others. At the same time, however, American independent cinema was already in the process of being shaken up dramatically by the impact of a cluster of factors linked together by advances in digital technology. While digital technology had already made its presence felt in film production in the independent sector as early as in the late 1990s (at the same time as indiewood filmmaking was establishing its dominance) and had continued to make significant inroads in the early 2000s, it nonetheless did not start providing a significant alternative to indiewood until the end of the decade and especially early in 2010s, when it also started changing the rules of film distribution. By that time other interrelated technology-led developments that started affecting the sector, the film industry at large and media industries in general, such as the rapid rise of social media, the extraordinary pervasiveness of smart screen technologies, the increasing affordability of high-quality digital shooting hardware and the dramatic improvement of content delivery infrastructure, created the conditions for a huge outburst of filmmaking activity. This activity, which took place primarily at the margins of the sector, reignited American independent cinema in a number of ways and inevitably expanded the discourse of independence to a dramatic extent.

Industrially, this activity brought independence again away from the conglomerated majors' specialty film divisions and standalone superpowers such as Lionsgate to artisanal companies, formal and informal communities and cooperatives of filmmakers and even individual entrepreneurs, many of whom tried to exploit new and emerging approaches to distribution. One element that linked these approaches was the bypassing of the theatrical distribution and exhibition circuit that traditionally has been controlled by the conglomerated majors and their subsidiaries. Not surprisingly, a lot of this activity has not been seen anymore as 'cinema' or 'filmmaking' but rather as media-making, which can circulate fluidly in a multitude of digital platforms in order to reach as easily as possible the smart screen technologies through which an increasing number of audiences watch independent and Hollywood films as well as other 'content'. Indeed, writing as early as in 2005, Patricia R. Zimmermann was calling for 'independent narrative film … to be rethought as a form of cinema that moves across different platforms and through different audiences and economies, rather than the more static model of a feature-length film on celluloid that plays in theatres and film festivals',[4] while three years later filmmaking consultant Peter Broderick was triumphantly proclaiming 'the New World of Distribution', which, fuelled by 'the fundamental importance of the internet or its disruptive power', 'empower[ed] [filmmakers] to keep control of their "content"'.[5]

Furthermore, the impact of this activity can be seen also in the aesthetic and ideological dimensions of independent films (which together with the industrial dimension represent the three axes of orientation upon which other scholars have based their approach to American independent cinema, especially King[6]). Indeed, one could argue that, since the late 2000s, filmmaking activity at the margins of the independent sector has done nothing short of 'de-institutionalising' and destabilising American independent cinema. With the number of films produced and available via various distribution outlets being in the tens of thousands (perhaps more) in the past decade, it is clear that any effort to define aesthetic tendencies and identify ideological proclivities across such an expansive independent film sector are bound to be thwarted. Simply put, the field is now too vast to be studied methodically and systematically, and can therefore encompass works that can be located within the parameters of any aesthetic paradigm and at any point imaginable within the ideological spectrum. In this respect, by default this articulation of American independent cinema lacks the precise characteristics that have helped scholars such as King, Newman, myself and others to identify distinct trends within the sector such as 'indie' and 'indiewood' (or 'Indiewood') cinema.[7]

This chapter, then, provides an overview of these recent developments and places them within another discourse, that of 'media convergence', a term that started being popularised in the mid-2000s following the publication of Henry Jenkins' influential *Convergence Culture* in 2006 (although its effects were under way much earlier than that).[8] With media convergence conceptualised by Jenkins as involving 'the flow of content across multiple media platforms, the cooperation between multiple media industries, and the migratory behaviour of media audiences who will go to almost anywhere in search of the kinds of entertainment experiences they want', and therefore manifesting itself at a technological, industrial and sociocultural levels,[9] like in the rest of this book, the chapter will focus primarily on how changes materialised at an industrial level. On the one hand, it will argue that the emergence and success of indiewood were in many respects part of the conglomerated majors' strategy to expand their output across media platforms in an effort to capture as big a share as possible of a seemingly ever expansive (thanks to new technologies) media market.[10] As a result, the indiewood phase of American independent cinema, from the late 1990s onwards, was not only a development in the US independent film sector but, much more broadly, it was a development within the US media industries' efforts to recalibrate, in order to maintain their com-petiveness within a global media landscape.

On the other hand, despite destabilising American independent cinema as it had been institutionalised under the auspices of indiewood and providing a huge range of often alternative and oppositional voices, the outburst of activity at the margins of the sector did not necessarily take place away from the purview of the conglomerated majors, their sister companies and their corporate parents. This is because these companies and a number of other entertainment conglomerates quickly asserted their control over most of the physical infrastructure through which 'content' circulates worldwide. In this respect, although many of these new 'low-end' independents have managed to find novel ways to connect with audiences, very few of these cases were of a 'crossover' kind. Indeed, with the exception of 'mumblecore', a group of films produced primarily in the second half of the 2000s and associated with the SXSW Festival in Austin, Texas, which achieved wide critical recognition but little commercial success, this part of the American independent cinema sector has had few other success stories that have resonated culturally or commercially in the US and internationally. As a result, American independent cinema as part of a media convergence discourse is a constantly evolving category of filmmaking that continues to be shaped at the most basic level by developments instigated by global entertainment conglomerates.

The success of indiewood

In Chapter 8, the label 'indiewood' was introduced as a 'grey area between Hollywood and the independent sector', 'a brand of independent filmmaking' that emerged because of the presence of a strong industrial and institutional infrastructure and as a 'hybrid form of cinema' that mixes practices associated with the majors with elements associated with independent filmmaking. The introduction to this chapter also referred to indiewood as an intensification of elements that were originally associated with American independent cinema when it started to become increasingly commercialised, popularised and institutionalised in its 'indie' phase during the early and mid-1990s. With stardom, genre, auteurism, marketing strategies, the involvement of the Hollywood majors and increasing production and marketing costs becoming much more prominent in the sector towards the end of the 1990s and in the 2000s than before, indiewood could also be seen as a new phase in contemporary (post-1980) American independent cinema. Indeed, it could be seen as an 'enhanced' version of the indie phase that came to dominate the discourse of independent filmmaking in the US from the late 1980s onwards. This section will discuss indiewood in some more depth than Chapter 8, focusing primarily on the ways in which it can be seen as a symptom of media convergence.[11]

Although indiewood as the dominant discourse in American independent cinema became particularly pronounced in the late 1990s, when a string of films produced and/or distributed primarily by the majors' specialty film labels met with huge critical and commercial success, including *Good Will Hunting* (Van Sant, 1997, Miramax), *Shakespeare in Love* (Madden, 1998, Miramax), *Magnolia* (P.T. Anderson, 1999, New Line Cinema) and *Traffic* (Soderbergh,

2000, USA Films), its origins can be located a few years earlier. Specifically, its genesis can be traced to 1989–90, when Hollywood cinema started becoming even more deeply integrated within the structures of entertainment conglomerates than before, signalling the arrival of a new phase in the history of the US (and international) media industries.[12] After an approximately 25-year period of old-style conglomeration (see Chapters 4 and 6) and a restructuring and realignment of their parent companies' emphasis on communication and media, in the late 1980s the Hollywood majors found themselves under new ownership yet again. This time, however, the parent companies constituted a new group of conglomerates that targeted global domination of all media markets. Whether these new conglomerates originated in the media industries (News Corporation and Time) or the consumer electronics one (Sony and Matsushita), their target was to acquire the major producers of media content (film, network, cable and satellite television, music, print media, etc.) in order to support their other business segments, which tended to focus on media delivery systems that targeted the home (cable and video in particular).

This 'reconglomeration' came into full force in 1989–90 with Sony's takeover of Columbia (1989), the Time Warner merger (1989), the takeover of MCA Universal by Matsushita (1990) and Disney's aggressive expansion to other media segments following the 1990 announcement of the 'Disney Decade', a corporate plan to reinvent and expand Disney on a global scale in the 1990s. Within this climate of extraordinary transformation across the media landscape, characterised primarily by an intensified convergence of all media industries under the corporate umbrella of a handful of entertainment-focused conglomerates, and with regulatory frameworks increasingly loosening (culminating with the 1996 Telecommunications Act), it is not surprising that American independent cinema started changing too at around the same time. In this respect, the rise of Miramax, the enhanced popularity of the Sundance Film Festival, the increasing commercial success of films such as *sex, lies, and videotape* and other developments should not be seen as exceptional. Instead, they should be understood as yet another symptom generated by deep and far-reaching changes across the media industries that were taking place during the same time. Consequently, the arrival of the more commercial 'indie' cinema of the early 1990s should also be seen within a context in which a small number of entertainment conglomerates set out to bring a diverse range of 'filmed entertainment' to the home, primarily through cable, video and on-demand services.[13] In this picture, indie cinema's role was to provide product differentiation as well as keep busy the entertainment conglomerates' distribution pipelines across an expanding number of media platforms. This was an especially important role given that the Hollywood majors financed, produced and distributed directly only a relatively small number of films per year.

The establishment of the second wave of the majors' specialty film divisions (Fine Line Features, Sony Pictures Classics and Miramax) can also be understood more fully within the context of media convergence than as developments strictly within the independent film sector. Trading now not only in different media markets and segments (film, television, music, etc.) but also in different types of product for the same market (in the case of film – special effects-driven blockbusters, star- and genre-driven high-concept films that were distributed in saturation releases, as well as cheap 'indie' film and even non-US art-cinema productions that opened in a small number of theatres in platform releases) the entertainment conglomerates changed completely the rules of the industry. On the one hand, they brought together modes of production and distribution that had developed and existed in relative separation in previous decades, and therefore started to erase some of the significant differences that historically characterised media products made away from Hollywood from the ones created by the Hollywood major players. On the other hand, the conglomerates' prowess in marketing in tandem with their control of distribution and delivery systems on an increasingly global scale allowed them not only to tap into numerous niche markets, but also to succeed in popularising American independent cinema to an extent never seen before in the sector (with *Pulp Fiction*, another early sign of the imminent arrival of indiewood, being a key example).

More specifically, these divisions represent a move on behalf of the entertainment conglomerates towards further vertical integration within a specific media market segment (film), while at the same time providing further opportunities for synergies between themselves and their other established media branches, strengthening therefore their integration on a horizontal level too. Sony Pictures Classics provides an excellent illustration of the benefits these specialty film divisions offered their parent companies, as the introduction of this specific film division in 1992 provided Sony with a number of advantages over some of its competitors. First, Sony ensured its presence in both key markets in American cinema: that of wide releases, through its major finance, production and distribution company Columbia Pictures, and the increasingly lucrative American specialty film market, which would be served by its new subsidiary.[14] Sony Pictures Classics would also continue to trade in non-US art-house films in an effort to be present in that niche but prestigious market too.

Second, with the introduction of SPC, Sony quickly increased the number of its theatrical releases by a third (and in later years almost doubled them). Specifically, by 1996, next to Columbia and TriStar's 40 US film releases during that particular calendar year Sony could also boast an additional 18 releases by SPC, which contributed an extra $40 million in US theatrical box office gross next to Columbia-TriStar's $580 million.[15] Arguably more important than the theatrical receipts, however, the SPC releases increased the speed with which Sony's library of titles expanded, therefore adding value to the company as a whole.

Third, SPC provided additional product for Sony Pictures Home Entertainment, Sony's division that traded in the area of home video. During a time when video was the only alternative to cable, and given Sony's absence from the cable market due to its historical emphasis on the video market, the additional titles helped Sony expand its home entertainment audience. This is because art-house and independent films have targeted traditionally older and more upmarket audiences, who were not served satisfactorily by the franchise and star and genre films of the majors, which tended to target primarily younger audiences.

Fourth, the expanded library of titles also meant that the parent company had more options and more diversity of product to use as leverage in pushing its consumer electronic products in various markets. This became an extremely important factor later in the 1990s and 2000s, when DVD technology started taking off, as Sony could use its titles to push DVD players. With SPC having amassed a large number of films from around the world, including the commercially ultra-successful *Crouching Tiger, Hidden Dragon* (Ang Lee, 2001), Sony's consumer electronics division had both the number and the diversity of titles to market its DVD players and support them with the right product globally. Finally, the establishment of SPC also invited potential synergies with Sony's other subsidiaries (e.g., with Columbia Records, later Sony Music Entertainment), which helped exploit particular properties from a number of perspectives, while also maximising the commercial exploitation of some of its titles. For instance, the film *Capote* (Miller, 2005), which SPC co-financed and distributed outside the US, benefited from an original soundtrack from RCA, which at that time was under the umbrella of Sony BMG, Sony's music division.

By 1995, the six conglomerated majors, together with their specialty film subsidiaries (Miramax, SPC, Fox Searchlight, Gramercy – a specialty film label co-founded by European conglomerate Polygram and Universal – New Line Cinema and its own subsidiary, Fine Line Features) and former major MGM controlled 96.47 per cent of the North American theatrical box office,[16] with the rest of the 23 film distributors vying for the remaining 3.53 per cent. However, out of this 96.47 per cent, the specialty film distributors that have been associated heavily with the American independent film sector (Miramax, New Line, Gramercy, Fine Line, Sony Pictures Classics and Fox Searchlight) accounted for 11.78 per cent of the theatrical market, representing both a very healthy picture for the sector and a significant contribution to their conglomerate parents' bottom line. In this respect, the influx of new specialty film divisions, which started with the establishment of Fox Searchlight in 1994 and Paramount Classics in 1998, came to enhance that picture, as it created even more competition in the market and therefore a need for more commercially minded independent films. These films would continue to provide product differentiation from the majors' blockbusters but would also continue to supply their parents' distribution companies with content, while at the same time standing out in a marketplace that was increasingly populated by an expanding number of distributors and therefore an increasingly large number of titles in release.

Nine years later and at the peak of indiewood, in 2004, the theatrical film market and independent film's place in it was in some ways very similar to 1995.[17] This time the conglomerated majors (the Big Six together with Dreamworks SKG and MGM) occupied 78.55 per cent, while the group of their specialty subsidiaries, which at that time included 10 companies (Miramax, New Line Cinema, Fox Searchlight, Focus Features, Sony Pictures Classics, Paramount Classics, Rogue Pictures, Dimension Films, Fine Line Features and Warner Independent Pictures) captured 12.01 per cent. Together, then, the majors and their subsidiaries were responsible for 90.56 percent. But while this seems to suggest that a little less than 10 per cent of the theatrical market was up for grabs by the rest of the distributors, indicating a fairly competitive film market, the truth was different. With large standalone companies Newmarket Films and Lionsgate capturing together another 7.61 per cent, it meant that the rest of the distributors had to fight for the remaining 1.83 per cent of the market, around half of the 3.53 per cent available to them in 1995. More importantly, while in 1995 just 23 distributors were vying for that 3.53 per cent, in 2004 that number had increased nearly five-fold, to 112.

While all the distributors other than the Hollywood majors were releasing an assortment of films, it was the star-featuring, genre-adhering, auteur-driven, increasingly expensive and carefully marketed indiewood films that attracted the lion's share of critical attention and of box office receipts in the independent/specialty film market. For instance, while long-established standalone distributor First Run Features released 12 features (eight documentaries and four fiction films) in 2004, their total box office gross was less than $0.5 million.[18] On the other hand, films such *Sideways* (Payne, 2004, Fox Searchlight), *Eternal Sunshine of the Spotless Mind* (Gondry, 2004, Focus Features), *Kinsey* (Condon, 2004, Fox Searchlight), *Before Sunset* (Linklater, 2004, Warner Independent) and *Napoleon Dynamite* (Hess, 2004, Fox Searchlight) grossed approximately $176 million in total, received multiple nominations for Academy Awards as well as awards specifically focused on independent film, and became exemplary of an indiewood cinema in a number of ways (see Case study 9.1).

Figure 9.1 The commercial appeal of *Sideways* was enhanced by the 'big laughs' afforded by the golf scene, among others.

Case study 9.1 At the peak of Indiewood: Alexander Payne and *Sideways*

> *Sideways* (Payne, 2004, 126 min.) produced by Michael London Productions and Sideways Productions, distributed by Fox Searchlight.

By 2003, Fox Searchlight, News Corporation's specialty film division in the American film market, had become a significant force in American independent cinema, with its films recording substantial box office success and the company itself getting kudos for its work and perceived as 'the very model of how a studio specialty division should operate' ('Searchlight Feasts', 2003, p. 13). A new management regime installed in 2000, six years after the company's establishment in 1994, had been working to rebrand Searchlight as a company that releases films with 'more market awareness' than in the past but without eschewing the 'tradition of artistic risk-taking' that had been the trademark of the division under the direction of Lindsay Law in the 1990s (Duke, 2000, p. 9). Indeed, if films such as *One Hour Photo* (Romanek, 2002) and *The Banger Sisters* (Dolman, 2002) were decidedly star-driven genre pictures that received wide distribution with the help of sister company 20th Century Fox, films such as *Antwone Fisher* (Washington, 2002), *The Good Girl* (Arteta, 2002) and *Kissing Jessica Stein* (Herman-Wurmfeld, 2002) were clearly 'indiewood' productions that combined the artistic risk-taking (through difficult or offbeat subject matter, introspective narratives, slow pace, etc.) with the increased market awareness that the company wanted (clear generic frameworks, the presence of Hollywood stars, strong production values, etc.).

With all the company releases in 2002 achieving in total a US theatrical box office gross of over $130 million (Tzioumakis, 2012a, p. 146), Fox Searchlight intensified this business strategy in 2003, lining up a schedule of ambitious releases that, among others, included *In America* (Sheridan), *Bend It Like Beckham* (Chadha) and *28 Days Later* (Boyle). The critical and commercial success of these films too made Searchlight a top destination for creative filmmakers, at a time when Miramax, the undisputed leader in the American independent film market in the 1990s, had moved to much more expensive productions that competed against the Hollywood majors, including *Gangs of New York* (Scorsese, 2002) and *Chicago* (Marshall, 2002). It was at this time that writer-director Alexander Payne and his collaborator Jim Taylor brought to Searchlight *Sideways*, an adaptation of the titular novel by Rex Pickett.

Having established a reputation as a key indiewood filmmaker following the critical and commercial success of *Election* (1999), which, despite having been financed and distributed by Paramount, was hailed widely as a key example of indiewood filmmaking (see, for instance, King, 2009, p. 191) and *About Schmidt* (2002), which starred Jack Nicholson against type and was released by New Line Cinema, Payne and Taylor were in a particularly strong position to make their next film in an indiewood-led American independent cinema sector (Tzioumakis, 2013a, pp. 36–8). Even before being involved with *About Schmidt*, Payne, together with producer Michael London, had optioned the (then unpublished) Rex Pickett's novel for £12,500 (Pickett, 2012a), with independent producer-distributor Artisan reportedly interested in financing the production with a budget of $10 million (Pickett, 2012b). However, Payne ended up committing to *About Schmidt*, while by the time of that film's release Artisan was in financial trouble and on the way to a corporate takeover by Lions Gate a year later, in 2003 (Waxman, 2003), which meant that whatever deal was in place was voided.

Following the success of *About Schmidt* (which in the US alone grossed $65 million), Payne went back to *Sideways* and together with Taylor invested further in the property's development by writing the script and casting the film, choosing little-known Paul Giamatti and Thomas Haden Church as the main leads (Goldstein, 2003). With a complete package in place, London, Taylor and Payne pitched the film to a number of companies, both studio specialty film divisions such as Focus Features and Hollywood majors such as Paramount and Dreamworks SKG (Kunz, 2007, p. 114). In the end, the project ended up at Searchlight, which greenlit the film in the autumn of 2003 with a budget of $18 million (Goldstein, 2003). Part of the reason the film was rejected by the other companies was its casting, which was not star-led. On the other hand, Searchlight, which wanted to work with Payne as part of its strategy to continue to attract creative filmmakers, not only accepted the film package as was, but reportedly broke its 'ironclad $15 million budget ceiling by $3 million' (Thompson, 2004) to secure the film.

In many ways *Sideways* is a textbook example of an indiewood film, combining an in-depth character study (expected in many independent films) with an appealing plot about two friends spending a week together in beautiful Californian wine country before one of them gets married (which locates the film firmly within well-established narrative tropes and generic traditions, including the pre-wedding stag-do, the buddy film and the road movie). This confirms fully King's definition of 'Indiewood' as a practice where 'some markers of distinction often remain present but in combination with more mainstream/accessible characteristics than might generally be associated with examples of art or less indie film' (2009, p. 21) that targets an audience 'receptive to the presence of some markers of difference or distinction [but] within the context of frameworks broadly familiar from the Hollywood mainstream' (p. 35).

In terms of the former approach, the narrative pays particular attention to a number of details that reveal the main characters as complex individuals, not easily reducible to stereotypes or understood as narrative functions. For instance, Miles (Giamatti) is a considerate, eloquent, well-read man, with exceptional abilities in wine tasting, and is clearly placed as the main point of identification for the viewer. At the same time, he is seen to steal money from his mother's savings to finance the trip with his friend, is an avid reader of *Barely Legal* and succumbs all too often to the temptation to see things with dark-tinted glasses. Jack (Haden Church), on the other hand, is presented as ultra-confident, successful professionally, ready to marry in to a well-off family and always with a positive disposition, a clear counterpoint to Miles. However, he is also very shallow, while his positive qualities are revealed to be a façade when towards the end of the film he collapses in despair, realising that he might lose his future wife because of his infidelities.

These rich characterisations, however, are contained within a linear narrative (with the days of the week the friends spend together clearly marked through intertitles), driven by causality and spiked by a number of comedic moments that lighten considerably the otherwise pensive and introspective tone that permeates the film. Jack's crazy run with the golf club, the two friends' inability to fake a car accident, the stark naked man who runs after them following Miles's effort to retrieve Jack's wedding ring after yet another example of the latter's infidelities and several other scenes provide big laughs in a film that also uses many sequences with minimalist piano music and no dialogue to depict the characters' emotions and feelings. Furthermore, the film makes the most of the very appealing Californian landscape, with a number of scenes taking place in sun-kissed vineyards, picturesque villages, upscale wineries and inviting restaurants and bars. As a result, the character studies are often subsumed in wider formal structures determined by genre conventions, especially those associated with the road movie (driving through these areas, which become a very prominent background for the plot to unfold against). In the end all goes well. Despite cheating on his future wife repeatedly and having his face smashed by one of his conquests when she finds that he is getting married, Jack's wedding takes place on schedule and without a hitch, with Miles as the best man. Miles, on the other hand, is eventually forgiven by his own lover during the trip, after not having told her the truth about his and Jack's trip. As expected in road movies, both men have learned a lot about themselves during this trip and are ready to 'grow up' and form adult relationships.

If narrative and genre allow small and sometimes contradictory details of the characters' lives to open up avenues through which viewers can question identity formations only for these to be couched by stronger narrative and generic conventions such as the happy ending, the development of self-knowledge, the formation of the heterosexual couple and so on, visual style is similarly utilised often unconventionally but overall within the classical mode of storytelling. This is particularly evident in a scene where the two main characters drive through the Californian wine country and a montage sequence composed of split screens consisting of asymmetrical shots of vineyards and grape harvesting and accompanied by an upbeat music soundtrack appears out of nowhere. The sequence, which lasts about 30 seconds, adds little to the narrative while the split-screen technique is not used again in the film. However, it highlights in an emphatic way the beauty of the landscape, the glorious sunshine (which sometimes is reflected in the camera's lens) and the significance of the vineyards in local wine production. With the film's plot unfolding primarily in the Santa Ynez Valley, which is full of vineyards and wineries, the sequence does not look out of context, despite contributing little to the narrative and breaking away from the rules of classical editing that have been structuring the film's visual economy throughout.

On the other hand, the technique and its emphasis on highlighting the landscape represents an invitation to discerning audiences to make comparisons with other such instances where these elements are mobilised, especially the films of the Hollywood Renaissance, such as *The Thomas Crown Affair* (Jewison, 1968) and a number of buddy/road movies such as *Scarecrow* (Schatzberg, 1971) and *Thunderbolt and Lightfoot* (Cimino, 1974). According to the film's production notes, Payne was influenced by 'the maverick, gritty and deeply personal American filmmaking of the 1970s that led to the explosion of road movies in the first place' and collaborated closely with his director of photography, Phedon Papamichael, to achieve a 'retro' style characterised by 'a certain softness and pastel quality to the colors that you see in 60s and 70s films' (*Sideways* Production Notes, no date). And with Hollywood Renaissance films considered predecessors to a considerable part of contemporary American independent cinema, thanks to a number of popular books (Mottram, 2006, Biskind, 2005) and TV documentaries ('The Movie Brats, Take Two') that make this connection, it is clear that *Sideways* played up this angle, as the film's production notes also confirm.

The film was a commercial and critical triumph, grossing over $100 million at the worldwide theatrical market, receiving a very large number of awards and eventually becoming Fox Searchlight's most commercially successful and award-winning film in its history to that time ('*Sideways* Is Fox Searchlight's Most Successful Film', 2005). Equally important, it was a major contributor to what can be seen retrospectively as a golden age of indiewood filmmaking in the mid-2000s together with a number of titles that found similar success and defined the sector: *Lost in Translation* (S. Coppola, 2003), *Eternal Sunshine of the Spotless Mind* (Gondry, 2004), *Napoleon Dynamite* (Hess, 2004), *Brokeback Mountain* (Ang Lee, 2005), *Crash* (Haggis, 2005), *Good Night, and Good Luck* (Clooney, 2005), *Capote* (Miller, 2005).

In the aftermath of this success, both the filmmaker and the company went from strength to strength, with Payne continuing his personal/commercial filmmaking with *The Descendants* (2011) and *Nebraska* (2014), while Fox Searchlight not only survived the 2008 closure of most of the majors' specialty film divisions, but became the undisputed leader in the vastly reshaped independent film sector of the 2010s, continuing to back clearly indiewood filmmaking with such critical and commercial successes as: *Juno* (Reitman, 2007), *Slumdog Millionaire* (Boyle, 2008), *The Grand Budapest Hotel* (Anderson, 2014) and *Birdman* (or *The Unexpected Virtue of Ignorance*) (Iñárritu, 2014).

Finally, many indiewood films participated in and benefited from a number of practices that were becoming commonplace across the media industries as the impact of media convergence started to be felt in the 1990s and 2000s. Extensions, synergies and franchise-building, practices that Jenkins identifies as hallmarks of corporate media convergence and once associated only with the conglomerated Hollywood majors,[19] started to become increasingly visible in the indiewood-dominated independent film sector at the time. For instance, the majors' specialty film divisions 'extended' their market substantially by gaining entry to all delivery systems and platforms controlled by their parent companies, giving them a significant advantage over standalone companies that did not have access to these platforms. Productions such as *Capote*, which was distributed by Sony Pictures Classics, tried to benefit from synergies, including the release of a soundtrack by RCA, as mentioned above. Even franchising, arguably the least expected practice in the independent film sector, eventually found its way in it. Perhaps most famously Kevin Smith has tried to exploit the cultural cachet of his 1994 film *Clerks*, with two sequels, a six-episode TV show, merchandising and the establishment of his well known Askewniverse, while his *Jay and Silent Bob Strike Back* (2001), itself originally based on a comic book, so far has produced two TV movie spin-offs: *Jay and Silent Bob Get Old* (2012) and *Jay and Silent Bob Get Irish* (2013) (both directed by himself). With other independent films such as *The Blair Witch Project* (Myrick and Sanchez, 1999) and *My Big Fat Greek Wedding* (Zwick, 2002) having a rich history of efforts towards franchising, with films such as *Before Sunrise* (1995) expanding into trilogies and lending their characters' to filmmaker Richard Linklater's other film *Waking Life* (2001) and with films such as *The Darjeeling Limited* (W. Anderson, 2007) attached to prequels such as *Hotel Chevalier* (2007) the concept of franchising has certainly become significant in more recent American independent cinema.[20]

The studio pullout and the demise of Miramax

With indiewood films becoming increasingly expensive to produce and market and finding often spectacular commercial success, especially during the mid- and late 2000s, a number of conglomerated majors started questioning the *raison d'être* of their specialty film divisions. More specifically, by 2007 the average marketing costs for a specialty film release in the US alone had reached $25 million, up 44 per cent from the previous year. This meant that studio divisions might find themselves spending this amount of money as print and advertising (P&A) costs for films that could have cost only $10 million to produce, making it increasingly difficult to break even.[21] If this was difficult to achieve for low-budget films, it was equally, if not more, difficult for studio divisions to recoup costs if the films they released were expensive productions. With almost all studio divisions eventually turning to production and with the average production costs hitting $49.2 million in 2007,[22] it was clear that a film needed to reach $100 million at the very minimum for its producers to start thinking of profits (after theatres kept part of the box office revenues, the distributor had deducted its fee, advertising and marketing costs were accounted for and production costs were paid). And even though the sector had started seeing an expansive list of box office hits grossing over $100 million – *Pulp Fiction, Good Will Hunting, Shakespeare in Love, Traffic, March of the Penguins* (Jacquet, 2004), *Fahrenheit 9/11* (Moore, 2004) – this was still a rare occurrence even in the heyday of indiewood.

With the availability of such enormous amounts of distribution and marketing funds at their disposal and with the need to utilise increasingly wide release methods for their specialty product, both in order to stand out in a congested marketplace and because the commercial elements of many of these films often merited them, a number of these divisions started looking increasingly like major releasing organisations. In this respect, their corporate parents started to question whether it made financial sense to maintain two different film-releasing divisions and their respective infrastructures and overhead costs if both used the same distribution methods and practices. Even if some films had originally to have a platform release, to build the word of mouth and to receive positive reviews that they could use when eventually expanding widely (in over 1,000 engagements), the long-established former studios would be able to handle such a process, especially as the marketing mix of such films included an emphasis on stardom, genre and authorship, elements that major releasing organisations knew well how to sell.

At the same time, the sector started facing problems that pointed to a dark future for indiewood. The first was a product glut, with the number of theatrical releases and the distributors behind them increasing exponentially. Indeed, compared with only the previous year, 2007 had witnessed 18 additional releases in the specialty film sector, while the number of releases in the US in general had leapfrogged from 449 in 2002 to 590 in 2007, with the major studios being responsible for only a fraction of this incredible 30 per cent increase in five years.[23] More spectacularly, in the same five-year period, the number of distributors in the US theatrical market more than doubled, from 74 releasing organisations in 2002 to 154 in 2007,[24] which explains clearly the need for higher budgets and marketing costs for a film to be noticed in such a competitive marketplace.

A second problem was access to theatres as the franchise blockbusters of the conglomerated majors increased in number. For instance, during one week in the summer of 2009, the top three films at the US theatrical box office, all released by Hollywood majors – *Harry Potter and the Half-Blood Prince* (Yates, Warner Bros.), *Ice Age: Dawn of the Dinosaurs* (Saldanha and Thurmeier, Fox) and *Transformers: Revenge of the Fallen* (Bay, Paramount) – claimed 12,000 theatres,[25] a little less than one-third of all the available screens in the US that year.[26] With the other releases of the majors claiming a comparable number of theatres and screens and with their more commercial films promising exhibitors a higher volume of ticket sales than even the top indiewood titles, it is clear that this was also a substantial problem in terms of the extent to which investment in indiewood film could continue at the same intensity.

Finally, the producers and distributors both of franchise blockbusters and of independent films had to get to grips with the alarming slowdown of DVD sales, which had become a key ancillary market, especially in the first half of the 2000s. Indeed, an indiewood film such as *Sideways* was not only a box office smash in the theatres, it also sold 1.5 million units in DVD (a fraction of which was in VHS) on the first day of its home-video release, thus providing Fox Searchlight with significant additional revenue.[27] However, after consecutive years of huge increases in penetration levels, DVD technology quickly reached saturation. By 2006, sales of films on DVD were growing only by 2 per cent per annum, while by 2010 there was a fall in sales of approximately 20 per cent compared with the figures in 2006.[28] With no alternative home-delivery technology advanced enough to anticipate a turnaround, by 2008 the Hollywood majors, their specialty film labels and independent producers and distributors were seeing their biggest ancillary market shrinking. With the majority of independent films already finding it increasingly difficult to assert themselves in the theatrical marketplace it was becoming clear that their chances of being 'discovered' in the home-video market a few months later were diminishing.

This complex combination of rising costs, increasing competition, diminishing market and replication of operations provided the rationale for the corporate parents of the specialty film divisions to start pulling out of the indiewood-dominated independent film market, starting with Time Warner, which in February 2008 brought New Line Cinema's distribution operations within the fold of Warner Bros. while allowing it to continue producing films under that brand name. With New Line Cinema having become increasingly focused on franchise films such as the *Rush Hour* (1998–2007) and *Austin Powers* (1998–2003) trilogies it was not surprising that it was the first such division, a major independent, to cease to operate as a distributor, given that Warner Bros. could easily oversee similar franchises and films such as *Sex and the City: The Movie* (King, 2008) and *Sex and the City: The Movie 2* (King, 2010). However, if the end of New Line Cinema was not surprising given that Warner Bros. could rather easily assume the former's operations, Time Warner's decision to close a few months later (June 2008) both its other specialty film labels, Warner Independent Pictures (after a five-year presence in the market) and Picturehouse (three years after its establishment), caught the industry by surprise, as it meant that it was pulling out of the independent film market completely. As I have discussed elsewhere in detail, neither Warner division had performed particularly well financially, despite an early success with the documentary *March of the Penguins*, while both divisions had been latecomers in the independent film market and therefore had found it difficult to compete with established powers such as Fox Searchlight and Focus Features.[29]

If Time Warner's exit from specialty and independent filmmaking surprised the industry, Viacom's decision to do the same a few days later with its own subsidiary, Paramount Vantage, shows clearly the problems of the indiewood-focused specialty film divisions of the conglomerated Hollywood majors. In the 1998–2005 period, Viacom had maintained the rather low-profile Paramount Classics, a subsidiary that had not followed its fellow studio specialty film divisions in pursuing primarily indiewood film production and instead was relying primarily on acquisitions of independently produced films from festivals – a practice associated with the previous wave of studio divisions, in the early 1990s. But in 2005, with the success of indiewood films sweeping the industry, Viacom established Paramount Vantage with the explicit intention of competing in that market. In many respects, Paramount Vantage was a rebranded Paramount Classics, though the latter continued to exist after 2005 as a production outfit, albeit it made only a handful of films, which were released by Vantage. With the new division finding itself in both the production and the distribution business of films that were much more commercial than the releases of Paramount Classics, it is clear that the company underwent a major identity change while also requiring strong financial returns in its investment in order to remain viable. These returns, however, did not materialise, despite the company's association with such key indiewood films of the mid-2000s as *Babel, There Will Be Blood, No Country for Old Men* (Coen and Coen, 2007) and *Into the Wild* (Penn, 2008). According to industry critics, the majority of the division's releases after *Babel* barely broke even, if they did not lose money,[30] while its participation in the multi-award winning and commercially successful *No Country for Old Men* entailed only its exploitation in international markets and not the US, where the film recorded a very strong box office gross of just under $75 million.[31]

While the closures of these four companies clearly demonstrated a rapidly changing landscape in 2008, the sector's restructuring took a new turn two years later when Disney shuttered Miramax Films, the company most closely associated with the indie and indiewood iterations of contemporary American independent cinema, especially during the 1990s. After a protracted period of speculation about its future, Disney sold its specialty film division for a reported $660 million to a consortium of equity investors interested in exploiting its library of titles and not in running the company as a theatrical distribution organisation.[32] The sale took place almost five years after Bob and Harvey Weinstein, Miramax's founders and top executives for almost 25 years, had walked out of the company following a well-publicised fall-out with Disney's chairman, Michael Eisner, over a number of issues.[33] However, despite the nature of these problems, the issue in hand was Miramax's incredible expansion and success, to the extent that in the 2000s critics debated if it was part of the independent cinema scene following releases of films that had cost upwards of $100 million to produce, such as *The Aviator* (Scorsese, 2004) and *Cold Mountain* (Minghella, 2003), and attaching to it a range of labels, including: 'mini major,' 'semi indie company,' and 'quasi studio' (see Introduction), while, as discussed in this book, following Wyatt (1998a), film scholars have considered it together with New Line Cinema as a major independent.

But since the Weinstein brothers' departure in 2005 and until its sale in 2010, Miramax had been transformed from the undisputed leader of the specialty film market to a small-scale producer-distributor that was finding it increasingly difficult to remain competitive in the market it had helped create. The company was releasing on average eight films per year, with *No Country for Old Men* (which it co-produced and co-distributed with Paramount Vantage) being its only major critical and commercial success during that time. In this respect, and in line with decisions by Time Warner and Viacom, Disney's move to offload its once market-leading and market-defining subsidiary was hardly surprising, especially as the conglomerate also stood to make $660 million from a company it had originally bought in 1993 for $60 million.

A further chapter in the Hollywood majors' pullback from the independent film sector took place in late 2013, when Comcast restructured Focus Features, recalibrating it as a company with interests beyond indiewood when once it had thrived with such defining indiewood films as *Lost in Translation, Eternal Sunshine of the Spotless Mind* and *Brokeback Mountain*. With the company's more recent releases including horror sequels such as *Sinister 2* (Foy, 2015) and *Insidious: Chapter 3* (Whannell, 2015) and erotica such as *Fifty Shades of Grey* (Taylor-Johnson, 2015), Focus Features now specialises in theatrical releases of international films in the English language such as *The Danish Girl* (Hooper, 2015) and *Suffragette* (Gavron, 2015). Indeed, the rebranded division's increasing dissociation with indiewood was formally underwritten recently (2016) by its merger with Universal Pictures International Productions, a move designed to bring it even closer to worldwide specialty film production and distribution than to production and distribution associated with independent filmmaking in the US.[34]

As is clear, these developments have reshaped the independent film sector radically, leaving a consolidated indiewood realm that is now dominated by the remaining two Hollywood studio specialty divisions (Fox Searchlight and Sony Pictures Classics) as well as a small number of standalone companies such as Lionsgate, Summit Entertainment (with the two merging in 2012 to create a very large entertainment company without any ties to the Hollywood majors), the Weinstein Company, FilmDistrict, Open Road, A24, STX and a few others. However, a substantially consolidated sector in terms of the number of specialty film companies does not necessarily mean the production of fewer indiewood titles, and certainly does not mean the end of indiewood as the dominant expression of American independent cinema since the late 1990s. Indeed, as I will also discuss in the epilogue to the present volume, indiewood films have been increasingly financed, produced and distributed by the Hollywood majors themselves, which means that the 'indiewood' label is now also becoming a Hollywood major film category as well as an independent film one.

With such a shift suggesting a vastly bigger identity crisis in the independent film sector than in the 1990s, when the emergence of the 'indie' label prompted a number of critics to question the term 'independent', it has fallen increasingly on the multitude of filmmaking activity at the very margins of the sector to lay claim to the label and shift the discourse of independence to a different expression of filmmaking. This expression, thanks primarily to the advent of new digital technologies, has been moving increasingly away from the theatres and to the digital screens of YouTube and on-demand services, creating in the process a new landscape in the sector, one nonetheless that has been increasingly difficult to map and understand.

Beyond indiewood: digital filmmaking and the regeneration of American independent cinema

Despite making its appearance in the early 1990s, digital film production started receiving critical attention in the independent film sector in the US after films produced under the Dogme 95 banner such as the Danish titles *Festen* [*The Celebration*] (Vinterberg, 1998) and *Idioterne* [*The Idiots*] (von Trier, 1998) caused a stir with their unconventional film techniques, controversial subject matter and anti-mainstream cinema politics.[35] But it was not until the early 2000s that digital independent film production took off in the sector with a number of initiatives established to support it. According to King, by 2003, 30 per cent of all feature films submitted to the Sundance Film Festival were shot in digital video,[36] demonstrating clearly the potential of the technology to contribute towards a paradigm shift in American independent cinema. This was especially as new online and other distribution platforms for many of these films had started making their dissemination easier than in the past – a chronic problem for most low-budget independent films given their limited chances for theatrical distribution, a field historically dominated by Hollywood studio films and of course the increasingly commercial indiewood productions, as we saw in the previous section. With scholars like Zimmermann calling as early as 2005 for a reconsideration of independent film as a form of cinema that moves beyond celluloid and exhibition in theatres and festivals,[37] it was clear that digital technology was changing the fabric of the independent film sector as the latter was experiencing the long-term effects of media convergence.

Zimmermann's argument became particularly evident a few years later, when the mobility of exhibition and consumption of film and other media content increased exponentially, especially after the appearance and rapid market pervasiveness of tablets, smartphones and other mobile technologies that were used as exhibition platforms. This opened many new doors for low-budget independent films. As Hayley Trowbridge has noted, during a short but transformative period in the second half of the 2000s numerous

distribution-related trends emerged, including but not limited to: the implementation of digital distribution practices (e.g. distributing film via hard drives
and digital downloads) and marketing strategies (e.g. use of QR codes and viral
campaigns); an increased visibility and viability of non-theatrical distribution
models (especially online distribution through a number of outlets) and the
utilisation of new marketing avenues (especially through the use of social
media); the entry of new companies and platforms into the distribution field
(YouTube, Amazon, iTunes, SnagFilms, Filmdoo, IndiePix and others) and
marketing arena (again social media, especially MySpace up to the late 2000s,
Twitter and Facebook); and a general reinvigoration of DIY and grassroots
distribution models and marketing strategies that enabled an unprecedented
number of filmmakers to disseminate their work to particular audiences.[38]
Of course, conventional distribution and marketing methods are far from
becoming extinct, with the overall revenues from theatrical distribution
increasing steadily, from $9.3 billion in 2003 to $11.1 billion in 2015 in the
US alone.[39] Still, all these new developments have been changing, on some
occasions radically, the rules of the game for both Hollywood and independent
filmmakers. With the latter now able to locate often directly audiences through
social media and to publicise their films to often very precisely calculated niche
demographics, it is clear that this is a time when low-budget independent
filmmakers do not have to consider extremely expensive theatrical releases as a
necessity, especially as the number of people who watch films on new mobile
exhibition technologies is constantly increasing.

Although not many of these films have crossed over to the mainstream in
the same way that some of the indiewood titles mentioned earlier have, the
low-budget digital independent film sub-sector has an increasing number
of success stories, of films that beat the odds and in the process connected
with substantial audiences through a variety of distribution methods and
exhibition platforms, while also achieving respectable remuneration. For
instance, *Tarnation* (Caouette, 2003), a film that reportedly cost just $300 to
produce, and *Four Eyed Monsters* (Buice and Crumley, 2005) epitomised what
Geoff King has called the 'digital desktop aesthetic'; that is, they were created
primarily with non-professional equipment which provided these generally
autobiographical films with a strong identity.[40] Distributed in novel ways,
both films attracted significant attention, which translated into respectable
commercial success. Furthermore, the now famous 'mumblecore' cycle of
films, with titles such as *The Puffy Chair* (Duplass, 2005), *Mutual Appreciation*
(Bujalski, 2005) and *Alexander the Last* (Swanberg, 2008), which took its name
from the often inaudible and incomprehensible way many of the characters in
these films talk, consisted primarily of films that were not distributed in the
theatres. Yet, these films developed a substantial following in other platforms

on which they were released, demonstrating that for this type of independent filmmaking theatrical distribution and exhibition were considered anachronistic,[41] even though they were utilised to some extent and for some titles in particular markets. Furthermore, digital independent film production has had significant success in the documentary feature genre, as a number of documentarians have used the advent of digital filmmaking not just to make films on a number of important subjects, but also to distribute them online and to encourage activism for the various causes their films have championed.[42]

If there is anything at the core of these developments, besides the presence of the digital technology that facilitates them, it is an emphasis on the new forms of finance, production, distribution and exhibition that bypass the significant barriers to entry associated with professional filmmaking. This is especially important given the increasingly expensive indiewood productions that often have been considered as having few points of contact with what I have called elsewhere the 'low-key and low-budget quality independent film' that exemplified the formative years of American independent cinema movement in the late 1970s and most of the 1980s.[43] In this respect, efforts to locate new sources of finance, to develop novel and cheap methods of tackling the logistics of production, to come up with creative approaches to distribution and marketing and to develop new exhibition practices have become increasingly prominent at the margins of a sector that has been changing at a rapid pace. The rest of this section will provide an overview of these efforts.

In terms of the realm of production finance, American independent cinema has always had success stories of filmmakers who, against all odds, managed to come up with inventive and creative ways to raise the necessary funds to produce their films (see, for instance, Case study 6.2, on John Sayles and *Return of the Secaucus 7*, and Case study 8.2, on Kevin Smith and *Clerks*). While such partly self-finance models have continued and intensified in the digital era, by far the most significant new development has been the emergence of crowdfunding. As defined by *Forbes*, this practice involves the 'funding a project or venture by raising many small amounts of money from a large number of people, typically via the Internet'.[44] With independent film projects requiring a relatively small investment for their production, crowdfunding became a very significant source of funding for thousands of films, especially when two major internet platforms dedicated to this kind of practice emerged in the late 2000s, Kickstarter in 2009 and the aptly named Indiegogo a year earlier. Indeed, by the end of 2012 and in Kickstarter alone, according to data from the platform more than $100 million had been pledged to almost 5,000 feature-length films by approximately 900,000 people, 86 of these films received theatrical distribution and 49 were among the official selection of titles for the 2011 Sundance Film Festival.[45] Such results prompted the trade press in

2013 to pronounce crowdfunding as becoming 'more and more the standard for independent film projects'[46] and popular publications such as *Wired* to proclaim in 2014 that 'Kickstarter ha[d] changed indie moviemaking for good' and that '"crowdfunding" [had] entered the popular lexicon as it expanded from funding DIY endeavors to multimillion-dollar celebrity projects and [had] become one of the most exciting — and polarizing — developments in pop culture'.[47] By 2015, the number of all film project campaigns launched in Kickstarter had reached the 48,000 mark, with almost 25,000 reaching their target goal in terms of funding,[48] demonstrating, besides the wild success of this method of funding, the difficulties involved in mapping out the terrain of independent film in the US given the volume of films being made.

If production finance has undergone such dramatic changes that have made access to funds easier than ever before, similar developments can be seen in the field of production itself. Digital technology has moved in giant leaps since the late 1990s when the introduction of digital video (DV) first demonstrated the potential for the development of an independent cinema at the margins of the sector. Writing in 2005, Chris Holmlund argued that by that time both established and new filmmakers were adopting digital video technology, which had a number of advantages, especially in terms of reducing costs but also because of the ways it enabled filmmakers to maintain control of their work, both creative and financial. This is because, on the one hand, that technology was becoming increasingly affordable for individual filmmakers, while, on the other hand, a number of organisations, companies and institutions were being established to provide resources for and support this type of filmmaking.[49] As King remarked, by the early 2000s digital cameras capable of producing good-quality images were available for as little as $1,000, while editing software packages had been developed for use in personal computers.[50] However, as by that time distribution was still defined primarily by theatres, home video and cable television, channels that were controlled by major entertainment conglomerates and their affiliated gatekeepers, digital productions had few opportunities to circulate widely. This was especially because the flat image of DV made them look like cheap, amateurish productions compared with the ones produced by professional equipment, which partly explains why even films with a star-studded cast such as *Tadpole* (Winick, 2001) and *Tape* (Linklater, 2001) found little commercial success in the theatres, with the former recording a box office gross of $2.9 million and the latter a little less than $0.5 million.[51]

However, as online distribution started becoming increasingly accessible from the late 2000s onwards with the introduction of video sharing platforms such as YouTube and as the aspect of media convergence that wanted consumers to be able to seek media experiences online started materialising increasingly, it was clear that digital filmmaking had a much better opportunity to create spaces where it could be consumed and appreciated than in earlier years. This was especially as the technology to make films continued to improve and become increasingly inexpensive, while also being incorporated in user-friendly devices such as smartphones that made image capture and editing easy (see also Case study 9.2). With video-making and video-sharing becoming quickly cultural phenomena in all parts of the world where people have access to and can afford the devices and the technology, it is not surprising that low-budget digital filmmaking in the US (and elsewhere) also has broken away from the margins of the industry and found itself in a much more central place in the American independent cinema landscape than in the mid-2000s. This can be seen clearly in the increased emphasis placed on digital film productions by key institutions in support of independent filmmaking. For instance, in 2010 the Sundance Film Festival introduced its NEXT category, which, through an emphasis on films that combine 'digital tech with unfettered creativity', targeted filmmakers working at the margins of the sector.[52] Indeed, such has been the impact of low-budget digital filmmaking, not just in the sector but in the media landscape at large, that by 2014 popular magazines such as *Rolling Stone* were reporting on the 'post-Sundance, post-SXSW, post-digital cinema era', an era when 'we take the notion of non-Hollywood moviemaking for granted'.[53]

If finance became increasingly easy given the level of micro-budgets that many filmmakers became accustomed to in the digital age and the means of production became increasingly accessible, it was arguably the field of distribution that underwent the most radical change since the late 2000s. While DVD had been instrumental in providing low-budget digital films with a strong alternative to theatrical distribution for most of the 2000s and filmmakers routinely set up websites through which they can sell their films directly to interested parties or utilise online marketplaces such as Amazon, by the late 2000s this particular distribution technology was becoming increasingly obsolete in the face of an increasingly pervasive on-demand culture. Indeed, as mentioned above, DVD sales had already plateaued in 2006 and started declining the following year. On the other hand, increasing access to broadband internet (for both filmmakers and film audiences) and the constant and rapid improvement in bandwidth ushered the meteoric rise of download and streaming technologies.[54] Besides being able almost immediately to challenge DVD as the key film exhibition channel in the home, these technologies answered a demand for film exhibition on the go, via mobile platforms such as smartphones and tablets, which were also being introduced in the marketplace at around the same time (with the first iPad tablet introduced by Apple in April 2010).

These developments dovetailed with the entry to the independent film market of a number of new companies, which provided access to online

Figure 9.2 American independent film in the age of the smartphone: *Tangerine* was shot entirely on enhanced iPhone5 cameras.

Case study 9.2 From professional cameras to smartphones: new opportunities for independent filmmakers in the micro-budget sector – *Tangerine*

> *Tangerine* (Baker, 2015, 86 min.) produced by Duplass Brothers Productions and Through Films, distributed by Magnolia Pictures.

Contemporary American independent cinema has been notorious for the frequent critical and commercial success of micro-budgeted films, shoestring productions that were produced and distributed commercially, despite great obstacles and constraints, primarily because of the persistence and ingenuity of the filmmakers. Robert Rodriguez and *El Mariachi* (1993), Kevin Smith and *Clerks* (1994), Ed Burns and *The Brothers McMullen* (1995) and especially Jonathan Caouette and *Tarnation* (2003), with the last film allegedly having cost $300 to produce, have made for greatly entertaining success stories in the sector and have been cited time and again by filmmakers and critics as inspirational. As Kleinhans put it, working on shoestring films that eventually become box office hits represents 'a much-hyped aspect of independent features' that nonetheless distorts the bigger picture (1998, p. 318). Indeed, as we saw in Case Study 8.2, on *Clerks*, the original cut of the film might have cost approximately $27,000 but Miramax invested over four times this figure to blow it up from 16mm to 35mm and therefore make it suitable for commercial exhibition.

Although these success stories have persisted in more recent years, with films such as *Four Eyed Monsters* (Buice and Crumley, 2005), *Paranormal Activity* (Peli, 2007) and several titles associated with the 'mumblecore' film cycle acquiring legendary status, what is different from the earlier titles of the 1990s is that the crossover success of the more recent films has not depended primarily on securing theatrical exhibition (though some of these films did receive a theatrical release). Instead, success has often been ascribed to the persistence, ingenuity and entrepreneurship of their makers, both in terms of arranging the means of production and, perhaps more importantly, in terms of securing distribution deals through new (digital) avenues and platforms as well as exploiting opportunities provided by social media. *Tangerine* is certainly one such recent example of a micro-budgeted film having managed to become both critically acclaimed and commercially successful, including through release in theatrical markets in the US and other countries.

Prior to *Tangerine* writer-director Sean Baker had a number of credits, including four other micro-budgeted independent features, the budgets for which has been estimated in the range of just $3,000 for *Take Out* (2004) (http://www.imdb.com/title/tt0391483/business?ref_=tt_dt_bus) to $235,000 for *Starlet* (2012) (Jacobs, 2015). Although Baker was not looking to make another such low-budget production he nonetheless was offered production finance by Mark and Jay Duplass to make another such film under their Duplass Brothers Productions banner, a production company that supported inexpensive productions (Jacobs, 2015) and had achieved significant visibility in film and television in the 2010s, especially as one of its TV properties, *Togetherness* (2015–16), had been optioned by HBO around the same time (Watercutter, 2015).

At that point Baker and frequent collaborator and screenwriter Chris Bergoch did not have a script but were interested in making a film that takes place in a very specific part of west Los Angeles, the corner of Santa Monica Boulevard and Highland Avenue. Being aware of the fact that the area is used by transgender sex workers Baker and Bergoch decided to come up with a story that takes place in that particular milieu, including having transgender actors playing the leads. Not knowing any of these workers, but wanting to make the film 'responsibly and respectfully' (Watercutter, 2015), the filmmakers started talking to a number of transgender people in a nearby LGBT centre. This is where they met Mya Taylor (who plays Alexandra), who introduced them to Kitana Kiki Rodriguez (who plays Sin-Dee), both African American, and through discussions and interviews with them Baker and Bergoch came up with the core of a story that revolves around the efforts of a transgender sex worker to track down the cisgender person her boyfriend cheated on her with and confront them both. This story is supplemented and interestingly juxtaposed with a second story, that of an Armenian taxi driver who often buys the services of transgender sex workers, despite being married with children, and who in his turn tries to track down Alexandra.

With an extensive treatment of the story prepared and with Taylor and Rodriquez unconventionally cast in the main leads, despite not having prior acting experience, the Duplass brothers gave Baker $100,000 (Jacobs, 2015), which, while it guaranteed some of the costs, was not sufficient for the kind of film Baker had in mind, a significant portion of which relied on extensive location shooting. Baker needed either more funds to be able to afford the equipment, crew and other logistical details of the shoot or to reconfigure the story in such a way that it would not depend on characters moving along the streets of Los Angeles.

It was at this point that Baker decided to explore the possibility of shooting the film not with a professional camera but with a smartphone camera, specifically the iPhone 5 camera. By that time (early 2014), there were already films that had been shot with an iPhone, such as the micro-budgeted *King Kelly* (Neel, 2012), which was partly shot with an iPhone 4 (McCauley, 2012), while in the more avant-garde milieu of independent cinema, artist Jamie Jenkinson had used the iPhone5 for a series of experimental short video works (Hamlyn, 2015, pp. 44–51). However, given the limitations of the iPhone camera, especially its inability to select focus (which means that everything in the recorded image is in sharp focus no matter how far or close to the lens) but mainly because of the fact that its use has been synonymous with amateur videos that have overwhelmed digital platforms and social media, it had not been utilised fully in commercial feature filmmaking.

Deciding that it was the only way to make the kind of film they wanted to make with the budget they had, Baker and Radium Cheung (who are credited together as co-directors of photography) set out to enhance substantially the iPhone5 camera's ability and tailor it to the demands of *Tangerine*. Starting with looking at videos with iPhone experiments on a Vimeo channel, Baker noticed a Kickstarter campaign for Moondog Labs, which provides anamorphic lenses, which allow filmmakers using iPhones to be able to shoot in 'true scope widescreen ratio' and which, according to Baker, could 'elevate' his film's look to 'a cinematic level' (quoted in McGarry, 2015, p. 136). The filmmakers also used an app called Filmic Pro, which allowed them 'more control over the captured image' and which was responsible for creating the film's grainy look (Sciretta, 2015), and a 'Steadicam Smoothee', a small stabiliser that provides a Steadicam shot effect (McGarry, 2015, p. 136). Furthermore, sound was recorded separately and with professional equipment as the iPhone does not have the capacity to record sound with the fidelity required for a professional film, while the celebrated-by-critics orange hue that characterises the film's aesthetic and refers indirectly to the film's title was achieved in post-production through professional colour correction. As is clear, then, despite the headlines focusing on the fact that the film was made with three iPhones, the actual technology involved to make the film 'cinematic' and to give its look involved a lot more than that.

Managing to come up with the necessary (digital) means of production that would allow them to make the film as they envisaged it, the filmmakers concentrated on the other aspects of production. Its unconventional casting practices (which were devised partly because the budget did not allow for a casting director) extended to other parts in the film and made extensive use of social media, with Instagram star Francis Lola featuring in a scene, while Chelcie Lynn, who appears in a small part as the makeshift brothel's madam, was cast through Vine (SeanBakerTangerine, 2015). Vine was also used as a starting point for the arrangement of the film's soundtrack, with Baker locating a number of artists whose original compositions were uploaded in Soundcloud and contacting them directly with a view to use their work in the film. In this respect, *Tangerine* stands as a particularly strong example of a film that was made possible with the help of social media platforms.

The focus of the film's narrative is life in the margins of society. In following Sin-Dee's efforts to find the woman that her boyfriend cheated on her with, Baker takes the spectator on a trip in a seldom seen Los Angeles, which is 'not defined by the picturesque palm trees and the Hollywood sign' (Watercutter, 2015). Indeed, what makes *Tangerine* particularly interesting and is responsible to a substantial extent for its critical success is not so much that it puts an almost completely ignored identity minority, transgender people of colour, centre stage, or even that it has chosen actual transgender actors to perform the key characters in the film, whereas well-known indiewood films such as *Boys Don't Cry* (Peirce, 1999) and more recently *Dallas Buyers Club* (Vallée, 2013) have had white, straight actors performing such roles. Instead, it is its depiction of the environment within which these people live, work and circulate, an environment that is presented with an unflinching determination and a raw energy that matches fully the protagonists' efforts to survive in it. Whether in dramatic scenes such as the one where Sin-Dee bursts into a DIY brothel to find the cisgender person with whom her boyfriend had sex or in more comic scenes such as when the Armenian taxi driver is disgusted by the revelation that the sex worker he picked up was not transgendered, what becomes particularly evident is the ugliness of the world they inhabit. One could go as far as to argue that the camera often assumes an ethnographic function, moving relentlessly from street to street in west Los Angeles and revealing in every step of the way, in every corner, a world that bears little, if any, resemblance to the Los Angeles presented in Hollywood films, the Los Angeles of opportunities, the place where even sex workers such as Vivian in *Pretty Woman* (Marshall, 1989) can dream of a better future. Add to this the over-saturated colours that make the representation of the city extreme on an aesthetic level, and the viewer is treated to a spectacle that, as one reviewer put it, 'perfectly matches the drug-tinged hyperreality of its protagonists' (Mullen, 2015, p. 88). In this respect, the politics of representation is certainly a key issue in the film but that is not its real focal point, which, among other things, enables the film to avoid being exploitative of its subjects.

The film premiered in the NEXT category of the Sundance Film Festival in 2015, which admits 'pure, bold works distinguished by an innovative, forward-thinking approach to storytelling' ('Sundance Institute Announces Films in Competition and NEXT for 2016 Sundance Film Festival', 2015). In that section, *Tangerine* caused a 'minor stir' (Smith, 2015), initially because of the revelation that it was shot using iPhones, the first such film to be submitted to the Festival. Following reported interest by both a specialty film division (IFC Films) and an independent distributor (A24), the film's distribution rights were eventually acquired by Magnolia Pictures, a specialty film division of 2929 Entertainment, a diversified media conglomerate (Canfield, 2015). The company released the film theatrically in the summer of 2015 in a limited number of screens, achieving a respectable box office gross of $700,000. However, with Magnolia Pictures' forte being alternative release models that 'capitaliz[e] on non-theatrical revenue streams' (2929 Entertainment, no date), it is very likely that *Tangerine* generated a much higher revenue in VOD platforms, returning a profit both to its producers and to the distributor. In many ways, it is a paradigmatic independent film in the post-media convergence/social media era and, in the words of Ben Roberts, director of the BFI Film Fund, making a film like this is 'within any enterprising filmmaker's reach' (Roberts, 2015, p. 16).

distribution based on a variety of financial models. For instance, under the banner of 'Broadcast Yourself', YouTube has allowed filmmakers free access to market their films while also providing them with an opportunity to use the platform creatively as a potential exhibition window for their actual films; King and Tryon discussing extensively how independent films such as *Four Eyed Monsters* became commercially successful by utilising the platform for both marketing and exhibition.[55] However, in the ever-changing online media environment YouTube quickly also assumed practices associated with subscription-supported services by renting and selling films organised in channels that target particular demographics.[56] SnagFilms, on the other hand, is an online distribution company specialising specifically in low-budget independent fiction films and documentaries. Established in 2008 with a library of just 450 titles,[57] SnagFilms expanded exponentially, reaching 4,000 films by 2013 and receiving an award for the most 'promising private technology company' that is 'positioned to grow at an explosive rate'.[58] Operating with capital raised by investors and supported by advertising, SnagFilms has seen particular success with documentary titles, especially ones that fulfil the company's mission to promote social change. With the company specialising in connecting particular titles to charities and other activist organisations from the start, it quickly developed a reputation as a destination for documentarians willing to sell their films' digital rights to a company that also advertises links to and partnerships with some of the media industry's biggest names, including: Comcast's Xfinity.com, AOL, Hulu, Yahoo!, the Starbucks Digital Network, as well as a network of more than 110,000 affiliates such as news companies, non-profit organisations, bloggers and others.[59] Add to this the fact that SnagFilms is also the corporate parent of *Indiewire*, one of the key publications in support of independent cinema since the 1990s (see Chapter 8) and it is no surprise that so many independent filmmakers sell the digital rights to their films (and often other rights too) to the company. Indeed, as SnagFilms' founder and CEO Rick Allen has stated, some of the company's bigger titles have been sold to television, others have been released theatrically, while a selection of its films is also available on key pay platforms such as Amazon, iTunes and Netflix.[60]

In their effort to secure the digital rights of a large volume of films, companies such as SnagFilms have been advising filmmakers to 'be entrepreneurial on [their] own behalf', especially in terms of trying actively to locate niche audience demographics that could help make their films a commercial success.[61] With the advent of social media making possible the cultivation of a direct relationship between filmmakers and audiences and with the latter also potentially functioning as conduits for the publicity of films via their participation in a variety of social media networks, it is clear that, in theory at least, there are enhanced opportunities for creative filmmakers to publicise their films effectively and, more broadly, to exert a higher degree of control on the distribution aspect of the independent filmmaking business than in the past. Such developments closely follow neoliberal conceptualisations and definitions of creativity as a form of increasingly individualised entrepreneurship that, as Angela McRobbie argued, involves characteristics such as multi-skilling and speeded up pace of work.[62] Arguably, they have found their most obvious realisation in Peter Broderick's call to independent filmmakers to partake in 'the New World of Distribution', a two-part polemic that (coincidentally?) was first published in *Indiewire* in 2008.[63] This is how Broderick opens his article:

> Welcome to the New World of Distribution. Many filmmakers are emigrating from the Old World, where they have little chance of succeeding. They are attracted by unprecedented opportunities and the freedom to shape their own destiny. Life in the New World requires them to work harder, be more tenacious, and take more risks. There are daunting challenges and no guarantees of success. But this hasn't stopped more and more intrepid filmmakers from exploring uncharted territory and staking claims.[64]

Such a conceptualisation places distribution within a binary that, on the one hand, includes the 'Old World', equated here with a system through which established distributors seek to acquire film rights in all or most markets (theatrical, video, cable, on-demand/digital, terrestrial TV, foreign, etc.), which often allows the distributor to make a profit at the expense of the filmmaker. This is primarily because any profits tend to be offset by costly theatrical releases, which, for Broderick, are not essential in the contemporary converged media landscape. The 'New World', on the other hand, enables filmmakers to divide the rights of their films themselves and having sought and located particular audiences through the use of social media to tailor their films' distribution to these audiences in the most cost-effective way, through the use of the most appropriate distribution window(s). This can take the form of selling on-demand rights in a local market that has a special interest in a film (for instance, a documentary film that depicts a particular community) and it can even include theatrical releases in markets where filmmakers have located a strong interest and demand for their films. In extreme cases, such releases can extend to national, full-fledged theatrical distribution campaigns, as was the case with the micro-budgeted, digitally shot, independent horror film *Paranormal Activity* (Peli, 2008). Utilising an online campaign that encouraged 'moviegoers to demand via eventful.com that the movie play in their local town' with the view to arrange screenings for audiences in the locations that generated the most 'demands',[65] *Paranormal Activity* generated significant hype, forcing the company that had acquired the film's theatrical rights (in this case Hollywood major Paramount) to consider releasing the film nationwide. After 1 million 'demands', Paramount released the film theatrically in the North American market with staggering success, recording a box office gross of approximately $108 million.[66] However, successes like this have been rare. Nearly a decade after the publication of Broderick's polemic, the 'New World of distribution' is a reality that has not managed to prove nearly as revolutionary, successful and paradigm-shifting as its author wanted it to be. Equally, the 'Old World of distribution' has remained firmly in place, while the most visible US independent (low-budget and indiewood) films of the last few years have been firmly associated with that particular distribution model.

However, when it comes to American independent cinema, one element of distribution not associated with Broderick's 'Old World' that has become increasingly important in the contemporary world of converged media is the enhanced role and function of film festivals. As Cindy Hing-Yuk Wong has argued, since the turn of the century film festivals have advanced their symbiosis with markets in order to ensure 'programming, participation, and publicity'.[67] This has been particularly the case in North America, with festivals such as the Sundance Film Festival and especially the Toronto International Film Festival widely recognised as the loci where established distributors identify the key independent films seeking distribution.[68] Despite such practices pointing to established, 'Old World' models of distribution of American independent films, more recently several film festivals went much further than just premiering films and functioning as markets for film sales and distribution deals. Specifically, they partnered with on-demand services and other online distributors, effectively becoming distributors themselves. For instance, in

2009, the Austin-based SXSW Festival made a deal with established distributor IFC Films to screen five festival films in IFC Films' video on-demand (VOD) service at the same time as these films were premiering at the festival.[69] A year later, Sundance's decision to follow the same practice again through partnering with IFC Films' VOD service was hailed by the trade press as heralding the changing function of the film festival in a converged and connected media world.[70] This was especially as at the same time Sundance had also partnered with YouTube in order to make available three other selected films on the video-sharing platform, even before their premiere at the festival, while its collaboration with YouTube extended to the latter's sponsorship of Sundance's NEXT category, which had been introduced in the same year.[71]

With such partnerships and collaborations expanding in the 2010s, especially as the number of online distributors has been increasing and as 'New World' distribution models are constantly being refined, it is clear that distribution in the low-budget independent film sector in the US will continue to be influenced to a substantial extent by developments in the realm of film festivals. This is especially as the number of festivals continues to increase (with the New York Film Academy having recently calculated the number of film festivals in the US alone to be 465)[72] and as new players specialising in content streaming, such as Netflix and Amazon, have become particularly active in the festivals circuit to secure rights to low- and even high-budget films. Writing immediately after the end of the 2016 Sundance Film Festival, *Indiewire* journalist Chris O'Falt proclaimed that 'if you recently watched an independent or documentary film, [chances are] you more than likely watched it on Netflix',[73] demonstrating both the importance of festivals in showcasing films that otherwise have few opportunities to connect with a decent audience and the increasing significance of online distribution. With both Netflix and Amazon increasingly buying films from festivals (as well as financing and producing their own titles) in order to provide for their expanding VOD and subscription VOD (SVOD) services both in the US and internationally, it is clear that at least the established film festivals will continue to play a major role in shaping American independent cinema's distribution landscape in the age of converged media.

Conclusion: consolidation and independence, oligopoly and autonomy

The impact of media convergence on American independent cinema has been deep and far-reaching. On the one hand, and like it did with its Hollywood cinema counterpart, media convergence brought American independent cinema increasingly close to other previously distinct media industries, which were also restructured, realigned and reshaped under the impact of convergence. The takeover of standalone independent film companies such as Miramax and New Line Cinema by global entertainment conglomerates, the establishment of other similar specialty film divisions by the rest of the global media players and the operation of these divisions alongside other conglomerate subsidiaries specialising in music, games, cable television, print media and, significantly, Hollywood major film productions made a very substantial faction of American independent cinema an integral part of global media industries. Exemplified primarily by the indie and later indiewood film productions that were increasingly financed and produced by companies with corporate ties to the major entertainment conglomerates, this faction of American independent cinema found itself deeply determined by developments affecting similar companies in other industries at a global level. These developments included: American independent films being defined increasingly by the vertical and horizontal structures of the conglomerates that owned the key indiewood producing and distributing companies; benefiting from synergies between these companies and other divisions under the same corporate umbrella; finding themselves distributed in any new distribution windows, delivery systems and digital platforms that extended their life cycle and increased the profits of the companies behind them; assuming the role of specialised product that was used to feed the immense distribution pipelines of the conglomerates that owned their makers; and being used as leverage to support other business segments or interests associated with these conglomerates. In other words, American independent cinema during its indie and indiewood phases became a significant constituent element of a transnational entertainment economy.

In this respect, it is certainly understandable that indie and indiewood cinema evolved as increasingly commercialised categories of filmmaking that had few points of contact with the 'low-key, low-budget' independent cinema as this emerged in the late 1970s and early 1980s. Indeed, as Thomas Schatz put it: 'the rise of Conglomerate Hollywood involved not only the acquisition of the major studios but also the annexation of key factions of the indie movement by a new breed of media giants',[74] with both categories of filmmaking used to support the distribution of entertainment content around the world and in a variety of media markets.

However, once this process coalesced and the independent film sector started becoming almost fully defined by indiewood, despite the continuous presence of other types of independent cinema at the margins of the industry, American independent cinema also started experiencing a regeneration. The tensions between consolidation and independence, oligopoly and autonomy that Schatz has identified as the key structuring element in the American film industry (and the media industries more broadly) came into full play.[75] The introduction of digital technology initially in the field of production lowered the entry barriers to filmmaking to an unprecedented level and drew an increasing number of people to commercial filmmaking. But it was only a few years later, during the late 2000s and early 2010s, that distribution started providing the makings of a paradigm shift. Helped immensely by the ubiquity of social media, the pervasiveness of mobile exhibition technologies, the constant improvement in media delivery services and cultural changes in media consumption, this other faction of American independent cinema started slowly to stake its claim, not just in the sector but in the whole media ecosystem. And while not many films from that type of independent filmmaking have become major crossover successes or household names, they have nonetheless redefined the sector by their sheer volume (calculated in the tens of thousands of titles, possibly more) and, not surprisingly, by expanding vastly the terrain of what can be considered independent filmmaking in the US. As a result, and despite the persistence of indiewood as the most visible expression of independent filmmaking, American independent cinema as a whole has, by and large, become a much more fluid, less stable and less institutionalised category of filmmaking than in the heyday of indie and indiewood cinema in the 1990s and 2000s. Once again, since consolidation and oligopoly started defining the sector, autonomy and independence have found new ways to reassert themselves.

Notes

1 Tzioumakis, 2017, p. 243.
2 See, for instance, King, 2005, p. 47, Levy, 1999, p. 506 and Biskind, 2005, p. 470.
3 Tzioumakis, 2012a, p. 8.
4 Zimmermann, 2005, p. 246.
5 Broderick, 2008.
6 King, 2005, p. 2.
7 See for instance King, 2005, Newman, 2011 and Tzioumakis, 2012a.
8 Jenkins, 2006.
9 Jenkins, 2006, p. 2.
10 Dwyer, 2010, pp. 2–3.
11 The discussion of indiewood that follows in this section of the chapter was first published in 2013 as part of an article entitled 'American Independent Cinema at the Age of Convergence'. The article featured in a special issue under the title 'Et le cinéma indépendant?' of the *Revue française d'études américaines*, no. 136, edited by Anne Hurault Paupe and Céline Murillo.
12 For a detailed account of how this new chapter in media industry conglomeration affected independent cinema in the early 1990s, see Schatz, 2013, pp. 125–39.
13 See also Schatz, 2013, pp. 130–1.

14 During the 1990s, Sony had a third division (TriStar Pictures), which specialised primarily in star- and genre-driven film productions.

15 The figures are obtained from The Numbers, online, http://www.the-numbers.com/market/Distributors1996.php (accessed 10 January 2012).

16 All the figures for 1995 are taken from The Numbers, online, http://www.the-numbers.com/market/1995/distributors (accessed 1 August 2016).

17 All the figures for 2004 are taken from The Numbers, online, http://www.the-numbers.com/market/1995/distributors (accessed 1 August 2016).

18 The figures are taken from The Numbers, online, http://www.the-numbers.com/market/2004/distributor/First-Run-Features (accessed 1 August 2016).

19 Jenkins, 2006, p. 19.

20 For a good discussion of franchising and indiewood see Jess-Cooke, 2009, pp. 90–109.

21 McClintock, 2009.

22 Hazelton, 2008, pp. 6–7.

23 The figures are taken from the MPAA Entertainment Industry Market Statistics 2007, online, https://wikileaks.org/sony/docs/03_03/Mktrsch/Market%20Research/MPAA%20Reports/2007%20Market%20Statistics.pdf (accessed 19 November 2016).

24 The figures are taken from The Numbers, online, http://www.the-numbers.com/market/2002/distributors and http://www.the-numbers.com/market/2007/distributors (accessed 19 November 2016).

25 The figures are taken from Boxoffice Guru, online, http://www.boxofficeguru.com/072009.htm (accessed 1 November 2016).

26 The figures for the number of screens in the US in 2009 are taken from the MPAA Theatre Market Statistics 2010, online, https://wikileaks.org/sony/docs/03_03/Mktrsch/Market%20Research/MPAA%20Reports/2010/2010%20Theatrical%20Market%20Statistics.pdf (accessed 1 November 2016).

27 The figure is taken from Coming Soon, online, 8 April 2005, http://www.comingsoon.net/dvd/news/9094-sideways-elektra-off-to-good-start# (accessed 1 November 2016).

28 Belson, 2006.

29 Tzioumakis, 2012a, pp. 198–226.

30 Thompson, 2008.

31 The figure for the film's North American box office is taken from the IMDb, online, http://www.imdb.com/title/tt0477348/?ref_=nv_sr_1 (accessed 19 November 2016).

32 Quinn, 2010.

33 Roston, 2005, p. 49.

34 Rainey, 2016.

35 For more on Dogme 95 see Roman, 2001.

36 King, 2005, p. 53.

37 Zimmermann, 2005, p. 246.

38 Trowbridge, 2015, pp. 14–15.

39 The figures are taken from Box Office Mojo, online, http://boxofficemojo.com/yearly (accessed 1 December 2016).

40 King, 2014, p. 216.

41 Van Couvering, 2007.

42 See, for instance, the work of Robert Greenwald and his company Brave New Films (http://www.bravenewfilms.org).

43 Tzioumakis, 2013a, p. 32.

44 Prive, 2012.

45 Strickler et al., 2013.

46 '*Indiewire* Ultimate Guide to Crowdfunding', 2013.

47 Wood, 2014.

48 Follows, 2015.

49 Holmlund, 2005, pp. 9–10.

50 King, 2005, p. 52.

51 The figures are taken from the IMDb, online, for *Tadpole* http://www.imdb.com/
    title/tt0271219/?ref_=fn_al_tt_1   and   for   *Tape*   http://www.imdb.com/title/
    tt0275719/?ref_=fn_al_tt_1 (both accessed 19 November 2016).

52 For more information about NEXT see the Sundance Institute, online, http://www.
    sundance.org/festivals/sundance-film-festival/program (accessed 16 November 2016).

53 'Declaration of Independents: The 30 Greatest American Indie Films', 2014.

54 Tryon, 2009, p. 96.

55 King, 2014, pp. 81–8, Tryon, 2009, pp. 119–21.

56 Lang and Gilman, 2013.

57 Dahl, 2014.

58 SnagFilms, 2013.

59 Ellington, 2013.

60 Dahl, 2014.

61 Krinsky, no date.

62 McRobbie, 2002, p. 519.

63 Broderick, 2008.

64 Broderick, 2008.

65 Thompson, 2009.

66 The figure is taken from the IMBb, online, http://www.imdb.com/title/tt1179904/
    ?ref_=nm_flmg_prd_15 (accessed 19 November 2016).

67 Wong, 2011, p. 138.

68 Wong, 2011, p. 138.

69 Hernandez, 2009.

70 Hernandez, 2010a.

71 Hernandez, 2010b.

72 New York Film Academy, 2015.

73 O'Falt, 2016.

74 Schatz, 2013, p. 127.

75 Schatz, 2013, p. 127.

Epilogue: from independent cinema to specialty content

In the epilogue to the book's first edition in 2006 I suggested that American independent cinema should stop being examined in isolation from other types of niche filmmaking and considered instead as part of a larger category of specialty cinema that would also include films not produced or distributed by the conglomerated Hollywood majors, in particular non-US film imports. My rationale for this suggestion stemmed from the fact that the label 'independent' and its derivatives, especially 'indie', were being questioned severely by numerous institutions that contribute to definitions of independence in American cinema, prompting consideration of other, less charged, alternatives such as 'specialty' or 'niche'. At the same time, non-US films such as *La vita è bella* [*Life Is Beautiful*] (Benigni, 1999), *Wo hu cang long* [*Crouching Tiger, Hidden Dragon*] (Lee, 2001), *Ying xiong* [*Hero*] (Zhang, 2003) and *El laberinto del fauno* [*Pan's Labyrinth*] (del Toro, 2006), all handled by the same specialty film divisions of the Hollywood majors (Miramax, Sony Pictures Classics, Miramax and Picturehouse, respectively), which were also producing and/or distributing 'independent' films, were breaking records in terms of theatrical box office success and enjoying unprecedented visibility. Together with more modest but still significant critical and commercial successes such as *Le fabuleux destin d'Amélie Poulain* [*Amélie*] (Jeunet, 2001), *Monsoon Wedding* (Nair, 2001), *Y Tu Mamá También* (Cuarón, 2002), *Diarios de motocicleta* [*The Motorcycle Diaries*] (Salles, 2004), *Kung fu* [*Kung Fu Hustle*] (Chow, 2004) and *Volver* (Almodóvar, 2006), they were pointing to the presence of a very strong niche film market for international (commercial) productions, which looked like it was complementing the market for American independent (mostly indiewood) films, especially as both markets were dominated by the majors' specialty film divisions.

At that time, these divisions (which included Miramax, New Line Cinema, Fox Searchlight, Paramount Vantage, Focus Features, Warner Independent, Picturehouse, United Artists, Screen Gems and genre labels such as Dimension

Films and Rogue Pictures) were at the peak of their power and there seemed to be little that could threaten their domination. This is especially as low-budget digital production had yet to make its mark culturally or in terms of box office success (with the exception of a small number of films such as *The Blair Witch Project* that had become runaway hits), despite representing a very substantial percentage of all production in the sector. As I wrote at the very end of the first edition of this book:

> the label [independent cinema] might have changed (or be in the process of changing) but the type of film it signifies continues to thrive and represent the most likely source of original and challenging material in American cinema. The difference is that this type of film is now accompanied by, and competes against, other such films originating outside the United States.[1]

Although the events that followed have pointed much more forcefully to the need to stop examining independent filmmaking in the US in isolation from other 'similar' examples of cultural production than I had envisaged originally, my suggestion of placing American independent cinema together with foreign film imports under the label of 'specialty filmmaking' proved rather hasty. What in 2006 looked like a sustainable international film boom in US screens after decades of little penetration beyond a core number of art houses in major metropolitan markets, only a couple of years later seemed to have been all but finished. *Crouching Tiger, Hidden Dragon* and *Life Is Beautiful* have yet to be threatened in terms of box office success by any other film since their release at the turn of the century, while only three films released since 2007 have achieved notable commercial success, with the Mexican comedy *Instructions Not Included* (Derbez, 2013) being the only one that achieved a crossover status.[2]

Although a detailed examination of the reasons behind the failure of non-US films to penetrate further the American film market in the late 2000s and 2010s is beyond the scope of this epilogue, Chapter 9 has already suggested two of the key factors that contributed to it. The first was the closure of most of the conglomerated Hollywood majors' specialty film divisions, which took place in the late 2000s and which limited substantially the number of well capitalised and resourced companies with significant experience in releasing foreign films in the US market. The second one was the stratospheric increase in advertising and marketing costs of releases by the studio specialty film divisions in the late 2000s, which made all the companies in the sector become much more conservative in terms of the types of films they would invest in than they were in the earlier years of the decade, when these costs were much lower. Add to this the impact of the global financial crisis of 2008, which forced distributors to seek ways to minimise risk even further, and it is clear that the market for imports was much changed in the latter part of the 2000s and 2010s compared with the late 1990s and early 2000s.

However, in hindsight, one can certainly put at the top of this list of factors the ways in which media convergence realigned the American film industry as a content-producing industry that found itself in competition not just with other film industries but mostly with other media industries for the attention of demographics that were increasingly consuming media in the home and on the go via mobile devices. In this picture, American independent cinema found itself not only in competition with foreign film imports but also with serial television (with the 2000s generally considered a golden age for quality television drama), video games (an industry that has long surpassed cinema in terms of revenue and profits)[3] and more broadly with user-generated media such as those available on video-sharing platforms and even social media engagement as an increasingly widespread cultural practice. In this respect, if American independent cinema needs to be examined together with competing forms of media, these had only partially to do with non-US films and much more with what I would like to call 'specialty media content', produced by other media industries that were vying for the same type of discerning consumer, who could access this content often through the same device.

Arguably the biggest competitor (though the word 'competitor' is accurate only if seen from one particular perspective, as I will state at the end of this epilogue) for American independent cinema in this converged media environment has been quality television. With premium and even some basic cable channels developing a strong reputation as hubs for creative programme making and as US cable television as a sector has been enjoying a renaissance of sorts linked to a number of cable providers' increasing emphasis on original programming tailored to particular demographics, it is not surprising that talent once associated primarily with American independent cinema started being attracted to cable (and later web-based) television. Whether this attraction has involved well-established filmmakers who became showrunners in serial shows such as *Togetherness* (M. and J. Duplass, 2015–16, HBO) or in mini-series such as *Olive Kitteridge* (Cholodenko, 2014, HBO) and *Mildred Pierce* (Haynes, 2011, HBO), who produce and occasionally direct shows such as *The Knick* (Soderbergh, 2015–17, Cinemax) and *Boss* (Van Sant, 2011–12, Starz!) or who are simply employed as directors of individual episodes of shows such as *Mad Men* (2007–14, AMC – Lynn Shelton) and *Enlightened* (2011–13, HBO – Miguel Arteta and Nicole Holofcener), cable television has had a very significant number of independent filmmakers 'migrating' to it, either when between films jobs or potentially in more permanent arrangements. Indeed, such has been the 'haemorrhaging' of talent from American independent cinema to television that both trade and popular press have dedicated significant attention to the phenomenon, with an article published in *Time* in 2015 tellingly entitled 'Why TV Is the Perfect Place for

Indie Filmmakers' explaining this both in terms of potential for business and in terms of 'the indie aesthetic' being transferred easily to the other medium.[4] With content-streaming players such as Netflix and Amazon having also started developing original programming based on serial television formats and having already attracted filmmakers such as Woody Allen (Amazon), David Wain (Netflix) and Jason Reitman (Hulu) to produce their own shows it is clear that such migration will continue. This is especially as the landscape of television (and what constitutes it) continues to expand, while the future of independent cinema (and what constitutes it) is becoming increasingly unclear.

American independent cinema's place within this converged and realigned industry and especially its proximity to cable television and content-streaming business is confirmed by a number of recent initiatives undertaken by key institutions associated with the sector. For instance, the Independent Filmmaker Project's Film Week expanded in 2016 to include 'television, digital, web, V[irtual] R[eality] and app-based series', that decision having been motivated by the increasing recognition that storytelling by independent (film)makers is not limited to the medium of film.[5] This recognition has been endorsed by recent scholarship. Writing specifically about Miranda July and her professional identity as an independent filmmaker in the twenty-first century, Kathleen McHugh highlighted that July is not 'of any single medium' but instead 'her creative work is both diffused and integrated across different platforms', and includes a wide variety of artefacts from narrative films to web-based pieces to online digital photo compilations, among other examples that define her work.[6] Claudia Pederson and Patricia Zimmermann, moreover, have argued about the importance of other media that go 'beyond the screen' and are part of an 'independent media arts ecology' as providing more opportunities for women and other groups marginalised by the American film industry, including its indiewood-determined independent film sector. This is because independent media arts encourage less hierarchical systems of production, including 'collectives, collaborations, transmedia and interfaces' that allow 'feminist practices to flourish'.[7] In this respect, decisions by institutions to 'open up' to converged media not only underline the increasingly blurred boundaries between film and other storytelling media, they also create more opportunities for massively under-represented identity groups than a more strictly defined American independent cinema.

Still, despite some emphasis to links with other (new) media, independent cinema's increasing proximity to television has been by far the most visible recent development from an industrial perspective. Like the IFP, the Sundance Film Festival also announced in 2016 the introduction of 'Virtual Reality' and 'Episodic Content' categories, with the latter including submission of content for both broadcast and web-based television. As the Festival's press release put it:

> with so many areas of creative production converging to redefine how we view content in the current landscape, it feels like the right time to open up our submissions process to innovative, independently produced episodic projects. New technologies have made it more common to see series created outside of the studio system, and we're excited to present this work at the Festival.[8]

And both the IFP and the Sundance initiatives were preceded by SXSW's introduction of the 'Episodic' category in 2014 to account for the fact that television was 'getting more thematically complex and cinematic, with people crossing over more and more frequently from the feature world and with audiences readily consuming film and television on the same screens',[9] while similar categories were introduced by major festivals outside the US. One such example is the Berlin Film Festival, which in 2015 introduced its Berlinare Special Series as a platform to showcase quality television.[10]

Under these circumstances, my original suggestion to start examining American independent cinema as part of a specialty cinema needs to be modified and under the continuing impact of media convergence to be seen as part of a vastly expanding specialty media content that is to a substantial extent produced by talent that moves between the two (and often other) media. Such a conceptualisation allows independent cinema and television to cease to be competitors (as I indicated above) and become instead defined by symbiosis, mobility of talent, further loosening of the borders between the two media and even a similar aesthetic (as the article from the *Time* magazine suggested).[11] This of course means the end of any efforts to map, classify or in any way order American independent cinema as a distinct category in the way that some studies in the 1990s and 2000s did,[12] unless such efforts are attempted as part of long-term, well-resourced research projects. But then again, such efforts would be difficult even if scholars continued to examine American independent cinema in isolation. Given the vast numbers in terms of production and the fact that distribution of the majority of these films takes place away from the theatres, it is close to impossible to locate and examine all the films in the sector, the number of which is in the tens of thousands, perhaps more.

Finally, any future examination of the still dominant, most visible and theatrically released indiewood cinema is also bound to raise significant challenges to researchers and scholars. This is because such films have been associated primarily with the Hollywood majors' specialty film divisions,[13] the majority of which, as we have seen in Chapter 9, have now closed. With their place being taken by a host of new standalone companies and divisions of media corporations other than the Hollywood majors, indiewood has managed to survive, led by Fox Searchlight and its several critical and commercial successes, most recently with *12 Years a Slave*, *Birdman* and *The Grand Budapest Hotel*. However, to that list of indiewood distributors one should also add the Hollywood majors, which since the closure of their specialty divisions have been surprisingly active in the field. If in the past titles such as *The Fight Club* (Fincher, 1999, Universal), *Election* (Payne, 1999, Paramount) and *Three Kings* (Russell, 2000, Warner Bros.) were seen as rare excursions of the Hollywood majors onto indiewood turf,[14] in more recent years pillars of indiewood filmmaking have chosen the Hollywood majors to have their films produced and distributed by. Examples include Jason Reitman (*Up in the Air*, 2009; *Young Adult*, 2011; *Labor Day*, 2013; and *Men, Women and Children*, 2014; all for Paramount), Alexander Payne (*Nebraska*, 2013; also for Paramount), Paul Thomas Anderson (*Inherent Vice*, 2015; for Warner Bros.), Joel and Ethan Coen (*True Grit*, 2011 and *Hail Caesar*, 2016; for Paramount and Universal, respectively), David O. Russell (*American Hustle*, 2013 and *Joy*, 2015; both for 20th Century Fox), Spike Jonze (*Her*, 2013; for Warner Bros.) and George Clooney (*The Monuments Men*, 2014; for Columbia).

However, rather than directing and producing blockbuster films that are part of franchises or expensive star-genre vehicles, as other independent filmmakers did in earlier years when they were recruited by the Hollywood majors following commercially successful indie films,[15] the above filmmakers have continued to work on relatively inexpensive indiewood films. And while such an arrangement has been beneficial for both parties (for the Hollywood majors it means the occasional prestige-level film and the possibility of awards, while for the filmmakers it means they can continue to receive finance to make the films they want to make), it has also demonstrated clearly that the indiewood category has been moving increasingly closer to the Hollywood majors than previously was the case. In this respect, besides placing a huge shadow upon the future of this type of filmmaking as part of an independent sector, this new relationship between key indiewood filmmakers and the Hollywood majors provides yet another motivation to question the usefulness of the label 'independent' in American cinema.

In the contemporary converged media landscape, American independent cinema is losing both its identity and its specificity. However, given its proven ability to regenerate, or as Geoff King put it, to continue to thrive while seemingly in permanent crisis,[16] it will not be surprising if it manages to survive as a discourse, a brand or a label that continues to signify quality for a particular group of feature films, irrespective of who makes these films, how and where.

Notes

1 Tzioumakis, 2006, p. 284.
2 *Instructions Not Included* is currently the fourth most commercially successful non-US release in the US theatrical market. The other two post-2007 films that achieved significant commercial success, *Under the Same Moon* (Riggen, 2007) and *Dangal* (Tiwari, 2016), only just broke into the top 20 of US International releases. For the list of the top 20 most commercially successful releases of foreign films in the North American theatrical market, see Box Office Mojo, online, http://www.boxofficemojo.com/genres/chart/?id=foreign.htm (accessed 12 April 2017).
3 Nath, 2016.
4 Poniewozik, 2015. See also Bernhard, 2011 and Gatchman, 2015.
5 McNary, 2016.
6 McHugh, 2016, p 246.
7 Pederson and Zimmermann, 2016, p. 305.
8 'Sundance Film Festival: Introducing Virtual Reality and Episodic Content Categories', 2016.
9 Willmore, 2014.
10 Danish Film Institute, 2016.
11 This last element is only speculative at this point. Much more research is needed in terms of the elements that define the specificity of the two media before one starts talking seriously about aesthetic similarities.
12 See in particular Levy, 1999.
13 An argument also made by King, 2009, p. 4, when he talks about his slightly different conceptualisation of 'Indiewood' (with capital I, unlike in this book, in which a lower case 'i' is used).
14 King, 2009, p. 191.
15 See, for instance, Bryan Singer, Doug Liman and Jon Favreau, who, following the success of their independent films, started working for the majors and directing among others *X-Men* (2000), *The Bourne Identity* (2002) and *Iron Man* (2008), respectively.
16 King, 2013, pp. 41–52.

Bibliography

Aberdeen, J. A. (2000) *Hollywood Renegades: The Society of Independent Motion Picture Producers*, Cobblestone, Los Angeles.

Adams Sitney, P. (2000) 'The New American Cinema', in P. Adams Sitney (ed.), *Film Culture Reader*, First Cooper Square Press, New York, pp. 71–2.

Allen, Michael (2003) *Contemporary US Cinema*, Longman, London.

Allen, Robert C. and Douglas Gomery (1985) *Film History: Theory and Practice*, Alfred Knopf, New York.

Anderson, Nate (2007) 'Netflix Offers Streaming Movies to Subscribers', in *Ars Technica*, online, 16 January, http://arstechnica.com/uncategorized/2007/01/8627/ (accessed 20 December 2016).

Andrew, Geoff (1998) *Stranger than Paradise: Maverick Film-makers in Recent American Cinema*, Prion, London.

Angell, Elizabeth (2006) 'The History and Legacy of the AIVF', in *The Independent*, online, 1 July, http://independent-magazine.org/2006/07/history-and-legacy-aivf-association-independent-video-and-filmmakers/ (accessed 13 July 2016).

Arroyo, José (1993) 'Death Desire and Identity: The Political Unconscious of the "New Queer Cinema"', in Joseph Bristow and Angelia R. Wilson (eds), *Activating Theory: Lesbian, Gay and Bisexual Politics*, Lawrence and Wishart, London, pp. 70–96.

Badley, Linda, Claire Perkins and Michele Schreiber (eds) (2016) *Indie Reframed: Women's Filmmaking and Contemporary American Independent Cinema*, Edinburgh University Press, Edinburgh.

Balio, Tino (1976) *United Artist: The Company Built by the Stars*, University of Wisconsin Press, Madison.

Balio, Tino (1985) 'Retrenchment, Reappraisal and Reorganisation, 1948–' in Tino Balio (ed.), *The American Film Industry*, revised edn, University of Wisconsin Press, Madison, pp. 401–47.

Balio, Tino (1987) *United Artists: The Company that Changed the Film Industry*, University of Wisconsin Press, Madison.

Balio, Tino (1990) 'New Producers for Old: United Artists and the Shift to Independent Production', in Tino Balio (ed.) *Hollywood in the Age of Television*, Unwin Hyman, Boston, pp. 165–83.

Balio, Tino (1995) *Grand Design: Hollywood as a Modern Business Enterprise, 1930–1939*, University of California Press, Berkeley.

Belson, Ken (2006) 'As DVD Sales Slow, Hollywood Hunts for a New Cash Cow', in *New York Times*, 13 June.

Belton, John (1994) *American Cinema/American Culture*, Rutgers University Press, New Brunswick.

Bernhard, Josh (2011) 'Is Indie TV the New Indie Film?', in *Tribeca*, online, 30 November, https://tribecafilm.com/stories/51af7770f527048a77000001-is-indie-tv-the-new-indie (accessed 14 December 2016).

Bernstein, Matthew (1993) 'Hollywood's Semi-independent Production', in *Cinema Journal*, vol. 32, no. 3, spring, pp. 41–54.

Bernstein, Matthew (1994) *Walter Wanger: Hollywood Independent*, University of California Press, Berkeley.

Berra, John (2008) *Declarations of Independence: American Cinema and the Partiality of Independent Production*, Intellect, Bristol.

Biskind, Peter (1998) *Easy Riders, Raging Bulls: How the Sex 'n' Drugs 'n' Rock 'n' Roll Generation Saved Hollywood*, Bloomsbury, London.

Biskind, Peter (2005) *Down and Dirty Pictures: Miramax, Sundance and the Rise of Independent Film*, Simon and Schuster Paperbacks, London.

Bogdanovich, Peter (1975) 'Edgar G. Ulmer ', in Todd McCarthy and Charles Flynn (eds), *Kings of the Bs: Working Within the Hollywood System*, E. P. Dutton and Co., New York, pp. 377–409.

Boorman, John and Walter Donohue (1997) 'Three Portraits in the Form of a Homage', in *Projections* 7, Faber and Faber, London, pp. 87–92.

Bordwell, David, Janet Staiger and Kristin Thompson (1985) *The Classical Hollywood Cinema: Film Style and Mode of Production to 1960*, Routledge, London.

Bowser, Eileen (1994) *The Transformation of Cinema 1907–1915*, University of California Press, Berkeley.

Brady, Thomas F. (1946) 'Out Hollywood Way', in *New York Times*, 8 September.

Broderick, Peter (2008) 'Welcome to the New World of Distribution', in *Indiewire*, online, 17 and 18 September, http://www.peterbroderick.com/writing/writing/welcometothenewworld.html (accessed 19 July 2016).

Brodesser, Claude (2004) 'Niche Pics Stole Summer Heat', in *Variety*, 8 March, p. 53.

'Broidy Asks Lower Pay Scale on "B" Films to Insure Profit' (1947) in *Hollywood Reporter*, 5 June.

Brown, Colin (2002) 'Shoestring Films Get Knotted', in *Screen International*, no. 1384, 6 December, p. 10.

Canfield, David (2015) 'Magnolia Pictures Acquires Duplass Brothers-Produced "Tangerine" After Acclaimed Sundance Debut', in *Indiewire*, online, 27 January, http://www.indiewire.com/2015/01/magnolia-acquires-duplass-brothers-produced-tangerine-after-acclaimed-sundance-debut-65818/ (accessed 16 July 2016).

Carney, Raymond (1985) *American Dreaming: The Films of John Cassavetes and the American Experience*, University of California Press, Berkeley.

Carney, Raymond (1994) *The Films of John Cassavetes: Pragmatism, Modernism and the Movies*, Cambridge University Press, Cambridge.

Carver, Benedict (1999) 'UA Films to Make "Things": Garcia Helming Ensemble Cast', in *Variety*, online, 10 August, http://variety.com/1999/film/news/ua-films-to-make-things-1117750215/ (accessed 16 July 2016).

Chang, Chris (1994) 'Absorbing Alternative', in *Film Comment*, vol. 30, no. 5, September–October, pp. 47–53.

Chute, David (1986) 'Wages of Sin', in *Film Comment*, vol. 22, no. 4, July–August, pp. 32–4.

Cleary, Chip (1940) 'Republic, the Industry's Baby', in *Hollywood Reporter*, 4 October.

Cohen, David S. (2005) 'Is the Force Still with Him?', in *Variety*, 14 February, pp. 1, 58–9.

Conant, Michael (1976) 'The Paramount Decrees Reconsidered', in Tino Balio (ed.), *The American Film Industry*, University of Wisconsin Press, Madison, pp. 346–70.

Cook, David A. (2000) *Lost Illusions: American Cinema in the Shadow of Watergate and Vietnam 1970–1979*, University of California Press, Berkeley.

Corman, Roger and Jim Jerome (1998) *How I Made A Hundred Movies in Hollywood and Never Lost A Dime*, Da Capo Press, New York.

Crafton, Donald (1999) *The Talkies: American Cinema's Transition to Sound 1926–1931*, University of California Press, Berkeley.

Cripps, Thomas (1997) *Hollywood's High Noon: Moviemaking and Society Before Television*, Johns Hopkins University Press, Baltimore.

Dahl, Darren (2014) 'The SnagFilms Story: A Q&A with CEO Rick Allen', in *The Coca-Cola Journey*, online, 28 October, http://www.coca-colacompany.com/stories/the-snagfilms-story-a-q-a-with-ceo-rick-allen (accessed 10 December 2016).

Danish Film Institute (2016) 'New TV Drama Premiering in Berlin', in *Danish Film Institute Film Magazine*, online, 25 January, http://www.dfi.dk/service/english/news-and-publications/news/january-2016/splitting-up-together-in-berlin.aspx (accessed 14 December 2016).

Daressa, Lawrence (1986) 'Maintaining Independence Over the Long Term', in *Journal of Film and Video*, vol. 38, no. 1, winter, pp. 54–9 and 77.

Davies, Philip (1981) 'A Growing Independence', in Philip Davies and Brian Neve (eds), *Cinema, Politics and Society in America*, Manchester University Press, Manchester, pp. 119–35.

Davis, Glyn (2011) *Far from Heaven*, Edinburgh University Press, Edinburgh.

Davis, Ronald L. (1997) *Celluloid Mirrors: Hollywood and American Society Since 1945*, Harcourt Brace College Publishers, London.

Dawes, Amy (2003) 'DVDs Lead the Way to Recovery for Indie Film', in *Variety Supplement AFM 2003*, 17 February, pp. 13 and 32.

'Declaration of Independents: The 30 Greatest American Indie Films' (2014) in *Rolling Stone*, online, 3 July, http://www.rollingstone.com/movies/pictures/declaration-of-independents-the-30-greatest-american-indie-films-20140703 (accessed 10 December 2016).

DiOrio, Carl (2003) 'Indies Form Powerhouse', in *Variety*, 3 November, p. 16.

Dixon, Wheeler (1976) 'In Defense of Roger Corman', in *Velvet Light Trap*, no. 16, fall, pp. 11–14.

Dixon, Wheeler (1986) *Producers Releasing Corporation: A Comprehensive Filmography and History*, McFarland, Jefferson.

Doherty, Thomas (1988) *Teenagers and Teenpics: The Juvenilization of American Movies in the 1950s*, Unwin Hyman, Boston.

Duke, Paul F. (2000) 'The Recharge of the "Light Brigade"', in *Weekly Variety*, 1 May, p. 9.

Dwyer, Tim (2010) *Media Convergence*, McGraw-Hill and Open University Press, Maidenhead.

Earnest, Olen J. (1985) '*Star Wars*: A Case Study of Motion Picture Marketing', in Bruce A. Austin (ed.), *Current Research in Film: Audiences, Law and Economics, Volume 1*, Ablex Publishing, Norwood, pp. 1–18.

Ebert, Roger (1975) 'Joe Solomon: The Last of the Schlockmeisters', in Todd McCarthy and Charles Flynn (eds), *Kings of the Bs: Working Within the Hollywood System*, E. P. Dutton and Co., New York, pp. 135–46.

Ebert, Roger (1998) '*Psycho*', online, http://www.rogerebert.com/reviews/great-movie-psycho-1960 (accessed 9 July 2016).

Edgerton, Gary (1986) 'The Film Bureau Phenomenon in America and Its Relationship to Independent Filmmaking', in *Journal of Film and Video*, vol. 38, no. 1, winter, pp. 40–7.

Ellington, Annlee (2013) 'SnagFilms Snags $6 million', in *The Biz*, online, 18 January, http://www.bizjournals.com/losangeles/news/2013/01/18/snagfilms-snags-6-million.html (accessed 10 December 2016).

'Fact on Pacts' (2004) in *Variety*, 15 November, p. 71.

Farber, Manny (1975 [1952]) 'Blame the Audience', in Todd McCarthy and Charles Flynn (eds), *Kings of the Bs: Working Within the Hollywood System*, E. P. Dutton and Co., New York, pp. 44–7.

Fernett, Gene (1973) *Hollywood's Poverty Row: 1930–1950*, Coral Reef Publications, Satellite Beach.

'Film-Makers' Cooperative' (1966) in *Film Culture*, no. 42, fall, pp. 46–52.

Finler, Joel W. (2003) *The Hollywood Story*, third edn, Wallflower Press, London.

Flynn, Charles and Todd McCarthy (1975a) 'The Economic Imperative: Why Was the B Movie Necessary', in Todd McCarthy and Charles Flynn (eds), *Kings of the Bs: Working Within the Hollywood System*, E. P. Dutton and Co., New York, pp. 13–43.

Flynn, Charles and Todd McCarthy (1975b) 'Roger Corman', in Todd McCarthy and Charles Flynn (eds), *Kings of the Bs: Working Within the Hollywood System*, E. P. Dutton and Co., New York, pp. 301–11.

Follows, Stephen (2015) 'The Statistics Behind Film Crowdfunding, Part 1', online, 17 November, https://stephenfollows.com/film-crowdfunding-kickstarter-statistics/ (accessed 10 December 2016).

'Fox Searchlight Acquires Jason Reitman's Debut Feature "THANK YOU FOR SMOKING" from David O. Sacks' Room 9 Entertainment' (2005) in *BusinessWire*, 12 September.

Fuchs, Andreas (2004) 'Sundance Spotlight', in *Film Journal International*, online, 27 October, http://www.filmjournal.com/sundance-spotlight (accessed 16 July 2016).

Gaines, Jane (2003) 'The Colored Players', in *African Americans in Cinema: The First Half Century*, CD-ROM, University of Illinois Press, Champaign.

Gatchman, Dina (2015) 'Forget Indie Film – How Indie TV Is Changing the Content Landscape and Producers Are Getting Pilots Made', in *SSN*, online, 10 April, http://www.ssninsider.com/forget-indie-film-how-indie-tv-is-changing-the-content-landscape-producers-are-getting-pilots-made (accessed 14 December 2016).

'Getting $1,000,000 for 7-Yr License; Mono Plans Own TV-Distribution in Future' (1951) in *Daily Variety*, 20 June.

Getze, John (1974) 'Horror or Horrid Films, AIP Quickies Score at Box Office', in *Los Angeles Times*, 20 February.

Goldstein, Patrick (2003) 'Moving "Sideways" to Stay on Track', in *Los Angeles Times*, online, 16 December, http://articles.latimes.com/2003/dec/16/entertainment/et-gold16/2 (accessed 1 August 2016).

Gomery, Douglas (1986) *The Hollywood Studio System*, St Martin's Press, New York.

Goodridge, Mike (2001a) 'Developing World', in *Screen International*, no. 1318, 27 July, pp. 17–18.

Goodridge, Mike (2001b) 'The New Hollywood Way: A Business of Co-dependents', in *Screen International*, no. 1330, 26 October, p. 1.

Goodridge, Mike (2002) 'Top 20 Independent Movies of All Time', in *Screen International*, no. 1343, 8 February, p. 33.

Grant, Barry K. (1985) 'The Classic Hollywood Musical and the Problem of Rock 'n' Roll', in *Journal of Popular Film and Television*, vol. 13, no. 4, pp. 195–205.

Grimes, Teresa (1986) 'BBS: Auspicious Beginnings, Open Endings', in *Movie*, no. 31/32, winter, pp. 54–66.

Grindhouse Cinema Database (no date) 'William Castle: Grandmaster of Exploitation Cinema', in Grindhouse Cinema Database, online, https://www.grindhousedatabase.com/index.php/William_Castle:_Grandmaster_of_Exploitation_Cinema (accessed on 9 July 2016).

Guerrero, Ed (1993) *Framing Blackness: African American Image in Film*, Temple University Press, Philadelphia.

Hagopian, Kevin (1986) 'Declarations of Independence: A History of Cagney Productions', in *Velvet Light Trap*, no. 22, pp. 16–32.

Hamlyn, Nicky (2015) 'Imperfect Scans: Jamie Jenkinson's iPhone Video Works', in *Journal of Visual Art Practice*, vol. 14, no. 1, pp. 44–51.

Hampton, Benjamin B. (1970) *History of the American Film Industry From Its Beginnings to 1931*, Dover Publications, New York.

Hanke, Ken (1989) *Charlie Chan at the Movies: History, Filmography and Criticism*, McFarland, Jefferson.

Hanna, David (1941) 'The Little Acorn Has Grown', in *New York Times*, 2 February.

Hanson, S. (1985) 'Orion: Looking to the Stars', in *Stills*, February, pp. 24–5.

Harris, Dana (2002) 'Studio Dealmakers Still Stingy: Production Pacts Scarce But Warners, Columbia Revving Up', in *Variety*, 11 November, pp. 8–9.

Harris, Dana (2003) 'H'wood Renews Niche Pitch: Studios Add Fresh Spin as They Rev Up "Art" Divisions', in *Variety*, 7 April, pp. 1 and 54.

Harris, Dana (2004) 'Mickey Seems M'maxed Out: Weinsteins Prep for the Long Goodbye', in *Variety*, 11 October, pp. 1 and 15.

Hefferman, Kevin (2004) *Ghouls, Gimmicks and Gold: Horror Films and the American Movie Business, 1953–1968*, Duke University Press, Durham.

Hernandez, Eugene (2006) 'AIVF to Close: Org Hopes to Keep Magazine Alive', in *Indiewire*, 15 June.

Hernandez, Eugene (2009) 'The Future of Festivals?', in *Indiewire*, online, 7 December, http://www.indiewire.com/2009/12/eugene-hernandez-the-future-of-festivals-55658/ (accessed 12 December 2016).

Hernadez, Eugene (2010a) 'The Doctor Is In', in *Indiewire*, online, 11 January, http://www.indiewire.com/2010/01/eugene-hernandez-the-doctor-is-in-246000 (accessed 12 December 2016).

Hernandez, Eugene (2010b) 'Five Sundance Films, 3 From This Year's Fest, Coming to YouTube This Week' in *Indiewire*, online, 20 January, http://www.indiewire.com/2010/01/five-sundance-films-3-from-this-years-fest-coming-to-youtube-this-week-245930/ (accessed 12 December 2016).

Hillier, Jim (1986) 'The Economics of Independence: Roger Corman and New World Pictures', in *Movie*, no. 31/32, winter, pp. 43–53.

Hillier, Jim (1994) *The New Hollywood*, Continuum, New York.

Hillier, Jim (ed.) (2001) *American Independent Cinema: A Sight and Sound Reader*, BFI, London.

Hoberman, J. (1988) *Dennis Hopper: From Method to Madness*, Walker Art Center, Nineland Place.

Holmlund, Chris (2005) 'Introduction: From the Margins to the Mainstream', in Chris Holmlund and Justin Wyatt (eds), *Contemporary American Independent Film: From the Margins to the Mainstream*, Routledge, London, pp. 1–19.

Holmlund, Chris and Justin Wyatt (eds) (2005) *Contemporary American Independent Film: From the Margins to the Mainstream*, Routledge, London.

Horton, Andrew (1976) 'Turning On and Tuning Out at the Drive-In: An American Phenomenon Survives and Thrives', in *Journal of Popular Film*, vol. 5, no. 3/4, pp. 233–44.

Hurst, Richard Maurice (1979) *Republic Studios: Between Poverty Row and the Majors*, Scarecrow Press and Metuchen, London.

Imagine ... (2006) 'The Movie Brats, Take Two', produced by Alan Yentob, BBC Productions, BBC (first aired 6 November 2006).

'Independents Head East' (1933) in *Morning Telegraph*, 19 April.

'*Indiewire* Ultimate Guide to Crowdfunding' (2013) in *Indiewire*, online, 19 August, http://www.indiewire.com/2013/08/indiewires-ultimate-guide-to-crowdfunding-for-filmmakers-35750/ (accessed 10 December 2016).

Isenberg, Noah William (2004) 'Perennial Detour: The Cinema of Edgar G. Ulmer and the Experience of Exile', *Cinema Journal*, vol. 43, no. 2, winter, pp. 3–25.

Izod, John (1988) *Hollywood and the Box Office 1895–1986*, Columbia University Press, New York.

Jacobs, Diane (1980) *Hollywood Renaissance: The New Generation of Filmmakers and Their Work*, Delta Books, New York.

Jacobs, Matthew (2015) '"*Tangerine*" May Have Had a Tiny Budget, but the Film's Heart Is Bigger Because of It', in *Huffington Post*, online, 9 July, http://www.huffingtonpost.com/

entry/tangerine-movie-transgender_us_559bc990e4b05d7587e22881 (accessed 16 July 2016).

James, David E. (1989) *Allegories of Cinema: American Film in the Sixties*, Princeton University Press, Princeton.

Jancovich, Mark (1996) *Rational Fears: American Horror in the 1950s*, Manchester University Press, Manchester.

Jenkins, Henry (1995) 'Historical Poetics', in Mark Jancovich and Joanne Hollows (eds), *Approaches to Popular Film*, Manchester University Press, Manchester, pp. 99–122.

Jenkins, Henry (2006) *Convergence Culture: Where Old and New Media Collide*, New York University Press, New York.

Jess-Cooke, Carolyn (2009) *Film Sequels*, Edinburgh University Press, Edinburgh.

Kay, Jeremy (2002) 'Revolution: Master of Independents', in *Screen International*, no. 1367, 9 August.

King, Geoff (2005) *American Independent Cinema*, I. B. Tauris, London.

King, Geoff (2009) *Indiewood USA: Where Hollywood Meets Independent Cinema*, I. B. Tauris, London.

King, Geoff (2010) *Lost in Translation*, Edinburgh University Press, Edinburgh.

King, Geoff (2013) 'Thriving or in Permanent Crisis? Discourses on the State of Indie Cinema', in Geoff King, Claire Molloy and Yannis Tzioumakis (eds), *American Independent Cinema: Indie, Indiewood and Beyond*, Routledge, London, pp. 41–52.

King, Geoff (2014) *Indie 2.0: American Independent Cinema Since 2000*, Columbia University Press, New York.

King, Geoff (ed.) (2017) *A Companion to American Indie Film*, Wiley Blackwell, Oxford.

King, Geoff, Claire Molloy and Yannis Tzioumakis (eds) (2013) *American Independent Cinema: Indie, Indiewood and Beyond*, Routledge, London.

Kirkpatrick, Marshall (2006) 'Amazon Unbox Goes Live', in *Tech Crunch*, online, 7 September, https://techcrunch.com/2006/09/07/amazon-unbox-goes-live/ (accessed 20 December 2016).

Klain, Stephen (1983) 'Prods Over-Value US Art Mart: Classics Eye Upfront Stakes as Terms Stiffen', in *Variety*, 4 May, p. 532.

Kleinhans, Chuck (1998) 'Independent Features: Hopes and Dreams', in Jon Lewis (ed.), *The New American Cinema*, Duke University Press, Durham, pp. 308–27.

Knapp, Emily (2006) 'Apple Announces iTunes 7 with Amazing New Features', Apple press release, online, 12 September, https://www.apple.com/pr/library/2006/09/12Apple-Announces-iTunes-7-with-Amazing-New-Features.html (accessed 20 December 2016).

Koszarski, Richard (1994) *An Evening's Entertainment: The Age of the Silent Feature Picture, 1915–1928*, University of California Press, Berkeley.

Krämer, Peter (1998) 'Post-classical Hollywood', in John Hill and Pamela Church Gibson (eds), *The Oxford Guide to Film Studies*, Oxford University Press, Oxford, pp. 289–309.

Krinsky, Tamara (no date) 'Snagging Successfully: Online Portal Helps Filmmakers Find Their Audiences', in *Documentary Magazine*, online, no date, http://www.documentary.org/feature/snagging-successfully-online-portal-helps-filmmakers-find-their-audiences (accessed 16 November 2016).

Kunz, William M. (2007) *Culture Conglomerates: Consolidation in the Motion Picture and Television Industries*, Rowman and Littlefield, Lanham.

Lang, Brent and Greg Gilman (2013) 'The Wrap's Streaming Guide: From Netflix to SnagFilms, Where to Find Your Movies', in *The Wrap*, online, 17 March, http://www.thewrap.com/thewraps-streaming-guide-netflix-snagfilms-where-find-movies-you-want-81511/ (accessed 16 November 2016).

Lev, Peter (2003) *The Fifties: Transforming the Screen, 1950–1959*, Charles Scribner 's Sons, New York.

Levy, Emanuel (1999) *Cinema of Outsiders: The Rise of American Independent Film*, New York University Press, New York.

Lewis, Jon (1995) *Whom God Wishes to Destroy . . .: Francis Coppola and the New Hollywood*, Athlone Press, London.

Lewis, Jon (ed.) (1998) *The New American Cinema*, Duke University Press, Durham.

Leyda, Julia (2002) 'Black-Audience Westerns and the Politics of Cultural Identification in the 1930s', in *Cinema Journal*, vol. 42, no. 1, fall, pp. 46–70.

'Lippert Gets First Financing Morris Plan Ever Made Films' (1949) in *Variety*, 21 September.

Loosvelt, Derek (2005) 'Looking for Funds in All Possible Places: The Current State of Independent Film Financing', in *The Independent: A Magazine for Video and Filmmakers*, September, pp. 36–9.

Lowry, Ed (2005) 'Dimension Pictures: Portrait of a 1970s Independent', in Chris Holmlund and Justin Wyatt (eds), *Contemporary American Independent Film: From the Margins to the Mainstream*, Routledge, London, pp. 41–52.

Luers, Erik (2016) 'IFP Film Week Is Moving to Brooklyn', in *Independent Feature Project*, online, 31 March, http://www.ifp.org/press/ifp-film-week-is-moving-to-brooklyn/#. V4QeDJX6s5s (accessed 11 July 2016).

Lyons, Donald (1994) *Independent Visions: A Critical Introduction to Recent Independent American Film*, Ballantine Books, New York.

Maltby, Richard (1998) 'Post-classical Historiographies and Consolidated Entertainment', in Steve Neale and Murray Smith (eds), *Contemporary Hollywood Cinema*, Routledge, London, pp. 21–44.

Mann, Denise (2008) *Hollywood Independents: The Postwar Talent Takes Over*, University of Minnesota Press, Minneapolis.

Margulies, Ivone (1998) 'John Cassavetes: Amateur Director', in Jon Lewis (ed.), *The New American Cinema*, Duke University Press, Durham, pp. 275–306.

Mason, John (1976) 'The Making of *The Wild Angels*: An Interview with Roger Corman', in *Journal of Popular Film*, vol. 5, no. 3/4, pp. 263–72.

May, Lary (2000) *The Big Tomorrow: Hollywood and the Politics of American Identity*, University of Chicago Press, Chicago.

McCabe, John (1998) *Cagney*, Aurum, London.

McCauley, Scott (2012) 'Andrew Neel and Louisa Krause Talk *King Kelly*', in *Filmmaker Magazine*, online, 20 June, http://filmmakermagazine.com/47360-andrew-neel-and-louisa-kraus-talk-king-kelly/#.WBY3bJV745t (accessed 16 July 2016).

McGarry, Caitlin (2015) 'How to Make a Movie with an iPhone: An Interview with *Tangerine* Director Sean Baker', in *Macworld*, online, 18 August, http://www.macworld. com/article/2971675/video/how-to-make-a-movie-with-an-iphone-an-interview-with-tangerine-director-sean-baker.html (accessed 16 July 2016).

McGee, Mark Thomas (1989) *Beyond Ballyhoo: Motion Picture Promotion and Gimmicks*, McFarland Classics, Jefferson.

McGee, Mark Thomas and R. J. Robertson (1982) *The JD Films: Juvenile Delinquency in the Movies*, McFarland, Jefferson.

McGilligan, Patrick (1975) *Cagney: The Actor as Auteur*, A. S. Barnes and Company, New York.

McHugh, Kathleen (2016) 'Miranda July and the New Twenty-First-Century Indie', in Linda Badley, Claire Perkins and Michele Schreiber (eds), *Indie Reframed: Women's Filmmaking and Contemporary American Independent Cinema*, Edinburgh University Press, Edinburgh, pp. 239–53.

McNary, Dave (2004) 'Par Reinventing Classics', in *Variety*, 4 October, p. 5.

McNary, Dave (2016) 'IFP Week Expands to Include TV, Digital', in *Variety*, online, 20 July, http://variety.com/2016/film/news/ifp-film-week-expands-tv-digital-1201817933 (accessed 14 December 2016).

McRobbie, Angela (2002) 'Clubs to Companies: Notes on the Decline of Political Culture in Speeded Up Creative Worlds', in *Cultural Studies*, vol. 16, no. 4, pp. 516–31.

Medavoy, Mike, with Josh Young (2002) *You're Only as Good as Your Next One: 100 Great Films, 100 Good Films, and 100 for which I Should Be Shot*, Pocket Books, New York.

Medavoy, Mike (former Head of Worldwide Production of Orion Pictures [1978–90] and Chairman and co-founder of Phoenix Pictures [1995–present]) (2004) Interview with the author, 15 June, Los Angeles, CA, 1 hour.

Mekas, Jonas (2000) 'A Call for a New Generation of Filmmakers', in P. Adams Sitney (ed.), *Film Culture Reader*, First Cooper Square Press, New York, pp. 73–5.

Merritt, Greg (2000) *Celluloid Mavericks: A History of American Independent Film*, Thunder's Mouth Press, New York.

Messer, Arnold (President and Chief Operating Officer of Phoenix Pictures [1995–present]) (2004) Interview with the author, 15 June, Los Angeles, 30 minutes.

Miller, Don (1988) *B Movies*, Ballantine Books, New York.

Mohr, Ian (2005) 'Too Big for Their Niche: Specialty Arms Are Angst-ridden as Studios Shake Up Biz Plans', in *Variety*, 21 March, pp. 1 and 41.

Molloy, Claire (2010) *Memento*, Edinburgh University Press, Edinburgh.

Molloy, Tim (2016) 'Revolution Studios Acquires Rights to 5 GK Films', in *The Wrap*, online, 21 June, http://www.thewrap.com/revolution-studios-acquires-rights-to-5-gk-films (accessed 16 November 2016).

Molyneaux, Gerry (2000) *John Sayles: An Unauthorised Biography of the Pioneering Indie Filmmaker*, Renaissance Books, Los Angeles.

Monaco, Paul (2001) *The Sixties: 1960–1969*, University of California Press, Berkeley.

'Monogram Film Plans Disclosed' (1933) in *Los Angeles Times*, 13 May.

'Monogram Going Into Telepix: 1st Studio to Make Decision' (1950) in *Daily Variety*, 10 October.

'Monogram, Lippert Co May Merge; Negotiations Now in Progress' (1950) in *Variety*, 26 July.

'Monogram Marching On: Company Shows Swift Increase in Stature' (1943) in *Daily Variety*, 29 October.

'Monogram To Do 32 Movies' (1932) in *Hollywood Citizen-News*, 3 May.

Morris, Gary (1993) 'Beyond the Beach: Social and Formal Aspects of AIP's Beach Party Movies', in *Journal of Popular Film and Television*, vol. 21, no. 1, pp. 2–11.

Morris, Gary (2001) 'Edgar G. Ulmer's *Detour* on DVD', in *Bright Lights Film Journal*, online, no. 31, January, http://brightlightsfilm.com/edgar-g-ulmers-detour-dvd/#.V4ER7JX6s5s (accessed 9 July 2016).

Mottram, James (2006) *The Sundance Kids: How the Mavericks Took Over Hollywood*, Faber and Faber, London.

Mullen, Lisa (2015) '*Tangerine*', in *Sight and Sound*, December, pp. 88–9.

Murphy, J. J. (2007) *Me and You and Memento and Fargo: How Independent Screenplays Work*, Continuum, New York.

Murray, Rona (2011) *Studying American Independent Cinema*, Auteur, Leighton Buzzard.

'Mute Major' (1942) in *Time*, 20 March.

Nath, Trevir (2016) 'Investing in Video Games: This Industry Pulls in More Revenue than Movies and Music', in *Nasdaq*, online, 13 June, http://www.nasdaq.com/article/investing-in-video-games-this-industry-pulls-in-more-revenue-than-movies-music-cm634585 (accessed 14 December 2016).

Neale, Steve and Murray Smith (eds) (1998) *Contemporary Hollywood Cinema*, Routledge, London.

Needham, Gary (2010) *Brokeback Mountain*, Edinburgh University Press, Edinburgh.

'New Studio Chief Tells Expansion Plan' (1945) in *Hollywood Citizen-News*, 20 November.

New York Film Academy (2015) 'The Most Comprehensive List of Film Festivals on the Internet', online, https://www.nyfa.edu/student-resources/film-festivals (accessed 14 December 2016).

Newman, Michael Z. (2011) *Indie: An American Film Culture*, Columbia University Press, New York.

Nicholson, James H. (1970) 'AIP Formula – Not Foolproof, But It Pays Off', in *Daily Variety*, 27 October.

'Nicholson Forms New Distrib Unit' (1956) in *Hollywood Reporter*, 26 March.

O'Falt, Chris (2016) 'It's Complicated! How Netflix and Amazon Add a Big Wrinkle to Sundance Deal-making', in *Indiewire*, online, 21 January, http://www.indiewire.com/2016/01/its-complicated-how-netflix-and-amazon-add-a-big-wrinkle-to-sundance-deal-making-32496/ (accessed 12 December 2016).

Okuda, Ted (1989) *Grand National, Producers Releasing Corporation and Screen Guild/Lippert: Complete Filmographies with Studio Histories*, McFarland, Jefferson.

Oppelaar, Justin, (2002) 'Pangs of New York: Harvey Beefs Up, Slims Down', in *Variety*, 11 November, pp. 1 and 62.

Oppelaar, Justin (2003) 'New Line's Billion-Dollar Bet', in *Variety*, 2 January, p. 11.

Osgerby, Bill (2003) 'Sleazy Riders: Exploitation, "Otherness" and Transgression in the 1960s Biker Movie', in *Journal of Popular Film and Television*, vol. 31, no. 3, fall, pp. 98–108.

Peary, Gerald (1981) 'Sundance', in *American Film*, vol. 7, no. 1, October, pp. 46–51.

Pederson, Claudia Costa and Patricia R. Zimmermann (2016) 'Beyond the Screen: On Contemporary Feminist Media Re-articulations', in Linda Badley, Claire Perkins and Michele Schreiber (eds), *Indie Reframed: Women's Filmmaking and Contemporary American Independent Cinema*, Edinburgh University Press, Edinburgh, pp. 304–18.

Perren, Alisa (2012) *Indie Inc.: Miramax and the Transformation of Hollywood in the 1990s*, University of Texas Press, Austin.

Pickett, Rex (2012a) 'The *Sideways* Publishing Saga – The St Martin's Press Nightmare (Part I)', in *Huffington Post*, online, 16 April, http://www.huffingtonpost.com/rex-pickett/sideways-publishing-saga-_b_1274813.html (accessed 1 August 2016).

Pickett, Rex (2012b) 'The *Sideways* Publishing Saga – Part II: Exultation', in *Huffington Post*, online, 4 April, http://www.huffingtonpost.com/rex-pickett/the-sideways-publishing-s_b_1247255.html (accessed 1 August 2016).

Pidduck, Julianne (2003) 'After 1980: Margins and Mainstreams', in Richard Dyer, *Now You See It*, second edn, Routledge, London, pp. 265–93.

Pierson, John (1995) *Spike Mike Slackers and Dykes: A Guided Tour Across a Decade of American Independent Cinema*, Hyperion/Miramax Books, New York.

Pleskow, Eric (President and Chief Executing Officer of Orion Pictures [1978–90] and Chairman of Orion Pictures [1990–2] (2005) Interview with the author, 24 June, Weston, CT, 4 hours 30 minutes.

Polan, Dana (2002) '*Detour*', in *Senses of Cinema*, online, July, http://sensesofcinema.com/2002/cteq/detour/ (accessed 9 July 2016).

Poniewozik, James (2015) 'Why TV Is the Perfect Place for Indie Filmmakers', in *Time*, online, 26 January, http://time.com/3682354/tv-independent-film-sundance/n (accessed 14 December 2016).

Powers, James (1979) 'Dialogue on Film: Joseph E. Levine', in *American Film*, vol. 4, no. 10, September, pp. 39–47.

Pribram, E. Deidre (2002) *Independent Film in the United States, 1980–2001*, Peter Lang, New York.

Prince, Stephen (2002) *A New Pot of Gold: Hollywood Under the Electronic Rainbow, 1980–1989*, University of California Press, Berkeley.

Prive, Tanya (2012) 'What Is Crowdfunding and How does It Benefit the Economy' in *Forbes*, online, 27 November, http://www.forbes.com/sites/tanyaprive/2012/11/27/what-is-crowdfunding-and-how-does-it-benefit-the-economy/#20a311c84ed4 (accessed 10 December 2016).

Quart, Leonard and Albert Auster (2002) *American Film and Society Since 1945*, Greenwood Press, London.

Quigley, Martin J. (ed.) (1950) *The International Motion Picture Almanac 1949*, Quigley Publishing Co., Groton.

Quinn, James (2010) 'Walt Disney Offloads Miramax for $660 million', in the *Telegraph*, online, 30

July, http://www.telegraph.co.uk/finance/newsbysector/mediatechnologyandtelecoms/media/7918523/Walt-Disney-offloads-Miramax-for-660m.html (accessed 1 September 2016).

Rainey, James (2016) 'Peter Schlessel of Focus Features to Exit as CEO After Universal Pictures International Merger', in *Variety*, online, 4 February, http://variety.com/2016/film/news/peter-schlessel-exits-focus-features-universal-merger-1201697139/ (accessed 1 December 2016).

Regester, Charlene (1996) 'Black Films, White Censors', in Francis G. Couvares (ed.), *Movie Censorship and American Culture*, Smithsonian Institution Press, Washington, DC, pp. 159–86.

'Rep Plows Back Profits for Record Production Sked ...' (1941) in *Daily Variety*, 29 October.

'Rep Studio Open to Indie TV Prod'n; Rogers' TV-1st Run, 30G; Autry, 20G' (1951) in *Daily Variety*, 20 June, pp. 1 and 7.

'Republic Okays Old Films for Tele; Editing, Rescoring to Fit TV Needs' (1951) in *Weekly Variety*, 13 June, pp. 3 and 18.

'Republic Pictures Celebrates Its Tenth Anniversary' (1945) in *The Independent*, 23 June.

'Republic Stepping High' (1943) in *Daily Variety*, 29 October.

'Republic Will Release 58 at Cost of $25,000,000' (1946) in *Motion Picture Herald*, 22 June.

Rich, B. Ruby (1992) 'New Queer Cinema', in *Sight and Sound*, vol. 2, no. 5, September, pp. 30–4.

Richter, Robert (1986) 'Who Is an Independent Producer?', in *Journal of Film and Video*, vol. 38, no. 1, winter, pp. 21–3.

Roberts, Ben (2015) 'BFI Film Fund Insights', in *Sight and Sound*, December, p. 16.

Rodriguez, Elena (1988) *Dennis Hopper: A Madness to His Method*, St Martin's Press, New York.

Roman, Shari (2001) *Digital Babylon: Hollywood, Indiewood and Dogme 95*, Lone Eagle Publishing, Hollywood.

Rooney, David (2004a) 'Niche Biz Comes into Focus: U Specialty Label Marries Taste with Overseas Savvy', in *Variety*, 2 August, pp. 8 and 15.

Rooney, David (2004b) 'The Brothers Grim: Weinsteins Bridle at Disney Dictates', in *Variety*, 14 June, pp. 1 and 57.

Rosen, David, with Peter Hamilton (1990) *Off-Hollywood: The Making and Marketing of Independent Films*, Grove Weidenfeld, New York.

Roston, Tom (2005) 'Life After Miramax', in *Premiere*, March, pp. 48–51 and 122.

Ryan, Michael and Douglas Kellner (1990) *Camera Politica: The Politics and Ideology of Contemporary Hollywood Film*, Indiana University Press, Bloomington.

'Salesman' (1946) in *New York Times*, 10 February.

Sanders, Terry B. (1955) 'The Financing of Independent Feature Films', in *Quarterly of Film Radio and Television*, vol. 9, no. 4, summer, pp. 380–9.

Schamus, James (2002) 'A Rant', in Jon Lewis (ed.), *The End of Cinema As We Know It: American Film in the Nineties*, Pluto Press, London, pp. 253–60.

Schatz, Thomas (1993) 'The New Hollywood', in Jim Collins, Hilary Radner and Ava Preacher Collins (eds), *Film Theory Goes to the Movies*, Routledge and AFI, New York, pp. 8–36.

Schatz, Thomas (1996) *The Genius of the System: Hollywood Filmmaking in the Studio Era*, Metropolitan Books, New York.

Schatz, Thomas (1999) *Boom and Bust: American Cinema in the 1940s*, University of California Press, Berkeley.

Schatz, Thomas (2003) '*Stagecoach* and Hollywood's A-Western Renaissance', in Barry Keith Grant (ed.), *John Ford's Stagecoach*, Cambridge University Press, Cambridge, pp. 21–46.

Schatz, Thomas (2013) 'Conglomerate Hollywood and American Independent Film', in Geoff King, Claire Molloy and Yannis Tzioumakis (eds), *American Independent Cinema: Indie, Indiewood and Beyond*, Routledge, London, pp. 127–39.

Scheuer, Philip K. (1958) 'Shocker Pioneers Tell How to Make Monsters', in *Los Angeles Times*, 21 September.

Schickel, Richard (1999) *James Cagney: A Celebration*, Pavilion Books, London.

Sciretta, Peter (2015) 'Sundance Shocker: Sean Baker's Tangerine Was Shot Entirely on iPhone 5s', in *Slash Film*, online, 24 January, http://www.slashfilm.com/sean-bakers-tangerine-shot-on-iphone-5s/ (accessed 16 July 2016).

SeanBakerTangerine (2015) 'We Are the Actors and Filmmaker Behind Tangerine, Ask Us Anything', available through Reddit, online, https://www.reddit.com/r/IAmA/comments/3ckqwb/we_are_the_actors_and_filmmaker_behind_tangerine/ (accessed 16 July 2016).

'Searchlight Feasts with "28 Days"; "Beckham" Goals Ensure Fox Unit Has Momentum' (2003) in *Hollywood Reporter*, 4 September, p. 13.

Segrave, Kerry (1999) *Movies at Home: How Hollywood Came to Television*, McFarland, Jefferson.

'$17 Million Budget for 68 Rep Pix' (1944) in *Daily Variety*, 27 April.

Shiel, Mark (2003) 'Why Call Them "Cult Movies"? American Independent Filmmaking and the Counterculture in the 1960s', in *Scope*, online, https://www.nottingham.ac.uk/scope/documents/2003/may-2003/shiel.pdf (accessed 20 December 2016).

'*Sideways* Is Fox Searchlight's Most Successful Film Ever; Comedy's $46 Million Gross Topples *The Full Monty*' (2005), in *Business Wire*, online, 8 February, http://www.businesswire.com/news/home/20050208005250/en/SIDEWAYS-Fox-Searchlights-Successful-Film-Comedys-46 (accessed 1 August 2016).

'*Sideways* Production Notes' (no date) in *Cinema Review*, online, http://www.cinemareview.com/production.asp?prodid=2736 (accessed 1 August 2016).

Simpson II, Tyrone R. (2003) 'Dark Manhattan: Gangster Films', in *African Americans in Cinema: The First Half Century*, CD-ROM, University of Illinois Press, Champaign.

'Single Movie Billing Plans Bring Attack' (1933) in *Hollywood Citizen-News*, 31 July.

Sinwell, Sarah E. S. (2017) 'Go Digital or Go Dark: Crowdfunding, Independent Financing, and Arthouse Exhibition in Kickstarter', in Geoff King (ed.), *A Companion to American Indie Film*, Wiley Blackwell, Oxford, pp. 452–67.

Sklar, Robert (1975) *Movie-Made America: A Cultural History of American Movies*, Random House, New York.

Smith, Nigel M. (2015) '*Tangerine* Is a Big Deal, Not Just Because It Was Shot on an iPhone', in *Guardian*, online, 10 July, https://www.theguardian.com/film/2015/jul/10/tangerine-film-iphone-buddy-comedy-transgender-prostitutes (access 16 July 2016).

SnagFilms (2013) 'SnagFilms Wins 2013 Red Herring Top 100 North America Award', in *PR Neswire*, online, 24 May, http://www.prnewswire.com/news-releases/snagfilms-wins-2013-red-herring-top-100-north-america-award-208833141.html (accessed 9 December 2016).

Snyder, Gabriel (2003) '"Aviator" Ready For Take-Off: Scorsese, DiCaprio Reteam for Pricey Hughes Biopic', in *Variety*, 9 June, p. 9.

Staehling, Richard (1975) 'From *Rock Around the Clock* to *The Trip*: The Truth About Teen Movies', in Todd McCarthy and Charles Flynn (eds), *Kings of the Bs: Working Within the Hollywood System*, E. P. Dutton and Co., New York, pp. 220–51.

Staiger, Janet (1983) 'Individualism Versus Collectivism: The Shift to Independent Production in the US Film Industry', in *Screen*, vol. 24, nos 4/5, pp. 68–79.

Stam, Robert, Robert Burgoyne and Sandy Flitterman-Lewis (1992) *New Vocabularies in Film Semiotics: Structuralism, Post-structuralism and Beyond*, Routledge, London.

Stanfield, Peter (1998) 'Dixie Cowboys and Blue Yodels: The Strange History of the Singing Cowboy', in Edward Buscombe and Roberta E. Pearson (eds), *Back in the Saddle Again: New Essays on the Western*, BFI, London, pp. 96–118.

Stanley Kramer Papers (Collection 161), Department of Special Collections, Charles E. Young Research Library, University of California, Los Angeles.

Stein, Ruthe (1969) 'The Youth Phenomenon in Films', in *Cineaste*, vol. 3, no. 2, fall, pp. 13–16.

Strawn, Linda May (1975a) 'Steve Broidy', in Todd McCarthy and Charles Flynn (eds), *Kings of the Bs: Working Within the Hollywood System*, E. P. Dutton and Co., New York, pp. 269–84.

Strawn, Linda May (1975b) 'Samuel Z. Arkoff', in Todd McCarthy and Charles Flynn (eds), *Kings of the Bs: Working Within the Hollywood System*, E. P. Dutton and Co., New York, pp. 255–66.

Strawn, Linda May (1975c) 'William Castle', in Todd McCarthy and Charles Flynn (eds), *Kings of the Bs: Working Within the Hollywood System*, E. P. Dutton and Co., New York, pp. 287–98.

'Studio Chief Returns from Indie Meeting' (1934) in *Hollywood Citizen-News*, 14 April.

'Sundance Film Festival: Introducing Virtual Reality and Episodic Content Categories' (2016) in *Withoutabox*, online, 26 July, http://inboxcart.com/index/details/Sundance-Film-Festival---Introducing-Virtual-Reality---Episodic-Content-Categories/57a06b6d676 74b0464b39b3b (accessed 14 December 2016).

'Sundance Institute Announces Films in Competition (2015) in *Sundance Institute*, on-line, 2 December, https://www.sundance.org/blogs/news/competition-and-next-films-announced-for-2016-festival (accessed 15 April 2017).

Tasker, Yvonne (1996) 'Approaches to the New Hollywood', in James Curran, David Morley and Valerie Walkerdine (eds), *Cultural Studies and Communications*, Arnold, London, pp. 213–28.

Taves, Brian (1995) 'The B Film: Hollywood's Other Half', in Tino Balio (1995) *Grand Design: Hollywood as a Modern Business Enterprise, 1930–1939*, University of California Press, Berkeley, pp. 313–50.

'The 1980s: A Reference Guide to Motion Pictures, Television, VCR, and Cable' (1991), in *Velvet Light Trap*, no. 27, spring, pp. 77–88.

'30 Years of Sundance Film Festival' (2015), online, http://www.sundance.org/festivalhistory (accessed 11 July 2016).

Thompson, Anne (1987) 'Rise and Shine: Mike Medavoy Interviewed by Anne Thompson', in *Film Comment*, vol. 23, no. 3, pp. 54–62.

Thompson, Anne (2004) 'Indiewood', in *Backstage*, online, 10 August, http://www.backstage.com/news/indiewood (accessed 1 August 2016).

Thompson, Anne (2008) 'Niche Distrib Crunch Claims Par Vantage', in *Variety*, 9 June.

Thompson, Anne (2009) 'With *Paranormal Activity*, Paramount Sets New Marketing Model', in *Indiewire*, online, 15 October, http://www.indiewire.com/2009/10/with-paranormal-activity-paramount-sets-new-marketing-model-239421 (accessed 10 December 2016).

Thompson, Kristin (1999) *Storytelling in the New Hollywood: Understanding Classical Narrative Technique*, Harvard University Press, Cambridge.

Trowbridge, Hayley (2015) *From the Cinema Screen to the Smartphone: A Study of the Impact of Media Convergence on the Distribution of American Independent Cinema 2006–2010*, unpublished PhD thesis, University of Liverpool.

Tryon, Chuck (2009) *Reinventing Cinema: Movies in the Age of Media Convergence*, Rutgers University Press, New Brunswick.

Tryon, Chuck (2017) 'Crowdfunding, Independence, Authorship', in Geoff King (ed.), *A Companion to American Indie Film*, Wiley Blackwell, Oxford, pp. 433–50.

2929 Entertainment (no date) 'Magnolia Pictures', online, http://www.2929entertainment.com/magpictures.aspx (accessed 16 July 2016).

Tuska, Jon (1982) *The Vanishing Legion: A History of Mascot Pictures: 1927–1935*, McFarland Classics, Jefferson.

Tzioumakis, Yannis (2004) 'Major Status – Independent Spirit: A History of Orion Pictures (1978–1992)', in *New Review of Film and Television Studies*, vol. 2, no. 1, pp. 78–135.

Tzioumakis, Yannis (2006) *American Independent Cinema: An Introduction*, Edinburgh University Press, Edinburgh.

Tzioumakis, Yannis (2008) 'Edgar G. Ulmer: The Low-End Independent Filmmaker Par Excellence', in Gary Rhodes (ed.), *Edgar G. Ulmer: Detour on Poverty Row*, Lexington Books, Lanham, pp. 3–23.

Tzioumakis, Yannis (2009) *The Spanish Prisoner*, Edinburgh, Edinburgh University Press.

Tzioumakis, Yannis (2012a) *Hollywood's Indies: Classics Divisions, Specialty Labels and the Independent Film Market*, Edinburgh, Edinburgh University Press.

Tzioumakis, Yannis (2012b) 'Style Developing and Product Upgrading: Monogram Pictures, the Ambitious B Film and Joseph H. Lewis's Three Contributions to the East Side Kids Film Series', in Gary Rhodes (ed.), *The Films of Joseph H. Lewis*, Wayne State University Press, Detroit, pp. 11–37.

Tzioumakis, Yannis (2013a) '"Independent", "Indie" and "Indiewood": Towards a Periodisation of Contemporary (Post-1980) American Independent Cinema', in Geoff King, Claire Molloy and Yannis Tzioumakis (eds), *American Independent Cinema: Indie, Indiewood and Beyond*, Routledge, London, pp. 28–40.

Tzioumakis, Yannis (2013b) 'American Independent Cinema in the Age of Convergence', in *Revue française d'études américaines*, no. 136 (special issue: 'Et le cinéma indépendant?/ Independence and Cinema', ed. Anne Hurault Paupe and Céline Murillo), pp. 52–66.

Tzioumakis, Yannis (2017) 'From Independent to Indie: The Independent Feature Project and the Complex Relationship between American Independent Cinema and Hollywood in the 1980s', in Geoff King (ed.), *A Companion to American Indie Film*, Wiley Blackwell, Oxford, pp. 233–56.

Van Couvering, Alicia (2007), 'What I Meant to Say', in *Filmmaker*, online, spring, http:// www.filmmakermagazine.com/archives/issues/spring2007/features/mumblecore.php#. VBK6ZRVwaM9 (accessed 12 September 2016).

Watercutter, Angela (2015) '*Tangerine* Is Amazing – But Not Because of How They Shot It', in *Wired*, online, 7 July, https://www.wired.com/2015/07/tangerine-iphone/ (accessed 16 July 2016).

Waters, John (1983) 'Whatever Happened to Showmanship?' in *American Film*, vol. 9, no. 3, December, pp. 55–8.

Waxman, Sharon (2003) 'With Acquisition, Lions Gate Is Now Largest Indie', in *New York Times*, online, 16 December, http://www.nytimes.com/2003/12/16/movies/with-acquisition-lions-gate-is-now-largest-indie.html (accessed 1 August 2016).

Wiener, Thomas (1975) 'The Rise and Fall of the Rock Film, Part 1', in *American Film*, vol. 1, no. 2, pp. 25–9.

Wiese, Michael (1992) *Film and Video Financing*, Michael Wiese Productions in association with Focal Press, Studio City.

Williams III, Wade (1988) 'Best of the Low Budget "B"s: Edgar Ulmer's Dark Excursion into the Nightmare World of Fatal Irony', in *Filmfax: The Magazine of Unusual Film and Television*, no. 11, n.p.

Willmore, Alison (2014) 'Why SXSW Is Introducing "Episodic", a Program Dedicated to Digital and Television Series', in *Indiewire*, online, 30 January, http://www.indiewire. com/2014/01/why-sxsw-is-introducing-episodic-a-program-dedicated-to-digital-and-television-series-30607 (accessed 14 December 2016).

Wood, Jennifer M. (2014) 'Kickstarter Has Changed Indie Moviemaking for Good', in *Wired*, online, 22 January, https://www.wired.com/2014/01/crowdfunding-2013/ (accessed 10 December 2016).

Wood, Robin (1984) *Hollywood from Vietnam to Reagan*, Columbia University Press, New York.

Wong, Cindy Hing-Yuk (2011) *Film Festivals: Culture, People and Power on the Global Screen*, Rutgers University Press, New Brunswick.

Wyatt, Justin (1994) *High Concept: Movies and Marketing in Hollywood*, University of Texas Press, Austin.

Wyatt, Justin (1998a) 'The Formation of the "Major Independent": Miramax, New Line and the New Hollywood', in Steve Neale and Murray Smith (eds), *Contemporary Hollywood Cinema*, Routledge, London, pp. 74–90.

Wyatt, Justin (1998b) 'From Roadshowing to Saturation Release: Majors, Independents, and Marketing/Distribution Innovations', in Jon Lewis (ed.), *The New American Cinema*, Duke University Press, Durham, pp. 64–86.

Wyatt, Justin (2002) 'Independents, Packaging and Inflationary Pressure in 1980s Hollywood', in Stephen Prince, *A New Pot of Gold: Hollywood Under the Electronic Rainbow 1980–1989*, University of California Press, Berkeley, pp. 142–59.

Yeaman, Elizabeth (1934) 'Monogram Aiming at 52 Pictures Per Year ', in *Hollywood Citizen-News*, 23 October.

Zimmermann, Patricia R. (2005), 'Digital Deployment(s)', in Chris Holmlund and Justin Wyatt (eds), *Contemporary American Independent Film: From the Margins to the Mainstream*, Routledge, London, pp. 245–64.

Index